SOME LA
THEORIES OF THE EUCHARIST

SOME LATER MEDIEVAL THEORIES OF THE EUCHARIST

Thomas Aquinas, Giles of Rome, Duns Scotus, and William Ockham

MARILYN MCCORD ADAMS

OXFORD
UNIVERSITY PRESS

Great Clarendon Street, Oxford, OX2 6DP,
United Kingdom

Oxford University Press is a department of the University of Oxford.
It furthers the University's objective of excellence in research, scholarship,
and education by publishing worldwide. Oxford is a registered trade mark of
Oxford University Press in the UK and in certain other countries

First published 2010
First published in paperback 2012

Impression: 1

British Library Cataloguing in Publication Data
Data available

Library of Congress Cataloging in Publication Data
Data available

ISBN 978–0–19–959105–3 (Hbk.)
ISBN 978–0–19–965816–9 (Pbk.)

Printed in Great Britain by
MPG Books Group, Bodmin and King's Lynn

To Terri and Tim, Elizabeth and Rachel,
Connor, Elliott and Betsy,
with thanks for eucharistic camaraderie!
Pange lingua...

Acknowledgments

Book projects incur debts. Mine are first to Oxford University and to Christ Church, the institutions between which my appointment as Regius Professor of Divinity and residentiary canon was split. Thanks are due to them for three terms of sabbatical (Michaelmas 2006, Michaelmas 2008, and Hilary 2009), during which this project was conceived and completed. I am likewise grateful for the generous hospitality of the Philosophy Programme at the Australian National University in Canberra, where I was a visiting fellow in July–December 2006. Their tradition of lively philosophical engagement, their remarkably well-stocked modern library, and the terrific IT support created a wholesome environment for fruitful work. My friend and colleague Francesco del Punta generously supplied me with a copy of Giles of Rome's *Theoremata de Corpore Christi* years ago, and more recently went above and beyond the call of the house-sitter's duty in sending me some Scotus books that I had neglected to bring. My third term of sabbatical leave (Hilary 2009) was underwritten by an AHRC grant, which I could not have received but for the willing help of Dr Alexandra Lumbers, who compensated for my lack of computer literacy by uploading my application. I am also grateful to the readers for Oxford University Press, whose comments provoked some improvements in the manuscript. Thanks of another kind are due to those parishes where I have attended and/or celebrated many eucharistic liturgies. Years of experience have allowed me to reflect on many questions, as it were, from the inside.

M.M.A.

Feast of Corpus Christi, 2009

Contents

PART THREE: WHAT SORT OF UNION?

Introduction

This book is driven by twin passions—eucharistic piety and an appetite for philosophical analysis—passions that I share with the medieval authors on whom I focus. It is a work of historical theology and history of philosophy, which aims to analyze and clarify the views of certain medieval thinkers, not to develop constructive theories of my own. Because many who pick up this book will resonate to one and not the other of my motives, I have tried to write it in a way that will allow readers to select what is most useful and enjoyable for them.

For the thirteenth- and fourteenth-century authors on whom I mostly concentrate, the eucharist is one of seven Christian sacraments (the others being baptism, confirmation, ordination, penance, matrimony, and extreme unction) and arguably their consummation. If other sacraments single out people for participation in worship and fit them for Christian living and dying, the eucharist offers the risen and ascended Christ keeping His promise to believers to be with them always to the end of the age (Matt.28: 20). In the eucharist, the Body and Blood of Christ come to be really present on the altar, giving faithful participants an opportunity for communion with Him in the here and now.

Because thirteenth- and fourteenth-century Christian philosophical theologians believed this to be true, they felt obliged to try to reconcile it with what else they held to be true—not only with surrounding faith commitments, but also with their metaphysical convictions and with then up-to-date theories in natural science. The core of this book (Part Two, Chapters 4–9) examines the metaphysics and physics of real presence as analyzed by Thomas Aquinas, Giles of Rome, John Duns Scotus, and William Ockham. For these authors, Aristotle was the philosophical authority: his works were the place to begin in forwarding theories in metaphysics and natural philosophy. Accordingly, I begin (in Chapter 1) with a sketch—for the benefit of students and scholars less familiar with Aristotelian thought—of some of the distinctive conceptual machinery on which my authors draw. Specialists may wish to skip this chapter, but equally some may find it a welcome review.

Historians may wonder why I do not widen my scope to include in-depth treatments of earlier (ninth- and eleventh-century) eucharistic controversies. My answer is that—without leaving earlier thinkers entirely out of account—my interest is in what happens to philosophy and theology when core doctrines are subjected to rigorous analytical attention. Before the reintroduction of Aristotle's wider corpus, philosophers and theologians did not have the analytical tools needed to give their discussions the precision that such a project requires. Some would object that sacramental theology does not call for scholastic distinctions, but a posture of contemplation that trades in types and symbols. They regret the emphases and the subsequent influence of the authors I have chosen.[1] My response is that, while philosophical analysis is a different activity from contemplation, so much so that it may not be possible to engage in both at once, analysis is not the enemy of contemplation. Human theorizing itself requires both analysis and imagination: the latter to furnish the model and the former to spell out its meaning. For Aristotle, vigorous analytical work culminates in the enjoyable contemplation of the understanding at which it arrives. For Bonaventure, analytical results not only inform contemplation, but can be juxtaposed in ways that provoke it by boggling the mind.

Just as late-nineteenth-century experiments confronted physicists with data that Newtonian theory had not been designed to handle, so Aristotle had forwarded his system to manage the deliverances of ordinary experience and natural reason, and was in no position to consider various tenets drawn from Christian revelation—for example, the Body and Blood of Christ come to be really present on altars where bread and wine were and still seem to be. Just as Einstein's theory represented a breakthrough that could both account for the new data and explain why Newtonian physics had worked so well in the region of the data to which it had been responsive, so my authors fiddled with the axioms, sometimes making small-scale adjustments and other times

[1] Henri Cardinal de Lubac SJ seems to press this point of view in his *Corpus Mysticum: The Eucharist and the Church in the Middle Ages*, trans. Gemma Simmonds CJ with Richard Price (London: SCM Press, 2006), II. 9. 220–1; II. 10. 228–37, 250, 256–60.

trying for systematic reintegrations. I will close my discussion of eucharistic real presence (in Chapter 10) by overviewing the conceptual modifications my authors propose and considering to what extent they achieved theoretical coherence and to what extent they contented themselves with ad hoc modifications. Thus, in this part of my book, my vision is binocular, with one eye on the meticulous details of their analyses and the other on their method in philosophical theology. Philosophers and historians of philosophy may read Chapters 3–10 to discover fascinating developments in the philosophy of body and in conceptions of causality. Historical theologians may look to this part for an accurate read of difficult and technical developments in eucharistic theology; likewise students doing the medieval paper for the Final Honours School in Theology at Oxford! Christian philosophers may profit from the methodological lessons, even if their philosophical attention is principally directed to other topics and problems.

Such gargantuan efforts at philosophical accommodation found their motivation in a wider theological frame from which they drew their religious inspiration. Accordingly, I shall follow the philosophical preliminaries (in Chapter 1) with a sketch of Western medieval commonplaces about what sacraments *are* and what they are *for* (Chapter 2) and how and in what sense Christian sacraments were supposed to be more effective (Chapter 3). Medieval Christian believers hoped for union with God. Having dealt in detail with eucharistic real presence (in Part Two), I shall move on to consider eucharistic eating and drinking, which somehow take Christ in (Chapter 11). Then (in Chapter 12) I shall win further insight into the point of sacraments by considering what it will be like in the life to come, when we have to do without them, and by asking how tightly my authors integrate their understanding of sacraments into their analyses of human nature and eschatology. Historical and systematic theologians should find it useful to ponder their example. Readers with purely philosophical interests may wish to pass over the theologial issues surveyed in Chapters 2, 11, and 12, but they may instead find their curiousity tweaked and wish to discover what lured my authors into such thought experiments.

My own conclusion is that, where the metaphysics and physics of eucharistic real presence are concerned, my authors were strikingly bold and remarkably resourceful. By contrast, they proved much less imaginative when it came to integrating medieval Christian insistence on material cult with traditional and emerging understandings of human nature and destiny.

I

Aristotelian Preliminaries

The focus of this book is on some medieval theories of the eucharist. The principal authors on which it concentrates work out their theories of sacramental causality and eucharistic real presence within a broadly Aristotelian philosophical frame. To appreciate their worries and to applaud or critique their results demand familiarity with some fundamental Aristotelian conceptual machinery. Since issues about bodies and their placement loom the largest (and will occupy Chapters 4–10 below), what follows overviews two topics: Aristotelian conceptions of the metaphysical structure of corporeal things, and Aristotelian conceptions of place. Coverage begins but does not stop with Aristotle himself. Where relevant, it goes on to what ancient, Arab, and medieval Latin commentaries made of his ideas. The aim of this chapter is modest: not to exhaust its subjects or debate and defend interpretations, but to orient students and non-specialists to ways of thinking that our principal authors took for granted.

I. The Metaphysical Structure of Corporeal Things

Experience acquaints us with bodily things in wide variety: earth, air, fire, and water; rocks, flowers, and trees; worms, birds, and lizards; cats and mice, lions and lambs; sun, moon, and stars; and, of course, human beings. Two items cry out for explanation: difference and change. Broadly speaking, antiquity sponsored two strategies for explaining difference and change among bodily things: atomism and hylomorphism. *Atomism.* Atomism treats macro-objects (rocks, trees, and cows) as made up of micro-objects (atoms) of fundamentally different kinds. Differences among macro-objects are explained as different arrangements of different kinds of atoms; changes, as their rearrangement. Thus, Democritus and Lucretius held that the universe consists of atoms and the void. Macro-objects result from chance collisions and hooking-together of atoms of the same and/or different types. Changes are a function of locomotion, of other chance collisions, of couplings and decouplings.

Aristotle rejected atomism, because he thought it could not explain the macroscopic world as we know it. Ancient atomism identifies atoms as the basic entities of the universe. Their theory treats atoms as literally indivisible and indestructible, and therefore as having paradigmatic unity. The macro-objects of our experience are reduced to chance aggregates, with no more intrinsic unity than a heap of stones or the links of a chain. By contrast, Aristotle identifies living organisms, plants, and animals as having paradigmatic unity. He was impressed by the fact that plants and animals have characteristic life cycles, organic structures, and functional activities, and by the fact that they breed true. Chance collisions cannot explain such "always or for the most part" regularities. If chance collisions were all that was involved, we should expect random arrangements of arms and legs, eyes and ears. We should not be surprised if some cows lasted for only five minutes while others carried on for five years. Yet, where the material world is concerned, Aristotle insisted, it is the functional unity and consistency of plants and animals that demands explanation.[1]

Hylomorphism. The alternative to which Aristotle turned was to treat corporeal things as shaped-up stuff. His governing metaphor is the sculptor in his or her studio, who takes a lump of clay and shapes it into a statue. The clay is the stuff or the matter (*hyle*), and the shape is the form (*morphe*). Hylomorphism is the theory that all corporeal things are like the statue in being shaped-up stuff, formed matter. Differences in structure are explained as differences in form. Changes are analyzed as changes of form in which the matter is transformed, analogous to the way a sculptor might reshape the nose of a statue to achieve a better likeness or turn a horse figurine into a giraffe figurine instead.

To convert the metaphor into a theory requires several further steps. First, if corporeal things are formed matter, 'form' does not refer simply to the static distribution of material parts. Cows differ from violets, not only in static structure, but also in the shape of their functional dynamics. Violets

[1] For an excellent account that takes its cue, not only from Aristotle's *Metaphysics*, but also from its biological works, see Montgomery Furth, *Substance, Form, and Psyche: An Aristotelian Metaphysics* (Cambridge: Cambridge University Press, 1988).

have no stomachs. Cows not only have two stomachs; there is a characteristic process by which food is chewed, swallowed, regurgitated for cud to be chewed some more, before it descends again to be turned into cow fuel and cow parts. For Aristotle, static structure is there to make characteristic functions possible (the way that the "innards" of the car's engine are dictated by what it will take to make the car roll at certain speeds); the latter *explains* the former. Both static and dynamic shapes are included in what Aristotle means by 'form'.

The second step is to "reify" form and matter. Ordinarily, we do not think of the clay and the shape of the clay as different *parts* of the statue. We do recognize that the clay is separable from it shape, insofar as it can be reshaped into something else, but we do not speak of the shapes as distinct parts. Hylomorphism as a theory of corporeal things "reifies" matter and form by treating them as distinct metaphysical components or constituents of corporeal substances, and accordingly analyzes corporeal substances as "composites" of matter and form.

The third step is to recognize that corporeal things are multiply shaped. Theoretically interpreted, this means that their matter is subject to many forms, some of which make the thing to be the very thing it is and without which it could not exist, and others that it could exist without. Thus, Aristotle and Aristotelians partition shapes or forms into substantial forms (those that are essential to the individual thing) and accidental forms (those that they can exist without). Socrates cannot exist without being human, but he can lose his pallor by bronzing in the sun. Beulah the cow cannot exist without being bovine, but she once did weigh less than 300 pounds. Substantial form explains why an individual has the static structure and dynamic functions characteristic of its species, whereas accidental forms account for other features (pallor or whiteness) or functions (ability to play the violin or to speak Chinese).

So far, then, hylomorphic theorizing identifies the following layer-like structure within corporeal things:

accidental forms
inhere in
substantial form
prime matter

Matter is first shaped up into a thing by substantial form, and the composite is constituted as a substance with the paradigmatic unity that Aristotle was aiming for: *per se* unity. This hylomorphic composite is further shaped up by accidental forms, which are said by Aristotle to inhere in substance. A substance is united with its accidents, but, because it could exist without them, the substance together with its accidents (for example, white Socrates or half-a-ton Beulah) form a *per accidens* unity.

This theoretical sketch also exposes the bare bones of Aristotle's analysis of change. Parmenides had famously argued that change is impossible, because what came to be would have to come to be either from what is or from what is not. But what is, is already. And something cannot come to be from nothing. Aristotle replied with two distinctions. First, and absolutely fundamental in his philosophy, is the distinction between act and potency. The lump of clay in the sculptor's studio is not actually a statue, but it is (unlike water or the intellectual soul) the kind of thing that can be shaped into a statue and so is potentially a statue. Pale Socrates is actually pale, but Socrates is also the kind of thing that can be tan instead and so is potentially tan. This prime matter may actually be combined with the form of bovinity to constitute Beulah the cow, but it is the kind of thing that can be combined with any other substantial form that it could be naturally caused to have and so is potentially a constituent of Beulah's corpse.

The second distinction is between something's coming to be F from what in no way exists (what is not *simpliciter* or pure nothing) and what is potentially F coming to be actually F. Among corporeal things, change is potency actualization, in which what is potentially F comes to be actually F. For Aristotle, change is intelligible only because there is something that persists through the change and is first potentially but not actually F and then is actually F, or vice versa. Where the form is substantial form, the reshaped stuff is prime matter (or some composite of prime matter and lower-level substantial forms; see below); where the form is accidental, the reshaped stuff is the substance in which it inheres. Here below (bracketing Aristotle's special assumptions about the heavens), whatever shape matter has, it has the potentiality to be reshaped. Socrates cannot exist without being human, but the prime matter that constitutes Socrates can exist without constituting Socrates and can be informed by any form it could be naturally caused to acquire. This potency of matter for substantial forms it does not have means that all hylomorphic composites are the kinds of things that can come into being and pass away.[2]

[2] Aristotle, Physics I. 7–8 189^{b}30–192^{b}6.

Aristotle also uses his governing sculptor/sculpture metaphor to introduce his distinctive doctrine of the four causes. In *Physics* II.3 $194^{b}16$–195a3, he advances a model of explanation according to which an adequate account of changes in corporeal things here below involves four factors: *the material cause*, or that out of which a thing comes to be; *the formal cause*, which is usually the form or shape acquired; *the efficient cause*, or what makes what is made or makes the change to happen; and *the final cause*, or that for the sake of which change happens. Thus, when the sculptor shapes clay into a sculpture, the clay is the material cause; the shape or static distribution of the clay parts, the formal cause; the sculptor who shapes the clay, the efficient cause; and the existence of a monument to Socrates, the final cause. Medieval Aristotelians regularly identified material and formal causes as internal, insofar as they are constituents of what comes to be. By contrast, the efficient and final causes are often external: the sculptor is not the sculpture, health is not the activity of walking that Socrates undertakes for health's sake.

Unity versus Plurality of Substantial Forms. Aristotle was drawn to hylomorphism because he thought it could accommodate the paradigmatic unity he saw in plants and animals. But complications arise. Once matter and form are "reified" into parts or at least metaphysical constituents of composite substances, the question arises how paradigmatically *one* any *composite* could be. Why will not being composed of matter and form compromise unity as much as a plurality of atoms would? There is worse to come. For substantial form is supposed to stand behind essential structures and functions. Reflection on living things raised the question whether what it is to be a plant or animal substance does not already—accidents aside—involve multiple shapes and so a plurality of substantial forms. Where plants and animals are concerned, matter has to be shaped up into organic body. Plants and animals are also alive, both engaging in vegetative functions (nutrition, growth, and reproduction) with animals adding sensory cognition and appetite. Human beings are also rational and capable of abstract thought. All of these functions are essential. Surely, they must include some animating substantial form or soul. Does not this add up to a plurality of substantial forms as well as prime matter in living things? What, then, becomes of their paradigmatic unity?

Medieval Latin Aristotelians confronted these problems squarely and offered two basic solutions.[3] The first whittled the plurality of substance-

[3] For a detailed examination of the unity versus the plurality of substantial forms, see my *William Ockham* (Notre Dame: University of Notre Dame Press, 1987), ch. 15, pp. 633–70. For an

constitutors back to two—one substantial form and prime matter—and then extended Aristotle's act/potency distinction to remove the appearance of composition by reducing the ontological status of one of the components. The second approach recognized a plurality of substantial forms and prime matter each as really distinct actualities, but assigned them metaphysically primitive aptitudes to unite with one another to constitute something one *per se*.

The "Unitarian" Position. The first approach is developed by Aquinas, who concedes that two actual things make an aggregate (a heap of stones) or at best a *per accidens* unity (white Socrates or half-ton Beulah). Aquinas appeals to Aristotle's notion that composite substances get their being through form—it is substantial form that shapes stuff up into a thing—to motivate his doctrine that matter is neither actually substance nor nothing at all (*purum nihil*), but potency for being, which is actualized through its combination with substantial form. Matter is not an actual particular thing (a *hoc aliquid*) in and of itself the way ancient atoms are. Thus, a corporeal substance is not the aggregation of two actual things. Rather it is one actual thing *per se*, whose potency for being is actualized through its substantial form.

Such potency actualization constitutes the actuality of a particular substance. Aquinas reasons that any forms added after that will be accidental. This means that, if plants and animals were constituted by prime matter and the form of corporeity, then the animating principle or principles would be added as accidental forms. Positing a plurality of substantial forms would run counter to Aristotle's identification of plants and animals as the paradigm substances. Accordingly, Aquinas denies that there is a plurality of substantial forms in plants and animals with the form of corporeity at the base. Rather the sole substantial form of a plant or animal is its animating principle, which virtually contains the form of corporeity, in the sense that the animating principle has power (*virtus*) to organize matter in all the ways that the form of corporeity would, and power (*virtus*) to animate them besides. Where substantial forms are concerned, Giles of Rome joins Aquinas in supporting the unitarian position.

excellent analysis of earlier pluralist views, see Roberto Zavalloni, *Richard de Mediavilla et la controverse sur la pluralité des formes: Textes inédits et étude critique* (Louvain: Éditions de l'Institute Supérieur de Philosophie, 1951).

A Plurality of Substantial Forms? Scotus and Ockham found Aquinas's notion that matter is pure potency (a mean between what is actually something and nothing at all) *metaphysically* incoherent. Hylomorphism was posited to explain structure and change. If bodies are shaped-up stuff, the stuff to be shaped up has to be actually something that is capable of being (further) shaped! The potency posited by Aristotle's theory of change is the potency of stuff to be shaped in a way it is not now and so is parasitic on something actual (the stuff) that has the potency! Moreover, matter is supposed to be what persists through transformational changes. If matter got all of its actuality through the substantial form it has now, how could that very same matter get all of its actuality through a different substantial form? They wondered, what would be the same about it, what would be the "it" that persists?

Second, Scotus and Ockham join other pluralists in charging that unitarianism cannot save the phenomena involved in animal deaths, according to which fresh corpses regularly have the same size, shape, and qualities that the living body had. Both unitarians and pluralists agree: death means that the stuff that constituted the living body is no longer shaped by the animating principle or soul form. But, for unitarians, the animating principle or soul form was the only substantial form involved in shaping up that matter into a thing (for example, Beulah the cow). When the single substantial form is taken away, the original thing ceases to be, and a new substantial form shapes up the matter into a different thing. One consequence—explicitly drawn by Aquinas—is that the living body and the corpse are numerically distinct bodies. The question is, what explains why the fresh corpse has accidents of the same species as the living body had? If Beulah the cow and Elsie the cow and Billy the goat all are led to the same slaughter house, where they breathe the same air and have their throats slit with the same knife, why does the corpse that succeeds Beulah have black and white spots, and the corpse that succeeds Elsie have a horn broken the same way as hers was, and why does the corpse that succeeds Billy have a goat shape rather than a cow shape? Everyone agrees, accidents do not "migrate" from one substance to another. So, on the unitarian view, death strips the matter of all of the forms—substantial and accidental—that it had before. The environmental factors and the cause of death are the same. The unitarian view has no resources to explain these living body/fresh corpse similarities. By contrast, pluralists maintain that the accidents are of the same species, because the living and the dead bodies are numerically the same body.

Death involves the separation of the animating form, which leaves the composite of prime matter and the form of corporeity behind.

Pluralists further pointed to the *theological* advantages of their positions. The medieval church fostered the veneration of relics, which were said to be the dead bodies or body parts of the saints. But the unitarian view implies that the dead body is not numerically the same as the body the saint had. Why, then, venerate it? Likewise, the body taken down from the cross and laid in the tomb would not be Christ's body, the same one that Mary bore. During the three days between Christ's death and resurrection, unitarians would have to concede that Christ's body did not exist and so was not available to be really present anywhere during that time.

Thus, the pluralist position further complicates the above layer-like structure of composite substances, at least where living things are concerned. For human beings, the diagram would be as follows:

accidental forms
inhere in
intellectual soul
sensory soul
vegetative soul
corporeity
prime matter

Only early thirteeth-century pluralists posited all three soul forms in humans. Scotus denies that the sensory soul is really distinct from the intellectual soul and so posits only two substantial forms in human beings, while Ockham argues for two soul forms (sensory and intellectual but not vegetative) and so admits three substantial forms for human beings.

If these moves "save the phenomena" surrounding death and the veneration of relics, how can they satisfy Aristotle's theoretical *desideratum* that plants and animals exhibit paradigmatic unity? For Scotus and Ockham, matter and form are not only reified in the sense of being counted as metaphysical constituents. They are reified in the strong sense of being supposed to be really distinct things (*res*), each with an actuality of its own, each such that it is metaphysically possible for it to exist without the others. Scotus and Ockham agree that sometimes really distinct things combine to constitute mere aggregates (a heap of stones); sometimes, merely *per accidens* unities (Socrates and his pallor). Nevertheless, Scotus and Ockham contend, some really distinct things are nevertheless such that they have a natural aptitude to unite with the others to make something that is one *per se*. That things have an aptitude to unite to makes something one *per se* with some things and not others is a primitive intrinsic fact about them that requires no further explanation.

Both unitarians and pluralists go beyond what is explicit in Aristotle to develop his concept of corporeal substance in distinctively different ways. Pluralists stick with the shaped-up-stuff metaphor and insist that stuff must *be* something if it is to be there to be shaped. For them, each of the parts or constituents of the hylomorphic composite has an actuality of its own and an aptitude of its own to unite with the others to make something one *per se*. For pluralists, the parts are what they are prior to and independently of actually uniting to constitute the composite substance. Unitarians, by contrast, try hardest to show how plants and animals can exhibit paradigmatic unity. For them, it is not the case that the metaphysical constituents are actually what they are prior to the whole. Rather, it is the other way around: the whole is prior to the parts, insofar as substantial form gets its actuality by being the conduit through which the composite receives its actuality, and matter gets its actuality only insofar as the whole is actualized through its substantial form.

Reifying Which Accidents? If bodies are shaped-up stuff, formed matter, Aristotle's ten categories can be taken metaphysically as an attempt to classify what types of shapes there are.[4] Twice Aristotle produces a list of ten:[5] substance, quantity, quality, relation, place, time, state, being in a position, action, and passion. Aristotle's own remarks suggest at least two ways of arriving at this list. The first is to identify a set of basic questions that elicit distinct and non-overlapping ranges of answers. The suggestion is, for example, that answers appropriate to the question "when?" are never suitable for the question "where?" and vice versa. A second approach is to look at the various kinds of answers one gets when the question "what is it?" is pressed. For example, if I ask what Socrates is, the first answer may be "a human being." If I inquire further what a human being is, and so on, the answers will be "a rational animal" and so on until one gets to the last answer "a substance." Again, if I ask what mauve is, the first answer may be "a shade

[4] See Giorgio Pini, *Categories and Logic in Scotus* (Leiden, Bosto, and Cologne: Brill, 2002), where Pini shows how early thirteenth-century philosophers in the Latin West insisted that the *Categories* could be taken two ways: as a work of logic and as a work of metaphysics.

[5] Aristotle, *Categories* (c. 4, 1^b25 ff.) and *Topics* (I. 9 103^b20–39). In *Metaphysics* V. 7 1017^a22–7, however, he lists only eight.

of purple," then "a color," but ultimately "a quality."[6] It is at least arguable that Aristotle did not have much invested in this precise list or its length; at any rate he never defends it or the above-mentioned strategies for developing it. Nevertheless, however much medievals came to question and dispute them, Aristotle's ten categories had presumptive weight for them and was definitely the place to start.

Aristotle is clear that substance is the first category. He distinguishes primary substances or substance individuals (such as Socrates and Beulah the cow) from secondary substances (substance kinds).[7] In the *Categories*, primary substances are the subjects that are, on the one hand, constituted as the very individuals they are by their secondary substances, and that are characterized by added accidental shapes. Aristotle insists that

[P1] substance individuals are naturally prior to accidents

in that the accidental shapes depend for their existence on the existence of the substances (no shape without something's being shaped), but not vice versa (although he is notoriously less clear about whether an individual substance could exist without any accidental shapes at all).

Especially pertinent to this study is the question of which accidents to reify.[8] Some thirteenth-century Aristotelians (Richard Middleton among them) contended that not only substance but all nine categories of accidents must be reified. They took their inspiration from Aristotle's own remark that

[P2] there is no passage from contradictory to contradictory—it is not the case that a proposition is first true and then its contradictory opposite is true—without any change.

Because Aristotelian change is shape change, they inferred that

[P2′] there is no passage from contradictory to contradictory without the generation or corruption of some thing

and concluded that, not only secondary substance, but accident forms in all nine categories must be things really distinct from things in other categories.

[6] See J. L. Ackrill, *Aristotle's 'Categories' and 'De Interpretatione'* (Oxford: Oxford University Press, 1963), notes to ch. 4, pp. 78–80. Ockham notes this first approach in *Summa logicae* I, c. 41; Opera Philosophica (hereafter OPh) I. 107.

[7] Aristotle, *Categories*, 2 $1^a20–1^b9$; ch. 5 $2^a11–3^a21$.

[8] For more detailed analyses, see my *William Ockham*, chs. 5–8, pp. 143–285.

The authors on which this study focuses in Chapters 3–10 are less extravagant. They all reify substantial and sensible quality forms. Aquinas, Giles of Rome, and (usually) Scotus reify quantity. As Ockham would later charge, they treat quantity as a kind of "skin" between substance, on the one hand, and sensible qualities, on the other, to yield the following structure:

sensible qualities
inhere in
quantity
inheres in
substantial form(s)
prime matter

It is essential to dimensive quantity to have parts that are distinct and determinate, so that one part is at a distance from another. Quantity thus does double duty: it extends the sensible qualities that inhere in it, and it extends the substance (or at least the prime matter) in which it inheres, so that one part is at a distance from another. Aquinas and Giles of Rome assign quantity a further job, not only of extending the parts of sensible qualities or matter so that they have one part at a distance from another, but of dividing them into parts in the first place. Scotus and Ockham reject this idea, insisting that sensible qualities, prime matter, and material substantial forms are divided into parts of themselves. Ockham insists that locomotion by efficient causes can explain the distribution of parts so that one is at a distance from another. Once locomotion is brought into the picture as an additional change explainer, Ockham thinks the change argument will support at most the reification of substance and some qualities. Changes in the other eight categories can somehow be reduced to these.

The Problem of Universals. In his introduction to Aristotle's *Categories*, the Neoplatonist philosopher Porphyry identifies what I have been calling "shapes" as predicables, which are by nature common or sharable by many individuals. Porphyry treats the categories as highest genera under which a hierarchy of species are distinguished by means of differentiae. Porphyry's tree charts the branches under the category of substance, which divides the species into corporeal and incorporeal substance; corporeal substance (or body) into animate and inanimate; animate into plants and animals; and animals into rational and non-rational; and rational animals into mortal (human) and immortal. Reflecting on it, Porphyry distinguishes five types of predicables: genus, species, differentia, proprium, and accident, whose systematically different relations to their subject it is the philosopher's job to analyze. Throughout our period, medievals in the Latin West continued to shoulder this burden, among other things by producing many commentaries on the predicables.[9]

If Porphyry insists that the categories classify predicables, Aristotle is clear that primary substances or substance individuals are not predicables. They are the subjects, not the predicates. In his technical language, they are neither in a subject (the way accidents are) nor said of a subject (the way secondary substance is).[10] Yet, Porphyry and other ancient commentators already recognize that "predicable" is ambiguous, between a *semantic* relation that holds between concepts or linguistic entities in a sentence or proposition, and a *metaphysical* relation between a thing and its constitutor- and/or characterizer-properties. Everyone agreed that there are concepts of genera, species, differentiae, propria, and accidents. Everyone agreed that it belonged to the subject matter of logic to analyze the systematic differences among their semantic properties.[11]

Porphyry raises a further question. Seemingly, concepts have application only if they correspond to reality. If genera, species, differentiae, propria, and accidents were things, would not they have to be, not particular, but common things? If so, what sorts of things would non-particular predicable things be? Two alternatives came to his mind: either genera and species exist separately from individuals here below, the way Platonic forms were supposed to do, or they are not separate from individuals but are placed in them in such a way as to be constitutive of their essence, as Aristotle was believed to have taught. Following Augustine, Christian theologians did recognize eternal paradigms to exist in God's mind as Divine ideas. Nevertheless and unsurprisingly, by far the majority report among thirteenth- and fourteenth-century Aristotelians was the "Aristotelian" answer: that substance kinds exist in substance individuals in such a way as to be constitutive of their essence.

Boethius problematizes both answers. Focusing on Porphry's claim that predicables are common, Boethius contends that what it is to be common has to be resolved in terms of resemblance or identity. To say that human

[9] For more detailed discussions of the problem of universals, see my *William Ockham*, chs. 1–4, pp. 3–141.

[10] Aristotle, *Categories* 2 1^a20–1^b9.

[11] See Pini, *Categories and Logic in Scotus*, for an examination of the medieval research program that treated the *Categories* as a work on logic.

nature is common to Socrates and Plato is either (1) to say that human nature in Socrates is numerically distinct from but relevantly similar to human nature in Plato, or (2) to say that human nature in Socrates is numerically the same and identical in Socrates and Plato. But philosophical commonplaces:

[P3] If A is wholly and completely in B, and C is wholly and completely in D, and B and D are wholly and completely outside one another, then A is not numerically the same as C,

and

[P4] If X is similar to Y, there is something else Z that is the respect of their similarity.

Socrates is wholly and completely outside Plato, and Socrates' (Plato's) human nature is wholly and completely inside Socrates (Plato). So, by [P3], it follows that human nature is not numerically one in Socrates and Plato. But, if human nature is numerically distinct in Socrates and Plato, then to say that they have human nature in common must mean that human nature in Socrates is relevantly similar to human nature in Plato. By [P4], there must be something else (call it human nature*) with respect to which Socrates' and Plato's human natures are similar. Human nature* is common to Socrates' human nature and Plato's human nature. By [P3], this cannot mean that human nature* is numerically the same and identical in Socrates' human nature and Plato's human nature. Therefore, it must mean that the human nature* of Socrates' human nature is relevantly similar to the human nature* of Plato's human nature. By [P4], there must be something else (call it human nature**) that is the respect of their resemblance, and so on to infinity.

Adherents of this common opinion tended to take their cue from the solution that Boethius attributes to Alexander of Aphrodisias to claim that the same item—the species, for example, human nature—has a double mode of existence. It exists in the intellect as an object of thought and as such is an abstract general concept that is common and predicable of many simultaneously. It also exists in reality and is numerically multiplied in numerically distinct individuals (as [P3] implies). Yet, there is some one thing that is the respect of the resemblance between Socrates and Plato (as [P4] requires): namely, human nature existing in the intellect as an object of thought.

Individuation. If human nature is somehow common to numerically many individuals, and exists in each in such a way as to be constitutive of their nature, it must be that there is something else in individuals that "individuates" them (that is, that makes them to be numerically distinct) from one another.[12] As Scotus sometimes puts it, "something the same" entities also have to include among their metaphysical constitutors something distinct! If so, majority reporters faced two problems: first to identify what the individuator is, and second to explain what the relation between nature and individuator is within the individual thing constituted by them. *What Individuator?* Seemingly, given its function, the individuator itself will have to be unsharable. Seemingly, the theoretical options would be either to posit unsharable properties (which later Scotists dubbed "thisnesses") alongside sharable ones, or to construct an unsharable property from an aggregate of sharable properties.

In the twelfth century, William of Champeaux forwarded the intuitive idea that what individuates Socrates from Plato is their accidents. Socrates, say, is pale, short, fat, and ugly, while Plato is tall, dark, and handsome. Each accident—whiteness, 5-feet-tallness, ugliness—is sharable, but the whole package of accidents is unshared and unsharable. Medieval Aristotelians found two reasons to reject this proposal. The first and most widely accepted was that it runs contrary to Aristotle's claim that [P1] substance is naturally prior to accidents: that is, that accidents depend on substance for their existence, but not the other way around. If individual substances are individuated by packages of accidents, then Socrates would depend on accident packages to be distinct from Plato and so to be the very individual that he is. The second, urged by Duns Scotus, was that it is metaphysically impossible to construct an unsharable property out of sharable properties: if each property in the aggregate is sharable, the whole aggregate will be sharable, too! These two factors drove Scotus to posit primitive unsharable properties, properties not classified by Aristotle's ten categories of predicables, to do the individuator's job.

A significant plurality of medieval Aristotelians was attracted to another pair of intuitive ideas that had some currency among the ancient commentators: that matter and/or quantity play(s) the role of individuating corporeal substances.[13] Consider a shop counter of lookalike Eiffel Tower

[12] For a more extensive discussion of this topic, see my *William Ockham*, ch. 16, pp. 671–95.

[13] For an excellent presentation of the historical development of these alternatives, see M. D. Roland-Gosselin, OP, *Le "De Ente et Essentia" de S. Thomas D'Aquin: Texte établi d'après les manuscrits parisiens, introduction, notes, et études historiques* (Paris: Librairie Philosophique J. Vrin, 1948), "Le Principe de Individualité," 49–134.

models. It is tempting to say that what makes them numerically distinct is that this one was made from *this* hunk of metal and that one from *that* hunk of metal. Aristotelian hylomorphism does make prime matter the ultimate stuff that gets shaped up and hence the ultimate subject in which the forms exist. The trouble is that matter of itself is just as common as substantial forms are. What makes *this* hunk of matter to be numerically distinct from *that* in the first place? To many, quantity appeared to be the right answer, because it pertains to the essence of dimensive quantity to have parts that are distinct and determinate from one another. Aquinas says that dimensive quantity is such that, if only it could exist of itself, it would be individuated of itself. The problem is that quantity is an accident, and Aristotle teaches that accidents are naturally posterior to substance. For Aquinas, the answer was to put the two together—the individuator is matter "signed" by quantitative dimensions—and win the advantages of each. Matter is one of the metaphysical constituents of corporeal substance and the ultimate subject in which the forms exist. Quantity would be individuated of itself if only it could exist of itself. Quantity in matter divides matter into parts and distributes the parts at a distance from one another. Thus, matter signed by quantity is both substantial enough to overcome the natural priority argument, and individuated into distinct hunks. It is, therefore, able to individuate both the substantial and the accidental forms that inhere in it. These ideas loomed large for both Aquinas and Giles of Rome in their formulations of eucharistic theology (see especially Chapter 8 below).

How Related? If an individual corporeal substance is metaphysically constituted by a common nature and an individuator, the question becomes urgent, what is the relation between the two within that individual? Ockham could see only two alternatives: either the individuator is really distinct and separable from the nature, or it is not. Like Scotus, Ockham thought it was ridiculous to suppose that one thing could be made to be the very thing it is by anything really distinct from it. To say that X is really distinct from Y, is to say that X is one thing (*res*) and has its own integrity as the very thing it is, prior to and independently of any union with Y, and vice versa. But, if individuator and common nature are really the same within the individual, then human nature in Socrates is inseparable from the individuator in Socrates and so is no more common to many than the individuator is. If the natures existing in real individuals are not common, then why is an individuator needed?

This and many other detailed arguments convince Ockham that no such composition of common nature and individuator exists within the individual. Only individuals are real, and real individuals are individual in and of themselves. What makes individuals of the same species to be co-specific is not some common metaphysical constituent that exists numerically multiplied in numerically distinct individuals, and exists in the intellect as the species concept under which each and all of those individuals fall. What makes individuals members of the same species is that their individual natures are species-wise similar to one another. What makes them all fall under the species concept is that they are each and all relevantly similar to the concept. Boethius' argument against explaining the way genera, species, and so on are common in terms of resemblance fails, because [P4]—that, if X is similar to Y, there is something else Z that is the respect of their similarity—is false. The species-wise similarity of Socrates' humanity to Plato's does not have to be grounded in something else that is the respect of their similarity. Socrates' humanity and Plato's humanity are species-wise similar in and of themselves.

II. The Nature of Place

Eucharistic real presence—the doctrine that Christ's Body and Blood come to be really present on the altar where bread and wine still seem to be—challenges common sense as well as many philosophical theories of bodily placement. Here as elsewhere, the authors on which this study focuses in Chapters 3–10 took their cue from Aristotle, whose treatments of place were philosophically and exegetically vexed and in consequence already much commented upon.[14]

Aristotle's method in theory-construction is to begin with a list of commonly agreed *desiderata* that any adequate account ought to accomodate. Where place is concerned, he lists the following:

[i] place *contains* what is in place;
[ii] place is *not part of* what is in place;
[iii] the immediate place of a thing is *equal* to the thing;

[14] For an outstanding analysis of early English commentaries, see Cecilia Trifogli, *Oxford Physics in the Thirteenth Century (ca.1250–1270): Motion, Infinity, Place, and Time* (Leiden, Boston, and Cologne: Brill, 2000).

[iv] place is *separable* from what is in place;
[v] place is *immobile*.[15]

[i] seems to follow from what it means to say that one thing is *in* another. [ii] rules out saying that the whole body is in place through its own matter or through its own forms. [iii] dictates that the immediate place of a thing be equal to or commensurate with the thing. Ordinarily, we say that Christ Church Cathedral is in England or in the city of Oxford, but neither is its immediate and proper place, because the boundaries of England and Oxford do not coincide with those of the cathedral building; England and Oxford contain much else besides. Moreover, what is in place are *natural* bodies, and—in Aristotelian physics—what it means to call a body natural is that it has an inward principle of motion. So located bodies are by nature mobile, by nature not only capable of but naturally apt to change place. Hence, [iv] it will not work to identify place with anything a body takes with it when it goes (for example, its matter or form or its parts). Moreover, [v] in locomotion, place itself has to stay put while the body moves. Aristotle thinks of the universe as finite and bounded by the outermost celestial sphere, with cosmic markers of upward and downward directions.[16] Suppose air is located at a lower place P1 and moves upward to a higher place P10. If P10 were simultaneously to move upward as fast as the air, then the air's motion would be pointless, because the simultaneous motion of the place would keep the body from reaching its goal.

Two theories of what place is suggested themselves to Aristotle: that place is incorporeal continuous three-dimensional extension that is capable of receiving bodies; and that place is the limit of the containing body whose limit touches and is coincident with that of the body contained. Versions of the first were sponsored by ancient atomists and presented by Aristotle in *Categories*, ch. 6, 5^{a}6–14. The second is the position at which Aristotle arrives and which he defends in *Physics* IV. 4–5. Not only did these two accounts seem incompatible with each other; each was problematic in itself.

Three-Dimensional Place. To contemporary readers whose imaginations have been schooled to Cartesian coordinates and Newtonian absolute space, the first position is the more intuitive and seems more obviously to satisfy Aristotle's *desiderata* [i]–[v]. Certainly, the first position would seem to have

[15] Aristotle, *Physics* IV. 4 210^{b}34–211^{a}2, 212^{a}17–19.
[16] Aristotle, *Physics* IV. 4 212^{a}22–7.

an advantage over the second where [iii] is concerned. How could a two-dimensional surface be equal in quantity to a three-dimensional body?

Within the Aristotelian scheme of things, however, three-dimensional place poses deep-structure metaphysical difficulties. [1] First, it posits extension as existing independently (existing *per se*) of any and every body. But, for Aristotle, extension is one of the shapes that do not exist without something to shape. More technically, extension is a function of quantitative dimensions that are accidents and so dependent for their existence on their existence in body.[17] Aristotle concludes that, if place were three-dimensional extension, it would have to *be* body. [2] Second, Aristotelian bodies are impenetrable. Giles of Rome digs down to identify what he takes to be the reason: it is metaphysically impossible for two bodies to be extended in the same place at once, because it is metaphysically impossible that two quantitative dimensions exist in the same place at once. If place were three-dimensional extension, then—whether the quantitative dimensions existed *per se* or in a body—place would be impenetrable and unable to receive extended bodies after all.[18] Ironically, these very difficulties—of positing independent accidents and multiple quantities in the same place—number among the principal problems for the doctrine of eucharistic real presence as well (see Chapters 4–10 below).

Place as the Surface of the Containing Body. In *Physics* IV. 6–9, Aristotle rejects a three-dimensional approach to place and argues against the void. Instead, he defends the remarkable idea that place is the immobile limit or surface of the containing body, whose surface touches or coincides with the surface of the contained body.[19] One big advantage of this analysis is that it "locates" place in natural bodies, and so avoids positing any accidents existing independently of substance. Place so conceived can also be made to fit most of Aristotle's listed *desiderata*. The surface of the containing body does [i] *contain*. [iii] *Equality* of proper place means not equality in volume but commensuration between the surfaces of container and contained body so that surfaces of container and contained touch or coincide. The surface of

[17] See Ockham, *Expositio in Libros Physicorum Aristotelis* IV. 6. 12; OPh V. 70.

[18] Giles of Rome, *Theoremata de Corpore Christi* (Rome, 1554), Propositiones VII–VIII, fos. 4vX–5ra; *Commentaria in octo libros Physicorum Aristotelis* (Venice, 1502; Frankfurt: Minerva GMBH,, 1968), fo. 93va–b. See Cecilia Trifogli, "La Dottrina del Luogo in Egidio Romano," *Medioevo*, 14 (1988), 235–90, esp. 243–4. See also her *Oxford Physics in the Thirteenth Century*, ch. 3, pp. 142–64.

[19] Aristotle, *Physics* IV. 4 212^a5–6^a.

the container is [ii] *not part* of the contained body, and it is [iv] *separable from* the contained body. When the contained body moves, it leaves that container and moves through continuum many others.

Nevertheless, all is not well. Not only does this second account startle in the abstract; it yields counter-intuitive results in the concrete. Locomotion is change of place. From the *Physics-IV* definition, it seems to follow that a body is in motion if and only if there is continuous change in the surfaces that immediately contain it. Three counter-examples challenge this result. The first two are "river boat" paradoxes.

[Case 1] Suppose a boat is tied to the dock, but that the water around it is in continuous flux. Surely the boat is at rest, going nowhere. Yet, it is not at rest if place is the surface of the containing body, because the containing body is continuously changing. This example seems to show that place so defined is not [v] immobile. Ordinary intuition encourages the conclusion that changes in the containing surface are *not sufficient* for locomotion the way they should be if the definition were correct.

[Case 2.1] Suppose the boat is moving down the river, but that the water is also moving down the river at the same time at the same speed. Surely the body is in motion, but the surface of its container-body remains the same.

[Case 2.2] Suppose a full bottle of water is carried from the kitchen to the dining room. The water moves from one room to another, but its immediate containing surface does not change. Ordinary intuition supports the inference that changes in the immediate containing surface are *not necessary* for locomotion either.

[Case 3] Aristotelian cosmology itself features a moving body that—on this definition—is not in place at all. The outermost sphere of the heavens rotates eternally, but its convex surface is the limit of the universe and is not contained by anything. Aristotle declares explicitly, a body that does not have a container is not in place.[20]

The first three cases (1, 2.1, and 2.2) show that *"Aristotelian" place, understood simply as the limit of the container body, is not [v] immobile.* This is, as Averroes notes, a straightforward consequence of Aristotle's decision (in *Physics* IV. 4–5) to house place in natural bodies. *Natural* bodies are mobile by definition, because their make-up includes an "inward principle of motion." So all places will be mobile *per accidens*, insofar as they are the surfaces of bodies that are mobile *per se*! Moreover, the combined upshot of

[20] Aristotle, *Physics* IV. 5 212^{a}31–2.

the above cases (1, 2.1, 2.2, and 3) is that *locomotion is not, after all, a function of change of merely "Aristotelian" place.* Their startling implication is that bodily motion and rest will have to be reckoned relative to something else!

Aristotle himself dismisses the river-boat cases with the suggestion that the boat is at rest (Case 1) and in motion (Case 2.1) with respect to the river as a whole.[21] But this seems unsatisfactory, since Aristotle himself has distinguished common from proper places and insisted that place, strictly speaking, is to be identified with proper place.[22]

The more common strategy is to appeal to a cosmic frame of reference—to the north/east/south/west poles of the universe, to the outermost heavenly sphere that moves neither up nor down, and to the center around which it rotates—to secure some kind of measure for rest and motion. In [Case 1], the boat is in the same place because, even though the water is continuously flowing around it, the order of the surface of whatever water is there at the moment to the cosmic fixed points remains the same as the order of the immediately preceding and following water surfaces. Thus, Aquinas declares, even though the *material* changes (the water flows), the *order* (the relation to the cosmic fixed points) remains the same.[23]

Giles of Rome gives this strategy significant development when he distinguishes *material* place from *formal* place. Material place is the surface of the containing body, while *formal* place is the order of the surface to the cosmic fixed points. Giles makes Aquinas's idea more precise by identifying the relevant order as distance. Moreover, on Aristotle's definition in *Physics* IV, while the body is in a place, its surface and that of the container body coincide. In some passages, Giles shifts from seeing place as the distance from the *container* body surface to regarding it as the distance from the *contained*-body surface. Thus, in Case 1, the boat changes place materially, but not formally. The boat is at rest, because the boat's distance from the cosmic fixed points remains constant. Likewise for Cases 2.1 and 2.2, the material place of the boat and the water do not change, but they move nonetheless because they change place formally.[24]

[21] Aristotle, *Physics* IV. 4 212^{a}23–9. See Ockham, *Expositio in libros Physicorum* IV. 7. 1; OPh V. 79–80.

[22] Aristotle, *Physics* IV. 2 211^{a}23–9.

[23] See Trifogli, *Oxford Physics in the Thirteenth Century*, ch.3, p. 179; and "La Dottrina del Luogo in Egidio Romano," p. 262. She references Aquinas, *In Phys.* IV, lect. 6, nn. 14–15; Marietti, p. 227.

[24] Trifogli, "La Dottrina del Luogo in Egidio Romano," p. 265–6. See Ockham's summary of Gile's position in *Expositio in libros Physicorum* IV. 7. 2; OPh V.80.

Trifogli notes that what Giles has effectively done (without explicitly admitting it) is to set formal place, the distance of the located body from the cosmic fixed points, alongside "Aristotelian" place, the limit of the containing body, so that he is working with two distinct concepts of place. And it is to formal place, not "Aristotelian" place, that Giles assigns the important theoretical roles: formal place is the somehow immobile place, and formal place is the true measure of rest and motion.[25]

Scotus and Ockham begin with *Physics-IV* "Aristotelian" place.[26] They insist that the container body, not the contained body, is the site of place. If so, Aquinas's and Giles's appeal to order or distance relations to cosmic fixed points does not show how place can be literally [v] immobile. For order and distance relations are Aristotelian accidents: shapes that depend on what they shape for their existence. Moreover, for Aristotle,

[P5] accidents cannot migrate from subject to subject.

Numerically the same shape cannot first be the shape of this stuff and then the shape of that stuff, although this and that stuff can have shapes that are *specifically* the same (as numerically distinct lookalike Eiffel Tower statues do). If the containing surface is continuously changing, the order and/or distance relations to the cosmic fixed points are likewise continuously changing, each numerically distinct from those that came before.[27]

For their part, Scotus and Ockham still try to combine "Aristotelian" place with an appeal to some sort of cosmic reference to secure a measure for locomotion. Numerically distinct subjects make for numerically distinct accidents. Scotus contends, however, that what is relevant for locomotion is not whether the relations of the surrounding surface are *numerically* the same, but whether they are *specifically* the same. If they are specifically the same, then Scotus will say that the place is *the same*, not numerically, but *by equivalence*: so far as motion is concerned, it is as if they were numerically one place. It will not do, however, simply to declare that a body is at rest if

[25] Trifogli, "La Dottrina del Luogo in Egidio Romano, " pp. 235–7, 268–75.

[26] Scotus, *Ordinatio* II, d. 2, p. 2, q. 1–2, n. 219; Vaticana VII. 254; Ockham, *Quodlibeta* I. 4; Opera Theologica (hereafter OTh) IX. 24. For an extended examination of Scotus's views, see Richard Cross, *The Physics of Duns Scotus: The Scientific Context of a Theological Vision* (Oxford: Clarendon Press, 1998), ch. 11, pp. 193–213, esp. 202–13.

[27] Scotus, *Ordinatio* II, d. 2, p. 2, q. 1–2, n. 222; Vaticana VII. 255–6; Ockham, *Expositio in Libros Physicorum* IV. 7. 3; OPh V. 81–3. See also Trifogli, *Oxford Physics in the Thirteenth Century*, ch. 3, pp. 180–6.

and only if its places are equivalent in relation to motion, while a body is in motion if and only if its places are not equivalent in relation to motion. Some criterion of equivalence must be supplied.[28] Scotus takes his cue from Aristotle's own handling of the river-boat cases: just as Aristotle appeals to the whole river, so Scotus speaks of equivalence as calculated "in relation to the whole universe."[29] Most likely, Scotus has in mind that the Aristotelian universe finds its limit in the convex surface of the outermost sphere, which contains everything else the way the whole river contains everything in its waters. Even if the outermost sphere rotates on its vertical axis, so that different parts of it are at different times closer or nearer to surfaces containing objects here below, still the distances between the numerically distinct surfaces and the convex limit will be of the same species where the body is at rest and of different species where the body is in motion.[30] In Case 1, water may be flowing around the boat, but the relation to the whole universe of the surface of the water surrounding it at t_1 is specifically the same as that of the water surrounding it at t_2. Relative to the whole universe, the boat hasn't gone anywhere.[31]

For Scotus (as we shall see in Chapter 5 below), there are two sorts of locator relations involved in bodily placement and locomotion. There are the relations of the surrounding surfaces (the merely "Aristotelian" places) to the whole universe, which—by [P5]—are numerically distinct in numerically distinct container surfaces. And there are the presence or whereness relations of the contained bodies and/or their parts to the surrounding surfaces, where presence to *this* surface will be a numerically distinct relation from presence to *that* surface. Once again, a body stays put, when the surface(s)

[28] *Pace* Edward Grant, who declares the opposite in his in many ways helpful article "The Medieval Doctrine of Place: Some Fundamental Problems and Solutions," in *Studi sul XIV Secolo in Memoria di Anneliese Maier* (Rome: Edizioni di Storia et Letteratura, 1981), pp. 57–79; esp. pp. 66–7.

[29] Scotus, *Ordinatio* II, d. 2, p. 2, q. 1–2, n. 227; Vaticana VII. 258.

[30] Thus, I am unpersuaded by Richard Cross, who sees in this reference to "the whole universe" a daring move on Scotus's part: namely, that of dropping reference to particular cosmic fixed points—the outermost sphere, the poles, or the center—and seeing "the whole collection of places" as "fixed and immobile," so that "the identity of place" is "established by relations within the whole." See *The Physics of Duns Scotus*, p. 210. For interesting comparisons between Scotus's and Thomas Wylton's treatment, see Cecilia Trifogli, "Thomas Wylton on the Immobility of Place," *Recherches de Théologie et Philosophie médiévales: Forschungen zur Theologie und Philosophie des Mittelalters*, 65/1 (1998), pp. 1–39.

[31] Scotus, Op. Ox. II, d. 2, p. 2, q. 1–2, nn. 224–9; Vaticana VII. 256–9. See also Trifogli, *Oxford Physics in the Thirteenth Century*, ch.3, pp. 184–6; and Cross, *The Physics of Duns Scotus*, ch. 11, pp. 208–12.

to which it is present bear specifically the same locator relation to the whole universe; and a body undergoes locomotion, when the surface(s) to which it is present bear specifically distinct locator-relations to the whole universe.

Ockham agrees that [not-v] "Aristotelian" place is really mobile. The outermost sphere is a perfect example: it is an "Aristotelian" container place *par excellence*, but it rotates eternally. Nevertheless, its eternal rotation does not keep it from being a cosmic frame of reference, relative to which high and low can be calculated. What is important for this function is that the outermost sphere does not itself move up or down in rectilinear motion. Because it does not, the center around which it rotates is also a cosmic fixed point, which is always equidistant from all of the parts of the rotating sphere. The stuff actually in the center may change, but the center will remain *the same by equivalence*, because the distance from the outermost sphere of what is there now is equal to the distance from the outermost sphere of what was there before.[32] Gesturing towards Case 1, Ockham declares that other places really move (the surface of the water around the boat), but cosmic fixed references allow them to be *immobile by equivalence*. Moreover, not every body that is continuously in a different "Aristotelian" place is in motion, but only those that would be in a different place even if their place were not in motion (as the boat tied to the dock would not).[33] Turning to Case 2.2, Ockham says that what is moved in a vessel remains in *numerically* the same place, but that place is *diverse by equivalence*, because it is as if it were in different vessels moving through different places. That is how what is literally in numerically one place is nevertheless in motion.[34]

What about Case 3, the eternally rotating outermost sphere? Aristotle's response is that the heavens are not in place *per se*, but accidentally through their parts. In circular motion, the heavenly body as a whole does not change place and therefore as a whole does not need to be in place, but its parts do change place and so need to be in place. But what exactly is meant by 'parts'? Some medieval commentaries objected that the heavens can be divided into parts either by wedges or sections, or in concentric rings. If the former, then the outermost limit of each wedge is the convex surface of

[32] Ockham, *Expositio in libros Physicorum* IV. 7. 7–8; OPh V. 89–92.
[33] Ockham, *Expositio in libros Physicorum* IV. 7. 6; OPh V. 86–7.
[34] Ockham, *Expositio in libros Physicorum* IV. 7. 9; OPh V. 93.

the outermost sphere, which is not contained. It follows that it is not the case that all of the parts or wedges are in place, because none of them will be completely surrounded by anything. If, however, the parts are concentric rings, then not all of the parts will be in place, because the outermost one will not be.

Avempace proposed that the place of the outermost sphere is the convex surface of the sphere itself. But this violates [iv] the separateness condition listed among Aristotle's *desiderata*. The relation of the heavens to its own convex surface does not change, whether or not the heavens move.[35] By contrast, Averroes suggests that, because the motion of the heavens is circular, they are located by their relation to the center around which they move—namely, the earth—and the parts of the sphere bear different relations to different parts of the earth as the sphere rotates. Giles of Rome also seizes on distance from the center, insofar as it is determinative of formal place, which the outermost sphere has, by contrast with material place (a containing surface), which the outermost sphere lacks.[36]

Ockham strides into this dispute to bite some bullets. He straightforwardly declares that the heavens and other bodies are said to be in place equivocally, because the "Aristotelian" definition of place does not pertain to the outermost sphere either *per se* or *per accidens*.[37] The heavens are not *in* place *per se*; rather they *are* a place.[38] For the heavens to be in place *per accidens* is only for the heavens to contain something at rest that is in place *per se*.[39] Averroes grounds the circular motion of the heavens on their relation to the center. Ockham considers what would happen if there were nothing at rest in the middle of the universe. He answers that the heavens would still move, because the following counterfactuals would be true: "the heavens are such that if there were something at rest in the middle, its parts would be different distances from something at rest" and/or "if there were a body at rest surrounding it, the parts of the heavens would be continuously different distances from the body at rest" and "if there were a body at rest surrounding it, the body would be in place *per se*."[40] But for each of the heavenly

35 See Trifogli, *Oxford Physics in the Thirteenth Century*, ch. 3, p. 198.
36 Trifogli, "La Dottrina del Luogo in Egidio Romano," 266–7.
37 Ockham, *Expositio in libros Physicorum* IV. 8. 1; OPh V. 96–7.
38 Ockham, *Expositio in libros Physicorum* IV. 7. 7; OPh V. 90.
39 Ockham, *Expositio in libros Physicorum* IV. 8. 1; OPh V. 96–7.
40 Ockham, *Expositio in libros Physicorum* IV. 8. 1; OPh V. 97–8.

spheres, Ockham adds, it is accidental to it whether or not it is contained by anything.[41] The upshot is that neither actual "Aristotelian" container places nor an actual stable center is required for the heavens to rotate. Where circular motion is concerned, counterfactual relation to a locational frame of reference will suffice!

[41] Ockham, *Expositio in libros Physicorum*, IV. 8. 3; OPh V. 100.

PART ONE

Why Sacraments?

2

Sacraments: What, Why, and Wherefore

I. Material Cult, How Human?

Cross-culturally and trans-temporally, human beings have used material cult to house their (our) attempts to traffic with supranatural spiritual power. The basics are simple. Human life in this world is dangerous, fraught with difficulties beyond our ordinary coping capacities. Human beings in trouble need to call for help on powers beyond the perceived natural order, outside their social system. But this remedy has the vices of its virtues. To be of any use, such powers must outclass, not only us, but the this-worldly powers that threaten us. Precisely because extra-systemic powers are not part of our world, because they do not exemplify any of the natural kinds analyzable by scientific scrutiny and do not fill any identifiable social roles, precisely because they have no determinate order toward us, they are unpredictable. This fact puts humankind in a double bind: traffic with the supranatural is necessary for life, but at the same time is dangerous to our health!

Material cult is one deeply entrenched human solution to this problem. To the extent that *cult* is governed by rules and regulations, or at least by custom, cult imposes a conventional social order with semi-defined expectations from the human and the supranatural side. In the Bible, God is represented as showing mercy to humans by taking the initiative to institute various cultic rites (in the Hebrew Bible, circumcision and Mosaic/levitical temple regulations; in the Gospels, holy eucharist and baptism instituted by Christ).

Cult is characteristically *material*, because material stuff is thought to be able to "catch" spiritual power and thus to serve as a medium of transaction.

Where negative spiritual force (for example, guilt or contamination) is concerned, human beings may wish to make it "disappear." Cultic rites transfer the negative force to the material stuff, which is then burned or banished or eaten by clergy, thereby removing it from the participant's world. (For example, in the Bible, whole burned offerings and the Yom Kippur wilderness goat both banish sin; released birds fly away the contamination of disease.) Where positive spiritual force is concerned, humans want to benefit but fear that naked contact with the supranatural would be ruinously overwhelming. Material sacrifices offered to the powers-that-be both absorb the positive force from them and tone it down to a beneficial dose that can be accessed through sprinkled blood or a sacred meal. Human beings by nature are not only material but somehow spiritual. Participating in material rites allows human beings to cleanse themselves from or to "catch" the contagion of spiritual power to transform human dealings with supranatural beings, with nature, and with one another.[1]

Despite the logic in its favor, religious and philosophical objections to material cult are almost as ancient and equally persistent. (1) Philosophy charges that the idea—that material stuff "catches" or material rites confer on it spiritual power with which it then "infects" or wreaks havoc on other things—runs contrary to our scientific understandings of what material stuff is like. (2) Theology contends that such rites mistake who/what God is. Contrary to what some Bible stories suggest,[2] holiness does not just "break out" on trespassing humans, the way fire "breaks out" in nearby combustible material. God is not a natural cause that acts by natural necessity in relation to creatures. For Christians, the exercise of Divine power in relation to creatures is a function of God's free and contingent self-control. (3) Moreover, material cult misrepresents what God expects from human beings. In John's Gospel, Jesus Himself tells the Samaritan woman that "God is Spirit" and humans are meant to worship "in spirit and in truth" (John 4: 24). Jesus continues the prophetic critique of hypocrisy, that God is not interested in the mere performance of external material rites; God looks on the heart (Matt. 5–6, 23). According to Platonizing religion and

[1] Henri Hubert and Marcel Mauss, *Sacrifice: Its Nature and Function*, trans. W. D. Halls; foreword E. E. Evans-Pritchard (Chicago: Chicago University Press, 1898/1964).

[2] Cf. the stories of Nadab and Abihu, who are struck dead for unauthorized offerings of incense at the altar (Lev. 10: 1–3), and Uzzah, who was struck dead when he reached out his hand to steady the ark lest it topple from the cart (2 Sam. 6: 7), and the warnings not to touch Mt Sinai when God descended upon it to give Moses the law (Exod. 19: 12–13, 22–4).

monastic asceticism, what stands in the way of optimal Divine–human relations is human preoccupation with material things (see Chapter 12 below). Material rites would seem only to reinforce that tendency. Philosophy and theology join forces to stress that true religion should be about personal relations and moral performance, and so should be out to secure the dominance of the personal and spiritual over the material side of human being.

II. Sacraments Anyhow

In the medieval Latin West, philosophical theologians were alert to these issues and regularly rehearse them in their *pro* and *contra* arguments. Yet, the Christian Church as they knew it inherited and elaborated a material cult. Sacraments were part of that cult, involving as they do material stuffs, bodily actions, and sometimes spoken words.[3]

Signing the Sacred. In his twelfth-century theology textbook, the *Sentences*, Peter Lombard subsumes sacraments under the category of *signs*—something the cognition of which causes something else (the *significatum* or thing signified) to come into cognition. Broadly speaking, Augustine says that a sacrament is "a sign of a sacred thing."

[1] From Augustine's perspective, all creatures are *natural* signs of Godhead, because every creatable nature is a way of imperfectly resembling the Divine essence. The whole created universe is sacramental, broadly speaking.

Even though sacramental rites generally sign with the similar (in baptism, physical washing to signify spiritual washing; in the eucharist, bread and wine to signify spiritual food), ritual signs are essentially *conventional*, instituted by God.[4] They could be and have been different. Like the church fathers before them, medieval Latin authors go to great lengths to show why and how established rites are presently suitable, while others were apt for earlier times (for example, first circumcision, then baptism; first the sacrifice of bulls and goats, then penance and eucharist).[5]

[3] Aquinas, *Sent.* IV, d. 1, q. 1, a. 3, co [13351].

[4] Aquinas, *Summa Theologica* III, q. 60, a. 5, ad 1um & ad 2um; III, q. 64, a. 2, ad 1um; Bonaventure, *Breviloquium* pt. VI, c. 1; Quaracchi V. 265.

[5] Aquinas, *Summa Theologica* III, q. 60, a.5, ad 1um & ad 2um; Bonaventure, *Breviloquium* pt. VI, c. 1; Quaracchi V. 265; cf. Hugh of St Victor, *De Sacramentis*, trans. Roy Deferrari (Cambridge, MA: Medieval Academy of America, 1951), bk. I, pt. 9, c. 2, p. 155; Scotus, *Op. Ox.* IV, d. 1, q. 3, n. 2; Wadding VIII. 69.

[2] Immaterial things can be signs (one thought can regularly bring another into cognition), and—William Ockham observes[6]—God could have instituted spiritual signs of sacred things. But Lombard takes it for granted that sacramental signs are material, when he defines sacraments as "visible forms of invisible grace."[7] Hugh of St Victor and Aquinas explain: 'visible' must mean 'sensible'. Christian sacraments involve touch and hearing as well as sight.[8]

[3] Precisioning further, Lombard declares that, properly speaking, a sacrament not only signifies but *causes* invisible effects to be present.[9] Hugh of St Victor maintains that a sacrament is a corporeal or material element set before the external senses, one that represents by likeness, signifies by institution, and contains by sanctification spiritual grace.[10] Aquinas echoes this, writing that sacraments are sensible signs of sacred things[11] insofar as they are ordered to the sanctification of human beings.[12] Writing later, Duns Scotus distinguishes between speculative or theoretical signs (for example, *homo* is a sign of human nature) and practical signs that signify that the thing signified exists or is coming to be. Practical signs divide into equivocal or uncertain versus certain and efficacious signs. Certain and efficacious signs again split into those that signify their significata with quasi-necessary certainty (when the thing signified is always concomitant with the sign), and for-the-most-part certainty (when the thing signified is usually concomitant with the sign). Sacraments that signify supernatural spiritual effects in the soul, are for-the-most-part certain practical signs, insofar as sacramental participation confers these benefits unless there is some impediment in the participant.[13]

Nature versus History. If God has freely and contingently instituted material cult for human beings, medieval Latin theologians inferred, material cult must be *fitting for God and useful to us*.[14] What is fitting for God is a function, not only of what God is (that is, of the Divine essence), but also of what God

[6] William Ockham, *Quaest. in IV Sent.*, q. 1; OTh VII. 5.

[7] Peter Lombard, *Sentences* IV, d. 1, c. 2; Grottaferrata II. 232.

[8] Hugh of St Victor, *De sacramentis* bk. I, pt. 9, c. 2, p. 155. Aquinas, *Summa Theologica* III, q. 60, a. 4 c.

[9] Peter Lombard, *Sentences* IV, d. 1, c. 4, sec. 2; Grottaferrata II. 233.

[10] Hugh of St Victor, *De sacramentis* bk. I, pt. 9, c. 2, p. 155.

[11] Aquinas, *Summa Theologica* III, q. 60, a. 4 c.

[12] Aquinas, *Summa Theologica* III, q. 60, a. 3 c & ad 1um.

[13] Scotus, *Op. Ox.* I, d. 1, q. 3, nn. 2 & 9; Wadding VIII. 69–70, 77.

[14] Bonaventure, *Sent.* IV, d. 1, p. 1, a. 1, q. 1; Quaracchi IV. 12.

purposes in creation. Likewise, what is useful to us depends on what we are (that is, on human nature) and where we fit into the Divine scheme of things. *Prima facie*, it seems obvious that sacraments—as sensible signs of immaterial things—could prove useful *only* to creatures who have the cognitive capacity to grasp both sensible and immaterial things, and who need to or benefit from beginning with sensible things and coming to know the spiritual through the sensible. Angels are bodiless intellects that do not rely on sensibles for their knowledge of immaterial things, while non-rational animals are equipped only with external and internal senses and so have no cognition of immaterial things at all. By contrast, human beings are metaphysical straddlers by nature—composites of an animal body and an intellectual soul. Aquinas teaches that the same human being senses and understands,[15] and further that cognizing immaterial things through sensible things pertains to human nature.[16] So far as natural cognitive powers are concerned, humankind seems uniquely able to benefit from sensible signs pointing to immaterial things.

For medieval Latin theologians, however, human nature was not enough to explain why sacraments are useful. Human being has not only a nature but a history, which is "chaptered" into states. What makes sacraments skillful means for Divine ends is not simply what we are, but the state in which we find ourselves. So far as human history is concerned, the frame plot begins with a trial period of improvable excellence and resolves into a state of permanent perfection. This simple narrative is complicated by tragic failure to pass the test, which precipitates us into this present state. Thus, this present state has a prequel and a sequel. The prequel locates humankind in Paradise. The sequel divides Adam's race, relocating some in heaven (*patria*, the fatherland) and others in hell. The tragic plot complication is Adam's fall. In this present state, human beings are wayfarers or wanderers (*viatores*) struggling with the consequences of sin and moving toward their eternal destinies. Sacraments were not needed in Paradise because God creates Adam and Eve with lower powers so ordered to higher that they do not depend on sensation for their cognition of immaterial or spiritual things.[17] Likewise, sacraments will not be needed in glory, because the blessed will have unmediated vision of the Divine essence, while—after the judgment—the damned

[15] Aquinas, *Summa Theologica* I, q. 76, a.1 c.
[16] Aquinas, *Summa Theologica* III, q. 60, a. 4 c; q. 61, a. 1 c.
[17] Aquinas, *Summa Theologica* III, q. 61, a. 2 c.

will have lost all hope of seeing Christ or God.[18] It is our condition in this present state that explains why material cult is a good thing.

Plot Elaborations. Christian theologians filled out this schema with a variety of emphases. The Neoplatonist Pseudo-Dionysius—in his books *Divine Names, The Celestial Hierarchy*, and *The Ecclesiastical Hierarchy*—explains that God is self-diffusing Goodness, who creates whatever else there is out of generosity, and who is the source of the being and well-being of everything else.[19] God's goal for intelligent creatures is Godlikeness and union with God. Since like is known by like, deiformity is a precondition of communion. The "trial" involves intelligent creatures in an effort more and more to imitate God in their thinking processes and to concentrate their love, the better to enter into communion with Deity.[20] The metaphysical "size gap" between God and creatures would be enough to make the challenge daunting and success dependent upon Divine help. For humans, the task is made more difficult by our soul–body composition, which naturally pulls us in opposite directions: the soul yearning for what transcends reason and intelligence, and the body pulling us toward what the senses applaud.[21] The difficulty is aggravated by sin and failure. From the beginning, human nature has stupidly glided away from the good things bestowed by God and turned to a life of fragmented desires whose end is death.[22] In this present state of distraction with material things, Pseudo-Dionysius concludes, material signs and images must be enlisted to point us toward the spiritual, both by likeness (beauty here below moving us to seek beauty up above) and ridiculous unlikeness (bizarre descriptions in biblical apocalyptic writings) that stirs us up to inquire.[23] Baptism enrolls the candidate in an athletic contest, in which Christ as God arranges the match, Christ as sage lays down the rules, and Christ as Beauty is the victor's prize. To the initiated it belongs scrupulously to observe the rules of the game and to do battle with whatever stands in the way of deiformity and contemplative union.[24] Pseudo-Dionysius styles the eucharist as a *synaxis*

[18] Aquinas, *Summa Theologica* III, q. 61, a. 4 ad 1um.

[19] *Pseudo-Dionysius: The Complete Works*, trans. Colm Luibheid (New York: Paulist Press, 1987); *The Celestial Hierarchy* (hereafter =*CH*) c. 4.1, p. 156; *The Ecclesiastical Hierarachy* (hereafter =*EH*) c. 1, secs. 3–4, p. 198.

[20] Pseudo-Dionysius, *CH* c. 3, sec. 2, p. 154; c. 4, sec. 2, pp. 156–7; c. 7, sec. 2, pp. 162–3; *EH* c. 1, sec. 5, p. 199.

[21] Pseudo-Dionysius, *CH* c. 2, sec. 3, p. 151.

[22] Pseudo-Dionysius, *EH* I, c. 3, sec. iii. 11, p. 220.

[23] Pseudo-Dionysius, *CH* c. 1, sec. 3, p. 146; c. 2, sec. 1, p. 148; c.2, sec. 3, pp. 149–50; *EH* c. 1, sec. 2, p. 197.

[24] Pseudo-Dionysius, *EH* I, c. 2, sec. iii. 6, p. 207; I, c. 3, sec. iii. 11, p. 221.

or a gathering-together that re-establishes "One over many," of the fragmented parts of the self in subordination to Christ as well as the several individual human beings into Christ's Body-politic.[25] Sacraments grant Divine communion to both soul and body: to the soul by way of contemplation, together with an understanding of the rites; to the body by way of the imagery of the rite and the symbols of Divine communion.[26] Soul–body participation in the sacraments also foretells the resurrection, when as partners in the journey—whether in the struggle towards holiness or in the descent into impiety—they will be judged together.[27]

Hugh of St Victor, in his monumental work *The Sacraments* (*De Sacramentis*), complements Pseudo-Dionysius' picture of creation with a speculation about why God placed human souls in bodies. Self-diffusing goodness not only creates the environments—earth, sea, and sky—and "ornaments" them with inhabitants—cattle and snakes, fish and birds. Self-diffusing goodness opens the opportunity for the human soul to become more Godlike still by imitating God in the exercise of providence. Divine providence governs the whole cosmos. All creatures including human beings have an obligation of obedience to God. But God placed human souls in human bodies so that human reason would exercise prudence to govern not only the human body but also the whole earth.[28] Human beings were created in the middle, not only to serve but to be served, not only to inhabit the earth but to be its lord and possessor.[29] Thus, Hugh declares, the world was made for the sake of human beings, the soul for the sake of God, the body for the sake of the soul, and the material world for the sake of the body.[30]

According to Hugh, God endowed the first human beings with power to discern good and evil, with perfect knowledge of the nature and uses of sensible things, and with an enjoyable degree of contemplation. The "test" was that humans should exercise providence to preserve good order for a time and a season, meanwhile reproducing the human race. After satisfactory performance, they were to be transferred to a higher state of contemplation,

[25] Pseudo-Dionysius, *EH* I, c. 3, sec. i, p. 209; I, c. 3, sec. iii. 11–13, pp. 221–2.
[26] Pseudo-Dionysius, *EH* I, c. 7, sec. iii. 9, p. 257.
[27] Pseudo-Dionysius, *EH* I, c. 7, sec. iii. 9, p. 257.
[28] Hugh of St Victor, *De Sacramentis*, bk. I, pt. 1, c. 19, p. 23.
[29] Hugh of St Victor, *De Sacramentis*, bk.I, pt. 1, c. 25, p. 25; bk. I, pt. 2, c. 1, pp. 28–9; bk. I, pt. 6, c. 1, p. 94.
[30] Hugh of St Victor, *De Sacramentis*, Prologue III. 4; bk. I, pt. 2.1, pp. 28–9. Cf. Bonaventure, *Breviloquium* pt. II, c. 4; Quaracchi V. 221; pt. II, c. 9; Quaracchi V. 226–7.

while the younger generation repeated the exercise, and so on until the perfect population of the heavenly city was reached.[31] For Hugh, human nature was itself a sign reassuring human beings of their future destiny: if God could join such different natures as body and soul in union and friendship, God could overcome the metaphysical size gap and raise creatures to participation in Divine glory.[32]

Unfortunately, the human race failed the test at the beginning, when its primal ancestors did not preserve but violated right order by disobeying God's commandments. Insubordination of creature to God redounded in insubordination of the senses to reason and of body to soul. All members of Adam's race fall heir to the consequences: guilt of offense against God, psycho-spiritual disarray, weakness of body, and eventual death.

Christ's Saving Work. In *Cur Deus Homo*, Anselm shows how human sin threatens to put God in a double bind. On the one hand, it would have been unfitting for Divine Justice simply to pass over human sin without imposing negative consequences. For the seriousness of sin is a function, not only of the concrete act type (for example, eating fruit), but of the worthiness of the offended party. Since God is a being more worthy of honor than which cannot be conceived, any offense against God is immeasurably culpable. Human disobedience to God is no peccadillo but maximally indecent. On the other hand, it would be unfitting for God simply to leave Adam's race to its just deserts, because that would mean the frustration of God's original plan, which created human beings for deiformity and for communion with God. Since Wisdom does not start what it cannot finish, and Omnipotence can finish anything it starts, God has to find a solution to the "sin problem" that satisfies Justice but saves some of Adam's race for eternal bliss. Christian theology handed it down: God's own answer to sin is for God the Son to become a member of Adam's race and to die on the cross!

Medieval theologians worked with several explanations of how the Incarnation and passion of Christ were supposed to rescue Adam's race from the consequences of sin. Patristic theology contributed *the Ransom Theory*, according to which the devil has the right to kill and eternally

[31] Hugh of St Victor, *De Sacramentis* bk. I, pt. 6, cc. 12–14, pp. 102–3; bk. I, pt. 6, cc. 24–5, pp. 110–11. Bonaventure, *Breviloquium* pt. II, c. 10; Quaracchi V. 227–8; pt. IV, c. 1; Quaracchi V. 241.

[32] Hugh of St Victor, *De Sacramentis* bk. I, pt. 6, c. 1, p. 94.

torment any human beings whom he can seduce into rebelling against God's authority. It would be unfitting for Divine Justice to use Divine Power to reclaim fallen humans by force. Instead, Divine Wisdom outwits the devil by becoming human in Jesus. The devil over-reaches his entitlements by killing Jesus, who is God and who—in his human nature—has led a sinless life. The devil's mistake puts Divine Justice in a position to demand Adam's race in exchange and to exercise Divine Power to raise Jesus from the dead.[33]

Anselm and Abelard mocked the idea that the devil (or any other creature) has rights against God, much less that he could acquire such rights by persuading human beings to join his rebellion against their rightful Lord. Likewise ridiculous, Abelard thought, was the notion that the devil should exercise such rights over his moral betters, which the elect always were.[34] Equally repugnant, Anselm contends, is the suggestion that God, who is Truth itself, should stoop to trickery by making Christ's human nature "bait in the trap of the cross."[35] Lombard, for his part, tries to rehabilitate the Ransom Theory: the devil does not have rights against God, but God permits human sinners to fall into the devil's control. The devil does injury to God by abducting God's servants and holding them by force, injury to humans by deceiving us with false promises and leading us to a place of torment. Nevertheless, humans are justly held because human guilt deserves to suffer such things.[36] Moreover, God's seizing us by force would use the devil's methods, because the devil is a lover of power. God set us a better example by waiting until the devil's injustice gives occasion for our release.[37]

If the Ransom Theory involves God in offering something to the devil, Anselm's *Satisfaction Theory* represents fallen humanity as owing God a debt that it cannot pay. Anselm's argument turns on two premisses: the metaphysical size gap between God and creatures (in *Monologion*, c. 28, Anselm says that, in comparison with God, creatures are "almost nothing"[38]), and

[33] Anselm, *Cur Deus Homo* I. 7; Schmitt II. 55–9; *Meditatio redemptionis humanae*; Schmitt III. 84–91.

[34] Anselm, *Cur Deus Homo* I. 7; Schmitt II. 55–9; Abelard, *Opera Theologica: Commentaria in Epostolam Pauli ad Romanos* (Corpus Christianorum, Continuatio Mediaevalia XI; Turnholt: Brepols, 1969), 110–18.

[35] Anselm, *Meditatio redemptionis humanae*; Schmitt III. 85.

[36] Peter Lombard, *Sentences* III, d. 20, c. 4, sec. 1; Grottaferrata II. 127.

[37] Peter Lombard, *Sentences* III, d. 19, c. 2, sec. 5; Grottaferrata II. 120–1; III, d. 20, c. 2; Grottaferrata II. 126; III, d. 20, c. 3, secs. 1–2; Grottaferrata II. 126–7.

[38] Anselm, *Monologion*, cc. 28 & 31; Schmitt I. 46 & 49.

family solidarity in sharing guilt or merit and in general the consequences of individual members' actions. Anselm contends that God's purposes for Adam's race must be fulfilled. But offense against God must be set right by punishment or by satisfaction. Satisfaction owed is proportionate to guilt, and guilt is proportionate to the worthiness of the offended party. Thus, any offense against God makes the offender immeasurably culpable. But there is not enough to any mere creature for it to do or be anything immeasurably worthy; God alone can. Beneficiaries are beholden to their benefactors. Even if some superior creature had the capital, its making satisfaction for Adam's race would not restore Adam's race to its original dignity as being subject only to God. The solution is for God to become a member of Adam's race, and to render to God in His human nature what Adam's race always owed: a life of complete obedience to the Divine will. Because Christ is innocent, He did not owe it to God to die. Hence, His *death* is something extra, and because it is *His* (= God the Son's) death, it is immeasurably worthy. Because Christ is a member of Adam's race, His offering is not that of an external patron, but that of one family member on behalf of the whole clan. Hence the death of the God-man makes satisfaction for Adam's race and so makes it possible for God to carry out God's original purposes for Adam's race after all.

Abelard rejects the Satisfaction theory as a blasphemous misrepresentation of Divine character and purposes, as if God were an offended ruler who could not possibly adopt a favorable attitude toward humans unless and until satisfaction was paid. Moreover, if God really did stand in need of appeasement, how absurd to think that God would be placated by killing another innocent human being! On the contrary, God's basic posture toward us is love, and it does not change with the fall. Only human attitudes toward God change. The point of Christ's life, death, and passion is to exhibit the extent of Divine love and to rekindle a love for God in our hearts.[39]

Hugh of St Victor makes bold to harmonize the Ransom and Satisfaction theories by imposing a legal frame. On the Ransom scenario, both the devil and Adam's race stand convicted: the devil of doing injury both to God and to humans, while Adam's race has given offense only to God. Human beings therefore have a legal case against the devil, but they cannot bring suit without an advocate. The only lawyer available is God, but God is angry over human sin. The solution is for Adam's race to placate God, which is what happens

[39] Abelard, *Commentaria in Epistolam Pauli ad Romanos* II. iii. 26. 117–18.

when the passion of Christ makes satisfaction for sin![40] By contrast, Aquinas and Bonaventure identify satisfaction for sin as the centerpiece of Christ's saving work, while treating love-kindling and role-modeling as side benefits.[41]

In effect, such medieval accounts of Christ's saving work divide the "sin problem" into two parts: guilt removal and damage reversal. Forgiveness, rationalized or not by Ransom and/or Satisfaction, deals with the first. Damage reversal itself has two phases: restoring psycho-spiritual order within human beings, and re-establishing human dominion over the wider material environment. The second phase is postponed to the sequel. Cooperating with God on the first phase dominates the believer's agenda in this present state. Yet, the traditional plot is more complicated still. In both the prequel and the sequel to this present state, the order God establishes and the help God provides raise human beings above their natural norm to degrees of contemplation and cognitive access to spiritual things that lie beyond natural human powers. The trial period was supposed to be given over to a process of augmenting supranatural deiformity. Thus, besides plunging the human race below its natural norm, Adam's fall forfeits "original justice" and other anticipated supranatural benefits. Damage reversal means not only bringing us back up to our natural norm, but raising us above it. Fulfilling Divine purposes for the human race means using this present state, not only to recover what was left behind in Paradise, but to advance beyond it.

Sacraments for Adam's Fallen Race. For Ransom and/or Satisfaction theorists, it is Christ's saving work that makes it *fitting for God* to proceed with the original Divine project. According to the Western medieval church, sacraments are *how* God proceeds, because it is *useful to us.* It is right that saving benefits not rain down on individual members of Adam's race willy nilly. Applying for them through sacramental participation is an important step toward spiritual recovery. Sacraments are not merely dispensers of supranatural spiritual qualities and "soul ornaments." Participating in sacramental rites is itself an act of worship in which the believer assumes a more nearly correct posture toward God.

Specifically, *material* rites are seen to be useful to us for a trio of traditional reasons. First, because fallen humans are preoccupied with sensible things, it helps if some of them instruct reason by pointing beyond themselves to

[40] Hugh of St Victor, *De Sacramentis* bk. I, pt. 8, cc. 3–4, pp. 9–10.

[41] Aquinas, *Summa Theologica* III, q. 1, a. 2 c. Bonaventure, *Sent.* III, d. 20, a. 1, q. 2 c; Quaracchi III. 419–22.

where grace, the theological virtues, the spiritual gifts, even Christ Himself are to be found. Faith is stirred at the presentation of such material signs. Second, human disobedience is a sin of pride that prizes the lower good over the higher. Requiring human sinners to subject themselves to material rites (the higher to the lower) in order to get needed spiritual benefits is a salutary antidote, insofar as it requires the reverse posture of humility. Third, as a consequence of the fall, human attention and appetites are highly distractible and pulled in many different directions. Commandments and cult enjoin on humans many Godward things to do, and so combat sloth and leave us little leisure for vice.[42]

Material Rites in Developmental Sequence. If material rites are useful to Adam's fallen race, the Bible, the principal authority for Christians, tells how the cult varied down through the centuries. Theologians organized these data by dividing this present state into three periods by reference to the laws by which human beings are governed: the natural-law period from Adam to Moses, the old covenant or Mosaic law from Sinai to Christ, and the new covenant instituted by Christ and sealed by His passion. Their analyses are shaped by Christian claims to supercede Judaism: Church replaces synagogue and renders Jewish rites henceforth null and void.[43] Bonaventure sees an analogy between the history of the human race and the growth of a child from infancy to adulthood. All sacraments signify the passion of Christ, but there is an evolution from inchoate to explicit with the use of ever clearer imagery and eventually spoken words, to match an increase in human cognitive capacities to discern spiritual things.[44] More importantly, there is a difference in sacramental efficacy. Everywhere and always, God is the principal cause of spiritual benefits, and Christ's saving work is what makes it fitting for God to confer them on Adam's fallen race. But medieval Latin Christians questioned and disputed just how the succession of material cults mentioned in the Bible figured in the distribution of spiritual benefits to the participants. Looming large was the distinction between sacraments whose efficacy depends on the beliefs and motives of the participants (those that

[42] Peter Lombard, *Sentences* IV, d. 1, c. 5, secs. 1–5; Grottaferrata II. 234–5; Hugh of St Victor, *De Sacramentis* bk. I, pt. 9, c. 3, pp. 156–8; Bonaventure, *Sent.* IV, d. 1, p. 1, a. 1, q. 1; Quaracchi IV. 12; *Breviloquium* pt. VI, c. 1; Quaracchi V. 265; Aquinas, *Sent.* IV, d. 1, q. 1, a. 2 c [13324]; Scotus, *Op. Ox.* IV, d. 1, q. 3, n. 3; Wadding VIII. 70.

[43] Bonaventure, *Breviloquium* pt. VI, c. 2; Quaracchi V. 266–7.

[44] Aquinas, *Sent.* IV, d. 1, q. 1, a. 5, qc. 3 [13445]; IV, d. 1, q. 1, a. 3 c [13351]; *Summa Theologica* III, q. 60, aa. 6–8; III, q. 61, a. 3 ad 2um; Bonaventure, *Breviloquium* pt. VI, c. 2; Quaracchi V. 266; pt. VI, c. 4; Quaracchi V. 268.

work *ex opere operantis*) and those whose efficacy depends only or largely on the performance of the outward rite (those that work *ex opere operato*).

Natural Law. Thus, from Adam to Moses, there was no externally imposed legal system, but humans were left to govern themselves according to the natural law within.[45] Humans acted out their natural inclination to honor God in material rites: they bore witness to their faith in God as creator with offerings, in God as redeemer with sacrifices, and in God as rewarder with tithes.[46] These rites were volutary, celebrated out of devotion rather than obligation,[47] although there may have been Divine counsels about what would be pleasing.[48] During this period, faith was "counted as righteousness" for the removal of original sin. The patriarchs were saved by faith in Christ-to-come (*ex opere operantis*) and their cultic acts merely bore witness to the faith through which they were justified.[49]

Mosaic or "Old" Law. Two developments brought on the giving of the Mosaic law. First, as time wore on, human natural instinct was darkened (overlaid with socially reinforced sinful habits) so that natural-law precepts could no longer function as an adequate guide to right living. Explicit and burdensome precepts were necessary for correction and for punishment.[50] Likewise required were mandated sacraments of faith that used widely available low-cost materials and furnished sensible signs of Christ's passion.[51] Second, by the time of Moses, the community of the faithful had expanded beyond one man, his wives, and children, to a whole people. Bodies politic require to be governed by a system of law and to be marked off from others by exclusive external collective rites.[52]

The efficacy of old-law cult was a subject of debate. Lombard insisted that—apart from circumcision—old-law rites were mere signs, instituted by

[45] Aquinas, *Sent.* IV, d. 1, q. 2, a. 6, qc. 3 c [13602]; Bonaventure, *Sent.* IV, d. 1, p. 2, a. 1, q. 2 c; Quaracchi IV. 34.

[46] Hugh of St Victor, *De Sacramentis*, bk. I, pt. 12, c. 4, p. 191; Aquinas, *Sent.* IV, d. 1, q. 1, a. 2, qc. 3 c [13333] & ad 2um [13335]; Bonaventure, *Sent.* IV, d. 1, p. 2, a. 1, q. 3 c; Quaracchi IV. 35–6.

[47] Hugh of St Victor, *De Sacramentis*, bk. I, pt. 11, c. 3, p. 183; bk. I, pt. 11, cc. 5–7, p. 184.

[48] Hugh of St Victor, *De Sacramentis*, bk. I, pt. 11, c. 4, p. 183; Bonaventure, *Sent.* IV, d. 1, p. 2, a. 1, q. 2 c; IV, d. 1, p. 2, a. 1, q. 3 c; Scotus, *Op. Ox.* IV, d. 1, q. 7, nn. 3–4; Wadding VIII. 131.

[49] Aquinas, *Sent.* IV, d. 1, q. 1, a. 2, qc. 3 ad 2um [13335]; *Summa Theologica* III, q. 61, a. 4 c; III, q. 62, a. 6 c & ad 3um.

[50] Aquinas, *Sent.* IV, d. 1, q. 1, a. 5, qc. 3 [13445]; *Summa Theologica* III, q.61, a. 3 c ad 2um; Bonaventure, *Sent.* I, d. 2, p. 2, q. 1 ad 2um; Quaracchi IV. 38.

[51] Aquinas, *Summa Theologica* III, q. 61, a. 3 c & ad 2um.

[52] Aquinas, *Sent.* IV, d. 1, q. 1, a. 2, qc. 4 c [13336]; Scotus, *Op. Ox.* IV, d. 1, q. 3, n. 3; Wadding VIII. 70.

God only to signify. When patriarchs performed them out of love for God, the inner motive was meritorious, but the external act was not. Hugh of St Victor disagreed: the external act is not meritorious in itself (*per se*) as is the inner act of love for God; but external rites performed out of such motives could be said to justify *per accidens*. Thus, Abraham's sacrifice of Isaac was meritorious, but derivatively so. While finding Hugh's position more defensible, Bonaventure reasserts that there is no efficacious order between the performance of old-law rites and spiritual benefits, the way there is with new law rites. The merit comes from the internal act (*ex opere operantis*).[53] Aquinas and Scotus say the same.[54]

Circumcision. Circumcision was neither a natural-law dictate nor a Mosaic-law innovation. It was a command God gave to Abraham (Gen. 17). Moreover, medieval Latin Christian theologians generally conceded that God would at no time leave Adam's fallen race without an efficiacious remedy against original guilt.[55] Accordingly, they agreed, circumcision was efficacious *ex opere operato* for removing original guilt the way baptism is now. But they deployed a variety of strategies to show how circumcision was inferior to Christian rites. Three desirable spiritual effects were distinguished: guilt removal, grace conferral with its positive effect of making the recipient worthy of eternal life, and grace conferral with its effect of repressing concupiscence that impels one to sin. Lombard opted for guilt removal without grace conferral; William of Auxerre endorsed guilt removal and grace conferral but without any positive effects; Alexander of Hales and Bonaventure, guilt removal and grace conferral with the positive effect of making the recipient worthy of eternal life, but without full empowerment against concupiscence.[56] Aquinas confesses that he used to favor the last position, but, by the time he wrote the *Summa Theologica*, he had come around to the view that circumcision brought the removal of guilt and the conferral of grace with its full range of positive effects.[57]

Scotus declares that, while Mosaic-law rites were sacraments improperly speaking because they do not work *ex opere operato* but only *ex opere operantis*,

[53] Bonaventure, *Sent*. IV, d. 1, p. 1, a. 1, q. 5 c; Quaracchi IV. 25–6.

[54] Aquinas, *Summa Theologica* III, q. 62, a. 6 c; Scotus, *Op. Ox*. IV, d. 1, q. 6, n. 10; Wadding VIII. 124–225.

[55] Scotus, *Op. Ox*. IV, d. 1, q. 6, n. 2; Wadding VIII. 110; IV, d. 1, q. 7, n. 2; Wadding VIII. 130–1.

[56] Aquinas, *Summa Theologica* III, q. 62, a. 6 c; Bonaventure, *Sent*. IV, d. 1, p. 2, a. 2, q. 3 c; Quaracchi IV. 43–4.

[57] *Summa Theologica* III, q. 62, a. 6 c.

circumcision was a sacrament properly speaking because it confers grace *ex opere operato* and not only by virtue of the inner faith and motives of the circumcised.[58] When it comes to explaining away the authorities of the saints who denied that circumcision is properly a sacrament, Scotus explores three approaches. (1) One could say (as he understands Bonaventure to do) that circumcision does not confer as much grace as baptism. (2) Or one could say that circumcision was inferior to baptism because, in cancelling guilt and conferring grace, it was unable immediately to "open the doors" to heaven. But—Scotus adds—this was not because of any defect in the rite itself, but because of its location in time—namely, before the passion of Christ, which made satisfaction for Adam's race.[59] (3) Or one could acknowledge that circumcision confers grace only up to a certain degree and so does not always add grace—for example, to recipients (perhaps Abraham himself) who have otherwise received grace in that degree or higher.[60] If true, this would not necessarily distinguish circumcision from baptism. Consider the Blessed Virgin Mary, who was full of grace at the time of Jesus's conception. If she had been baptized later, baptism would not have conferred grace on her. Scotus suggests that baptism signifies the disjunction: not simply grace coming to be, but grace either existing or coming to be in the recipient.[61] Circumcision could signify disjunctively as well.

If circumcision is the cure for original sin from Abraham to Christ, what about the period from Adam to Abraham? If God never leaves Adam's fallen race without a remedy, what was it in the pre-circumcision period? Scotus agrees that, where adults are concerned, faith in God as redeemer or in Christ's future passion might suffice, apart from any external rite. But what about the infants who are too immature for such inner beliefs and motives? Scotus thinks there must have been some other external rite (analogous to circumcision and baptism) that could cancel guilt and confer grace *ex opere operato*. Systematic considerations demand it, even if the Bible does not record what such a rite was![62]

New-Law Sacraments. Scotus expresses Christian theological consensus, when he declares that the Gospel is adorned with perfect sacraments. All are instituted by Christ or God (although Scotus questions whether there is

58 Scotus, *Op. Ox.* IV, d. 1, q. 6, n. 10; Wadding VIII. 124–5.

59 Scotus, *Op. Ox.* IV, d. 1, q. 6, n. 11; Wadding VIII. 125.

60 Scotus, *Op. Ox.* IV, d. 1, q. 6, n. 11; Wadding VIII. 125–6.

61 Scotus, *Op. Ox.* IV, d. 1, q. 6, n. 12; Wadding VIII. 126.

62 Scotus, *Op. Ox.* IV, d. 1, q. 7, nn. 2–3; Wadding VIII. 130–1.

explicit biblical warrant for this).[63] All new-law sacraments have efficacy from God alone as principal cause.[64] The most perfect meritorious cause of grace is Christ completing His earthly career with us, a career that exhibits rather than merely promising benefits,[65] who merits our first union with God.[66]

If Cardinal Humbert of Silva Candida in the eleventh century was the first to insist that the number of new-law sacraments is seven[67]—baptism, confirmation, penance, eucharist, ordination, matrimony, and extreme unction—twelfth- through fourteenth-century theologians reached for numerous images in showing how these seven are apt. Like Aquinas, Scotus invites us to consider an analogy between corporeal and spiritual life. Just as, in natural life, individuals are first generated and then nourished, strengthened, and repaired; so, in the spiritual life, individuals are generated in *baptism*, nourished in the *eucharist*, strengthened in *confirmation*, repaired by *penance*, assisted in dying by *unction*.[68] Just as, in natural life, human communities need procedures for establishing people in ranks and roles necessary for life together; so, in the spiritual life, carnal reproduction to repopulate the community is housed in the sacrament of *matrimony*, while *ordination* provides clergy to administer the sacraments, which father the reproduction of spiritual being or grace.[69]

Bonaventure draws on a medical image to suggest how the seven sacraments are instituted for healing, restoration, and preservation of life.[70] As for healing, the sacraments are seven remedies against sevenfold disease: baptism against original sin, penance against mortal sin, extreme unction against venial sin, ordination against ignorance, holy eucharist against malice, confirmation against weakness, and matrimony against concupiscence.[71] As for restoration, seven sacraments cultivate seven (three theological and four cardinal) virtues: baptism leads to faith, confirmation to hope, holy eucharist to charity, penance to justice, extreme unction to perseverance,

[63] Scotus, *Op. Ox.* IV, d. 2, q. 1, n. 6; Wadding VIII. 138.
[64] Scotus, *Op. Ox.* IV, d. 2, q. 1, n. 6; Wadding VIII. 138.
[65] Scotus, *Op. Ox.* IV, d. 2, q. 1, n. 2; Wadding VIII. 135.
[66] Scotus, *Op. Ox.* IV, d. 4, q. 2, n. 4; Wadding VIII. 222.
[67] According to Henry Chadwick in "Ego Berengarius," *Journal of Theological Studies*, NS 40/2 (Oct. 1989), pp. 414–45; esp. p. 422.
[68] Scotus, *Op. Ox.* IV, d. 6, q. 10, n. 12; Wadding VIII. 359.
[69] Scotus, *Op. Ox.* IV, d. 2, q. 1, n. 3; Wadding VIII. 135–6; cf. Aquinas, *Summa Theologica* III, q. 65, a. 1 c; III, q. 65, a. 2 c.
[70] Bonaventure, *Breviloquium* pt. VI, c. 3; Quaracchi V. 267–8.
[71] Bonaventure, *Breviloquium* pt. VI, c. 3; Quaracchi V. 267.

which is a complement of courage, ordination to prudence, and matrimony to temperance.[72]

When it comes to preservation, Bonaventure overlays the medical with Hugh of St Victor's military image: the seven sacraments equip us for the battle of life with the ornaments of grace, which can be found only in the army of the Church. Since the troops are weak and vulnerable, sacraments are needed to fortify the combatants, restore the wounded, and revive the dying. Baptism strengthens those who are entering, confirmation those who are fighting, and extreme unction those who are leaving the fray. Holy eucharist restores the recuperating (from venial sin), while penance resurrects those who have fallen into mortal sin. Orders function to enlist new recruits, while matrimony brings future fighters into natural existence.[73]

Worship, the Human Vocation. For Aquinas, the focal rubric is worship: human beings are made for worship, ultimately for beatific vision and enjoyment, a form of communion that presupposes deiformity.[74] Sanctification is required to make human beings eligible to participate in the worship of God. "A holy God cannot dwell with an unholy people." Sacraments are signs that signify human sanctification: *commemorative* signs of the cause of our sanctification (namely, the passion of Christ), *demonstrative* signs of the form of our sanctification (namely, the graces and virtues conferred on participants), and *predictive* signs of the end of our sanctification (namely, eternal life together with God).[75] Sacraments work at two levels, negatively to remedy the consequences of sin, and positively to perfect the soul for worship.[76] So far as the Christian sacraments are concerned, all

[72] Bonaventure, *Breviloquium* pt. VI, c. 3; Quaracchi V. 267.

[73] Bonaventure, *Breviloquium* pt. VI, c. 3; Quaracchi. 267–8.

[74] Aquinas, *Summa Theologica* III, q. 60, a. 5 c.

[75] Aquinas, *Summa Theologica* III, q. 60, a. 3 c.

[76] Aquinas, *Summa Theologica* III, q. 63, a. 3 c; III, q. 63, a. 6 c; III, q. 65, a. 1 c. Gary Macy, in his *The Theologies of the Eucharist in the Early Scholastic Period: A Study of the Salvific Function of the Sacrament according to the Theologians c.1080–c.1220* (Oxford: Clarendon Press, 1984), focuses on how the eucharist was thought to function as a remedy for sin. He distinguishes three major types of theories, emerging in temporal succession: Paschasius' ninth-century theory that Christ's really present Body and Blood make "natural contact" and "mingle" with the body and blood of the recipient and thereby mediate the latter's contact with Godhead (defended by a succession of figures into the twelfth century (I. 27–8; II. 4 5); the mystical theory (allegedly exemplified by Hugh of St Victor) that eucharistic participation facilitates but is not necessary for a spiritual union of the soul with Godhead that requires faith working through love (III. 74–86); and the ecclesial theory (advanced by Lombard, Gilbert of La Porrée, and Abelard) that eucharistic participation results in the union of believers within the corporate institution of the Church (IV. 106–32). Macy wonders why an interest in real presence survived the waning of Paschasius' theory (IV. 131) and returns to his theory that real presence loomed large because of Church polemics against the

confer, restore, or intensify grace in the soul and the theological virtues—faith, hope, and charity—in the soul's powers. Such spiritual benefits are first acquired in baptism, lost by mortal sin, and restored by penance.

Aquinas maintains, however, that some sacraments single out recipients for certain roles in the Church and distinguish them by impressing an indelible spiritual character.[77] Thus, he holds that baptism, the rite of initiation, deputizes the baptized to a passive role in worship, and impresses the baptismal character, which is a passive power to receive spiritual benefits. Confirmation deputizes believers as soldiers of the Church militant to persevere in bold confession of the faith under hostile circumstances, and so confers the Holy Spirit and impresses a character that is an active power.[78] Likewise, ordination impresses a character that is active spiritual power to perform sacramental rites and thereby to make sacred things available to others.[79] If unmediated vision and enjoyment of Godhead is our supranatural end, holy eucharist is the consummation of our worship as wayfarers this side of the grave.[80] The eucharistic prayer of consecration ushers everyone around into the real presence of Christ's Body and Blood on the altar under forms of bread and wine, whereas worthy reception (by the baptized who have been absolved of any mortal sin in the meantime) brings on union with the mystical body of Christ.[81]

Among new-law sacraments, holy eucharist is distinctively different. The others are perfected in their *use*: baptism when someone is baptized, confirmation when someone is confirmed, ordination when someone is ordained, penance when someone is absolved, unction when the dying are anointed, matrimony when the couple is joined. Officiating clergy can go through the preliminaries, but there will be no baptism unless there is someone to be baptized! This is because what these sacraments produce *ex opere operato* are spiritual effects in the souls of appropriate receivers.[82] By contrast, the eucharist involves a double layer. The real presence of the Body and

Cathars (V. 137). What he leaves out of account is that the eucharist is an act of worship, and the real presence of Christ's Body and Blood greatly enhances worship!

[77] Aquinas, *Summa Theologica* III, q. 63, a.1 c & ad 1um & ad 2um; III, q. 65, a.5, ad 1um & ad 2um.

[78] Aquinas, *Sent.* IV, d. 7, q. 2, a. 1, qc. 2 c [14629]; *Summa Theologica* III, q. 65, a. 1 c.

[79] Aquinas, *Sent.* IV, d. 7, q. 2, a. 1, qc. 1 c [14625]; *Summa Theologica* III, q. 63, a. 2 c.

[80] Aquinas, *Summa Theologica* III, q. 65, a. 3 c; III, q.73, a. 3 c.

[81] Aquinas, *Summa Theologica* III, q. 65, a.3 c & ad 3um; Bonaventure, *Sent.* IV, d. 8, p. 1, a. 2, q. 2 c; Quaracchi IV. 186; *Breviloquium* pt. VI, c. 9; Quaracchi V. 274.

[82] Aquinas, *Sent.* IV, d. 7, q. 2, a. 1, qc. 3 ad 2um [14635].

Blood of Christ under forms of bread and wine is produced *ex opere operato*. After the consecration, the Body and Blood of Christ would be there, even if (as would be irregular) no one received the host or chalice (say, if the priest dropped dead as he finished the prayer of consecration and no other communicants were around) and even if those who receive are somehow indisposed (say because of unabsolved mortal sin). This is because the effect—the real presence of Christ's Body and Blood—does not exist in the souls of the receivers, but independently under as somehow contained by forms of bread and wine.[83] What indisposition in the receiver obstructs is the further effect of uniting the receiver with the mystical Body of Christ.[84] Put otherwise, in eucharistic consecration, the Body and Blood of Christ come to be really present on the altar, whether we are ready or not, and whether we recognize it or not. It is Christ's way of keeping His promise to be with us always, of continuing His corporeal presence with us even after He has ascended to the Father's right hand.[85]

Lombard distinguishes between the sacrament or sign and the thing signified or the thing (*res*) of the sacrament. In the eucharist, signs and significata are doubled. The eucharistic elements (the species of bread and wine) are signs. The real and really present Body and Blood of Christ are both things (*res*) and signs, because they are the things signified by the eucharistic species and yet are also signs of the mystical Body of Christ and the faithful receivers' union with it. The latter are things (*res*) of the sacrament that do not (in this context) signify anything else.[86] Thus, where the eucharist is concerned, the first thing signified (*res sacramenti*) will be produced whether or not the second thing signified (*res sacramenti*) is produced. This sacrament can be somehow perfected independently of worthy reception.

Scotus uses these points to focus his own account of the superiority of the eucharist. New-law sacraments are efficacious signs. Of these, the eucharist is the truest in signifying, because what it signifies—namely, the true Body of Christ—is always present when the rite is performed. Other new-law sacraments are only "for-the-most-part certain" signs, because whether or not the invisible effect is produced depends on the disposition of the

[83] Aquinas, *Sent.* IV, d. 7, q. 1, a. 3, qc. 3 ad 2um [14607]; IV, d. 7, q. 2, a. 1, qc. 3 ad 2um [14635]; IV, d. 8, q. 1, a. 1, qc.3 c [14768]; *Summa Theologica* III, q. 73 ad 3um.

[84] Aquinas, *Sent.* IV, d. 8, q. 1, a. 1, qc. 3 co [14768].

[85] Aquinas, *Sent.* IV, d. 8, q. 1, a. 3, qc. 3 c [14821]; *Summa Theologica* III, q. 73, a. 5 c.

[86] Lombard, *Sent.* IV, d. 8, c. 7, sec. 2; Grottaferrata II. 285.

receiver (for example, it is not produced when mortal sinners or the unbaptized receive the eucharistic species). All other sacraments consist in and therefore do not outlast their use or the performance of the rite. But the eucharist—the true Body and Blood of Christ—are somehow permanent (because really present under forms of bread and wine) before their use (before their being received), because Christ willed to be with us permanently.[87]

Thus, by the thirteenth century, leading Latin school theologians were taking their cue from Lombard and representing holy eucharist as the pinnacle of the typical wayfarer's worship experience (the contemplative heights of St Paul and a few others excepted).[88] Most thinkers took this estimate to depend essentially on two claims: namely, that new law sacraments "effect what they figure" (bring about what they signify), and that—after consecration—the Body and Blood of Christ are really present where the bread and wine were and still seem to be. Thirteenth- and fourteenth-century theologians subjected both to extensive philosophical analysis. They reasoned that, to be true, these claims would have to be consistent with the rest of what is true. Their job as philosophical theologians was to probe and discover whether and how this could be so.

[87] Scotus, *Op. Ox.* IV, d. 1, p. 3, q. 2, n. 9; Wadding VIII. 69–70, 77; IV, d. 8, q. 1, n. 5; Wadding VIII. 408–9.

[88] Gary Macy, in his *The Theologies of the Eucharist*, understands Hugh of St Victor and other twelfth-century adherents of the mystical theory to disagree, and to maintain that mystical union with Godhead is the peak worship experience at which the religiously serious among wayfarers should aim—an experience that could be had independently of sacramental participation. By contrast, Lombard and his thirteenth- and fourteenth-century followers embrace the "ecclesial" theory that the goal of worthy reception is deeper incorporation as a member in good standing of the institutional Church (III. 75–85; IV. 107–41).

3

Sacramental Causality: "Effecting What They Figure!"

I. Spiritual Powers in Material Stuff?

Sacraments are *material* rites, involving material stuffs (water, oil, bread, and wine), bodily actions (pouring water or smearing oil on people's heads, eating and drinking the eucharistic species), and sometimes (in new-law sacraments) spoken words. Sacraments are *signs*; in the Bible, signs that look backward or forward to the passion of Christ, whose self-offering makes it fitting for God to proceed with Divine plans for the human race, signs that signify grace in the souls of suitable participants and/or the real presence of Christ's Body and Blood on the altar. Medieval Christian theologians insist that new-law sacraments (most would add circumcision; see Chapter 2 above) are *efficacious* signs: they bring about what they signify; they "effect what they figure." Either they *contain* grace the way a vessel contains water, or they *cause* grace to exist in pious and well-prepared souls, or both. The eucharistic species *contain* the Body and Blood of Christ, which the performance of the rite makes to be really present *ex opere operato*. Medieval Christians stressed the causal efficacy of new-law sacraments, both as a way of marking the superiority of new-law sacraments over old, and as a way of reassuring the faithful. If sacraments *cause* spiritual benefits and/or real presence, then they *work* to guarantee that suitably prepared participants get what they need!

Nevertheless, the most obvious way to understand 'X is an efficient cause of Y' implies 'X has and exercises efficient causal power to produce Y'. And the idea that material rites possess efficient causal powers to produce spiritual benefits and/or real presence has proved perennially problematic. *Theological*

Ineptitudes. Granted that material rites are useful to Adam's fallen race in this present state. Would it not threaten Divine control over the soteriological process to suppose that grace-producing causal power belonged to the sacraments themselves? School theology held that dying in a state of grace guaranteed entrance into heaven. If new-law sacraments caused grace, would not sacramental participation force God's hand? Likewise, if celebrating the eucharistic rite *caused* Christ's Body and Blood to be really present, would that not give clerics the power to conjure God?

Moreover, theological consensus had it that the spiritual benefits delivered through the sacraments are *supranaturally infused.* Normally, Aquinas takes this to mean that there is no *natural* passive power to receive them, and no *natural* active power to produce them. Aquinas understood Aristotle to hold that natural passive powers and natural active powers are perfectly matched. Likewise, all agree, only Divine power can make the Body and Blood of Christ to be really present under forms of bread and wine, while they still remain in heaven. How, then, could sacraments be *efficient* causes of grace in the soul[1] or of the real presence of Christ's Body and Blood on altars where mass is said?[2]

Philosophical Obstacles. To Bonaventure, literally locating such efficient causal powers in the sacraments themselves borders on the metaphysically unintelligible. A host of difficulties circle around the nature of these powers: questions as to when, how, and into what they would be infused; questions as to how long they would last.[3] Where Bonaventure alludes, Aquinas spells out the objections in some detail. *Sacraments as Subjects of Inherence?* If there were such efficient causal power, it would have to be an accident, and so to exist in the sacraments as in a subject. But what is received is received according to the mode of the receiver. Sacraments are sensible signs and so material things. But grace-producing or grace-disposing power is power to produce something spiritual, and spiritual power cannot exist in a corporeal body as in a subject.[4] Here there are two worries. (1) The first is "the Characterization Problem": if material subjects could be characterized by spiritual powers, the distinction between material and spiritual might seem

[1] Aquinas, *Sent.* IV, d. 1, q. 1, a. 4, qc. 1; Parma 7. 1. 460–1.

[2] Aquinas, *Sent.* IV, d. 1, q. 1, a. 4, qc. 1; Parma 7. 1.461.

[3] Bonaventure, *Sent.* IV, d. 1, p. 1, a.u, q. 4; Quaracchi IV. 24; IV, d. 10, p. 2, a. 1, q. 3 c; Quaracchi IV. 232.

[4] Aquinas, *Sent.* IV, d. 1, q. 1, a. 4, qc. 2; Parma 7. 1. 461; *Summa Theologica* III, q. 62, a. 4.

to break down. (2) The second is "the Proportionate Subject Problem": between the subject of inherence and the inherent form, there must be a proper proportion. This is often interpreted to imply that the subject cannot be more complex than the inherent form—which is usually taken to imply that numerically the same form cannot inhere in numerically distinct subjects simulataneously. It also seems to follow that a spiritual form (which is simple and without parts) could not have a material and hence infinitely divisible subject of inherence.[5] *A fortiori*, no new-law rite—composed as it is of material stuffs, bodily actions, and spoken words—could be the subject of a single grace- or real-presence-producing power.[6]

Ontological Placement. If sacraments were the subject of genuine causal power, [3] *what Aristotelian category* would this causal power exist in? Not substance, nor any species of quality listed by Aristotle, nor quantity (which is not capable of acting this way). All of the other accidental categories are relatives, and Aristotle denies that relatives can be either the principle or the term of an action.[7]

Again, [4] metaphysical excellence comes in degrees, and creatable natures occupy higher and lower places on an excellence hierarchy, insofar as they are more or less Godlike. Moreover, the Causal Nobility Principle holds that, where cause and effect are different in kind, the cause must be of a more excellent kind than the effect is. *What degree of goodness*, then, would grace-producing or real-presence-effecting power have? Not the least, because grace is a noble effect. Not the best, because grace and virtues of the mind are better than any *created* power to produce them. Not in between, because the soul's powers can act well or badly, but grace-producing or grace-disposing power or real-presence-producing power would act only for good.[8]

Again, [5] *when* would such power be conferred? Not when the sacrament was instituted by Christ, because the actual sacrament (for example, a mass said or a baptism performed by Aquinas or Bonaventure) did not exist then. Not when the individual rite is being celebrated either. For, in the beginning, God created a world full of things with their own Aristotelian natures, and God decided on a policy of always-or-for-the-most part concurrence with

[5] The case of the intellectual soul informing the body, whole in the whole body and whole in each part, is taken as a special case that even Divine power would not repeat.

[6] Aquinas, *Sent.* IV, d. 1, q. 1, a.4, qc. 2; Parma 7. 1. 461; *Summa Theologica* III, q. 62, a. 4.

[7] Aquinas, *Sent.* IV, d. 1, q. 1, a. 4, qc. 2; Parma 7. 1. 461.

[8] Aquinas, *Sent.* IV, d. 1, q. 1, a. 4, qc. 2; Parma 7. 1. 461.

those natures. God is the first cause of the existence and activities of all creatures. But Divine policy is to keep non-concurrence and "solo Divine action" to introduce new entities to a minimum. God does regularly act to create a human soul *ex nihilo* when the human foetus is sufficiently developed, and God does act to produce grace, soul characters, and soul ornaments, and infused theological virtues in suitably prepared souls on the occasion of their sacramental participation. To suppose that God also infuses grace- or real-presence-producing power in the individual rite when it is being celebrated is to multiply such supranatural entity production beyond necessity.[9]

Medieval approaches to these difficulties divide into those that posit and those that deny any efficient causal power for supranatural effects in the sacraments. At stake among the five that follow is whether—where X is said to cause Y—positing efficient causal power in X is the only way to secure the relevant sort of explanatory connection between them.

II. The "Divine Assistance" Theory

Pacts instead of Powers! Bonaventure and Aquinas tell how one group of masters avoid the above difficulties by denying that properly speaking there is any grace-producing or grace-disposing or real-presence-producing power in new-law (or any other) sacraments. For, properly speaking, 'X possesses a power (*virtus*) to produce Y' implies that there is some absolute quality Q that is Y-producing power, and that quality Q inheres in X as in a subject. For all of the reasons just cited, assistance theorists maintain that there is no quality in new-law (or any other) sacraments that is efficient causal power to produce grace, or to dispose the soul for grace, or to make the Body and Blood of Christ to be really present under forms of bread and wine. Rather by a Divine pact, God causes grace and/or grace-disposing characters or ornaments in the soul when suitably prepared persons participate in the sacraments. Likewise, by a Divine pact, God makes the Body and Blood to be really present on altars where the prayer of consecration is said. Sacramental participation or (in the case of the eucharist) celebration of the sacramental rite itself furnishes the occasion. Divine power "assists" the sacrament to produce the effect.

[9] Aquinas, *Sent.* IV, d. 1, q. 1, a. 4, qc. 2; Parma 7. 1. 461.

Because the Divine pact turns their concomitance into a regularity, however, common usage speaks of the sacraments having power or causing in an extended sense. Assistance theorists are happy to acquiesce in this extended usage, so long as we understand that there is no supranatural power quality in the sacraments. Rather, what Divine pact establishes is *a relation*: a certain *efficacious ordering* of sacramental participation to spiritual benefits, and an efficacious ordering of the performance of the rite to the real presence of Christ's Body and Blood. This is—they claim—analogous to what happens when a king lays down a regulation that anyone who produces a certain sign (say a lead coin) should receive £100. The law does not add any new quality to the sign, but a new relation, because it is ordered to something to which it was not ordered before.

Reaching for a biblical analogy, assistance theorists turn to the story of Elisha and Naaman the leper (2 Kgs 5: 1–19). Elisha tells Naaman to wash seven times in the river Jordan and he will be cleansed. Naaman obeys and is healed. Assistance theorists say that no power quality inheres in Elisha's words or in the Jordan's waters. Rather, Naaman's devotion and obedience are disposing conditions, and Divine power produces the cure. If God had made a pact always to "assist" when prophets commanded and devoted and obedient lepers bathed in the Jordan, common usage would have had it that Jordan's waters cause cures and have curative power. Likewise, with the sacraments, there is no spiritual power in the celebrant's words or in the material stuffs, but the suitable participant's faith and obedience disposes and Divine power produces the spiritual benefits in the participant's soul.[10]

Mixed Reviews! After giving lengthy explanations of both "inherent power/absolute quality" and "assistance" theories of sacramental causality, and consigning "inherent power/absolute quality" theories to borderline unintelligibility, Bonaventure is surprisingly equivocal in drawing his conclusion. He allows that both theories are defensible (*probabile*), although the assistance theory is more reasonable and in no way contrary to piety. This estimate does not settle the issue for Bonaventure, because sacraments trade in miracles, and—where miracles are concerned—reasons have less weight![11] Later on, however, Bonaventure seems to prefer to reason from

[10] Bonaventure, *Sent.* IV, d. 1, p. 1, a. u, q. 4; Quaracchi IV. 23–4. See also Aquinas, *Sent.* IV. 1. 1. 4. 1; Parma 7. 1. 462; *De Veritate* q. 2, a. 4 c; *Summa theologica* III, q. 62, a. 1 c.

[11] Bonaventure, *Sent.* IV, d. 1, q. 1, a. u, q. 4; Quaracchi IV. 24.

the assistance theory rather than the inherent-power/absolute-quality theory, although he continues to mention both options.[12]

By contrast, Aquinas protests that the assistance theory turns even new-law sacraments into mere signs, because they do not really *do* anything either to introduce grace or to dispose the patient to receive it.[13] So far as Aquinas can see, the Divine pact confers on the sacraments no aspect of causality, but leaves all of the real action of grace- or real-presence production to God. To put his point more sharply, Aquinas turns to Aristotle's distinction between *per se* and *per accidens* efficient causality. For Aristotle, *per se* efficient causes are those on which the existence of the effect really depends by contrast with *per accidens* causes that have no explanatory connection with the effect. In his famous example, Aristotle identifies the sculptor as a *per se* cause of the sculpture, because the substance subject is denominated "sculptor" from sculpting power and the power to produce sculptures is what sculpting power essentially is. The same substance subject may be white, in which case it is also true to say that the white sculpts. But Aristotle says that the white is a *per accidens* cause of the sculpting because whiteness and the sculptor's being white are causally irrelevant to the existence of the sculpture. The sculpting could proceed and the sculpture come into existence even if the sculptor got a suntan.

On Aquinas's reading, the assistance theory turns sacramental participation and/or the celebration of sacramental rites into mere *sine quibus non* conditions of spiritual benefits or of the real presence of Christ's Body and Blood. Aquinas contends, if new-law sacraments were only causes *sine quibus non*, they would have no more genuine causal relevance than *per accidens* causes do.[14] Again, assistance theorists say that what the Divine pact adds to new-law sacraments is a certain order or relation to transubstantiation or to the production of grace in the soul. But Aquinas takes Aristotle (in *Physics* V, t. 19) to deny that any relation or substance qua having a relation can be a principle of action and so to rule out the possibility that any relative can be a power. Only absolutes—in particular, substances or qualities—can.[15]

12 Bonaventure, *Sent.* IV, d. 10, p. 2, a. 1, q. 3; Quaracchi IV. 232.
13 Aquinas, *De Veritate*, q. 24, a. 7 c.
14 Aquinas, *Sent.* IV, d. 1, q. 1, a. 4, qc. 1; Parma 7. 1. 462.
15 Aquinas, *Sent.* IV, d. 1, q. 1, a. 4, qc. 2; Parma 7. 1. 463.

III. Aquinas on Sacramental Causal Power

Having rejected the assistance theory, Aquinas concludes that he will have to explain how grace-producing, grace-disposing, and real-presence-effecting causal powers can be found in the sacraments after all. *Clarifying Distinctions.* Aquinas moves to reconcile Divine causal prerogatives with genuine sacramental causality, by helping himself to a pair of distinctions. [D1] Considered from the side of their *effects*, efficient causes can be distinguished into *disposing* causes that dispose the patient for but do not themselves "reach" the ultimate effect, and *perfecting* causes that introduce the last perfection, the term of the change involved.[16]

[D2] Considered from the side of the *cause*—its independence or dependence in causing—efficient causes are distinguished into *principal* agents or first movers, and *instrumental* agents or moved movers. Powers are defined by their objects—what distinguishes power to heat from power to cool is just that the former is power to *heat*, while the latter is power to *cool*. Aristotelian physics finds it natural to speak of causal powers having a certain directed intentionality or aim. Every efficient cause—whether principal or instrumental—has power that pertains to it *by its nature* and that aims its action at a certain effect. But an instrumental cause qua instrument is moved by and so participates in the power of the principal agent and thereby receives a further intentionality or direction, toward the end at which the principal agent aims. Taking an example from artisans' tools, Aquinas explains that a hatchet or saw has power to divide objects by virtue of its sharpness. But when the carpenter uses the hatchet or saw to shape the wood into bench parts, the hatchet acquires a further intentionality—bench parts or a bench—that reach beyond what pertains to it by its own natural powers.[17] Taking a case from nature, Aquinas says that it pertains to the heat of fire by nature to dissolve, consume, and so on. But when used as an instrument of the nutritive power of the vegetative soul, fire and/or its heat participate in the power and thereby the causal aim of the principal agent: namely, to generate flesh.[18] Sometimes the instrumental cause only disposes

[16] Aquinas, *Sent.* IV, d. 1, q. 1, a. 4, qc.1; Parma 7. 1. 462.

[17] Aquinas, *Sent.* IV, d. 1, q. 1, a. 4, qc. 1; Parma 7. 1. 463. *De Veritate*, q. 27, a. 4 c. *Summa Theologica* III, q. 62, a. 1, ad 2um.

[18] Aquinas, *Sent.* IV, d. 1, q. 1, a. 4, qc. 1; Parma 7. 1. 462.

the patient to receive the principal agent's intended effect; other times they "reach" it: for example, active and passive elemental qualities qua instruments may reach natural forms educible from the potency of the matter, but only dispose the matter to receive the intellectual soul.[19]

Both [D1] and [D2] identify *subordination* as a way to harmonize Divine with sacramental causal power: sacraments are instrumental disposing causes, while God is the principal cause of grace in the soul and of transubstantiation.[20] Divine pre-eminence is further underscored by depreciating the ontological status and emphasizing the derivative nature of the power in the sacraments. Here, Aquinas seems to deploy another pair of distinctions. [D3] Aristotelian physicists sometimes distinguish *permanent* things from *successives*. Permanent things—for example, substances, qualities, or quantities—are the kind of things all of whose parts can exist at once, by contrast with successives—for example, time and motion—that cannot have all of their parts existing at once. The principal agent acts according to the exigencies of its own form; its active power is a form or quality that is a permanent thing and has *complete esse* in nature. But the instrumental cause qua instrument acts only insofar as it is moved by another. Aquinas infers that the power that the instrument receives qua moved by another is *proportioned to motion*. But, in *Physics* III, Aristotle defines motion as the incomplete actualization of potency as such, and so—Aquinas understands—as a quasi-mean between act and potency and hence not a complete being. Therefore, Aquinas concludes, the power of the instrument insofar as it acts for an effect that goes beyond its nature, is not fully actual and so is not a complete being that has fixed *esse* but an incomplete being that has only incomplete *esse.*[21]

Aquinas's example seems to invoke a different contrast that promises to be helpful with the characterization problem. According to Aristotle's theory of vision, the living eye sees red by receiving the sensible form without the sensible matter (for example, a species of redness from the nearby red wall). Since the seeing eye does not *become* red, however, redness cannot exist in the eye in the same way it exists in the wall. [D4] Aquinas's label for this *inesse* that things can have in a subject without thereby

[19] Aquinas, *Sent.* IV, d. 1, q. 1, a. 4, qc. 1; Parma 7. 1. 462.

[20] Aquinas, *Sent.* IV, d. 1, q. 1, a. 4, qc.1; Parma 7. 1. 463.

[21] Aquinas, *Sent.* IV, d. 1, q. 1, a. 4, qc. 2; Parma 7. 1. 463. *De Veritate*, q. 27, a. 4, ad 4um. *Summa Theologica* III, q. 62, a. 3 c; III, q. 62, a. 4 c.

characterizing the subject they exist in, *intentional esse*. Thus, redness is said to have not natural, but intentional, *esse* in the eye, so that the eye *sees* red but does not *become* red. Parallel to this, stone nature has intentional *esse* in the intellects of humans and angels, so that they *understand* what it is to be a stone, without *becoming* stones. Since Aristotelian physics also ruled out action beyond a determinate distance, the form of redness in the wall could not act directly on the eye. Rather the sensible species of redness would have to be propagated through the illumined air. Since the air does not thereby *become* red either, Aquinas understands the sensible species to have intentional *esse* in the material medium as well as the animated sense organ.[22] Returning to the issue of instrumental causes, Aquinas takes the air to be an instrument of the nearby red wall or its redness in causing vision in the eye; and contends that the air's power qua moved by the external visible has intentional *esse* in the air, and so has something like the diminished *esse* that things have in the soul.[23]

Sacramental Applications. Aquinas agrees that God alone can be a *principal* cause with respect to grace production, but creatures can be *instrumental* causes. Distinguishing further between *external* instruments (for example, the carpenter's hatchet or saw) and *internal* instruments (for example, the carpenter's arm), Christ's human nature is an internal instrument of Divine power, while sacraments are external instruments.[24] Like other instruments, sacraments have a double action: one that pertains to them through their own form—for example, washing, anointing the body; the other that exceeds their own form and pertains to them by the power of the principal agent.[25] Yet, even by virtue of this instrumental power, sacraments are not perfecting but only disposing causes where grace is concerned.[26] For example, baptism acts qua instrumental cause to dispose the baptized, ordination the ordinand to receive grace by producing a spiritual quality, a character or "ornament" in the soul. As for the tag that equivocal causes are nobler than their effects, Aquinas distinguishes what is nobler *simpliciter* from what is nobler *secundum quid*. Equivocal causes do not have to be nobler absolutely, but only in relation to producing a given type of effect (for example, fire acts

[22] Aquinas, *Summa Theologica* I, q. 78, a. 3.

[23] Aquinas, *Sent.* IV, d. 1, q. 1, a. 4, qc. 2; Parma 7. 1. 463. *De Veritate*, q. 27, a. 4, ad 4um. Cf. *Summa Theologica* III, q. 62, a. 4 c.

[24] Aquinas, *De Veritate*, q. 27, a. 4 c.

[25] Aquinas, *De Veritate*, q. 27, a. 4, ad 2um.

[26] Aquinas, *Sent.* IV, d. 1, q. 1, a. 4, qc. 1; Parma 7. 1. 463.

on a human body but is not nobler *simpliciter* than it). Moreover, the effect is not proportioned to the instrumental cause, but to the principal cause. Noble agents often use low-grade instruments, when they serve the purpose.[27]

Aquinas also thinks his account can dispel worries about the *ontological status* of the conferred causal power. First, Aristotle says that being is divided into being in the mind and being outside the mind, and the second is divided into the ten categories. Having assigned sacramental grace-disposing or transubstantiation-disposing power to the status of intentional or diminished being like the being that objects of thought have in the mind, Aquinas must deny that instrumental power belongs to any category on its own and properly speaking. Rather, incomplete beings are in a genus only by reduction, and Aquinas envisions a variety of alternative ways to "lead back" instrumental powers into categorial housing. The imperfect may be reduced to the perfect, and so motion to the term of motion. Since instrumental powers are proportioned to motion, they may be led back to the genus of the effect to be produced. Or, since instrumental causes are moved movers and so imply an ordering of mover to moved, instrumental power may be reduced to the category of passion. Or, instrumental power qua instrumental may be reduced to the genus of the power of the principal agent—for example, to quality or to uncreated power that is not in a genus.[28] Since goodness converts with being, such incomplete, intentional beings would be assigned degrees of goodness by reduction as well.[29] As to *when* the power is conferred, Aquinas replies, inchoately when the sacrament is instituted, but completely when the sacrament is actually moved by the principal agent (as when the carpenter actually moves the saw).[30]

Returning to problems about how a single spiritual power could exist in a complex material subject of inherence, Aquinas insists, on the one hand, that the division corporeal versus incorporeal applies only to complete beings in fixed, natural *esse*—just as categorial divisions apply only to being outside the mind and not to diminished being in the mind. Instrumental powers qua instrumental are incomplete beings in flux (*in fieri*) and so are neither corporeal nor incorporeal, strictly speaking.[31] On the other

[27] Aquinas, *Sent.* IV, d. 1, q. 1, a. 4, qc. 1; Parma 7. 1.463; *De Veritate*, q. 27, a. 4, ad 11um.

[28] Aquinas, *Sent.* IV, d. 1, q. 1, a. 4, qc. 2; Parma 7. 1. 464. *Summa Theologica* III, q. 62, a. 4, ad 2um.

[29] Aquinas, *Sent.* IV, d. 1, q. 1, a. 4, qc. 2; Parma 7. 1. 464.

[30] Aquinas, *Sent.* IV, d. 1, q. 1, a. 4, qc. 2; Parma 7. 1. 464.

[31] Aquinas, *De Veritate*,1. 27, a. 4, ad 5um.

hand, Aquinas relies on his example of sensible species having intentional or spiritual *esse* in the medium (then a majority-report theory tracing its pedigree to Averroes), to argue that grace-disposing power can have intentional *esse* in the material signs that sacraments are.[32] To this, he adds a more dubious example, claiming that the spoken and audible words have existing in them according to spiritual or intentional *esse* the meanings that they are meant to cause in the soul.[33] As to the complexity of the sacramental subject, Aquinas appeals to the part/whole distinction: part of the power can exist in one part of the instrument, another part in another, but taken together they make one power because they are ordered to a common effect.[34]

IV. Metaphysical Obstacles, Persisting

Ingenious and imaginative as Aquinas's choice of philosophical machinery is, its physical and metaphysical coherence came under attack even within his own generation, and that on two main points: first, his claim that, while sacraments are not grace- or transubstantiation-producing, they are instrumental causes that produce *dispositions* for these effects; second, his contention that God the principal agent actually confers *supernatural power* on the sacraments.

Disposing Causes? Aquinas explains that sacraments *dispose* the soul to receive grace by producing characters or ornaments in the soul. Objectors counter that this is no less problematic than saying that sacraments produce grace itself. (1) The *Divine-prerogative problems* are just as bad. For the character or other alleged soul ornaments impressed on the soul at baptism or ordination are supranatural qualities, no more educible from the potency of the receiving subject than grace is. If—as Aquinas claims—infinite Divine power alone can create, transubstantiate, and bring non-educible forms into existence, the sacraments should have no more (even instrumental) power over sacramental characters or soul ornaments than over grace.[35]

[32] Aquinas, *Sent.* IV, d. 1, q. 1, a. 4, qc. 2; Parma 7. 1. 464. *De Veritate*, q. 27, a. 4, ad 4um. *Summa Theologica* III, q. 62, a. 4, ad 1um.

[33] Aquinas, *Sent.* IV, d. 1, q. 1, a. 4, qc. 2; Parma 7. 1. 464. *Summa Theologica* III, q. 62, a. 4, ad 1um.

[34] Aquinas, *Sent.* IV, d. 1, q. 1, a. 4, qc. 2; Parma 7. 1. 464. *Summa Theologica* III, q. 62, a. 4, ad 4um.

[35] Summarized by Scotus, in *Op. Ox.* IV, d. 1, qq. 4–5, n. 4; Wadding VIII. 81.

(2) Likewise, the *timing problems* are the same. For [i] genuine causes are simultaneous with their effects; otherwise, being would come from non-being. But [ii] new-law sacraments are metaphysical successives, insofar as the rites all involve strings of spoken words. Since successives cannot exist in an instant, successives have *external* limits: to say, for example, that motion begins at t_1 is to say that motion is occurring in intervals as soon as you like after but not including t_1; to say that motion ceases at t_{10} is to assert that motion is occurring in intervals as close as you like up to but not including t_{10}. Put otherwise, to say that motion occurs between t_1 and t_{10} is to make t_1 the last instant before and t_{10} the first instant after the motion. According to Western sacramental theology, however, [iii] characters, soul ornaments, and grace are all qualities produced in an instant; transubstantiation occurs as soon as the priest has pronounced the words of institution, likewise in an instant. Put otherwise, the first moment of the existence of the qualities or of the presence of the Body and Blood of Christ is an external limit of the rite or of participation in it. It follows [iv] that sacramental rites and whatever powers exist in them no longer exist when characters, soul ornaments, grace, or transubstantiation come into being, and so [v] the former cannot be genuine causes of the latter!

Laboring the details, Aquinas's challengers declare that it will not do any good to say that the last syllable of the sacramental formula does the causing, since that syllable itself takes time. Even if it did not, it would follow that all the other syllables were superfluous and not instrumentally active in producing the disposition for grace. Nor can it be said that the last syllable acts in the power of the preceding syllables, the way the last drop of water breaks through the rock in the power of all the others that went before it. For the previous water drops left some disposing effect in the rock, but the earlier syllables would leave no analogous disposition—in this case to receiving a character or soul ornament—in the soul.[36]

Turning to the special case of the eucharist where the term of the principal agent is transubstantiation, Aquinas's opponents are incredulous that bread accidents or spoken words could have any—even instrumental—causal efficacy with respect to turning the whole substance of bread into the Body of Christ. Not only do the spoken words of institution take time, but, even after the last syllable has been pronounced, it takes time for the vibrations of the air to be propagated from the region of the celebrant's

[36] Scotus, *Op. Ox.* IV, d. 1, qq. 4–5, n. 5; Wadding VIII. 82–3.

mouth to the bread. Thus, if the spoken words played a causal role, the bread would not be transubstantiated for some time after the celebrant had finished speaking—which is contrary to theological consensus.

Again, how could disposing conditions play any genuine causal role in transubstantiation. For, to do so, they would have to be simultaneous with it. But what would that disposing condition exist in? Not in the substance of the bread, because it no longer exists at the moment of transubstantiation. Not in the bread accidents. Surely, they say, not in the Body of Christ, because no such disposition exists there now.[37]

Thus, Aquinas's critics conclude, it is both physically and metaphysically "fictional" and "superfluous" to suppose that, while sacraments cannot be instrumental causes of grace or of transubstantiation, they are instrumental causes of disposing conditions instead.[38]

Supranatural Power (Virtus) in the Sacraments? Aquinas attempts to secure genuine causal efficacy for the sacraments by insisting that their appropriation by God as instruments brings with it conferral of supranatural power for effects beyond the scope of their own forms. Opponents return to metaphysical problems about proper proportion between inherent forms and their subjects, and conclude that there can be no such supranatural power *in* the sacraments.

Aquinas acknowledges, but attempts to finesse problems about how a spiritual (grace-disposing) power could exist in a corporeal subject by appeal to his notion that such instrumental powers have only intentional or diminished *esse* in their instrument subject. Critics press the point: why should the alleged intentional or diminished being of *what* exists in automatically solve problems about *how* it exists in, in the sense of how what inheres is proportioned to its subject? (1) They reassert that sacraments are material signs, spatio-temporally extended corporeal things. So, either the supernatural power would have to exist [a] whole in the whole and whole in each part, or [b] whole in the whole and part in each part. Not [b], because grace-disposing power is a spiritual power, which lacks parts and so cannot be extended. It might seem to follow further that a simple form cannot bear any proportion to an extended thing, and so that none can exist in any material subject whatsoever. But Christian hylomorphists had appealed to Augustine to make an exception for the intellectual soul, and to maintain

[37] Scotus, *Op. Ox.* IV, d. 1, qq. 4–5, n. 6; Wadding VIII. 83–4.
[38] Scotus, *Op. Ox.* IV, d. 1, qq. 4–5, n. 7; Wadding VIII. 84.

that it exists [a] whole in the whole and whole in each part of the living human being. Not wishing to multiply miracles beyond necessity, Aquinas's critics denied that spiritual (grace-disposing) power could exist in the sacraments the same way.[39]

(2) Again, they remind, many words are required in the sacrament. Therefore, either [a] the same power exists in each syllable, or [b] different powers exist in different syllables. If [a], then an accident would migrate from subject to subject (existing first in one syllable, and then—when it ceases to exist—the next syllable). Moreover, since it would remain after each syllable ceased to exist, it would be able to exist without each of its subjects and so would not have depended on that subject after all. If [b], then the sacrament consisting of the whole speech would not have any one power, but an aggregate of powers—which would compromise the unity of the sacrament because the power defines the sacrament. Critics query, is it plausible that such a temporally distributed aggregate of powers could produce any effect on the soul?

Aquinas's opponents have fingered an area on which he has been sketchy. Does he take for granted that the instrumental power in diminished being (which he occasionally calls spiritual *esse*) shares with the intellectual soul the capacity for existing whole in the whole and whole in each part of an extended subject of inherence? Would he regard the appeal to the authority of alleged philosophico-theological consensus as weak because insufficiently considered? In response to the idea that sacraments are complex, being constituted of words and things, Aquinas seems to envision many partial powers making a whole. But in what way partial? Is the power in the baptismal water of a different and complementary kind or of the same kind as the power in the baptismal words? If the former, what would the difference be? If the latter, why would both be needed?

(3) If Aquinas never considers the problems arising from the fact that the words of the sacrament exist successively in time, his opponents mock his example of audible words having power to convey meanings into the hearer's mind, because the meanings have intentional or diminished being in the spoken words. Spoken words are *conventional* signs, which have been imposed to signify something. All that imposition adds to the spoken sound is a relation of reason, which cannot be a principle of real production; no absolute form or real relation is involved. Again, if this were really so, then

[39] Scotus, *Op. Ox.* IV, d. 1, qq. 4–5, n. 8; Wadding VIII. 89.

spoken words should convey meanings to those who never learned the language, as much as to those who have—which is contrary to experience.[40]

V. Containment versus Inherence

Localizing Divine Power? Henry of Ghent agrees that "we have by faith to posit a super-eminence of power in new-law sacraments over old-law sacraments."[41] It will not do to hold that new-law sacraments are merely *sine quibus non* causes of grace, because this does not posit any grace-producing power *in* them. The correlation between sacramental participation and grace reception would hold only by virtue of some Divine pact or statute or ordinance.[42] Given the perceived problems with Aquinas's interpretation—that new-law sacraments are subjects of inherent supranatural grace-disposing power and actually *do* something toward the principal agent's intended effects—Henry proposes a different way for that power to be and act in the sacraments: that new-law sacraments *contain* what is *per se* creative of grace in the soul, because God is present in new-law but not in old-law sacraments to produce that effect.[43] New-law sacraments are vessels of grace insofar as they contain God who is the fontal source from whom grace emanates into those who receive them.[44]

Henry joins theological consensus that God is present in everything by the Divine essence and substance. To convince us that God is present in some things but not others to produce certain effects, Henry recalls Christ's curing a leper by touching him. Henry agrees with Aquinas that such miracles are accomplished only by Divine power. But Deity exists in the flesh and hence the hand of Christ through the grace of union. Preserving the language of principal versus instrumental causes, Henry declares that Deity existing in the hand of Christ is the principal cause, but the hand of Christ is the instrumental cause of curing the leper. Analogously, Henry insists, new-law sacraments are instrumental causes of grace, not because they are subjects of any supernatural power or because they do anything to produce grace, but because

40 Scotus, *Op. Ox.* IV, d. 1, qq. 4–5, n. 10; Wadding VIII. 90–1.

41 Henry of Ghent, *Quodlibeta* IV, q. 37 (Paris: Badius, 1518; repr. Louvain: Bibliothèque SJ, 1961), fo. 149vQ.

42 Henry of Ghent, *Quodlibeta* IV, q. 37, fos. 149v–150r R.

43 Henry of Ghent, *Quodlibeta* IV, q. 37, fo. 150rV.

44 Henry of Ghent, *Quodlibeta* IV, q. 37, fo. 150rV.

God exists in them in such a way that at their touch grace is conferred upon those who receive them. The eucharist is the paradigm case, because it contains Christ corporally. Other sacraments participate in this power by containing virtually what the principal sacrament really contains.[45]

Disanalogy or Impanation? Duns Scotus responds to Henry's proposal by insisting on a disanalogy between Christ's curing the leper by a touch of His hand, and God's using the sacraments to produce grace in the soul. As Henry himself points out, the Divine Word is *hypostatically united* to the human nature and hence to the flesh of Christ; while Scotus insists that God is not in the sacrament by His essence, presence, and power in any way different from that in which God is present in every body. Nor is it that presence in the sacrament somehow determines God to cause—among the many effects that God alone can cause—one effect rather than another. It is *self*-determination by the Divine will that disposes God to cause grace when the sacraments are received.[46]

Henry's analogy would hold good, only if the Divine Word were hypostatically united to eucharistic bread. Henry does not explicitly advance a theory of eucharistic impanation in *Quodlibeta* IV, q. 37 (see Chapter 11 below). On the contrary, he defends the alternative and incompatible doctrine of transubstantiation in numerous other quodlibetal questions.[47]

VI. Powerless Causes?

Much as Scotus disparages Henry's own solution, Scotus does take Henry's point that the *efficacy* of new-law sacraments is best separated from their reception or exercise of any grace-producing or grace-disposing or real-presence-effecting efficient causal power, since these are "not obviously possible."[48] Returning to the assistance theory, Scotus accepts both its negative thesis—that sacramental causality does not involve any power (*virtus*) in the sacraments themselves—and its positive contention—that by Divine institution sacraments are signs that have an efficacious ordering to some gratuitous effect. This efficacious ordering is not an absolute quality,

[45] Henry of Ghent, *Quodlibeta* IV, q. 37, fo. 150r V.

[46] Scotus, *Op. Ox.* IV, d. 1, qq. 4–5, n.11; Wadding VIII. 91–2.

[47] Henry of Ghent, *Quodlibeta* III, q. 7, fo. lvi L–N & fo. lvii Q; IX, q. 8, fos. ccclxv F–ccclxvi L & fo. ccclxxii P; IX, q. 9, fo. ccclxxi L; XI, q. 4, fo. cccccl L–O.

[48] Scotus, *Op. Ox.* IV, d. 1, qq. 4–5, n. 12; Wadding VIII. 94.

whether existing all at once or successively, whether having real or only intentional *esse*.[49] Rather, efficacious ordering is only a relation of reason of the sign (the sacramental rite) to the thing signified (grace in the soul or the real presence of Christ's Body and Blood).[50] Unlike earlier assistance theorists, however, Scotus does not want to write off talk of sacramental causality as a tolerable but strictly improper manner of speaking. Instead, Scotus draws on his own understanding of essential dependence to argue that—*pace* Aquinas—there is an essential explanatory connection between powerless sacramental causes and salvific effects.

Essential Dependence. According to Scotus, the difference between a heap and a universe is that items in the latter but not the former are essentially ordered to one another. Scotus recognizes two non-congruent essential orders. The order of eminence ranks essences on the basis of their intensive actuality (of how much being there is in them).[51] Scotus holds that, for any pair of natures, one is more perfect or nobler than the other, so that the domain of natures forms an excellence hierarchy with one and only one nature for each grade and the infinite being at the top.[52]

Important for present purposes is the second, the order of dependence, which is grounded in the essential active and passive causal powers of natures. *Familiar Categories*. Scotus begins with what he takes to be obvious: the essential dependence for its existence of the caused item (*causatum*) on its cause(s), and the essential dependence of causes on one another in causing a common caused item. Aristotle's distinction between *per se* and *per accidens* causes focuses on the first, the relation between causes and what is caused: X is a *per se* efficient cause of Y if X has and exercises causal power to produce Y.[53] Scotus famously dwells on the second, and attempts an explicit formulation of the distinction between essentially and accidentally ordered causes—between causes that are essentially versus those that are merely accidentally ordered to one another in causing the same caused item—in terms of three contrasts:

[49] Scotus, *Op. Ox.* IV, d. 1, q. 2, nn. 4–7; Wadding VIII. 58–60; IV, d. 1, q. 2, n. 11; Wadding VIII. 63.

[50] Scotus, *Op. Ox.* IV, d. 1, qq. 4–5, n. 19; Wadding VIII. 107.

[51] Scotus, *Op. Ox.* IV, d. 12, q. 2, n. 12; Wadding VIII. 732.

[52] Scotus, *De Primo Principio*, c. III, nn. 7, 9, 11; Wadding III. 232–4.

[53] Scotus speaks variously of "X producing Y *according to its own nature and not according to what is accidental to it*" and of X's acting through its own form possessed at rest (*in esse quieto*). See *Op. Ox.* I, d. 6, q. 5, n. 6; Wadding VIII. 321.

[1] in an essentially ordered series, the posterior cause depends on the prior cause *in causing* and not for its existence of something else; but in accidentally ordered series (for example, the series of fathers and sons) the posterior may depend on the prior for its existence or something else;

[2] in essentially ordered causes the prior is of another order and is of a higher and more perfect kind than the posterior, whereas this is not necessarily the case in accidentally ordered series;

[3] in essentially ordered causes, all of the causes are required to act simultaneously in causing the caused item, but this is not so with accidentally ordered series.[54]

Y and X are essentially ordered in the production of E, only if Y and X are by their very natures such that X depends on Y's exercising Y's causal power for X's exercising X's causal power with respect to E, or vice versa. When Jacob begets Joseph, God and the sun and Jacob's generative power form an essentially ordered series, but Abraham, Isaac, and Jacob form an accidentally ordered series in the production of Joseph, which happens after Abraham and Isaac are already dead!

Non-Obvious" Essential Dependence. Significantly, Scotus moves on from these to recognize other "non-obvious" types of essential dependence. [*Case 1: The Essential Dependence of the Posterior on the Prior Effect of the Same Cause*] Suppose some cause X is naturally apt to cause two caused items E1 and E2, but is naturally apt to cause them in a certain order—namely, E1 immediately and E2 only posterior to its having caused E1. E1 is the prior caused item and E2 is the posterior caused item. Scotus argues that, even if E1 neither has nor exercises any causal power to produce E2, E2 still essentially depends on E1, because E2 cannot exist unless E1 exists. This is because X's causal power is by nature ordered in such a way that it cannot produce E2 without first producing E1. E1 and E2 have an essential order of dependence to one another, not because either has or exercises any causal power in relation to the other's existence or causal activity, but because E1 and E2 are related to a third X that is the common cause of both. E2 is not related to X *simpliciter*, but to X qua having first produced E1. Thus, X can be said to be the remote cause of E2 and E2 the posterior effect of X, not because there is some other active causal power that intervenes to act together with X in

[54] *DPP*, c. III, n. 2; Wadding III. 230; Wolter ed., 3. 11.

producing E2, but insofar as X is first ordered to the prior caused item E1 and then to the posterior caused item E2.[55]

Having ventured to recognize essential dependence between items neither of which has or exercises causal power in relation to the other, Scotus extends the idea to other cases. [*Case 2: The Essential Dependence of the Remote on the Proximate Effect of the Same Cause*] Suppose E1 and E2 are essentially ordered to a common third Y, where Y is a proximate *per se* cause of E1, but Y is essentially ordered to X and X is the proximate *per se* cause in producing E2, and Y's causal power is by nature ordered in such a way that Y does not cooperate with X to produce E2 without first having acted immediately to produce E1. Once again, E2 will be essentially dependent on E1, because E2 cannot exist unless E1 exists.[56]

Making these extensions constitutes a radical theoretical move on Scotus's part: *what explains why E2 cannot exist without E1 is not their own active causal powers, but the naturally ordered active causal power of another. And it is the latter that essentially orders the prior and posterior caused items to one another in the essential order of dependence.*

Essentially Ordered Effects from Multiple Causes. Scotus's argument for the essential dependence of posterior on prior caused items treated the posterior's inability to exist without the prior as criterial for essential dependence. If so, we may wonder whether a common cause is really necessary, or whether multiple natural causes might do as well. [*Case 3: Sine Qua Non Conditions*] What if C1 were a *per se* cause of E1 and C2 were a *per se* cause of E2, but the intentionality of C2's causal power were so ordered that C2 would not act to produce E2 unless C1 had acted to produce E1? That is, what if the ordered intentionality of C2's causal power made it the case that the production of E1 by C1 were *a necessary condition* for the production of E2 by C2? Would that be enough for *the essential dependence* of E2 on E1, even if neither E1 nor E2 has or exercises efficient causal power in relation to each other? [*Case 4: Necessitating Dispositions*] What if C1 were a *per se* cause of E1 and C2 were a *per se* cause of E2, and C2 were by nature such that—given the production of E1 by C1 in the relevant environs—the production of E2 by C2 would follow *by natural necessity*? Would not that be enough for the *essential dependence* of E2 on E1 as well, even if

[55] *DPP*, c. I, nn. 203; Wadding III. 210–11; Wolter ed., 1. 9–1. 12.

[56] *DPP*, c. I, n. 4; Wadding III. 211; Wolter ed., 1. 14.

neither E1 nor E2 has or exercises efficient causal power in relation to each other?

In *Opus Oxoniense*, book IV, d. 6, q. 5, Scotus identifies some natural phenomena that are instances of both Cases 3 and 4 at once.[57] In Aristotelian optics, colored objects produce sensible species in nearby air, if and only if the air is illuminated. The sun (=C1) does the illuminating (=E1); the colored object (=C2) produces the sensible species (=E2). Here the illumination inheres in the air and is a "receptive basis" (*ratio receptivi*) that makes the air suitable for receiving further forms, namely, the sensible species. Thus, [Case 3] the illumination of the air is a necessary *sine qua non* condition of the air's receiving sensible species. Moreover, [Case 4] when the air is illumined, the production of sensible species in it by relevantly positioned colored objects follows by natural necessity. Again, a rock (= C1) may knock a piece of wood from its place, moving it (= E1) relevantly close to the fire (= C2) that burns it up (= E2). [Case 3] Proximity to the fire is a *sine qua non* of the wood's being burned up by it; and [Case 4], given the wood's proximity to the fire, its combustion follows by natural necessity. Illumination in the air and the motion of the wood are *sine quibus non disposing conditions*, which—given the presence of other relevant causal factors—naturally necessitate the second effect. But the naturally necessary sequencing of the effects—illumination and sensible species; motion and combustion—is explained not in terms of any active causal power of the prior effect (E1) or of its cause (C1) with respect to the posterior effect (E2), but in terms of the suitably situated active causal power of the second cause (C2).

Focusing on the fact that such phenomena satisfy the criteria for Case 4, Scotus does recognize some sort of *essential dependence* between the causes (C1) of such "naturally necessitating" dispositions (E1) and the posterior effect (E2), because he joins others in counting them (C1) *instrumental causes* of the posterior effect (E2)—and this, even though the cause (C1) of the disposing condition (E1) neither has nor exercises any active causal power with respect to the posterior effect (E2).[58] But Scotus extends the range of essential dependence and instrumental causality further still. Where "naturally necessitating" disposing conditions are concerned, some (for example,

[57] *Op. Ox.* IV, d. 6, q. 5, n. 6; Wadding VIII. 321–2; cf. IV, d. 1, qq. 4–5, nn. 12–15; Wadding VIII. 94–6.

[58] *Op.Ox.* IV, d. 6, q. 5, nn. 6–8; Wadding VIII. 321–2.

illumination in the air) are receptive bases (*rationes receptivi*), which condition the subject to receive further modification (for example, sensible species) and which must remain as long as the further modification remains (for example, sensible species are not produced or conserved in the dark). Others (for example, the motion of the wood close to the fire) are not receptive bases. Scotus focuses on naturally necessitating disposing conditions that are not receptive bases. He argues, not only that the posterior effect (E2) is *essentially dependent* on the disposing condition (E1), but also that the naturally necessitating disposing condition (E1) is "somehow *an active and instrumental cause*" of the posterior effect (E2), even though the disposing condition itself (E1) neither has nor exercises any active causal power in the production of the posterior effect (E2). Scotus notes that, generally speaking, the *per se* cause (C1) of a prior effect (E1) is not thereby said to be a cause of a posterior effect (E2), unless the prior effect (E1) itself is somehow a cause of the posterior effect (E2). If the cause of the naturally necessitating disposing condition counts as an instrumental cause of the further effect, the naturally necessitating disposing condition must somehow be a cause of the further effect, too![59]

Interim Review. It is time to take stock, before bringing these ideas home to the issue of sacramental causality. In *De Primo Principio*, Scotus moved from the essential dependence for existence of effects on their *per se* causes, and the essential dependence of posterior *per se* causes on prior *per se* causes in causing their common effect, to posit—in Cases 1 and 2—the essential dependence of a posterior effect on a prior effect of a common cause. This already gives us cases where essential dependence was not to be explained in terms of any active causal powers between the dependent and that on which it depends, but in terms of the active causal powers of something else. The naturally necessary order of prior and posterior effects is rooted in the ordered intentionality of the active causal powers of a third that is their common *per se* cause.

[59] *Op. Ox*. IV, d. 1, qq. 4–5, nn. 12–13; Wadding VIII. 94–5. Notice: In this argument, Scotus secures a causal connection between E1 and E2 by appeal to an accidentally ordered series. In the examples, the disposing condition (E1) depends on C1 for its existence, but E1 does not further depend on C1 for the exercise of its causal power to produce E2, because neither C1 nor E1 has or exercises causal power to produce E2. Rather C1 is said to be an instrumental cause of E2 because C1 is a *per se* cause of a disposing condition that—given other relevant causal conditions—naturally necessitates E2. Other powers set the causal context. All C1 has to do is act to produce the effect of which it is a *per se* cause, and the posterior effect is produced by the other powers. Put otherwise, the production of E1 by C1 removes an obstacle to the production of E2 by C2. Scotus reasons, if the disposing condition is the trigger, why should it not be an instrumental cause as well?

In *Opus Oxoniense* IV, d. 1, qq. 4–5, Scotus makes two further moves.[60] First, he identifies—in Cases 3 and 4—naturally necessary orders among the effects of different causes—where C2 is by nature apt to produce E2 when and only when C1 first produces E1 under relevant conditions of proximity—as cases of essential dependence. Second, he not only recognizes the relations of E2 to C1 and E2 to E1 as cases of essential dependence; he goes further to identify both C1 and E1 as "somehow active instrumental causes" of E2, even though neither C1 nor E1 has nor exercises any active causal power to produce E2. Rather the causal relevance of C1 and E1 to E2 is explained in terms of the ordered intentionality of the active causal powers of another (= C2).

In all of these cases, the ordering of effects to one another is said to be *naturally* necessary, and to find its explanation in the ordered causal propensities and capacities of some natural cause or other. Even though instrumental causes are not themselves *per se* causes of the posterior effect, the ordered intentionality of the natural causal aptitudes of other things in the wider causal context provide the explanatory connection that keeps such instrumental causes from being mere causes *per accidens*.

Sacramental Causality, One More Extension? In *Opus Oxoniense* IV, d. 1, q. 2, Scotus's strategy is to argue that sacramental causality is not *per accidens* causality, because it is sufficiently analogous to Case 4: that is, that sacramental participation is somehow a necessitating disposing condition of grace in the soul, and the celebration of the eucharist somehow a necessitating disposing condition of real presence.

To do this, Scotus feels he has to overcome an obvious disanalogy between sacraments, on the one hand, and his cited instances of Case 4, on the other: namely, the latter involve *natural* causes and *naturally* necessitating dispositions, while sacramental effects are not to be explained in terms of any *natural* cause, created or Divine! Scotus joins theological consensus in declaring that no creature or ordered aggregate of creatures can be a *per se* cause of supernatural infused qualities. If no creature can be a *per se* cause of supranatural infused qualities, then none can be a naturally necessitating disposing condition either. For no creatable causal power could explain the connection, because none would be ordered to produce supranatural grace in the soul upon the occurrence of some disposing condition. So, if there is a connection—if such human utterances and manipulations of material

[60] *Op. Ox.* IV, d. 1, qq. 4–5, n. 12; Wadding VIII. 94–5.

stuffs are that upon the occurrence of which grace in the soul follows—the "third" on which it depends is not a natural but a voluntary cause—the only voluntary cause able to be a *per se* cause of grace in the soul, the Divine will![61]

Ingeniously, Scotus contends, what makes sacramental disposing conditions *necessitating* is not the ordered intentionality of *natural* cause(s), but rather a *definitional* connection. His analogy is that, just as the real definition of the natures of natural *per se* causes links their nature with various causal activities and functional capacities, so the nominal definition of the sacraments links them with grace production. Scotus clarifies how it is not by virtue of their natural properties that things (or ordered aggregates of things, actions, and states of affairs) count as sacraments. Sacraments are signs—in the sense that Scotus is interested in, conventional signs. The differentia that turns a non-sign (for example, an uttered noise) into a sign (for example, a spoken word) is a relation of reason to the thing signified. The spoken sounds 'human being' enjoy no naturally necessary connection with human nature. But human language users impose 'human being' to signify by endowing 'human being' with a relation of reason to its significatum, thereby establishing a definitional connection between 'human being' and 'rational mortal animal'. Likewise, sequenced human utterances and manipulations of material stuffs enjoy no naturally necessary connection with supranatural grace in the soul. But Divine institution of soteriological statutes endows such activities with a relation of reason to supranatural grace in the soul, thereby establishing a definitional connection between sacraments/sacramental participation and grace production.[62]

Moreover, just as in the case of instrumental causality, naturally necessitating dispositions may be identified as causes of further effects with respect to which they neither have nor exercise any active causal power, so *de jure* sacraments/sacramental participation are a necessitating condition of grace in the soul even though neither the sacraments nor their participation neither have nor exercise any active causal power to produce it. The consequence between sacramental participation and grace in the soul is not secured by any absolute necessity. By absolute Divine power, God could have refrained from soteriological legislation, could have and indeed (under the old law) did institute different sacraments as disposing

61 *Op. Ox.* IV, d. 2, q. 1, nn. 5–6; Wadding VIII. 138.

62 *Op. Ox.* IV, d. 1, q. 2, nn. 4–10; Wadding VIII. 58–62; IV, d. 1, qq. 4–5, nn. 18–19; Wadding VIII. 106–7.

conditions.[63] But the connection between new-law sacraments/sacramental participation and supranatural grace in the soul *is* necessary with respect to God's ordered power (power exercised according to actual Divine statutes for the time after Christ's passion) and is underwritten by the necessity of immutability according to which Godhead necessarily is true to itself by being consistent of purpose *ad extra*.[64]

VII. Causes Sine Quibus Non

Parisian Considerations. Scotus's treatment of sacramental causality in his *Opus Oxoniense* focuses on Case 4 and only on examples of Case 3 that are also examples of Case 4. But his discussion of will and intellect in his *Reportata Parisiensia* II, d. 25, q. u, forwards an example of Case 3 that is not also an example of Case 4. In that passage—as Stephen Dumont has argued—Scotus came to regard as defensible a version of Henry of Ghent's position (also popular among leading Franciscans) that the will is related to acts of intellect as to causes *sine quibus non*.[65] The intellect and the object X (separately or together = C1) exercise efficient causal power to produce an act of understanding X (= E1). The will (= C2) is by its very nature such that it is able to produce acts of willing or nilling X (= E2) only if the intellect (C1) has presented the object X (E1). The act of understanding X (E1) is a *sine qua non* of the will's willing or nilling X (E2), even though (according to Henry and some Franciscans) neither the object X nor the intellect, not even the act of understanding X, has or exercises any efficient causal power to produce an act of will.[66] On this account, the relation between intellect and will is an example of Case 3, where the connection—E2 only if E1—is secured by the ordered intentionality of will power itself. But it is not an example of Case 4: the intellect's presentation of an object

[63] *Op. Ox.* IV, d. 6, q. 6, n. 2; Wadding I. 110–11; IV, d. 6, q. 6, n. 8; Wadding VIII. 118–20.

[64] *Op. Ox.* IV, d. 1, qq. 4–5, nn. 12–13; Wadding VIII. 95; IV, d. 1, qq. 4–5, n. 18; Wadding VIII. 106.

[65] Stephen D. Dumont, "Did Duns Scotus Change his Mind on the Will?" in Jan A. Aertsen, Kent Emery Jr., and Andreas Speer (eds.), *Nach der Verurteilung von 1277: Philosophie und Theologie an der Universität von Paris im letzten Viertel des 13. Jahrhunderts. Studien und Texte* (Berlin and New York: Walter de Gruyter, 2001), pp. 719–94. Thanks to Dumont, not only for the article, but for recalling the case of will and intellect to my attention in this connection.

[66] *Rep. par.* II, d. 25, q. u, nn. 15–18; Wadding XI. 370–1. See Dumont, "Did Scotus Change his Mind on the Will?" sect. V, pp. 744–58.

(E1) is not a *necessitating* disposition for any action on the will's part (E2). This is because will power is by nature a power that self-determines itself to action or inaction with respect to presented objects and likewise to willing or nilling them. The intellect's presentation of an object X can stand with an act of willing X, an act of nilling X, or with no action at all with respect to X.

The logic of Scotus's earlier reasoning ought to lead him to acknowledge Case 3 as involving non-obvious essential dependence. For he defended essential dependence in Cases 1 and 2 on the ground that the ordered intentionality of a causal power made it the case that E2 would not be produced without E1's having been produced. Thus, in Scotus's mind, it was enough for non-obvious essential dependence of E2 on E1 that E1 was a *sine qua non* of E2! The difference between Cases 1 and 2, on the one hand, and Case 3, on the other, is that the causal power whose ordered intentionality secures the essential connection between E2 and E1 in Cases 1 and 2 is itself a cause of E2 as well as of E1; while the causal power whose ordered intentionality secures the essential connection between E2 and E1 in Case 3 is the cause of E2 but not of E1.

This brings us to a further point, which Scotus could have exploited more fully to remove the supposed disanalogy between sacramental essential dependence and his usual examples of Cases 3 and 4. For Scotus, what distinguishes non-obvious essential dependence from *per accidens* causal connections is that the former but not the latter is grounded in the ordered intentionality of a causal power. But ordered intentionality can be built into a causal power by nature or by the will's choices. Nature builds it into colored objects that their species-producing power is power to produce species only when the medium has been illuminated. But the king's policy decision structures the intentionality of his will power, so that he wills to give $100 only to those who present specially minted lead coins. Naturally ordered intentionality is naturally necessary. Much of the ordered intentionality of will power is contingent and up to the agent. But how the power gets its ordered intentionality should make no difference to whether the dependence relation and to whether connection is essential. It is the fact of the ordered intentionality that explains why E2 cannot exist without E1 (Case 3) and/or why E2 exists when and only when E1 is produced (combined Cases 3 and 4). So far as I know, Scotus does not explicitly say so, but sacramental participation and eucharistic celebration do qualify as *sine qua non* conditions of grace in the soul and real presence on the altar, respectively. The fact that the ordered intentionality of the Divine will is free and contingent, while that of species-producing power is naturally necessary, should be irrelevant to whether a relation of non-obvious essential dependence obtains!

Streamlining with Ockham. William Ockham is the one who places sacramental causality squarely in the category of *sine qua non* causality. In doing so, he both builds on and critiques Scotus's position. Scotus's first move to extend essential dependence to [Case 1] prior and posterior effects of a common cause already forwarded a distinction between [a] cases where the essential dependence of X on Y is explained in terms of Y's active causal powers; and [b] those where the essential dependence of X on Y is explained in terms of the active causal powers of another Z. Against Scotus, Ockham advances epistemological reasons for denying that there are any cases of non-obvious essential dependence (of *sine qua non* causality) in nature. Ockham reasons that if—where X and Y are natural things—Y's being necessary for the existence of X is not enough to show that Y has and exercises causal power in the production of X, then we would "lose every way of persuading or knowing that one thing is an efficient cause of another." For example, we would not be able to infer that the heat in fire is and exercises efficient causal power to burn nearby combustibles, because we would have to allow for the possibility that God does all of the efficient causal work, while the heat in fire and the burning of combustibles are related to one another as prior and posterior effects of God.[67]

Nevertheless, Ockham does not think Scotus's division [b] is empty: there are cases in which the regular sequence between X's and Y's is explained, not by their own causal powers but by the will of some voluntary cause.[68] Civil law would furnish obvious examples, and so—Ockham thinks—would sacramental causality, where the Divine will is the other (Z) whose action secures the sequence between sacramental participation (Y) and grace in the soul (X). Thus, Ockham identifies sacramental causality as *sine qua non* causality. And—*pace* Aquinas but in agreement with Scotus—Ockham insists that the will of the other furnishes an explanatory connection

[67] Ockham, *Quaest. in Sent.* II, qq. 3–4; OTh V. 72–3; *Summula Philosophiae Naturalis* II, c. 3; OPh VI. 218; *Quaestiones in Libros Physicorum Aristotelis*, q. 141; OPh VI. 781.

[68] Ockham, *Quaest. in Sent.* IV, q. 1; OTh VII. 14; IV, q. 2; OTh VII. 33; IV, qq. 3–4; OTh VII. 60.

between X's and Y's and so keeps *sine qua non* causality from being merely causality *per accidens*.[69]

What started the whole discussion of sacramental causality was the notion that new-law sacraments differ from old-law sacraments (except for circumcision) in being efficacious signs that "effect what they figure." Scotus's and Ockham's views can preserve the contrast, but the difference will not be that there is efficient causal power in the former but not in the latter. Rather the difference lies in the ordered intentionality of the causal power of another: namely, the ordered intentionality of Divine will power with respect to each. Because new-law sacraments (and circumcision) work *ex opere operato*, the essential connection is between sacramental participation and grace in the soul or between eucharistic celebration and real presence. Because old-law sacraments function *ex opere operantis*, the essential connection will be between the participant's faith in Christ's passion and grace in the soul.

VIII. The Assistance Theory, Revived

Scotus and Ockham both counter Aquinas's contention that powerless "causes" are merely causes *per accidens*. The white is a *per accidens* cause of the sculpture because no causal power underwrites any connection between whiteness or possessing whiteness and sculpture production. But, in the case of the sacraments, the ordered intentionality of Divine will power does forge an explanatory connection between the sacraments and salvific effects. For Scotus, this makes non-obvious essential dependence essential all the same. For Ockham, it gives *sine qua non* causes explanatory power.

Two Scotists and rough contemporaries of Ockham—John Bassolis (+1347) and Franciscus Mayronis (+ after 1328)—find themselves unable to follow Scotus or agree with Ockham about this claim. Bassolis declares that the only real efficient causes are *per se* efficient causes: : that is, X is a real efficient cause of Y only if X has efficient causal power to produce Y and X exercises that power to produce Y in existence. Sacraments are not real causes of grace or real presence, because—for all of the reasons rehearsed in Section IV above and then some—they possess no grace-producing,

[69] Ockham, *Quaest. in Sent.* IV, q. 1; OTh VII. 8–9, 14.

grace-disposing, or real-presence-effecting causal powers.[70] Scotus's attempt to assimilate sacramental causality to [Case 4] non-obvious necessitating dispositions is "subtle," "defensible," even "beautiful," but all the same "doubtful" and in the end "wrong."[71] The Assistance Theory was right: sacraments can be called causes of grace or real presence, only improperly speaking.[72]

Likewise, Mayronis rehearses the usual arguments that there can be no absolute power in sacraments to effect anything in the soul.[73] But he tries to make the extended use of causal language seem more acceptable by noting its entrenchment with variable meanings across four distinguishable conceptual fields. [1] In *nature*, things are counted as efficient causes [i] at whose existence another follows, and [ii] that which gives being to a thing and/or conserves it in being. Mayronis insists that, to count as an efficient cause in nature, the effect must *really depend* on it.[74] [2] In *art* or crafts, things are counted as efficient causes, not because they receive efficient causal power, but because they receive the first effect—for example, motion from the principal agent,[75] as when the axe is swung by the carpenter to split the wood. [3] In *politics*, the whole connection between cause and effect is made by reason and will. Because the emperor legislates that flight is a capital offense, flight is said to be the cause of death. When the pope ordains that whoever crosses to the see of Alexandria is excommunicated, crossing to Alexandria is said to be the cause of excommunication.[76] [4] In *hierarchies*, the justice of the judge does not cause the penalty; the demerit of the criminal does. But the criminal's demerit is not a *natural* cause of his or her penalty. Rather it is so, because an authority has freely and contingently instituted laws to that effect, although the authority could have instituted different laws instead.[77] In both fields [3] and [4], the deeds gain explanatory flavor in relation to the wider explanatory framework of the established laws; just as in field [2] the first effect acquires an explanatory aura within the wider framework of the efficient causal activity of the principal agent.

70 Bassolis, *Sent.* IV, d. 1, q. 1; 1516, fos. 11ra–12vb.

71 Bassolis, *Sent.* IV, d. 1, q. 1; 1516, fo. 9rab & fo. 11ra.

72 Bassolis, *Sent.* IV, d. 1, q. 1; 1516, fos.11vb–12ra.

73 Mayronis, *Sent.* IV, d. 6, qq. 1–3; 1520, d. 7, q. 4; d. 9, qq. 1–2.

74 Mayronis, *Sent.* IV, d. 9, q. 2; 1520, fo. 187ra CD.

75 Mayronis, *Sent.* IV, d. 9, q. 2; 1520, fo. 187ra D.

76 Mayronis, *Sent.* IV, d. 9, q. 2; 1520, fo. 187ra D.

77 Mayronis, *Sent.* IV, d. 9, q. 2; 1520, fo.187rab DE.

Catching the spirit of Bassolis's conclusions, Mayronis declares that the last three categories are not *real* causes; only those in [1] the category of natural efficient causes are. In particular, [2] artisans' instruments are not real causes on which the effect depends.[78] The power that Christ claims after the resurrection, the power that Pilate had to crucify Him, was authority, and so not [1] natural, but [3] political and [4] hierarchical.[79] Likewise, the power over demons Christ gave to the disciples was [3] political and [4] hierarchical.[80] Christ gave them authority, so that, when they lay on hands, *God* heals and *God* expels Lucifer. In general, what is conferred in [3] politics is authority, which is not an absolute form, but a relation of reason and hence not an effective principle in [1] nature.

Applying these divisions to the sacraments, Mayronis declares that those who look for [1] a natural cause in the sacraments will labor in vain. All that is to be found there is [3] political or [4] hierarchical causation, which is in relation to a legislator. Sacramental acts or their reception cause the way something causes [3] in politics or [4] in hierarchies.[81]

78 Mayronis, *Sent.* IV, d. 6, q. 2; 1520, fo. 182vbP.
79 Mayronis, *Sent.* IV, d. 9, q. 1; 1520, fo. 186vb P.
80 Mayronis, *Sent.* IV, d. 7, q. 4; 1520, fo. 183rab DF.
81 Mayronis, *Sent.* IV, d. 9, q. 2; 1520, fo. 187rb E.

PART TWO

The Metaphysics and Physics of Real Presence

How Does it Get Where?

4

Explaining the Presence, Identifying the Change: Aquinas and Giles of Rome

I. Presenting Problems

New-law sacraments effect what they figure. They figure what is signified naturally but inchoately and indeterminately by their matter and more explicitly by their accompanying form of words. The sacrament of the altar is ordered, not simply to infusing grace in the soul—grace that is a participation of Christ's power and that prepares the soul for union with God. Aquinas contends that the sacrament of the altar is the consummation of other sacraments because its celebration makes the true Body of Christ to be really present, so that by eating the faithful are truly joined with Christ, their head, however veiled He may be from sight.[1] But how does the Body of Christ get there? How can it be there? Where, and in what sense of 'where', is it?

Among others, Aquinas, Giles of Rome, Scotus, and Ockham attempted detailed answers to these questions. They worked out their explanations within the framework of certain constraints. First, reliable *sense perception* under non-hallucinatory conditions of observation obviously confirms that

[T1] the bread accidents or "species" are still there on the altar, where they were before the consecration.

By Aquinas's time, *theological consensus* lays it down that

[1] See Aquinas, IV *Sent.* d. 10, q. 1, a. 1, qc 1 c [15163]; and *Summa Theologica* III, q. 75, a. 1 c & ad 2um.

[T2] by means of the consecration, the true Body of Christ (the very one that was born of Mary and crucified) comes to be "on the altar," "contained by the sacrament" "under the species" of bread that remain.[2]

Likewise, then-received Christology insisted that

[T3] the Body of Christ has ascended into heaven, where it will remain until Judgment Day,

and that

[T4] the risen and ascended Body of Christ is glorified and hence impassible.

By itself, [T4] seems to render [T2] problematic: however the Body of Christ gets to altars where eucharistic bread is being consecrated, it will have to be without undergoing any of the changes that impassibility disallows.

Moreover, *reason* assigned presumptive weight to twin *philosophical* theses about bodily location:

[T5] two bodies cannot be extended in the same place at once,

because a single body "fills" the place where it is by virtue of its quantitative dimensions, which exclude others. Conversely,

[T6] a single body cannot be extended in, or move toward, two distinct places at once.

Philosophically, [T5] seemed to follow from the metaphysical doctrine that matter signed by quantity is the principle of individuation. Likewise, even if x is a body of the same species as y, [T6] the very fact that x is in a distinct place from y at time t is enough to show that x and y are numerically distinct. Moreover, simultaneous multiple locations for the same body—contrary to [T6]—would seem to cause problems for Aristotelian physics, whose efficient causes act on relevantly close-by patients. The same water might be in a teakettle on the fire in London and in an ice tray in a freezer in Rome, and so take on and be the subject of contrary qualities simultaneously.

[2] Throughout his discussion, Aquinas's language moves back and forth among such phrases: IV *Sent.* d. 10, q. 1, a. 1, qc. 1, c [15163]; *Summa Theologica* III, q. 75, a. 1 c & ad 2um. Gary Macy, in *The Theologies of the Eucharist in the Early Scholastic Period: A Study of the Salvific Function of the Sacrament according to the Theologians c. 1080–c. 1220* (Oxford: Clarendon Press, 1984), recounts how it took some time to arrive at a consensus that the body on the altar was the very body that Mary bore and that died on the cross. He credits the influence of Paschasius' theory in the ninth century and the condemnations of Berengar of Tours in the eleventh century as contributing to its becoming a common-place assumption (I. 21–3, 36–7, 48; II. 68–9).

The very entrenchment of [T5] and [T6] make coherent eucharistic theology challenging philosophically. Whatever happens to the bread itself, [T1] the extended bread accidents remain. Will not their quantity "fill" the place and—by [T5]—exclude the dimensions of any other bodies, thereby preventing the true Body of Christ from being there at the same time—contrary to [T2]? Likewise, does not [T6] the ban on multiple location show that the Body of Christ cannot [T3] remain in heaven and at the same time [T2] exist on one or many altars where mass is being said? Add to these "multiple-location" problems the "size problem." Generally speaking,

[T7] a body is located in a place, only if its dimensions are commensurate with the dimensions of the place.

But the Body of Christ is almost always bigger than and differently shaped from the bread accidents on the altar. If [T7] holds, how can [T2] be true?

II. Transubstantiation, Provoked Ingenuity?

Aquinas promotes transubstantiation as the only viable solution to these problems—a solution that is theologically adequate because heresy-avoiding; one that is at once philosophically inventive and intelligible, developing Aristotelian insights to save the givens of faith (T2–T4) and experience (T1) all at once. *What Kind of Change?* Most medieval philosophers put it beyond question, not only that

[P6] contradictories cannot be simultaneously true,

but that

[P2] there is no passage from contradictory to contradictory—a proposition cannot be first true (false) and then its contradictory opposite be true (false)—without any change.

Therefore, if the Body of Christ is not on the altar before and is on the altar after the consecration, this must be due to some change. Seemingly the most obvious candidate would be *locomotion*. But this cannot explain how the Body of Christ comes to be on the many altars where the eucharist is simultaneously celebrated. Strictly speaking, for a body to change place requires it to leave the place where it was and to arrive at a different place where it was not, passing through the places in between. But—by [T3]—

the Body of Christ does not leave heaven, no matter what priests do at earthly altars. Likewise, by [T6], it is impossible for a single body to move towards two different places by two different routes at once.[3] Nor—by [T4]—can it be explained by some *internal change* in the accidents that inhere in the Body of Christ (say some qualitative or quantitative change).

How else can a proposition be true about something of which it was false before? Aquinas answers: something *x* can come to be where *x* was not before, if something else *y* that was there *gets converted* into *x*. For example, according to Aristotelian chemistry, fire can come to exist where it was not before, if the air there is converted into fire. But such generation of one element from another is an *Aristotelian substantial change*, in which prime matter is first informed by the substantial form of air and then by the substantial form of fire. The term-from-which and the term-to-which share *a common subject*; the term-to-which (=the fire) exists roughly where the term-from-which (=the air) existed before, because their common matter continues to exist roughly where it was before (I say "roughly" to allow for any rarefaction; Aristotelian air is denser than Aristotelian fire). Moreover, generation is a change in which the term-to-which (= the fire) comes to be *simpliciter*; it was not *there* before because it did not *exist* before.

Such *Aristotelian generation* cannot explain the post-consecration presence of the Body of Christ on the altar, because the Body of Christ has existed ever since it was formed in Mary's womb. The Body of Christ does not get there by coming into being for the first time. Nor does it get there by some metaphysical constituent of something on the altar (for example, the matter of the bread) becoming a metaphysical constituent of the Body of Christ instead. If the Body of Christ is to get there by conversion, it will have to be by some form of conversion in which nothing of what was converted (the term-from-which) persists in that into which it is converted (the term-to-which). Aristotelian physics recognizes no changes that meet that condition.

The Christian doctrine of creation has already required Christian theology to move beyond Aristotelian physics and metaphysics in conceptualizing Divine power. God's absolute power is over the whole being (*esse*) of created things. Divine power is power not merely to transform pre-existent matter by making it to be informed by first one substantial or accidental form and then another. Divine omnipotence includes power to create *ex nihilo* and to

[3] Aquinas, IV *Sent.* d. 11, q. 1, a. 1, qc.1 c [15304]; *Summa Theologica* III, q. 75, a. 2 c.

annihilate (to reduce to nothing without remainder). Bread is the item on the altar ripe for conversion: not the bread accidents, because experience shows [T1] that they remain; but *the substance* of the bread. Annihilation would be one way of converting the bread while making sure that none of its metaphysical constituents was preserved in the term-to-which of the change, because the term-to-which of annihilation is *purum nihil*! But, if annihilation would be a thoroughgoing way of getting the substance of the bread off the altar, it would be of no help in the positive project of getting the Body of Christ onto the altar, where it was not before.[4]

Aquinas's bold solution was to sponsor a further metaphysical innovation.[5] Created efficient causal power presupposes a mobile to move, a subject to transform. But Divine power is power over the whole being (*esse*) of created things. Aquinas suggests that Divine omnipotence includes not only power to create and to annihilate, but *power to convert the whole of one thing into the whole of another*. Relevant in the eucharist is power to *transubstantiate*: to convert the whole substance of the bread into the whole substance of the Body of Christ.[6] Of course, there is a sense in which Aristotelian substantial change converts one whole being into another, insofar as composite substances are one *per se*: the term-from-which (for example, the air) is one substance *per se* and the term-to-which (for example, the fire) is a distinct

[4] Aquinas, IV *Sent.* d. 11, q. 1, a. 2 c [15372]; *Summa Theologica* III, q.75, aa. 2–3 c.

[5] Not that Aquinas invented the term 'transubstantiation' or its use to signify turning one substance into another. *The notion* that the eucharistic bread and wine are substantially (*substantialiter*) changed into the Body and Blood of Christ appears already in the formula Berengar of Tours was made to swear in 1079. See H. E. J. Cowdrey, "The Papacy and the Berengarian Controversy," in Peter Ganz, R. B. C. Huygens, and Friedrich Niewöhner (eds.), *Auctoritas und Ratio: Studien zu Berengar von Tours* (Wiesbaden: Otto Harrassowitz, 1990), pp. 111–38. Joseph Goering, in his article "The Invention of Transubstantiation," *Traditio*, 46 (1991), pp. 147–70, traces the invention of *the term with this meaning* to Robert Pullen in the 1140s. *The term* was brought to prominence by Innocent III in the decrees issuing from the Fourth Lateran Council in 1215, but Gary Macy warns that this did not represent—as some scholars have suggested—*the dogmatizing* of the theory Aquinas later developed, because other theories continued to be tolerated and even presented as orthodox after 1215. Macy maintains that the point of Fourth Lateran language was not to rule out coexistence (or consubstantiation) and annihilation (the theory that the bread- and wine substances are annihilated at the consecration), but to insist on real presence in the face of the Cathar dualists who rejected material cult. See Macy, *The Theologies of the Eucharist in the Early Scholastic Period*, II. 58–9, 68–9; V. 137, 140–1. See also John C. Moore, *Pope Innocent III (1160/61–1216): To Root up and to Plant* (Leiden and Boston: Brill, 2003), ch. 9, pp. 239–40. What Aquinas does do is work out a philosophical formulation of transubstantiation in considerable detail, and I will refer to his philosophical analysis of it as "Thomistic" transubstantiation. David Burr, in his *Eucharistic Presence and Conversion in Late Thirteenth-Century Franciscan Thought* (Philadelphia: American Philosophical Society, 1984), claims that Bonaventure holds essentially the same theory as Aquinas develops (II. 8–15).

[6] Aquinas, *Summa Theologica* III, q. 75, a. 4 c & ad 1um & ad 2um.

substance *per se*. But, once again, Aristotelian substantial change involves a common subject that persists through the change, while the whole-being conversion that goes on in the eucharist is absolute and thoroughgoing: the *whole* substance of bread is converted into the *whole* Body of Christ, in such a way that the metaphysical constituents of the bread substance are converted into the metaphysical constituents of Christ's Body: the matter of the bread into the matter of Christ's Body; the substantial form of the bread into the substantial form of Christ's Body.[7] That means that neither the matter nor the substantial form of the bread remains after the consecration, either to lurk under [T1] the remaining species or to be metaphysical constituents of anything else. If the matter remained, that would mean that it had not been converted into the matter of Christ's Body, with the result that the matter of Christ's Body would not be there; if the substantial form remained, that would mean that it had not been converted into the substantial form of Christ's Body with the result that the substantial form of Christ's Body would not be there.[8] Thus, (what we might label) "absolute whole being conversion" in general, and transubstantiation in particular, are changes in which both terms (the term-from-which and the term-to-which) are positive beings, but neither term includes a metaphysical constituent that was or will be a metaphysical constituent of the other term.

Aquinas is urging medieval Aristotelians to welcome a new kind of change into their metaphysical taxonomy. He, therefore, pauses to compare and contrast absolute whole being conversion with already recognized kinds of changes. Unlike Aristotelian substantial or accidental transformations, but like creation and annihilation, absolute whole-being conversion does not involve a persistent subject that exists first in the term-from-which and then in the term-to-which. Absolute whole-being conversion is like annihilation in that nothing of the term-from-which remains in the term-to-which, but unlike it in that absolute whole-being conversion has something positive as its term-to-which. Like Aristotelian substantial and accidental transformations, absolute whole-being conversion does involve potency actualization: not the potency of a subject to receive a different form, but the obediential potency that a creature has to be absolutely converted into a

[7] Aquinas, IV *Sent.* d. 11, q. 1, a. 3, qc. 1 c [15351].

[8] Aquinas, IV *Sent.* d. 11, q. 1, a. 1, qc. 3 c [15313]; d. 11, q. 1, a.2 c [15327]; q.1, a.3, qc.1 c [15351]; *Summa Theologica* III, q. 75, a.3 c & ad 1um; q.75, a.5 c; q. 75, a. 6 c.

different whole-being by its Creator.[9] Insofar as it starts with a positive being whose obediential potency gets actualized, absolute whole-being conversion thus differs from creation *ex nihilo*, so that creation *ex nihilo* involves the greater exercise of Divine power.[10] Finally, absolute whole-being conversion is like Aristotelian substantial and accidental changes in involving change in the term-from-which, but unlike them in requiring no change in the term-to-which at all.[11]

Weeding the language for appropriate formulations, Aquinas offers two general rules:

[R1] change-expressing statements that merely imply an *order* of term to term should be conceded,

while

[R2] change-expressing statements that imply an *identity* of subject in the term-from-which and the term-to-which should not be granted properly speaking, but at most taken improperly and in an extended sense.

Aquinas thinks that statements of the form '*x* becomes *y*' or '*x* can be *y*' imply a common subject and—by [R2]—should be rejected; while statements of the form '*x* is converted into *y*' or 'from *x*, *y* comes to be' imply only an order of terms and so—by [R1]—should be accepted.[12]

Thus far, Aquinas has been laboring to identify a kind of change other than locomotion and Aristotelian substantial and accidental transformations that might get the [T3] ascended and forevermore [T4] impassible Body of Christ onto the altar. Transubstantiation also shares with annihilation the virtue of getting the bread substance off the altar. Aquinas thinks this is important if eucharistic veneration is not to turn into the idolatry of bread worship, and if Christ's own saying, "Hoc est corpus meum," is to be grammatically correct and true. If the bread were still present, Christ would not have said "*this* is My Body," because the bread is not His Body, but "*here* [*hic*] is My Body."[13] Further philosophical problems and puzzles require more explanations, which Aquinas thinks the theory of

[9] Aquinas, *Summa Theologica* III, q. 75, a. 4 c & ad 3um; q. 75, a. 8 c.
[10] Aquinas, IV *Sent.* d. 11, q. 1, a. 3, qc.3 ad 3um [15364].
[11] Aquinas, IV *Sent.* d. 10, q. 1, a. 1 ad 4um [15167]; d. 11, q. 1, a. 3, qc.1 c [15351].
[12] Aquinas, IV *Sent.* d. 11, q. 1, a. 4, qc. 4 c [15387].
[13] Aquinas, IV *Sent.* d. 11, q. 1, a. 1, qc. 1 c [15304]; *Summa Theologica* III, q. 75, a. 2 c.

transubstantiation (or, more generally, absolute whole-being conversion) can be developed to provide.

How is it "where"? It is evident to the senses that [T1] the bread accidents remain. Christ-with-us real presence means [T2] the Body of Christ is *under* them or *in* them or *contained by* them. These are location expressions. But, if they are taken literally, do not [T1] and [T2] run afoul of the philosophical doctrines that [T5] two bodies cannot be extended in the same place or [T6] one body extended in multiple places at the same time?

Decisive Distinction. Aquinas responds with a distinction between what is there (under/in/contained by the species) by the power of the sacrament (*ex vi sacramenti*) and what is there by natural concomitance (*ex naturali concomitantia*).[14] Briefly, only the direct term of the conversion is there by the power of the sacrament; there by natural concomitance or "quasi *per accidens*" is whatever is really united to the direct term of the conversion[15] and/or whatever the direct term of the conversion could not exist without.[16] Once again, new-law sacraments effect what they figure. In his *Sentence* commentary, Aquinas explains that what is there by the power of the sacrament meets two requirements: [i] as what is "figured," it bears a likeness to the term-from-which that is converted into it; and [ii] it is what is signified by the form of the sacrament. 'Hoc est corpus meum' signifies the Body of Christ. The Body of Christ does not bear any accidental likeness to the substance of the bread; it is like it only in being corporeal substance. Thus, it is only the corporeal *substance* of the Body of Christ that is there by the power of the sacrament. By contrast, Christ's Divinity (to which His Body is hypostatically united), His soul (which is the form of His Body while it is alive), and His accidents (which really inhere in His substance) are there by natural concomitance and quasi *per accidens*: that is, apart from Divinity which is of Itself everywhere, they are there by virtue of their real union with the Body of Christ, which is there by the power of the sacrament. Apart from Divinity which is everywhere of Itself, if they were not really united in these ways to Christ's Body—as His soul was not between His death and resurrection—they would not be under the species at all.[17]

14 Aquinas, IV *Sent.* d. 10, q. 1, a. 2, qc.1 c [15194]; *Summa Theologica* III, q. 76, a. 1 c.
15 Aquinas, *Summa Theologica* III, q. 76, a. 1 c.
16 Aquinas, IV *Sent.* d. 10, q. 1, a. 2, qc. 1 c [15194].
17 Aquinas, IV *Sent.* d. 10, q. 2, a. 3 ad 2um [15202]; *Summa Theologica* III, q. 76, a. 1 ad 1um.

There by the Power of the Sacrament. Aquinas wields this distinction to slice through both "multiple location" puzzles—about [T5] multiple bodies extended in the same place and [T6] a single body extended in multiple places at once—and "size" problems—about how the Body of Christ could fit under such a small and differently configured space. Interpreting [T7], Aquinas explains that the substance of a body is ordered to place by means of its own inherent quantitative dimensions: it is located in the place by the commensuration of *its own* quantitative dimensions with the dimensions of the place. Before the consecration, the bread substance was literally located on the altar because the bread quantity was commensurate with the dimensions of a place on the altar. When the bread substance is converted, the bread quantity remains commensurate with the dimensions of that place, with the result that the bread accidents remain literally located there as before. Likewise, according to [T3], the quantitative dimensions inhering in Christ's Body are commensurate with a heavenly place, so that Christ's Body is literally located there. What [T5] rules out is the dimensive quantities of two bodies being commensurate with the dimensions of the same place at the same time. What [T6] excludes is the dimensive quantity of a single body's being commensurate with the dimensions of multiple places at the same time. What [T7] rules out is a body's being ordered to a place by its own dimensions, when those dimensions are not commensurate with that place.

Aquinas insists that transubstantiation violates none of [T5]–[T7], because Christ's Body is not related either to the species or to the place where the species are by its own quantitative dimensions. The reason is that the quantitative dimensions of Christ's Body are not present on the altar by the power of the sacrament. Not only is Christ's own dimensive quantity not signified by the form of the sacrament—"Hoc est corpus meum!" Absolute whole-being conversion would get Christ's own accidents on the altar only if the bread accidents were converted into them. Because [T1] the *bread quantity* is still on the altar, it cannot have been converted into the dimensive quantity of Christ's Body. Christ's Body is not related to the species by means of its own dimensive quantity. Rather, the substance of the Body of Christ is ordered to the bread species *per se* and immediately, and so is related to them in the mode of substance. Aquinas explains, normally, where material substances are concerned, the whole nature of the substance is under each part of the dimensions under which it is contained. If human nature is defined as rational animal, we should not imagine that the genus animal is only under trunk and limbs while the differentia rational is only in the head; rather, the whole nature—rational animal—is found under the whole and the whole is found under each part. Likewise, under each part of air there is the whole nature of the air; under each part of bread, the whole nature of the bread. So also in the eucharist, the whole substance of Christ's Body is contained in the sacrament after the consecration, whole in the whole and whole in each part.[18]

Aquinas draws the further conclusion that Christ's Body is not literally in place on the altar, because it is not related to that place through any commensuration of *its own* quantitative dimensions with that place. Because Christ's Body is not the subject of the bread accidents the way the bread substance was, the substance of the Body of Christ is related to the place on the altar only through alien quantitative dimensions. Thus, the substance of the Body of Christ is in place on the altar only *per accidens*, by being present in the mode of substance to alien quantitative dimensions that are in place *per se*.[19]

Aquinas drives this point home by charting further consequences. Medieval Aristotelians had already identified different ways of being in place. For a body is *circumscriptively in a place* when its figure is circumscribed by the figure of the place. But—on Aristotle's categorial scheme—figure is a quality that pertains to quantity. If the dimensive quantity of the Body of Christ is not there by the power of the sacrament, its figure is not there in such a way as to be circumscribable. Aquinas concludes that the Body of Christ is not circumscriptively in the place where the bread species are, nor is it circumscribed by them. The fact that the Body of Christ is not said to be under the air that surrounds the bread accidents on the altar, is not a function of its being located in one place (where the bread accidents are) and not the other (where the air is), but only of the bread substance's having been converted into it while the air substance was not.[20]

Again, for something to be *definitively in a place* is for it to be in the place and for the place to be somehow commensurate with its quantity or power. Thus, a 2-cubit body is not definitively in a 1-cubit place, although it might be there somehow. Nor is the soul definitively in the hand, because the

[18] Aquinas, IV *Sent.* d. 10, q. 1, a. 2, qc. 3 c [15200] & ad 2um [15202] & ad 4um [15204]; qc. 4 c [15206]; *Summa Theologica* III, q. 76, a. 1 ad 3um; a.3 c.

[19] Aquinas, IV *Sent.* d. 10, q. 1, a. 2, qc. 3 ad 4um [15204]; *Summa Theologica* III, q. 76, a. 5 c.

[20] Aquinas, IV *Sent.* d. 10, q. 1, a. 3, qc. 1 c [15231] & ad 3um [15234]; *Summa Theologica* III, q. 76, a. 5 ad 1um.

hand does not define the scope of its power, which is exercised in other body parts as well. But an angel may be said to be definitively in a place, because its power is operative there and cannot be operative in other places at the same time.[21] Thus, the Body of Christ fails both tests for being definitively in place under the bread species: for it can be under bread species on many altars simultaneously; and it is not under them *as in place* on any altar at all![22] The size problem does not arise and no violation of [T7] is involved.

Once again, the Body of Christ is not under the accidents *repletively*, in such a way as to fill place, because bodies fill a place by virtue of the commensuration of their own quantitative dimensions with the dimensions of the place. But the quantitative dimensions of Christ's Body are not there by the power of the sacrament.[23]

When—in the eucharistic rite—the priest takes the consecrated hosts off the altar to distribute them to communicants, would not the Body of Christ under the species have to move with them if the eucharist is to fulfil its purpose of joining said communicants to Christ their friend and Head? Aquinas now predictably explains: because locomotion is change of place, locomotion requires the moved object to be in place. For something to move *per se*, it must be in place *per se*. *Per accidens* locomotion is of two sorts: one kind when the moved object is in place *per se* but moves *per accidens* (for example, the cargo in the ship moves *per accidens* when the ship moves *per se*); another when the object is not in place *per se* but is under/in/contained by something that is in place *per se*. Thus, the Body of Christ does not move *per se* because it is not under the host as in place *per se*. Nor does it move *per accidens* the first way, as the ship's cargo does. Rather it moves *per accidens* the second way by being under, in the mode of substance, the bread species, which are moved *per se*. Communicants encounter the Body of Christ, not as quantified, but in the mode of substance.[24]

Likewise clear is why the Body of Christ under the bread accidents is not itself visible or otherwise sense perceptible. Every bodily action requires contact, and bodily contact requires bodies to be present to one another and to place through their own dimensive quantities. Since the Body of Christ is

[21] Aquinas, *Summa Theologica* I, q. 52, a. 2 c; I, q. 53, a. 1 c.
[22] Aquinas, IV *Sent.* d. 10, q. 1, a. 3, qc. 2 c [15236]; *Summa Theologica* III, q. 76, a. 5 ad 1um.
[23] Aquinas, *Summa Theologica* III, q. 76, a. 5 arg 2 & ad 1um.
[24] Aquinas, IV *Sent.* d. 10, q. 1, a. 3, qc. 4 c [15244]; *Summa Theologica* III, q. 76, a. 6 c.

not present to the species or to places where the species are through its own dimensive quantity, its accidents are not able to act on the medium in the ways required for sense perception.[25] By the same token, the Body of Christ is not present under the species in such a way as to be causally affected by others: being present, not through its own dimensive quantity, but only in the mode of substance, the Body of Christ is not there in such a way that it can be broken by the hands of priests and torn by the teeth of the faithful—contrary to what Berengar of Tours was made to swear (see Chapter 11 below).[26]

Natural Concomitance? Aquinas's contention—that it is only the substance of Christ's Body that is there by the power of the sacrament, and that the substance of Christ's Body is there under the bread species only in the mode of substance—makes it sound as if the Body of Christ in heaven could be stripped down, denuded of everything but bodily substance—of Divinity, of soul, of the quantitative dimensions that would relate it to place, and of the accidents that would affect the senses. It is doubtful whether such a state of affairs would be metaphysically possible, given Aquinas's understanding that quantitative dimensions play a role in individuation and his (at least later) insistence on the unity of substantial forms, which makes the intellectual soul the one and only one substantial form of Christ's humanity.[27]

Even if such a strip-down were metaphysically possible, Aquinas denies that it is the case. The Divine Word never lays aside Christ's humanity. From the resurrection forward, Christ's soul is for ever more joined to His Body, and He exists extended, situated, quantified, and qualified in heaven. What priests do at earthly altars in no way affects the real union of Christ's humanity to His Divinity, of His soul to His Body, of His accidents to His substance. Even if they are not signified by the form of the sacrament, even if they are not there by the power of the sacrament, Christ's Divinity, His soul, and His accidents are there by real and natural concomitance, because of their (different sorts of) real union with the Body of Christ.

If so, if Divinity, soul, and accidents really are there, what do labels—'by the power of the sacrament', 'by natural concomitance'—matter? Christ's

[25] Aquinas, IV *Sent.* d. 10, q. 1, a. 4, qc. 1 c [15267]; *Summa Theologica* III, q. 76, a. 7 c & ad 1um.

[26] Aquinas, IV *Sent.* d. 10, q. 1, a. 1 ad 1um [15164].

[27] Aquinas, *Summa Theologica* I, q. 76, a. 4 c.

dimensive quantity will be there, Christ's human bodily shape and larger-than-host size will be there, Christ's color will be there after all. Will not the difficulties that Aquinas just tried to explain away rearise?

Aquinas insists, on the contrary, that the natural concomitance of Christ's bodily accidents solves more problems than it causes. One might think that the substance-mode presence of Christ's body under the species—whole in the whole and whole in each part—would rob Christ's Body of its organic structure, which requires parts to be at a distance from one another and attached to one another in a distinctive order (for example, head immediately to neck and not to foot). The natural concomitance of Christ's bodily accidents preserves the order of His bodily parts to one another and so keeps Christ's Body under the sacrament from being an unstructured heap.[28]

What, then, prevents problems about [T5] multiple bodies extended in one place from rearising? For Aquinas, everything turns on the priorities of *what orders what* to the bread species and their place. Metaphysically, Christ's Body is a layered hylomorphic composite, whose constituents are united by real unions. These guarantee that Christ's Body is organic wherever it goes. If the substance kernal were indirectly related by means of its own dimensive quantity to the place where the bread accidents are, then violations of [T5] and [T6] would arise. Moreover,à la [T7], the commensuration of its own dimensive quantity with the dimensions of that place on the altar would be impossible to achieve, because Christ's human body is differently shaped and larger than the bread was. Aquinas hopes to avoid all multiple location and size difficulties by inverting the ordering: the substance kernel is immediately ordered to the bread accidents in the mode of substance; the substance kernel is mediately ordered to the place on the altar by the bread species. Christ's bodily accidents, including His own quantitative dimensions and figure, are mediately ordered to the bread species by means of the substance kernel, which is mediately ordered to the place by means of the bread species. Once again, Christ's bodily accidents are there on the altar only in the sense of being really united to what is under the bread species in the mode of substance. There is no direct ordering of Christ's head to one part of the host/place and Christ's foot to another. So the misfitting shapes and sizes do not matter.

[28] Aquinas, IV *Sent.* d. 10, q. 1, a. 2, qc. 4 ad 3 [15208].

III. Giles of Rome: Explaining the Change, Putting the Mind to Rest

For Giles of Rome, the theology of the eucharist posed more difficulties than all of the other sacraments together. Writing his lengthy treatise *Theoremata de Corpore Christi* (38 incunabula folios in the Rome 1554 edition) from the posture of faith seeking understanding, Giles does not shoulder the foolhardy burden of proving the truth of a doctrine containing so much that is "beyond reason," but adopts the more limited goal of explaining apparent impossibilities away. His confidence of success rests on the intriguing if dubious inference that, since eucharistic doctrine is true (as authority assures us), and the limitations of human reason are universal, infecting those who would attack as much as those who defend it, human reason should be able to rebut purported refutations.[29] At the same time, his sense that full comprehension of the eucharist is impossible serves to loosen the boundaries of his metaphysical picture and allows him to entertain as "perhaps" possible ontological options that his predecessors would have dismissed.

Giles takes much from Aquinas: (i) the real distinction between essence and existence (*esse*) in creatures; (ii) unitarianism with regard to substantial forms; (iii) the endorsement of transubstantiation as the change that brings the Body of Christ to the altar(s); (iv) the distinction between "sacramental presence" and presence "by natural concomitance." Nevertheless, Giles draws on his extensive speculations in both metaphysics and physics, in an attempt to shed more light both on the nature of the change and on the manner of real presence.

The "How" of Transubstantiation. Aquinas explains the real presence of Christ's Body on the altar in terms of a whole-being substance-to-substance conversion, in which the whole bread substance is converted into the whole Body of Christ, form-to-form and matter-to-matter. Thomistic transubstantiation is difficult to understand because it differs from the substance-to-substance conversion of Aristotelian physics in two important ways. [i] Aristotelian efficient causal agents produce generation and corruption by *doing something to the matter* of the term-from-which. At first, the matter of

[29] Giles of Rome, *Theoremata de Corpore Christi* (Rome 1554), fo. 1ra.

the term-from-which is actualized by the substantial form of the term-from-which (for example, the substantial form of air) but is in potency with respect to any other substantial form that it could naturally acquire (for example, the substantial form of fire). The Aristotelian agent causes a new substantial form (for example, the substantial form of fire) to exist in the matter, a substantial form incompatible with the substantial form of the term-from-which (for example, the substantial form of air), so that the substantial form of the term-from-which (for example, the air) is driven out. On Giles's understanding, matter somehow includes or contains all of the substantial forms with respect to which it is in potency. The Aristotelian agent *educes* the form of the term-to-which from the matter of the term-from-which, and thereby *reduces* the form of the term-from-which to the potency of the matter of the term-to-which. Thus, Aristotelian physics can make generation and corruption intelligible because there is a common constituent that informed by the substantial form of air is the term-from-which but informed by the substantial form of fire is the term-to-which, where what the agent causes is its change of forms. But Thomistic transubstantiation deliberately rules out any such common constituent. How, then, does Divine power convert one term into the other? (Call this *the "No-Common-Constituent Problem."*) [ii] Moreover, the product of Aristotelian generation thereby comes into existence for the first time. But the Body of Christ came into existence long before mass was ever said and will continue to exist forever. (Call this *the "New-Existence Problem."*)[30]

Giles's bold contention is that transubstantiation does involve God's doing something to matter. The No-Common-Constituent and New-Existence problems can be explained away in terms of differences between Divine and created causal power. Aristotelian natural agents act to produce only what did not exist before and what does not exist already for two reasons. First, natural agents produce only through motion or transformation. Numerically the same motion or transformation cannot have a temporally interrupted existence. But numerically the same product cannot be naturally produced by numerically distinct motions or transformations. Thus, if a product came into being before and then ceased to exist, no natural agent can make that product exist again.[31] Second, natural agents can act on matter only insofar as it is quantified, and hence insofar as its parts

[30] Giles of Rome, *Theoremata*, Propositio I, fo. 1rab.
[31] Giles, *Theoremata*, Propositio I, fo. 1va.

are distinguished from one another by being located in distinct places. And it is metaphysically impossible for numerically the same form to inhere in numerically distinct hunks of matter at one and the same time. It follows that no natural agent will be able to produce a particular form F_1 in a hunk of matter M_2, if F_1 already exists in a hunk of matter M_1 at the same time.[32]

Suppose an Aristotelian agent acts on air to change it into fire. Natural agents could turn that fire back into air again, but not numerically the same air, because the change-producing motion or transformation would not be numerically the same as the first time. Again, having introduced the substantial form of air into *this* matter, those same natural agents might also simultaneously introduce the substantial form of air into *that* matter. But the substantial form of air in the former hunk would be numerically distinct from the substantial form of air in the latter hunk, because the hunks of matter in different places are numerically distinct.

Nevertheless, Giles declares that there is no impossibility in a created substance itself having temporally interrupted existence; the impossibility is with numerically the same interrupted process, not numerically the same interrupted product. *God can make numerically the same thing to return again, because Divine power does not have to act by motion or transformation.*[33] Thus, when fire was produced from air, the substantial form of fire was educed from the potency of the matter and the substantial form of air was reduced to the potency of that matter. But—starting with the fire—God could educe *numerically the same* substantial form of air from the potency of the matter, and so turn the fire back into *numerically the same air* as was there before.[34] This is one way God can convert one substance into another without the product's thereby existing for the first time.

Moreover, God can convert one substance into another that already pre-exists, because God is not restricted to acting on matter only insofar as it is quantified. Giles's daring thought is that *Divine power can reach beneath the quantification and the individuation to act directly on matter insofar as it is a quiddity*. Matter as a quiddity is indivisible, without parts, so that there is no "this" that differs from "that." In the spirit of Aquinas, Giles maintains that *what individuates matter is form*. Suppose a natural agent turns air in Rome into fire in Rome. God could convert air in London into numerically the

[32] Giles, *Theoremata*, Propositio I, fo. 1va; Propositio II, fo. 2ra.
[33] Giles, *Theoremata*, Propositio I, fo. 1va.
[34] Giles, *Theoremata*, Propositio I, fo. 1va.

same fire, the very one that exists in Rome. This is because Divine power reaches into the air, not only to its quantified matter, but beneath its quantity to act on the matter as a quiddity. By introducing numerically the same form of fire into the matter as quiddity as now exists in the matter in Rome, God can make numerically the same fire exist in London (where the London air was) as in Rome. Thus, God can convert one whole substance into another whole substance—form to form, matter to matter—by acting on matter as quiddity in a special way![35] Could not God do this with the eucharistic bread on altars where mass is being said?[36]

The No-Common-Constituent Problem is solved, because matter as quiddity is a metaphysical constituent of any and every material substance. But this does not turn transubstantiation into generation and corruption, because it is matter as quiddity and not matter as quantified that is common to the terms. The New-Existence Problem is solved because Divine power can act in the above ways to (re-)produce both what once existed and ceased to be, and what still exists elsewhere. Yet, as Aquinas warned, this sort of substance-to-substance conversion does not make the term-to-which to exist extended in many places at once, because it is the substance alone—and not the quantity or accidents—that is the term of the conversion.[37]

The Term-to-Which of Transubstantiation. Even if there were no problems about the manner of change in Thomistic transubstantiation, puzzles would arise about its term. Aquinas asserts repeatedly: the term-to-which of transubstantiation is the substance of Christ's Body; Christ's soul, His Divinity, His accidents are not included in the term-to-which, and so are there not by the power of the sacrament but by natural concomitance. Yet, in many of his works, Aquinas contends that there can be only one substantial form per individual substance thing (and so is a "unitarian" about substantial forms; see Chapter 1 above), and that in the case of human beings the substantial form is the intellectual soul. It seems to follow that the substantial form of Christ's Body is on the altar only by natural concomitance, and that the term-to-which of transubstantiation is its matter alone. But Aquinas thinks that prime matter is pure potentiality—as Giles says—a mean between being and nothing.[38] How then can matter without

35 Giles, *Theoremata*, Propositiones I–II, fos. 1va–2ra; see also Propositiones XXXI, fo. 19raBC.
36 The apparently obvious answer is "yes," but see the next section for more Aegidian surprises!
37 Giles, *Theoremata*, Propositio II, fo. 2rb.
38 Giles, *Theoremata*, Propositio XXIX, fo. 18vbC.

forms be the term-to-which of transubstantiation, and how could it be legitimate to identify it with the Body of Christ?

Giles responds with a series of distinctions. Since doctrinal formulae are set by ecclesiastical pronouncements, Giles is worried about what we can *say* as well as what we could mean. First, he reminds that the term 'body' can be taken three ways. [i] 'Body' can signify the three dimensions themselves (just as 'surface' signifies two and 'line' signifies one) and so is taken for quantity and is in the category of quantity and not in the category of substance, either *per se* or by reduction. [ii] 'Body' can be taken for the composite of matter and the form of corporeity, in which case it is in the genus of substance directly and is the genus of any animal. 'Body' thus taken for corporeal substance is predicated of its species as a whole and not as a part. [iii] 'Body' can signify matter alone, matter qua organized and under the form of soul.[39] When theological consensus says that the term-to-which of transubstantiation is the Body of Christ, 'Body' is not taken [i] the first way for quantity, because the quantity of Christ's Body is emphatically not the term-to-which or even part of the term-to-which of transubstantiation. Nor is it taken [ii] the second way for the genus of any animal. Rather in this context body is contrasted with soul as distinct and complementary animal parts. Giles wants to defend [iii] the third sense, and so needs to explain how it would be reasonable to take organized matter as the term of transubstantiation and still identify it with the Body of Christ.[40]

To this end, Giles forwards a second distinction, between things (*res*) and modes. Aristotle's categories classify things (*res*). Generally speaking, with the possible exception of Aristotelian actions and passions, which—some argue—are the same thing (*res*), Giles holds that

[P7] no thing (*res*) that through its nature is in a category can be in a category really different from it,

but

[P8] a thing in one category can have the mode of another category, because it is joined to another or related to another that pertains to that other category.[41]

[39] Giles, *Theoremata*, Propositio XXVI, fo. 16rab–va.
[40] Giles, *Theoremata*, Propositio XXVI, fo. 16va.
[41] Giles, *Theoremata*, Propositio XXVII, fo. 16vb.

Having (what we may call) an "alien" mode depends on conjunction or union or relations with what has or confers that mode by nature. Giles lists some examples:

[a] The *Liber de Causis* makes it an axiom that what is received is received after the mode of the receiver. Therefore, form receives the mode of that into which it is received.

[b] Knowledge insofar as it is a thing (*secundum rem*) is a quality, but it has the mode of relation insofar as it is related to the knowable.[42]

[c] Eucharistic accidents lack a real union to substance and so have existence in the mode of substance by Divine power.

[d] Hypostatic union makes Christ's human nature to have the mode of an accident.[43]

Giles reasons by analogy: just as [b] what is quality insofar as it is a thing (*secundum rem*) can have a relative mode, so what is substance insofar as it is a thing (*secundum rem*) can have a quantified or qualified mode.[44] Thus, extension *per se* and primarily pertains to quantity, and what is extended is extended only by means of quantity. Nevertheless, the parts of quantity are distinct from the parts of what is extended by quantity. For example, whiteness is extended through the surface, and according to this extension whiteness is quantified as much as the surface is. But the essence of whiteness differs from the essence of the surface, and the parts of whiteness essentially differ from the parts of the surface.

Returning to the case at hand, Giles agrees with Aquinas that matter of itself is pure potentiality, a mean between being and nothing. Considered in itself, matter is indivisible, does not have parts, and is not body in any sense.[45] Matter is extended by the extension of quantity and is divided the way its quantity is divided, just as the whiteness is extended and divided by its surface. But, although matter has parts *through* quantity, and could not continue to have parts *without* the inherence of quantity, the parts of matter are essentially different from the parts of quantity—just as the parts of whiteness would be essentially different from the surface, even if the parts of whiteness could not exist without the parts of the surface.[46] The intellect

[42] Giles, *Theoremata*, Propositio XXVII, fo. 16vb.
[43] Giles, *Theoremata*, Propositio XXVII, fo. 17raD–rbA.
[44] Giles, *Theoremata*, Propositio XXVII, fo. 17rbB.
[45] Giles, *Theoremata*, Propositio XXIX, fo. 18vbC; Propositio XXXI, fo. 19raBC.
[46] Giles, *Theoremata*, Propositio XXXIII, fo. 21vbD.

can separate them. Therefore, 'parts of matter' signifies only the essence of matter and does not signify the essence of quantity. Nor does 'parts of matter' signify a compound essence of quantity and matter together, because quantity and matter form a *per accidens* unity and do not constitute a third essence any more than the whiteness and its surface do.[47] The mode does not add any nature over and above the nature of the thing or make it to exist in a different category. Yet, the mode makes a real difference. Whiteness would be really different if it existed in a non-extended mode.[48]

From this analysis, Giles wants to draw a pair of coordinate explanatory conclusions. First, the term-to-which of transubstantiation is only the matter of the Body of Christ, taken in its quantitative mode. The bread substance is converted into matter alone; the quantity and the substantial form (the intellectual soul) of Christ's Body are *not* part of the term-to-which of the conversion. Second, and equally important, Christ's quantity and substantial form *are* on the altar by natural concomitance. Their real union with the matter is what keeps the matter from being pure potentiality and what keeps it divided into parts.[49] Moreover, the real union of the substantial form is—for Giles—what explains how the matter on the altar is numerically the same as the matter of Christ's Body in heaven (see the preceding section).

Because matter in the quantitative mode has parts and can be said to be organized as required for the inherence of the animating substantial form,[50] it qualifies as a whole of parts and as really composite and as a body in the third sense.[51] Thus, transubstantiation can still be described as the conversion of one whole composite into another whole composite, even if it is into the matter alone.

Relative to Aristotle, Thomistic transubstantiation is a piece of conceptual innovation in the first place. Giles argues that those who were willing to entertain whole being substance-to-substance conversions of matter to matter and form to form ought to find it easier to concede the conversion of the whole bread substance into the matter alone. (i) For starters, the conversion of bread form into the intellectual soul jars with hierarchical

47 Giles, *Theoremata*, Propositio XXVIII, fo. 17vbAB.

48 Giles, *Theoremata*, Propositio XXIX, fo. 18raD–rbAB.

49 Giles, *Theoremata*, Propositio XXVIII, fo. 17vbC; Propositio XXXIII, fo. 21vaD–vbA; Propositio XXXIV, fos. 22vbD–23raA.

50 Giles, *Theoremata*, Propositio XXVIII, fo. 17vbBC.

51 Giles, *Theoremata*, Propositio XXIX, fo. 18vbC.

considerations: nothing corporeal can be converted into something spiritual, Giles declares![52] (ii) More generally, conversions are easier to conceive of between the less opposed than between the more opposed. But the substantial forms of substance-to-substance conversions are incompatible with one another, while the substantial forms that matter does not actually have but can acquire already exist in the potency of the matter.[53] (iii) Again, the term-from-which is passive in the conversion. But—Giles contends—in composite substances, the matter is the locus of the passive power. Therefore, there is no more passive power in the composite of matter and substantial form than there is in the matter alone. It should be at least as easy to convert the bread substance into the matter alone as into the composite of matter and substantial form.[54]

Giles tries to talk us into his idea by taking us through a series of cases. *Case 1*. God can convert this air into this fire by educing numerically the same form that is in this fire from the matter of the air. Because matter differs through forms, if the matter that is in the air is informed by numerically the same form as is in this fire, the matter of the air is converted into the matter of the fire. *Case 2*. God can convert the whole substance of the bread into the matter alone, because God can reduce the substantial form of bread to the potency of the bread matter, and then convert the bread matter into the matter of the Body of Christ by acting on the matter as quiddity to make Christ's substantial form inhere in it. *Case 3*. Because the substantial form of bread does not contribute to the bread's passive potency for conversion, God does not have first to reduce the substantial form of bread to the potency of the bread matter. God can convert the whole bread immediately into the matter alone of Christ's Body.[55]

Giles is led to his startling proposal by his desire to salvage Thomistic transubstantiation, given Aquinas's doctrine of the unity of substantial forms. Giles does not imagine that his defense of it is conclusive. Nevertheless, he thinks that he has responded to the most powerful objections to it he can think of. In any event, Giles does not find the pluralist doctrine—that there are many substantial forms within a single substance thing—to be an intelligible idea.[56]

52 Giles, *Theoremata*, Propositio XXXII, fo. 20vaD–vbAB.
53 Giles, *Theoremata*, Propositio XXXII, fo. 21raAB.
54 Giles, *Theoremata*, Propositio XXXII, fo. 21rbABCD.
55 Giles, *Theoremata*, Propositio XXXIII, fo. 22raBC.
56 Giles, *Theoremata*, Propositio XXXIV, fo. 23raBCD–rbA.

The "How" of Real Presence. Real presence (in heaven and on each of many altars where mass is simultaneously said) gives rise to "multiple location problems," because standard philosophy of body lays it down that [T5] two bodies cannot be in the same place and [T6] one body cannot be in multiple places at once. The explanation of [T5] is that the dimensions of one body are essentially incompatible with those of another, and of [T6] that places circumscribe and define any body extended in it. Aquinas's reply is that [T5] and [T6] do not apply, because whole-being substance-to-substance conversion puts the Body of Christ on altars in a special way, otherwise than by means of its own dimensions. Giles calls this *per accidens* location, and imagines the objector posing an *Omni-Location Problem*: if the Body of Christ can have *per accidens* location on many altars at once, why could not God make it have *per accidens* location everywhere in the universe?[57]

Giles begins his clarification by expounding some familiar distinctions:

[D1] A body B is *definitively* in place P, if and only if the quantity of B is commensurate with the quantity of P and the quantity of B is not commensurate with that of any place other than P.

[D2] A body B is *circumscriptively* in a place P, if and only if the quantity of B is compared with the quantity of P, whole to whole and part to part.

[D3] A body B is *determined* to a place P, if the magnitude through which it is said to be in P is finite and that magnitude is not its own substance.[58]

Significantly, Giles understands all three as ways of relating a body to place, not immediately, but through some magnitude—whether the body's own quantity or through some other finite magnitude non-identical with the corporeal substance. Giles notes that [D2] being circumscriptively in place implies [D1] being definitively in place, which implies [D3] being determined to a place. But the inferences do not hold the other way around.

Illustrating these distinctions from the ontological hierarchy, Giles concludes:

[1] God is omnipresent by God's own infinite substance and so is not determined to place and does not exist in place definitively or circumscriptively;

[2] the Body of Christ is determined to and exists definitively and circumscriptively in its heavenly place, but—because it is not related to altar

[57] Giles, *Theoremata*, Propositio III, fo. 2rb–va.

[58] Giles, *Theoremata* Propositiones III–V, fos. 2va–3vb.

places by its own dimensive quantity but by the bread dimensions—it is determined to the place(s) on the altar(s) but does not exist in them definitively or circumscriptively;

[3] created intellectual substances are determined to place by their functional quantity (that is, the magnitude of their power to function) and exist in place definitively; and

[4] normal bodies are determined to place by their own dimensive quantities and exist in those places definitively and circumscriptively.[59]

On [D1], a body is definitively in a place only if it is confined to it and so is not simultaneously elsewhere. Consequently, on [D1] and [D2], a body can be definitively and/or circumscriptively in only one place at a time. Nevertheless, Giles declares (in response to the Omni-Location Problem), there would be no problem in the Body of Christ's being at one and the same time *determined* to many places—indeed to every place in the universe—by alien dimensions.[60] Presumably this would happen if God converted every other body into the Body of Christ!

Turning to the problem of how—if the parts of the Body of Christ are whole under the whole bread dimensions, and whole under each part—the Body of Christ can avoid being a heap of flesh bits and remain an organic body on the altar, Giles replies with a further distinction between quantitative and categorial position:

[D4] the quantitative position of a body is the order of the body parts to one another and to the whole and of the whole to the parts;

[D5] categorial position is the order of the parts of body to place.[61]

Giles reckons that these orderings of parts to whole and whole to parts, and of body parts and whole to the parts and whole of place, are certain relations. There can be no whole or relation of whole to parts without the relation of parts to one another. Nor can there be certain kinds of part-to-part relations without there being a whole and relations to the whole. But—Giles contends—the whole-part and parts-to-parts relations of a body can exist without that body's being related by its own dimensive quantity to place.[62]

[59] Giles, *Theoremata*, Propositio III, fo. 3vab.

[60] Giles, *Theoremata*, Propositio III, fo. 2vb; Propositio V, fo. 3rb–va.

[61] Giles, *Theoremata*, Propositio VI, fo. 4rab; Propositio XII, fo. 7va. Burr, in *Eucharistic Presence and Conversion*, finds similar distinctions in Godfrey of Fontaines (IV. 30), John Pecham (V. 42), Richard Middleton (VI. 61), and William of Ware (VI.73).

[62] Giles, *Theoremata* Propositio VI, fo. 4rab; Propositio XII, fo. 7va.

To persuade us, Giles offers an analogy. Sometimes up and down, higher and lower relations among parts and whole within a body run in the same direction as they do relative to the wider universe (both relative to other parts of the body and relative to the universe, the human head is higher and the feet lower). Other times, they are reversed (the trees roots are its mouth and so are higher relative to the whole tree and other tree parts, but—relative to the universe—the roots are lower than the branches). If the quantitative position can run in the opposite direction to its categorial position, then why could not a body have quantitative position without any categorial position at all?[63] Giles proposes that this is what happens in the eucharist. The Body of Christ exists under the host *quantified*, with head immediately connected to neck and not to ankles, but it is not there *quantitatively* because it does not exist there by means of its own dimensive quantity. Its organized parts are related to one another and not to place.[64]

Returning to the philosophical dictum that [T5] two bodies cannot exist in the same place at once because dimensions resist dimensions, Giles counters that dimensions are not essentially incompatible with and do not resist one another in and of themselves. Rather the resistance arises because of *the relations of quantity to externals* (to other bodies or to place). Just as heat can make a body hot without actually being a principle of heating something else, so dimensions can make a body to be quantified without actually resisting other dimensions. There is resistance only if one quantified body is related to another quantified body *by means of quantity*. But, if a body is there *by means of substance and not through its quantity*, there is no resistance. Giles concludes that, where one body is present by means of substance, there can be two or infinitely many bodies present by means of substance; likewise, where there is one part present by means of substance, two or all the parts can be present the same way.[65]

Having made extravagant claims for multiple location by means of substance, Giles goes on in a later theorem to propose limits on multiple location after all. His analogue of [T5] is what Scotus refers to as a "famous" proposition held also by Richard Middleton and William of Ware[66] that

[63] Giles, *Theoremata*, Propositio XII, fo. 8ra. Burr, in *Eucharistic Presence and Conversion*, cites William of Ware as giving the example of a man turned upside down with his feet higher than his head in relation to place, but lower than his head in relation to his whole body (VI. 73).

[64] Giles, *Theoremata*, Propositio VI, fo. 4rab.

[65] Giles, *Theoremata*, Propositio VIII 8, fo. 5va.

[66] Scotus, *Lectura* II, d. 2, p. 2, qq. 3–4, n. 255; Vat XVIII. 177; *Op. Ox.* II, d. 2, p. 2, q. 4, n. 275, 282; Vat VII. 274–5, 278.

[T8] multiple things whose relations to place have the same kind of foundation (*ratio*) cannot thereby be in the same place at once.

Giles illustrates what does and does not count as a different kind of foundation with the following examples. [i] An angel and a body can be in the same place, because the angel is related to place by the magnitude of its functional power, while a body is related by its own quantitative dimensions. [ii] An angel and a soul can coexist with a body because they are differently related to the body in question: an angel at most as its mover, but the soul as its form. [iii] God can be and is in the same place as any and every creature, because God is there by the unique immensity of Divine substance.[67] [iv] But two souls cannot be in the same body; nor can two angels be in the same place. [v] Postponing his analytical treatment to some later work, Giles assumes that glorified bodies are related differently to place, so that a glorified body can exist in the same place as a non-glorified one (for example, Christ's resurrected body passing through closed doors). [vi] Nevertheless, two glorified bodies cannot be in the same place except by a special miracle,[68] with the consequence that [vii] Christ's Body in heaven cannot exist in the same place as another glorified body except by a special miracle, although it can coexist in the same place with a non-glorified body. By contrast, [viii] the Body of Christ under the host cannot exist in the same place as a non-glorified body because it is present to the place through the bread dimensions, which resist another non-glorified body, but it can be in the same place with a glorified body because the host dimensions are compatible with it.[69]

Causal Exposure. In Aristotelian physics, causal exposure to acting and being acted upon requires that the body be related to place by means of its own quantitative dimensions, because qualities can act and be acted upon only when they are present in their quantitative mode. The Body of Christ under the host is not present by means of its own quantitative dimensions, with the result that its own accidents are not present in a quantitative mode. This explains why humans cannot see the Body of Christ under the host: not with the bodily eye, because the Body of Christ is not relevantly placed to cause sensible species in the medium and thence in the bodily eyes of

[67] Giles, *Theoremata*, Propositio XIV, fo. 9ra.
[68] Giles, *Theoremata*, Propositio XIV, fo. 9rb.
[69] Giles, *Theoremata*, Propositio XIV, fo. 9va.

those around the altar.[70] Not with the mind's eye, because for *ante-mortem* humans intellectual cognition requires proportioned phantasms and so begins with sensation.[71] Christ Himself as He is under the host cannot see things around the altar with His bodily eye, because it is not extended on the altar.[72] Nor can Christ as He is on the altar acquire sensory species of His Body as it is on the altar, for the same reason. But Christ does see His Body with the bodily eye in heaven, and the sensible species He acquires there are on the altar by natural concomitance.[73] Separate substances do not begin with sensation and do not require their objects to be extended in place and so can have an intellectual vision of Christ's Body under the host, unless Divine power prevents them (as perhaps happens in the case of devils).[74] Likewise, Christ as He exists under the host can have intellectual cognitions of intentional contents and spiritual things, because their mode of existing imitates His there.[75]

70 Giles, *Theoremata*, Propositiones XV–XVI, fo. 10vb.
71 Giles, *Theoremata*, Propositio XVIII, fo. 11vb.
72 Giles, *Theoremata*, Propositio XV, fo. 10rab.
73 Giles, *Theoremata*, Propositio XVII, fo. 11rab.
74 Giles, *Theoremata*, Propositio XIX, fo. 12ra–va.
75 Giles, *Theoremata*, Propositio XX, fo. 13rbB & D.

5

Duns Scotus on Placement Problems

I. Querying the Physics, Misidentified Change!

Focusing on Thomistic transubstantiation, Giles worried about how God gets the term-to-which out of the term-from-which, and how the term-to-which could be Christ's Body, given Aquinas's commitment to the unity of substantial forms. Scotus begins by raising a different worry: when one accurately identifies the term-to-which required in eucharistic conversion, it appears that Aquinas has seized on the wrong change! Recall that Aquinas argues for transubstantiation from the principle that

[P2] there is no passage from contradictory to contradictory—a proposition cannot be first true (false) and then its contradictory opposite be true (false)—without any change.

But Christ's Body first is not and then is really present on altars where mass is being said. And—by [T3] and [T4]—this cannot be accounted for by any locomotion, any quantitative or qualitative change, any generation or corruption in the Body of Christ. Aquinas proposes transubstantiation—which he understands as absolute whole being substance-to-substance conversion—to fill the explanatory gap. Aquinas himself has insisted: in transubstantiation, the term-from-which is the whole bread substance, and the term-to-which is the whole substance of Christ's Body.

Scotus protests, what needs explaining in the eucharist is not the whole being (*esse*) of the substance of Christ's Body, but its *real presence*—its being here (*esse hic*)—on altars where priests consecrate the eucharistic bread. Changes are partly defined by their essential (*per se*) terms. What changes essentially explain are their essential (*per se*) terms-to-which. Transubstantiation as Aquinas understands it cannot do the explanatory job for which it was invented!

Substance-to-substance conversion is—as Aquinas sees it—not only a skillful means but the only metaphysically possible means to the real presence desired. Reasoning by analogy with natural generation and corruption, he contends that the product of conversion is where what was converted into it used to be. Just as the bread substance was present under the bread accidents, whole to the whole and whole to the parts, so the Body of Christ comes to be present under the bread accidents, whole to the whole and whole to the parts.[1] But—as noted before—this analogy is unsupportable on their own accounting: fire is roughly where the air was because the matter that persists through the change as a metaphysical constituent of each in turn remains in roughly the same place. In Thomistic transubstantiation, by design, there is no metaphysical constituent common to the terms.[2] Anyway, Scotus quips, where X is converted into Y the result shares the conditions of Y, not X. Converting the bread into the Body of Christ would put the bread in heaven, not the Body of Christ on the altar![3]

Scotus denies any necessary concomitance or consequence between real presence and substance-to-substance conversion. The change whose *per se* terms are the absolute being (*esse simpliciter*) of a substance is logically and metaphysically independent of the change whose term-to-which is being here (*esse hic*), and vice versa. Scotus thinks that the most obvious reason for this is that real presence is an external relation. Where x is R to y, R is an internal relation if and only if it is impossible for x and y to exist and have whatever absolute properties they have and yet x not be R to y. Equality and similarity are *internal* relations because it is impossible for two cubic-meter cubes to exist without being equal or two white things to exist without being similar. In general, all relations in Aristotle's category of relation are internal. By contrast, where x is R to y, and it is possible for x and y to exist and have whatever absolute properties they have and yet x not be R to y, then R is an *external* relation. Being present or proximate or distant in place is a paradigm external relation. In general, Scotus maintains, all respects in

1 Scotus, *Op. Ox.* IV, d. 10, q. 1, n. 5; Wadding VIII. 498.

2 Scotus, *Op. Ox.* IV, d. 11, q. 2, nn. 6–7; Wadding VIII. 598.

3 Scotus, *Op. Ox.* IV, d. 10, q. 1, n. 8; Wadding VIII. 499. See David Burr, *Eucharistic Presence and Conversion in Late Thirteenth-Century Franciscan Thought* (Philadelphia: American Philosophical Society, 1984), where Burr finds the latter argument mentioned by William de la Mare (V. 36) and Vital de Furno (VI. 65).

Aristotle's last six accidental categories are external relations.[4] It follows that the change whose *per se* term is substance has no necessary connection with a further change whose term is an external relation of that substance, because—by definition—the external relation is one the substance could exist without.[5] Thus, substance conversion could occur without anything's acquiring a new place. Divine power over the whole being of the bread substance should mean that God has power to convert it into the Body of Christ as it is in heaven, in which case the Body of Christ (the substance *per se* term-to-which of the conversion) would exist without the external relation of being here on some altar where mass is being said.[6]

Aquinas denied that there are any changes whose *per se* terms-to-which are relations. Does not Aristotle declare, "in ad aliquid, non est motus"? Aquinas takes this tag to have implications about the ontological status of real relations among creatures. If real relations like equality or similarity or proximity were things (*res*) really distinct from their foundations (the quantities or qualities of their subjects), then—since things come to be related that were not before—such really distinct relation things would be the *per se* terms of some change. Aquinas concludes that real relations among creatures are not really distinct from, but really the same as and distinct in reason from, their foundations. When things come to be related that were not before, this is a concomitant or consequent side effect of a change of some other kind. Moreover, Aquinas maintains, that change need not involve a change in the existence or inherent properties of *both* relata; the Eiffel Tower stays put while the tourist comes closer to it. Thus, Aquinas thought, the Body of Christ could come to be present on the altar as a consequence of a non-relational substantial conversion of something else.

Scotus replies that the Aristotelian tag applies only to internal relations, which are housed in Aristotle's category of relation. The tag applies because changes in internal relations are always founded on absolutes (that is, on the substance, quantity, or quality of their relata). Thus, changes in internal relations are always *per accidens* consequences of *per se* changes in the absolutes. But Aristotle's remark does not apply to the external relations housed in the last six categories of accident, because these relations can vary

[4] Scotus, *Op. Ox.* IV, d. 10, q. 1, n. 11; Wadding VIII. 502; *Quodlibet* XI, nn. 13–14; Wadding XII. 268–9.

[5] Scotus, *Op. Ox.* IV, d. 10, q. 1, nn. 67; Wadding VIII. 498–9.

[6] Scotus, *Op. Ox.* IV, d. 10, q. 1, n. 8; Wadding VIII. 499.

even when the absolutes (substance, quantity, quality) of their relata remain the same.[7]

Having rejected Aquinas's proposal—whole-being substantial conversion of the bread substance into the Body of Christ—along with other familiar candidate changes, Scotus insists that what gets Christ's Body onto the altar is a change in really distinct external relations. To convince us that this is so, Scotus offers a more careful analysis of the component changes involved in changes of place. He distinguishes three cases. *Case 1.* When a body moves from place to place and another body is expelled, there are four motions or changes and eight terms: two in the expeller body and two in the body to be expelled. Suppose the expeller body B1 moves from P1 to P2, and the expelled body B2 moves from P2 to P3. B1 undergoes a loss-motion from having P1 to being deprived of P1; and B1 undergoes a gain-motion from being deprived of P2 to having P2. Likewise, for B2 with respect to P2 and P3, respectively. *Case 2.* Suppose B1 moves from P1 to P2, but does not expel B2 from P2. In that case, there are only two motions: the loss-motion by which B1 loses P1 and the gain-motion by which B1 gains P2. *Case 3.* Suppose B1 does not lose P1 but does acquire P2. In that case there will be only one motion: the gain-motion by which B1 acquires P2. Scotus declares that it is unintelligible that a body acquire a place that it lacked before, apart from instantiating one of these patterns.[8]

Scotus concludes that what happens with the Body of Christ in the eucharist is like Case 3: by [T3], the Body of Christ undergoes no loss-motion; nor—by [T1]—does the Body of Christ expel the extended bread species on the altar. Rather there is one gain-motion by which the Body of Christ acquires a new external relation of presence to the bread accidents and/or their place.[9]

Happily, Scotus's own, independently arrived at philosophy of relations accommodates [P2] and fits with this conclusion. Suppose x is R to y. Quite apart from any worries about the eucharist, Scotus's philosophy of relations maintains that—except where the subject x cannot exist without being R to y (for example, creatures cannot exist without being efficient causally dependent on God)—real relations among creatures are things (*res*) really

[7] Scotus, *Op. Ox.* IV, d. 10, q. 1, n. 11; Wadding VIII. 502; *Quodlibeta* XI, nn. 13–14; Wadding XII. 268–9.

[8] Scotus, *Op. Ox.* IV, d. 10, q. 1, n. 9; Wadding VIII. 501.

[9] Scotus, *Op. Ox.* IV, d. 10, q. 1, n. 10; Wadding VIII. 501.

distinct from and inherent in their foundations in their subjects. Consequently, they are the *per se* terms of some changes. When the Body of Christ comes to be newly present on altars where mass has been said, new real presence relations come to inhere in it, *pace* [T4].[10]

II. Modes of Presence

Unextended but Organic? Aquinas wants to hold—in accordance with [T4]—transubstantiation does not strip the Body of Christ of those things (*res*)—Divinity, soul, quantity, and other accidents—that are (in different ways) really united with it. But, because of multiple location, size, and causal vulnerability problems, Aquinas insists that its quantity and other accidents are not there in their natural mode. Aquinas therefore distinguishes between what is there *by the power of the sacrament*—only the substance, existing in the mode of substance—and what is there *by natural concomitance*—by virtue of being (in different ways) really united to substance. Multiple location, size, and causal vulnerability problems are supposed to be solved because quantity is there only by means of the substance and so is not there in the quantitative mode but in the mode of substance.

Giles of Rome and Henry of Ghent agree with both parts of Aquinas's conclusion: namely, that transubstantiation does not strip the Body of Christ of its accidents, and that its accidents are not there in their natural way. What they want to do is offer an explanation of *why* items that are really united should be related to the bread accidents or to their place in different ways. Distinguishing between the *primary* and *secondary* terms of a change, they say that the primary term comes to exist in its own proper mode, while secondary terms come to exist in the mode proper to the primary term. Thus, the substance of the Body of Christ is there in the mode of substance, because it is the primary term of transubstantiation, while quantity is there not in its natural quantitative mode but only in the mode of substance, because it is only a secondary term of the substance-to-substance conversion.[11]

Scotus rejects this proposal: whether something is the primary or a secondary term of an agent's action does not affect the nature of the

[10] Scotus, *Op. Ox.* IV, d. 10, q. 1, n. 11; Wadding VIII. 502.
[11] Scotus, *Op. Ox.* IV, d. 10, q. 1, n. 12; Wadding VIII. 503.

product. A quantified substance such as a stone or a cow can be produced either by God who creates it or by a natural process of generation. Either way, substance will be the primary term and quantity in the mode of quantity will be its naturally necessary concomitant.[12]

Another view denies that the Body of Christ remains quantified while existing in the host. Adherents reason that, just as it is possible for Divine power to bring it about that body exists together with body (as in the virgin birth or when Christ passes through closed doors), so Divine power could make all of the least parts of Christ's Body exist together under the host in such a way that there is no extension of part outside part.[13]

Scotus counters that this would turn the Body of Christ into a heap of flesh bits, whereas some parts being at different distances from others and having different shapes within the whole are necessary for an organic body, which is a necessary for animation. But, except for any consecrations between Christ's Good Friday death and Easter Sunday resurrection, Christ's Body under the host is not dead, but living.[14]

Two Kinds of Position. Working out his own account, Scotus borrows Giles of Rome's distinction between *quantitative position* (position that is a differentia in the genus of quantity), which implies an order of the parts of a whole to one another, and *categorial position* (position that presupposes quantitative position and signifies an order of parts to place, so that the whole is related by commensuration to the whole place and the parts to the parts of place). David Burr finds this distinction in other precursors: Godfrey of Fontaines, John Pecham, William de la Mare, and William of Ware.[15] Bodies that have categorial position in a place are said to exist there in *a dimensive or quantitative mode*, which is required for a body to be located in place properly speaking.[16] Without maintaining that quantitative position is essential to bodily substance, Scotus declares that

[12] Scotus, *Op. Ox.* IV, d. 10, q. 1, n. 12; Wadding VIII. 303; d. 10, q. 1,n. 17; Wadding VIII. 506.

[13] Scotus, *Op. Ox.* IV. d. 10, q. 1, n. 13; Wadding VIII. 503–4. See Burr, *Eucharistic Presence and Conversion*, V. 41, where he cites John Pecham as saying that this is possible for Divine power.

[14] Scotus, *Op. Ox.* IV, d. 10, q. 1, n. 13; Wadding VIII. 504.

[15] Burr, *Eucharistic Presence and Conversion*, IV. 30, V. 42, VI. 73.

[16] Scotus, *Op. Ox.* IV, d. 10, q. 1, n. 16; Wadding VIII. 506. Scotus worries about the categorial housing and labelling for these respects. Sometimes it looks as if the relation of the whole to the whole place belongs to the category *ubi*, while the relation of the parts to the parts of place to the category of position (Quodlibeta XI, nn. 5–6, 13–14; Wadding XII. 263, 268–9). Sometimes Scotus notes how philosophers define 'ubi' as a relation that a body can have to at most one place at a time, whereas the Body of Christ is present as a whole to many at once (*Op. Ox.* IV,

[T9] quantitative position is essential to *quantified* bodies.

It is unintelligible that a body be dimensionally quantified without there being any order of parts in the whole. It follows that, if Christ's Body does not get stripped of its accidents when it becomes really present on the altar, then Christ's Body retains quantitative position after the eucharistic consecration, so that His head is attached immediately to His neck and not to His foot, just as before.[17]

Next, Scotus argues that

[T10] quantitative position is logically and metaphysically independent of categorial position,

and that

[T11] categorial position is *not* essential to quantified body.[18]

For to have categorial position over and above quantitative position is just for the whole quantified body to have an external real relation of presence to the whole of the containing place, and for the parts of the quantified body to have external real relations of presence to the parts of the containing place. But God could make an organic body (whose parts have quantitative position in relation to the whole and to one another) exist outside the Aristotelian universe and so apart from any containing surfaces. Such a body would lack any external real relations to place because there would be no places to contain it. Consequently, it would have quantitative position without categorial position.[19]

Digging down to expose the metaphysical basis of this example, Scotus argues from the following—to his mind, necessary—premiss:

[P9] if a nature is contingently related to each form of another genus taken absolutely, then it is contingently related to the whole genus.

d. 10, q. 1, n. 11; Wadding VIII. 502). Other times, he speaks as if *ubi* pertains properly only to extended things, while broadly speaking it can also cover the simple presence of an angel to place (*Quodlibeta* XI, n. 17; Wadding XII. 272), so that position would entail *ubi* but not vice versa (*Op. Ox.* IV, d. 10, q. 1, n. 16; Wadding VIII. 506). See Burr, *Eucharistic Presence and Conversion*, VII. 76–81. See also Richard Cross, *The Physics of Duns Scotus: The Scientific Context of a Theological Vision* (Oxford: Clarendon Press, 1998), ch. 11, pp. 193–213.

[17] Scotus, *Op. Ox.* IV, d. 10, q. 1, n. 14; Wadding VIII. 505.

[18] Scotus, *Op. Ox.* IV, d. 10, q. 1, n. 17; Wadding VIII. 506.

[19] Scotus, *Op. Ox.* IV, d. 10, q. 1, n. 14; Wadding VIII. 505.

Put the other way around, Scotus's thought is that, if there were a necessary connection between *N* and some genus *G*, this would have to be explained by there being a necessary connection between *N* and some determinate species S_j of *G*; *N* would have to include within itself some cause that necessarily connected it with S_j. There is no necessary connection between a nature *N* and the disjunction of species coordinate under *G*—'Necessarily, *N* is either S_i or S_j or S_k . . .'—unless, for some species *S*, there is a necessary connection between *N* and *S*. But if, for each species *S* of *G*, *N* could exist without *S*, then *N* could exist without *G* as well.

Scotus recognizes that some may find [P9] counter-intuitive and pauses to clear away two putative counter-examples. [i] The first is that the genus number is necessarily connected with the disjunction odd-or-even, but it is not the case that number is necessarily odd and not the case that number is necessarily even. Scotus agrees that odd-or-even is necessarily connected with number, but thinks this is to be explained by the fact that each number has a necessary connection with one of the disjuncts: 3 is necessarily odd, while 4 is necessarily even. Hence, this example is not really counter to his understanding of [P9]. [ii] The second is that a surface is necessarily colored but contingently related to each color. Scotus bites the bullet and denies that surfaces are necessarily colored, insisting that there is nothing definitionally internal to what it is to be a surface that would make it contradictory for a surface to exist without any color at all.[20]

Given [P9] as the major premiss, Scotus adds the minor: since bodies are mobile, there is no particular place in which they are necessarily situationally or categorially positioned (whole in the whole, part in the parts). Therefore, Scotus concludes, quantified bodies bear a contingent relation to situational or categorical position in general, and so could exist without any categorial position at all. Even where (as in the natural case) bodies have both quantitative and categorial position, the relations of parts to one another and the relation(s) of the whole and/or its parts to place are different properties: the definition (*ratio formalis*) of one does not contain the other.[21]

On Scotus's metaphysical analysis, what it is for quantity or for quantified body to exist without categorial position is for the absolute thing to exist (with its parts ordered to one another within the whole) and not to have the external relations to place that would make it coextensive with the place

[20] Scotus, *Op. Ox.* IV, d. 10, q. 1, n. 15; Wadding VIII. 505.
[21] Scotus, *Op. Ox.* IV, d. 10, q. 1, n. 15; Wadding VIII. 505–6.

(the whole present to the whole place, and parts to the parts of place). Scotus recognizes two ways for this to happen: [a] one, as in the above example of God's creating a body outside the universe, when the absolute thing does not bear external presence relations to any place at all; [b] the other, when the whole body bears a presence relation to the whole place, but the parts of the body do not bear presence relations to the parts of the place. In this second case, the body may be said to coexist with the place because the whole is related to the whole; but the body lacks categorial position because the parts are not related to the parts.[22]

Christ's Body is present in the eucharist [b] the second way: the whole bears a presence relation to the whole place, but its parts do not bear presence relations to the parts of the place. Accordingly, Christ's Body *coexists with* the place and with the bread accidents in the place, but is *not coextensive with* the place or with the bread accidents in the place. It is thus really present but lacks situational or categorial presence.[23]

Solving the Presence Problems. From a sufficiently high level of abstraction, Scotus's conceptual machinery—the distinction between quantitative and categorial position, and the conceptualization of presence in terms of external relations—seems to provide ready solutions to the problems surrounding the real presence of Christ's Body in the eucharist. [i] Christ's Body is not a heap: it has quantitative position; its parts are ordered within the whole and to one another as before, naturally prior to whatever relation it may have to place. [ii] The fact that Christ's Body is of a larger size and a different shape from most eucharistic hosts makes no difference, because Christ does not have categorial position on the altar: Christ's Body is present as a whole but is not extended in the place; commensuration and configuration are not required. [iii] Nor does Scotus's analysis of eucharistic presence imply—contrary to [T5]—that two bodies or quantities (the bread quantity and the quantity of Christ's Body) are extended in the same place at once. [iv] Likewise, why should there be any problem about Christ's Body being really present on many altars? If the same foundation can have many internal relations of the same species to different terms at once (for example, this whiteness may be the foundation of similarities to many white things; this quantity, of many equality relations to other quantities), why cannot the same foundation have many external relations

[22] Scotus, *Op. Ox.* IV, d. 10, q. 1, n. 16; Wadding VIII. 506.
[23] Scotus, *Op. Ox.* IV, d. 10, q. 1, nn. 16–17; Wadding VIII. 506.

to different terms at once? A body's presence in a place is only a matter of its bearing an external relation to that place. Why suppose a body's capacity for founding a presence relation to a place is used up by the inherence of one such presence relation? God can bring about anything that does not involve a contradiction. Why not say that the whole Body of Christ bears relations of presence to the whole host place on many altars where mass is said simultaneously?[24]

The Perils of Multiple Location. In fact, Scotus's effort to sustain these conclusions leads him to develop his philosophy of body in still more radical directions. Whatever philosophical presumption there was in favor of

[T5] two bodies cannot be extended in the same place at once,

and

[T6] a single body cannot be extended in, or move toward, two distinct places at once,

Scotus thinks the givens of Christian theology should bring us to the conclusion that both [T5] and [T6] are false.[25] They appear true, because they accurately describe the limits of created natural powers: none of them can bring it about that two bodies are extended in the same place at once, or that one exists in and/or moves toward two distinct places at once. [T5] and [T6] do not reckon with Divine omnipotence, however, which can bring about whatever does not involve a contradiction. Scholastic theories of the eucharist have attributed to God power to make the Body of Christ to be really present in a non-natural way on altars where eucharistic bread has been consecrated. That is, God is able to make the Body of Christ to be present in a non-natural way (unextended, without categorial position) in the place where the bread accidents are present in a natural way (extended, with categorial position) at one and the same time. Moreover, since mass is said in many places simultaneously, God is able to make the Body of Christ to be present in a non-natural way on many altars at once. On this much, Aquinas, Giles, Henry, and Scotus are all agreed.

[24] Scotus, *Op. Ox.* IV, d. 10, q. 2, nn. 11–12; Wadding VIII. 513–14; d. 10, q. 3, n. 4; Wadding VIII. 528).

[25] See Burr, *Eucharistic Presence and Conversion*, where he identifies Peter Olivi (V. 48) and William of Ware (VI. 70) as thinking such extended multiple location possible by Divine power.

Scotus contends,

[P10] wherever God can make a natural substance to exist not under its natural mode or under a mode opposite to its natural mode, God can make it to exist under its natural mode.

On all accounts, the coming-to-exist of Christ's Body on the altar is miraculous, because no Aristotelian natural change could get it there while allowing it to remain in heaven. Scotus declares that presence in a non-natural mode constitutes a further miracle. God's making Christ's Body to be present on altars in a non-natural mode involves two miracles, while making it to be there in its natural mode would involve only one![26] Scotus concludes that Divine power can make the Body of Christ to be present *in its natural mode* in the place where the bread accidents are simultaneously extended—contrary to [T5]—and Divine power can make the Body of Christ to be present *in its natural mode* on many altars at once—contrary to [T6].[27] Moreover, the simultaneous natural-mode existence of two bodies in the same place or of one body in many places is to be attributed to Divine power, causing it to have relevant presence relations (of the whole body to the whole place, and of parts of the body to parts of the place), and does not require the whole-being conversion of one thing into another.[28]

This argument proceeds at a very high level of abstraction, however. Scotus and his interlocutors are agreed, Divine omnipotence does not include power to make contradictories true simultaneously. To secure his conclusion, Scotus must rebut arguments that the natural-mode existence of a body in many places at once would lead to contradiction. Broadly speaking, the considerations advanced by others in favor of [T6] are of two types.

[*1*] *Arguments from Finitude.* Aquinas, Giles, and others argue that it necessarily pertains to the finitude of a creature that it is able to exist and exercise power from only one location at a time. If the gift of subtlety could make it possible for risen bodies to pass through closed doors (the way Gospel narratives say Christ did), Aquinas insists, even glorified and risen bodies have determinate situational position and are circumscribed by and limited to existing in one place at a time.[29] Likewise, Giles insists, their place

[26] Scotus, *Op. Ox.* IV, d. 10, q. 3, n. 4; Wadding VIII. 528–9.

[27] Scotus, *Op. Ox.* IV, d. 10, q. 2, n. 9; Wadding VIII. 512–13; d. 10, q. 3, n. 2; Wadding VIII. 528; d. 10, q. 3, n. 4; Wadding VIII. 528–9.

[28] Scotus, *Op. Ox.* IV, d. 10, q. 2, n. 10; Wadding VIII. 513; d. 10, q. 3, n. 2; Wadding VIII. 528.

[29] Scotus, *Op. Ox.* IV, d. 10, q. 2, n. 5; Wadding VIII. 511. For a fuller discussion of glorified bodies, see my "Why Bodies as Well as Souls in the Life to Come?" forthcoming in a volume for

marks their boundary or limit; if it could exist elsewhere at the same time, it could exist outside of and beyond its limit.[30] As immaterial, angels cannot be extended in place (they have no parts to be distributed, part to one and part to another part of place), but they can exist definitively in place (whole in the whole and whole in each part). But—Giles argues—their finitude means that they are capable of exercising functional powers from only one determinate position at a time.[31] Put otherwise, God alone is infinite and omnipresent, able to act everywhere and always. But, if Divine power could make a body exist in its natural mode in two places at once, God could make it exist everywhere at once and so share in Divine omnipresence.[32]

[2] *Causal Exposure Arguments.* Aristotelian causal interaction requires corporeal agents and patients to be extended (to have categorial position) in proximate places. Putting Christ's Body on altars in a non-natural mode (for Aquinas, in the mode of substance; for Scotus, with quantitative but not categorial position) makes it invulnerable to local causal interaction because it is not extended there. But one body extended in many places—with not only quantitative but categorial position—would be vulnerable to causal interaction in each and all of them, and so open the possibility that the same body might undergo contrary changes at the same time. Aquinas retails some problematic possibilities: water might be in the freezer in Rome and on the boil on a London stove and so be simultaneously cold and hot; an animal might find nothing to eat in one place and food in another, and so be at once hungry and satisfied; it might get sick from bad weather in one place and grow strong and healthy in good weather elsewhere, might experience fatal blows one place and not die in another. Whether you say it has both conditions in each place, or one in one place and the other in another, it is still the same body that has contraries simultaneously.[33]

[3] *"Improved" Arguments for* [*T6*]. Wishing to attack the opposing position in its strongest form, Scotus himself formulates additional—he claims, better—causal arguments in defense of [T6]. Three elaborate the consequences of multiple causal vulnerabilities. [3.1] First,

the Wippel-fest medieval colloquium series, School of Philosophy, Catholic University of America.

[30] Scotus, *Op. Ox.* IV, d. 10, q. 2, n. 3; Wadding VIII. 509.

[31] Scotus, *Op. Ox.* IV, d. 10, q. 2, n. 3; Wadding VIII. 509.

[32] Scotus, *Op. Ox.* IV, d. 10, q. 2, n. 2; Wadding VIII. 509.

[33] Scotus, *Op. Ox.* IV, d. 10, q. 2, n. 2; Wadding VIII. 509. See Burr, *Eucharistic Presence and Conversion*, where he identifies William de la Mare (V. 36) and Vital de Forno (VI. 66) as having raised and rejected the force of some such causal exposure arguments.

[P11] it is impossible for the same matter to be under two substantial forms simultaneously.

But, if the same body could be in two places at once, the same food could be eaten by a cow in one place and a horse in another. Digestion would turn the same matter into cow flesh in one place and horse flesh in another. Again, if the same wood existed in two places and were relevantly proximate to fire in each of the two places, it would be reduced to ashes in two places. Because

[P12] efficient causal overdetermination is impossible,

however, the two fires would produce numerically distinct substantial ash forms in the matter at one and the same time.[34] [3.2] Suppose an animal exists in two places and finds food in one place and not in another. Shall we infer with Aquinas that it is hungry in one place and satisfied in another? Suppose it found food and ate in both places. Should we alternatively conclude that it was overstuffed with food?[35]

[3.3] Again, if a body could be extended in many places simultaneously, it would follow that the smallest fire could consume all of the combustibles in the world. For, if there were different fires in different places, they would together consume all of the combustibles. Let the combustibles be divided into parts as small as the fire. If the fire could exist in all of the places, it could consume them all.[36]

A further argument is from locomotion. [3.4] Attending once again to the essential (*per se*) terms of change, Scotus notes that

[P13] a natural agent does not *per se* intend the corruption of the term-from-which, but only *per accidens*, because the term-from-which is incompatible with the term-to-which.

Suppose a body B1 exists at P1, and a natural agent causes B1 to exist at P2. If place relations were not incompatible with one another, then, in causing B1 to exist at P2, the natural agent would not cause B1 not to exist at P1, and a body could exist in two places at once by natural agency. But this is impossible. Therefore, place relations must be incompatible, just as [T6]

[34] Scotus, *Op. Ox.* IV, d. 10, q. 2, n. 4; Wadding VIII. 510.
[35] Scotus, *Op. Ox.* III, d. 10, q. 2, n. 4; Wadding VIII. 510.
[36] Scotus, *Op. Ox.* IV, d. 10, q. 2, n. 4; Wadding VIII. 510.

implies.[37] Likewise, if two bodies could be extended in the same place at once, then a natural agent would not expel one body by moving another into its place.[38]

Multiple Location, Made Safe and Sane. Against these arguments, Scotus's defense of multiple natural-mode location is based on three theses. The first reflects his ever-sharp sensitivity to natural priorities and posteriorities:

> [T12] whatever are essentially prior to place relations (*ubi*) inhere in the body uniformly, even though the place relations are diverse.

Scotus explains that the essentially or naturally prior are not varied and multipled because of any variation in the essentially posterior, but rather the other way around; the naturally simultaneous vary together. A body's substance (its prime matter and substantial form) and its absolute accidents (its quantity and qualities and their *per accidens* union with substance) are naturally prior to its placement relations. Therefore, the substance, quantity, and qualities of a body are not rendered numerically distinct or different by the mere numerical distinction or difference of place relations.[39]

The other two theses tell us to calculate the consequences of multiple-location causal exposure the same way we would if the agents and patients were all together in the same region.

> [T13] Just as a patient existing in one place receives a form from two agents acting on it, so the patient existing in two places will suffer from proximate agents in both places.
>
> [T14] Just as a body existing in one place is related as an active power to different things close to it in that place, so the same body existing in two places would be related to the same things existing in two places close enough to it.

Whether in one place or in two, the patient has the same passive potency to receive absolute form, and the agent has the same active potency to confer forms on nearby patients. Therefore, the patient is acted upon by all of the agents close enough to it, whether they be in one place or in two.[40]

[37] Scotus, *Op. Ox.* IV, d. 10, q. 2, n. 4; Wadding VIII. 510. It seems that a 'not' is left out of the text, which should read 'if one *ubi* were not incompossible with another *ubi*' rather than 'if one *ubi* were incompossible with another *ubi*'.

[38] Scotus, *Op. Ox.* IV, d. 10, q. 2, n. 21; Wadding VIII. 523.

[39] Scotus, *Op. Ox.* IV, d. 10, q. 2, n. 13; Wadding VIII. 518; d. 10, q. 2, n. 17; Wadding VIII. 520.

[40] Scotus, *Op. Ox.* IV, d. 10, q. 2, n. 13; Wadding VIII. 518. See Burr, *Eucharistic Presence and Conversion*, where he identifies William de la Mare (V. 36) and Vital de Furno as deploying a similar strategy.

Answering the Causal Exposure Arguments. Heat and cold are absolute qualities. Therefore, by [T12], the water that is simultaneously in London (on the stove) and in Rome (in the freezer) will have the same quality in London and in Rome. Which quality will depend on whether the fire in London is stronger than the freezer in Rome. Were they matched, the water would be lukewarm in both places. By [T13] and [T14], the same thing would happen if both fire and freezer were simultaneously acting on the water in London.[41] Likewise, according to Aristotelian biology, hunger is a function of the qualities heat and dryness, which—by [T12]—are the same whether the animal is singly or multiply placed. Thus, if the animal finds food and his appetite ceases in one place, the animal's hunger will cease wherever it is.[42] Again, by [T13] and [T14], the degree of health or sickness in the animal will depend on the relative strengths of the sickness—causing agents in one place and health-producing agents in the other. The Hawaian beachcomber may be of only average health if he or she is also in Antarctica.[43] Again, life and death are a function of absolutes, of whether the dominant substantial soul form does or does not inhere in the organic body to form a complete substance that is one *per se*. By [T12], this is naturally prior to location and so will not vary with different place relations. If the animal dies here, it dies wherever it is.[44]

Against [3.1], Scotus denies the inference that two substantial forms—of the same or of different species—would exist in the same matter. By [T13] and [T14], the case is the same as if the food were in two stomachs in the same place or as if—by Divine power—there were two fires together in the same place close to the wood. Which body the food turned into would depend on the relative strengths of the digestive agents.[45] In the case of the wood, either the fires would act together to produce a more perfect effect than either would alone, or each fire would be a partial cause of the effect, since—by [P11] efficient causal overdetermination is impossible[46]—it is not possible for there to be two total efficient causes of altogether the same effect.

[41] Scotus, *Op. Ox.* IV, d. 10, q. 2, n. 15; Wadding VIII. 519.

[42] Scotus, *Op. Ox.* IV, d. 10, q. 2, n. 16; Wadding VIII. 519.

[43] Scotus, *Op. Ox.* IV, d. 10, q. 2, n. 16; Wadding VIII. 519–20.

[44] Scotus, *Op. Ox.* IV, d. 10, q. 2, nn. 15–17; Wadding VIII. 519–20; d. 10, q. 2, n. 22; Wadding VIII. 532.

[45] Scotus, *Op. Ox.* IV, d. 10, q. 2, n. 22; Wadding VIII. 523–4.

[46] Scotus, *Op. Ox.* IV, d. 10, q. 2, n. 23; Wadding VIII. 524.

To [3.2], Scotus replies that, when the animal eats in only one place, the locomotion of the food to the animal's stomach would be different in one place and the other because locomotion involves relations to place, but, once in the stomach, the substantial change from food to animal flesh will be the same in both places by [T12]. By the same token, Scotus should say that, when it eats in both places, it gets twice as much food as it needs in both places. But he hesitates and allows the further alternative: that in one place it gets one part and in the other place the other part, and it is satisfied in both places.[47]

To [3.3], Scotus maintains that—by [T14]—the fire located in many places would act on all of the nearby combustibles the same way it would if the fire were in only one place and the combustibles were nearby there. Since

[P14] natural power is less over more than over fewer, and less over many than over one,

the fire would act on the many in a more reduced degree than it would act on one alone.[48]

Answering the Finitude Arguments. Scotus agrees that God alone is immense, necessarily everywhere (if there is any *where* to be) according to Divine power, presence, and essence. But that does not mean that a creature could not in fact be everywhere by Divine power. Nor should his opponents deny it. For Giles says that Divine power could make Christ's Body to exist everywhere sacramentally by converting each and every body in the universe into the Body of Christ. And—by [P9]—there is no more limitation on a body's being *extended* somewhere than there is on a body's being somewhere *sacramentally*. From Scotus's point of view, for God to do one rather than the other is only for God to cause in the body more or fewer external relations to place. And God could do that with or without the instrumental causality of sacramental rites.[49] Likewise, by Divine power, an angel could exist in more than one place definitively.[50]

Answering the Locomotion Arguments. Most problematic for Scotus is [3.4] the argument from [P13] that, if it is multiple place relations in the same body and place relations to the same place in multiple bodies are not incompatible,

[47] Scotus, *Op. Ox.* IV, d. 10, q. 2, n. 23; Wadding VIII. 524.
[48] Scotus, *Op. Ox.* IV, d. 10, q. 2, n. 24; Wadding VIII. 524.
[49] Scotus, *Op. Ox.* IV, d. 10, q. 2, n. 15; Wadding VIII. 519.
[50] Scotus, *Ord.* II, d. 2, p. 2, q. 3, n. 264; Vat VII. 271; *Op. Ox.* IV, d. 10, q. 2, n. 18; Wadding VIII. 521.

then natural agents should be able to produce multiple location. Scotus replies briefly with a distinction between terms that are absolutely incompossible, whose coexistence involves a contradiction, and those that are incompossible relative to created power. There is no created power to produce two bodies in one place at the same time, and no created power to produce one body in multiple places at the same time.[51] Multiple locations are *virtually* incompatible relative to created causal power.[52]

This answer seems incomplete, however. Recall Scotus's own analysis of the multiple changes involved in locomotion. The action of the hypothetical natural agent C explains why B1 acquires place relations to P2. But it does not explain why B1 thereby loses place relations to P1, and why B2 loses place relations to P2 and gains place relations to P3. Perhaps Scotus wants to say that a natural agent C has the power to produce place relations to P2 in B1 only when C also acts to cause B1 to lose place relations to P1 and B2 to lose place relations to P2 and to gain place relations to P3; C cannot move B1 to P2 without intending other loss and gain changes at the same time. Divine power can produce the gain without any losses. Created power can produce the same gain only in a more complicated way—one that involves doing more things and so perhaps involves the exercise of greater causal power.

Scotus concludes that it is the philosophers, the ones who purport to follow natural reason, who sponsor [T5] and [T6], denying the metaphysical possibility of two bodies' being *extended* in one place or one body's being *extended* in two places at once. Yet, careful metaphysical analysis that respects Aristotelian natural priorities of substance over accidents and of absolutes over relatives shows that both sorts of multiple location are metaphysically possible after all. Scotus scolds and warns: it is not the impossibility of *understanding*, but their inability to *imagine* multiple location that underwrites [T5] and [T6]. But following where imagination leads is childish![53]

Sacramental-Mode versus Natural-Mode Presence. Even if it is metaphysically possible for multiple bodies to be extended in the same place and a single body extended in multiple places simultaneously, Scotus does not think that the Body of Christ is extended on the altars where mass is said. Rather, [T3]

51 Scotus, *Op. Ox.* IV, d. 10, q. 2, n. 21; Wadding VIII. 523.

52 Scotus, *Op. Ox.* IV, d. 49, q. 16, nn. 5–6; Wadding X. 612–13.

53 Scotus, *Op. Ox.* IV, d. 10, q. 2, n. 11; Wadding VIII. 513.

the Body of Christ has *natural-mode existence* (is extended, with situational or categorial as well as quantitative position) in heaven and [T2] exists on the altars *sacramentally* (unextended, without categorial position). Theological consensus thus presumes that natural-mode existence in one place is compatible with sacramental-mode existence in one or more others. Scotus's next question is, therefore, whether the Body of Christ necessarily has *the same parts and properties* in sacramental-mode existence as it has in natural-mode existence? By 'parts' Scotus refers to the metaphysical constitutents that make up Christ's Body: on Scotus's pluralist conception, prime matter and the form of corporeity unite to make Christ's Body; Christ's soul is the dominant substantial form that unites with them to make *per se* one human being. By 'properties,' Scotus means the absolute (non-relational) accidents of Christ's Body, its quantity and qualities. Scotus further distinguishes two ways the necessity operator can be taken: for absolute necessity, and for necessity *secundum quid*.

So far as absolute necessity is concerned, Scotus's answer to the question is negative:

[T15] it is *not* absolutely necessary that, if something has parts and properties under the natural mode, it has the same parts and properties under the sacramental mode; and

[T16] it is *not* absolutely necessary that, if a body has parts and properties under the sacramental mode, it has the same parts and properties in natural existence.

[T15] should be non-controversial: in the general resurrection, sacraments will cease (see Chapter 12 below); Christ's Body will exist and have parts and properties in the natural mode but will exist under the sacramental mode no more.[54] Scotus holds that [T16] is true for the same sort of reason: it is possible for Christ's Body to exist and to have parts and properties in the sacramental-mode existence without having natural-mode existence anywhere. The two modes of existence are logically and metaphysically independent, and Christ's Body is indifferent to each and both![55]

Scotus recognizes that [T16] is something Aquinas et al. will contest. For they understand sacramental-mode existence to be the result of substance-to-substance conversion. The term-to-which Y has natural-mode existence

[54] Scotus, *Op. Ox.* IV, d. 10, q. 4, n. 4; Wadding VIII. 533.
[55] Scotus, *Op. Ox.* IV, d. 10, q. 4, n. 4; Wadding VIII. 533.

somewhere P1. The term-from-which X has natural-mode existence elsewhere P2. The whole-being conversion of X into Y results in Y's existing at P2 sacramentally. On this account, natural-mode existence somewhere is presupposed for sacramental existence elsewhere.

Scotus argues against this conclusion, contending that

[P15] nothing X essentially depends on another Y unless either [a] Y pertains to the essence of X, or [b] Y is a cause of X.

Re [P15a], natural-mode existence does not pertain to the essence of sacramental-mode existence. For—on Scotus's analysis—natural-mode existence involves both quantitative and categorial position; categorial position requires not only that the whole body be related by a presence relation to the whole place, but that the parts of the body are related by presence relations to the parts of the place. Sacramental-mode existence requires quantitative position and a relation of the whole body to the whole of the place, but not presence relations of parts of the body to parts of the place. Thus, sacramental-mode existence is not defined by and does not include natural-mode existence; rather, sacramental-mode existence involves fewer presence relations than natural-mode existence does. Re [P15b], Scotus declares, God alone is the efficient cause of Christ's sacramental-mode existence; Christ's natural-mode existence has no causal role to play.[56]

Christ's Body is indifferent to natural-modes and sacramental-modes of existence, because, given the real existence of Christ's Body, whether it has one or the other is a function of how many and what kind of external presence relations inhere in it! This means that, *just as Christ's Body could have natural-mode existence without sacramental-mode existence, so Christ's Body could have sacramental-mode existence without having natural-mode existence at the same time*. Scotus tries to make this point vivid by drawing two further corollaries.

[Cor 1] the eucharist could have been before the Incarnation just as much as now, both so far as its signification and insofar as the contained and signified thing is concerned; and

[Cor 2] after the Incarnation, the Body of Christ could cease in its natural mode and yet remain truly in the eucharist, both so far as the truth of the sign and the reality of the contained thing are concerned.

[56] Scotus, *Op. Ox.* IV, d. 10, q. 4, n. 5; Wadding VIII. 533.

If the Body of Christ could exist without presence relations that would extend it in any place, it could exist in the sacramental mode before it existed in the natural mode, and it could continue to exist in the sacramental mode after it had ceased to exist in the natural mode.[57] In favor of [Cor 1], Scotus argues from

[P16] wherever a temporal thing can have real existence, there it can begin to be,

to the conclusion that the Body of Christ could have its first existence under the sacrament. When it came to have natural-mode existence, it would not begin to be *simpliciter* but rather would begin to be extended in place and so only begin to be *secundum quid*. Likewise, Scotus maintains, there are two ways for a thing to cease to be in a place: first, by the substantial change that separates its absolute parts (its prime matter from its substantial form) and—by [T12]—makes the thing cease to be wherever and however it really existed. Second, a thing can cease to be in place by losing its external relations to that place, while continuing to exist elsewhere. Scotus insists, a thing could lose the external relations whereby it existed—whether in natural or sacramental mode—in one place, without losing the external relations whereby it existed—whether in natural mode or sacramental mode—in another. Hence, it is possible for a body to exist in sacramental mode only after as well as before being extended somewhere.[58]

Having argued that a body's natural-mode and sacramental-mode existence are logically and metaphysically independent of one another, Scotus returns to the other interpretation of the original question: is it necessary *secundum quid* or hypothetically that, if a body has both natural-mode and sacramental-mode existence, it has the same parts and properties in both? For his answer, Scotus returns to his principle

[T12] whatever are essentially prior to place relations (*ubi*) inhere in the body uniformly, even though the place relations are diverse.

The absolute parts (prime matter and substantial form) and properties (quantity and qualities) of a body are naturally prior to any of its external relations to place. Consequently, for any given time, the body will have

[57] Scotus, *Op. Ox.* IV, d. 10, q. 4, n. 6; Wadding VIII. 533–4.
[58] Scotus, *Op. Ox.* IV, d. 10, q. 4, n. 8; Wadding VIII. 534–5.

those same absolute parts and absolute properties wherever it exists, whether naturally or sacramentally. It would be contradictory to say otherwise.[59]

Primary Presence versus Natural Concomitance. Wishing to deny that eucharistic consecration strips Christ's Body of its accidents, Aquinas et al. distinguish between what is primarily present *by the power of the sacrament* (namely, the primary significatum of the sacrament; the term of the whole being substance-to-substance conversion) from what is present *by natural concomitance* (what is really joined to the primary significatum; what the term of the substantial conversion could not have natural-mode existence without).

Having insisted that quantity inheres in Christ's Body as truly in its sacramental-mode existence as in its natural-mode existence in heaven, Scotus then recognizes that each of the really distinct things that is really united to Christ's Body as a part or a property is itself apt to be the foundation of its own external presence relation. Thus, for example, Christ's Body (the composite of prime matter and substantial form) as a whole could have a presence relation to the whole place of the species, without Christ's soul or His quantity and various qualities having any presence relation to that place. In that case, it would be true to say that Christ's Body existing here on the altar sacramentally is animated (is perfected by the soul form in both places) and quantified (perfected by quantity in both places), but not by a soul or a quantity that exists in both places, but rather by a soul or a quantity in heaven.[60]

Elsewhere (in the very next question), Scotus draws a different distinction for multiple location cases: where a body B1 exists at P1 and P2, some absolute properties F, G, . . . pertain to B1 at P1 *primarily as at P1* and to B1 at P2 *only concomitantly*; while others may pertain to B1 at P2 *primarily as at P2* and pertain to B1 at P1 *only concomitantly*. Scotus's thought seems to be that an absolute property F pertains to B1 primarily as at P1, if B1 would be F, even if P1 were the only place B1 existed at the moment. But F pertains to B1 concomitantly at P1 if F pertains to B1 primarily as elsewhere.[61] If so, his distinction does not seem to be well drawn. For B1's essential parts or properties would pertain to B1 even if B1 existed in only one place. Yet, if B1 did exist in two places (P1 and P2) at once, it would seem wrong to say

[59] Scotus, *Op. Ox.* IV, d. 10, q. 4, n. 11; Wadding VIII. 540.
[60] Scotus, *Op. Ox.* IV, d. 10, q. 4, n. 15; Wadding VIII. 542.
[61] Scotus, *Op. Ox.* IV, d. 10, q. 5, n. 2; Wadding VIII. 547.

that those essential parts or properties pertained to B1 primarily as at P1 and only concomitantly at P2; rather they would pertain to B1 "primarily" in both places.

Scotus's imprecision may be explained by the fact that he is not thinking about a body's essential parts or properties, but about differences in a body's causal exposure that arise from its having natural-mode versus sacramental-mode existence in a place. To be causally vulnerable to Aristotelian change, a body has to be extended in a place that is relevantly proximate to the agent. Properties or parts pertain to a body *primarily as here*, if this is the place where it was caused to have them. Such properties pertain to the body in sacramental-mode existence *only concomitantly*.

Sacramental Presence and Causal Exposure. Scotus proceeds to apply this distinction—between what pertains to the Body of Christ *primarily* as in the eucharist versus *only concomitantly*—with respect to four further cases: immanent actions, outgoing actions, bodily motion, and being seen. *Actions.* What can Christ as sacramentally present in the eucharist do? Scotus distinguishes Christ's *corporeal* from His *spiritual* powers. Human beings are soul–body composites. Merely spiritual powers—intellect and will—pertain primarily to the soul, but to the whole human being *per se* through the soul. Corporeal powers are not in the soul *per se* but in the soul–body composite: some pertain to the nature of mixed body, while others pertain to animate body as such.[62] Powers of both kinds pertain to the perfection of human nature, and it is an excellence in a human being to have them whether or not he or she has occasion to use them.[63] Scotus further contrasts *immanent* actions (for example, of cognition and appetite) that are absolute qualities of the agent itself, and *outgoing* actions that affect something else (for example, by moving it).

Where immanent actions are concerned, Scotus advances three theses:

[T17] every action that pertains to Christ primarily as in heaven pertains to Christ as in the sacrament concomitantly;

[T18] no sensation pertains primarily to Christ as in the sacrament;

[T19] the spiritual functions of intellect and will can inhere in Christ primarily as in the sacrament.[64]

[62] Scotus, *Op. Ox.* IV, d. 10, q. 7, n. 2; Wadding VIII. 560.
[63] Scotus, *Op. Ox.* IV, d. 10, q. 7, n. 6; Wadding VIII. 561.
[64] Scotus, *Op. Ox.* IV, d. 10, q. 5, n. 2; Wadding VIII. 547.

[T17] is an instance of [T12], given Scotus's understanding of immanent acts as absolute qualities that inhere in the agent naturally prior to external presence relations, and so pertain to Christ wherever Christ is. Christ's Body has natural-mode existence and so is extended in heaven. Christ's soul is definitively in the place—whole in the whole and whole in each part—where Christ's Body is extended. Scotus understands the scope of [T3] Christ's post-resurrection impassibility to be compatible with His being acted upon to sense things that are nearby to produce sensory cognitions and intellectual intuitive cognitions that pertain to Him primarily as He is in heaven. Because a sensation is an *absolute* form, Christ's being causally exposed to receiving sensations somewhere is enough for His having them concomitantly elsewhere, in places far away from the sensed object where Christ exists only in the sacramental mode.[65]

[T18] follows because sensation is the act of a corporeal power of an animate body and requires a proximate corporeal object in natural-mode existence to act on the sense organ. But Christ's Body does not have natural-mode existence in the eucharist.[66]

By contrast, if Christ's soul does have its own presence relation to the place on the altar, it will be present the only way spiritual beings (which have no parts) can be present to a place: namely, definitively, which Scotus defines as 'present whole to whole and whole to part'. For spiritual beings, this suffices for causal exposure. Scotus further distinguishes between intellects that are functionally separate from bodies (angels, separate and post-resurrection souls) and those that are "bound by the senses" because of their attachment to corruptible bodies that weigh them down. For human souls attached to corruptible bodies, intellectual cognition always runs by way of sensory cognition, and *ante mortem* mere humans can have intellectual intuitive cognitions only of those objects of which they have sensory cognitions. But Christ's post-resurrection soul is liberated from these aggravations and is able to have intellectual intuitive cognitions of existent and present objects that act on the intellect directly.[67] Moreover, since Christ's soul as definitively present on the altar is causally exposed to objects too far away to affect Christ's soul as it is in heaven, [T19] some spiritual acts can

[65] Scotus, *Op. Ox.* IV, d. 10,1. 5, nn. 3–4; Wadding VIII. 547.
[66] Scotus, *Op. Ox.* IV, d. 10, q. 5, n. 5; Wadding VIII. 550.
[67] See Scotus, *Op. Ox.* IV, d. 10, q. 8, n. 7; Wadding VIII. 566.

pertain to Christ's soul primarily as on the altar and only concomitantly as it is in heaven.[68]

Outgoing Actions. Predictably, where outgoing actions are concerned, Scotus maintains that

[T20] Christ in the eucharist cannot use any active corporeal power, whether it is merely corporeal (as those conseqent on the nature of mixed bodies are) or corporeal (as those consequent on the nature of animate bodies are),

because the exercise of corporeal powers requires the natural-mode existence of bodies and proportioned proximity between agent and patient. But Christ's corporeal powers as in the sacrament are not extended in place in the required way.[69] By contrast,

[T21] Christ in the eucharist can use any active spiritual power,

because their action does not require them to be extended in place. Thus, if an angel were definitively present to Christ in the eucharist, Christ could use His spiritual power to illumine the angel's intellect and to speak to the angel. Moreover, angels and separate and post-resurrection human souls have the power to move bodies—not power to move them organically, one part after another and one part by means of another, the way the conjoined soul does; but rather power immediately to move the whole body at once. Indeed, the human soul always possesses this power, but its conjunction with a corruptible body regularly obstructs the *ante-mortem* exercise of this power. The blessed exercise it in heaven and move their bodies not only organically but also the whole at once. Scotus speculates that Christ may have used that power during his earthly ministry when he escaped his enemies who wanted to throw him off the mountain (Luke 4: 29–30). Likewise, in the eucharist, the soul of Christ could use this power to move the bread accidents or the host immediately.[70]

Bodily Change. Taking 'change' (*motus*) to cover both instantaneous and progressive transitions, Scotus distinguishes strict-sense change, which includes only the Aristotelian quartet—substantial, quantitative, qualitative, and place change—from broad-sense change, which covers change with respect to any form, absolute or relative. What changes can the Body of

[68] Scotus, *Op. Ox.* IV, d. 10, q. 5, n. 5; Wadding VIII. 550.
[69] Scotus, *Op. Ox.* IV, d. 10, q. 7, n. 2; Wadding VIII. 560.
[70] Scotus, *Op. Ox.* IV, d. 10, q. 7, n. 5; Wadding VIII. 561.

Christ in the eucharist undergo, and what can cause them? So far as changes in the Body of Christ primarily as in heaven are concerned, [T12] predicts concomitance for changes in absolute forms and lack of concomitance for changes involving natural-mode relations to heavenly places.[71] Once again, created power to act on bodies to produce strict-sense or broad-sense changes requires that the body acted upon have natural-mode existence somewhere nearby—which the Body of Christ in the eucharist does not.[72]

Nevertheless, Scotus insists that God can act immediately to produce both strict- and broad-sense changes in the Body of Christ primarily as it is in the eucharist.[73] To be sure, given God's necessary omnipresence, if the Body of Christ had both sacramental-mode existence on altars and natural-mode existence in heaven, it is not clear how Divinely produced changes in absolute forms would pertain to the Body of Christ primarily more as it is in one place than as it is in another. What Scotus means is that God could produce such changes in the Body of Christ even if it existed only sacramentally in the eucharist and did not have natural-mode existence anywhere. Where absolute forms are concerned, Scotus's reasoning is clear: the Body of Christ in the eucharist has all of the dispositions for receiving absolute forms that it has in heaven. So, even if the Body of Christ existed only in the eucharist, God could actualize these dispositions, and the Body of Christ could, for example, become hot primarily as it is in the eucharist.[74] Likewise, sacramental-mode existence involves whole-to-whole presence of the Body of Christ to the place where the bread accidents are. When the priest moves the host off the altar and into the hands and mouths of the faithful, God acts immediately to produce a series of new whole-to-whole presence relations in the Body of Christ, and these relational changes pertain to the Body of Christ primarily as it is in the eucharist and not as it is in heaven. Indeed, Divine power could make the Body of Christ have whole-to-whole presence relations to places where the bread accidents never exist, and so Divine power could move it to any part of the universe.[75]

Scotus denies that the priest moves the Body of Christ *per accidens* by moving the host *per se* the way the pilot moves the cargo or the ship's really inherent whiteness or naturally consequent heaviness by moving the ship.

[71] Scotus, *Op. Ox.* IV, q. 6, n. 2; Wadding VIII. 552.
[72] Scotus, *Op. Ox.* IV, d. 10, q. 6, n. 2; Wadding VIII. 552.
[73] Scotus, *Op. Ox.* IV, d. 10, q. 6, n. 2; Wadding VIII. 552; n. 6; Wadding VIII. 554.
[74] Scotus, *Op. Ox.* IV, d. 10, q. 6, n. 3; Wadding VIII. 552.
[75] Scotus, *Op. Ox.* IV, d. 10, q. 6, n. 3; Wadding VIII. 553.

Rather, the Body of Christ is sacramentally present wherever the bread accidents are extended, not by any naturally necessary concomitance, not by real inherence, not because it is itself there as extended and movable and contained in something larger that is extended and movable. Rather, it is there that way only by a free and contingent act of the Divine will. Suppose an angel voluntarily decided to be present wherever a certain stone is present. If I move the stone *per se*, *I* do not move the angel at all, because I have no power to move other incorporeal substances. The relocation of the angel is not a naturally necessary consequence of the motion of the stone, nor does the angel inhere in the stone as an accident or the other way around, nor does the stone contain it. Nor does Divine production of the series of new presence relations mean that miracles are being multipled beyond necessity. Rather they are all consequences of the original Divine policy decision to make Christ's Body really present under the post-consecration bread species as long as they last.[76]

Present but Unseen? Christ's Body has real sacramental-mode existence on the altar. But can Christ's Body be seen as it is there? That the senses *do not* perceive it is an empirical fact. Thus, Aquinas wrote, "taste and touch and vision to discern Thee fail." *Ante-mortem*, humans have no intellectual vision of it either. Rather, Aquinas continued, "faith that comes by hearing pierces through the veil!" For Scotus, whether or not the Body of Christ can be seen as it is in the eucharist is a function of two factors: whether or not the Body of Christ existing sacramentally is the kind of thing that can be seen; and what the cognitive capacities of the would-be seer are.

So far as *sensory* vision by the bodily eye is concerned, bodies are visible only in their natural-mode existence (extended in place). Thus, the Body of Christ existing sacramentally is not the kind of thing that can be the cause or the term of a sensory intuitive cognition, because each requires a body to be extended in place and relatively close by. Even if the Body of Christ existed only in the sacrament, God could cause a sensory vision of it in the eyes of glorified and non-glorified bodies. But not even God could cause sensory vision to be of the Body of Christ primarily as it is in the eucharist![77]

So far as *intellectual* vision is concerned, the Body of Christ existing sacramentally passes the visibility test. Scotus has contended—against Aquinas and others—that being is the proper object of the intellect. But sacra-

[76] Scotus, *Op. Ox.* IV, d. 10, q. 6, n. 6; Wadding VIII. 553–4.
[77] Scotus, *Op. Ox.* IV, d. 10, q. 9, n. 5; Wadding VIII. 576.

mental-mode as opposed to natural-mode existence does nothing to take away the entity and hence does not obstruct the intelligibility of Christ's Body.[78] We *ante-mortem* humans do not see Christ's Body in the eucharist with our mind's eye, because our intellects are "bound by the senses," while Christ's Body existing sacramentally is unextended and hence unable to produce sensations. But created intellects not bound by sense—angels, separate souls, beatified humans—can naturally see the Body of Christ as it is in the eucharist,[79] even if bad angels are somehow obstructed from exercising that ability.[80] Nevertheless, this is not what the blessed see by the beatific act. According to our authors, the blessed are beyond sacraments: what contributes to their happiness is not seeing Christ's Body under bread accidents, but seeing Christ's Body existing in its natural mode—first and foremost, seeing the Divine essence itself (see Chapter 12 below)![81]

[78] Scotus, *Op. Ox.* IV, d. 10, q. 8, nn. 7–8; Wadding VIII. 566.
[79] Scotus, *Op. Ox.* IV, d. 10, q. 8, n. 7; Wadding VIII. 566.
[80] Scotus, *Op. Ox.* IV, d. 10, q. 8, n. 12; Wadding VIII. 570.
[81] Scotus, *Op. Ox.* IV, d. 10, q. 8, n. 10; Wadding VIII. 570.

6

Duns Scotus on Two Types of Transubstantiation

I. Drawing the Distinction

In medieval theology, ecclesiastical pronouncements were taken as laying down what had to be *said*, while underdetermining what the statements in question might *mean*. The Nicene Creed was compatible with many philosophical formulations of the doctrine of the Trinity; the Chalcedonian definition, with competing theories of the metaphysics of the Incarnation. Scotus understands the Fourth Lateran Council to require theologians to call eucharistic conversion 'transubstantiation'.[1] Scotus subsumes his own theories under this rubric by distinguishing *productive* from *translative transubstantiation*[2] and analyzing each in turn.

The Metaphysical Possibility of Productive Transubstantiation. Scotus begins with a definition:

[1] This remark of Scotus's may be the earliest evidence we have of a medieval author's taking Fourth Lateran this way. It was and is controversial what force Fourth Lateran's pronouncement about transubstantiation was taken to have when issued. Gary Macy argues that its point was to assert real presence against the Cathars and not to dogmatize the mode of presence. Three alternatives—the coexistence theory (the substances of the bread and of the Body of Christ exist together on the altar), the annihilation theory (the substance of the bread is annihilated at the consecration), and transmutation (the substance of the bread is changed into the substance of the Body of Christ)—continued to be debated as permissible options well after 1215, although the coexistence theory was losing out by the end of the thirteenth century. Macy emphasizes that Fourth Lateran specified the word 'transubstantiation' but did not dogmatize the theory that Aquinas later defended. See Gary Macy, *Treasures from the Storeroom: Medieval Religion and the Eucharist* (Collegeville, MN: Liturgical Press, 1999), ch. 5, pp. 81–5, 137–41; *The Theologies of the Eucharist in the Early Scholastic Period: A Study of the Salvific Function of the Sacrament according to the Theologians c.1080–c.1220* (Oxford: Clarendon Press, 1984), introduction, pp. 1–8.

[2] The distinction is made fully explicit only in *Op. Ox.* IV, d. 11, q. 4, n. 15; Wadding VIII. 666–7.

[D6] productive transubstantiation is the transition of a whole substance into a whole substance.

Like his predecessors, Scotus acknowledges that 'whole' is ambiguous. It can be taken for what is integrated from parts, in which case Aristotelian generation would count as productive transubstantiation, because its terms-from-which (for example, air) and to-which (for example, fire) are complete substances. But 'whole' can also be taken to refer to each part, so that each part of the term-from-which is converted, with the result that nothing that was part of the term-from-which is found in the term-to-which.[3] Here, Scotus is interested only in the latter interpretation. Scotus further emphasizes that both terms of transubstantiation are *substances*. Whole-being conversions of accident to accident would be called "transaccidentation."[4]

Given this definition, Scotus advances two theses:

[T22] productive transubstantiation is possible;
[T23] productive transubstantiation is possible only for Divine power acting immediately.

In defense of [T22], Scotus contends that the following sequence is metaphysically possible: substance S_1 wholly ceases to exist, whereupon a wholly new substance S_2 comes to exist for the first time. Whatever can be wholly new—not only the composition of its parts, but each of the parts themselves—can come into existence when another wholly ceases to be—not only that its parts cease to be united, but also that each of them ceases to exist. When each whole is a substance, the transition counts—by [D6]—as productive transubstantiation.[5]

The further inference to [T23] is easy, because productive transubstantiation requires the whole being and non-being of each term to be within the power of any agent that effects it. But

[P17] created powers all presuppose a subject on which to act and so are powers only to transform a subject.

Divine power alone is power over the whole being and non-being of a substance.[6]

[3] Scotus, *Op. Ox.* IV, d. 11, q. 1, n. 2; Wadding VIII. 586.
[4] Scotus, *Op. Ox.* IV, d. 11, q. 1, n. 3; Wadding VIII. 586.
[5] Scotus, *Op. Ox.* IV, d. 11, q. 1, n. 4; Wadding VIII. 587.
[6] Scotus, *Op. Ox.* IV, d. 11, q. 1, n. 4; Wadding VIII. 587.

These (by now familiar) thoughts about agent-causal power lead Scotus to two further theses about the possible scope of whole-being conversions:

[T24] Deity cannot be converted into any creature,

because Divine being and non-being are not subject to Divine power. Divine power ranges only over the possible, but—according to Scotus's elaborate cosmological argument—everything intrinsic to God is necessary and the non-existence of God is metaphysically impossible.[7] Thus, Incarnation is not to be construed as whole-being conversion of the Divine Word into a human being. Rather Incarnation involves the Divine Word becoming the term of an individual human nature's real relation of essential dependence.[8]

By contrast,

[T25] it is metaphysically possible for any creature to be wholly converted into any other,

because God has power over the whole being and non-being of each and every creatable thing. Divine power can make one first exist and then not exist at all, and God can make the other exist without using any previously existing components.[9] In natural generation and corruption, there is a limit on what can come to be from what, because something of the term-from-which survives in the term-to-which (there has to be a "suitability" of their common subject), and because created natural agents can introduce new forms into matter only in a certain order and not otherwise. No natural agent can produce an elephant immediately from rotting corn. But in whole-being conversion, nothing of the term-to-which survives in the term-from-which, and Divine power is not bound by such natural

[7] Scotus, *Op. Ox.* IV, d. 11, q. 2, n. 3; Wadding VIII.597.

[8] Scotus, *Op. Ox.* III, d. 1, q. 1, n. 4; Wadding VII. 1. 7; *Op. Ox.* IV, d. 11, q. 2, n. 4; Wadding VIII. 597. See Richard Cross, *The Metaphysics of the Incarnation* (Oxford: Oxford University Press, 2002), chs. 8–10, pp. 189–229; likewise, my *Christ and Horrors: The Coherence of Christology* (Cambridge: Cambridge University Press, 2006), ch. 5, pp. 108–13, 123–38.

[9] Scotus, *Op. Ox.* IV, d. 11, q. 2, n. 3; Wadding VIII. 597; see d. 11, q. 3, nn. 16–17; Wadding VIII. 619. David Burr, in *Eucharistic Presence and Conversion in Late Thirteenth-Century Franciscan Thought* (Philadelphia: American Philosophical Society, 1984), cites Scotus's predecessor William of Ware as saying that he does not understand what others mean by 'transubstantiation', but, if it is only a function of the successive annihilation of one thing and presence of another, then it would be possible for bread to be transubstantiated into Divinity (VI. 69, 74). Ware's definition is a hybrid of Scotus's two definitions, insofar as it focuses on the being of what is converted and the presence of the term. Ockham's definition [D11] fits Ware's more than Scotus's in this respect (see Chapter 7 below).

sequences. Thus, not only can Divine power convert any body into any other;[10] Scotus wants to say that God can convert spirit into body.[11] Not only can God convert quantity into quantity (for example, of the bread into that of the Body of Christ);[12] God can convert an absolute thing (a substance, quantity, or quality) into a relative thing, together with its foundation and term. For whatever X is converted into something else Y, Y will have its own mode of existing and will be brought into being in that mode.[13]

It seems to follow directly from [T25] that the whole-being conversion of eucharistic bread into the Body of Christ is metaphysically possible. Yet, two obstacles already raised by Giles of Rome stand in the way of treating eucharistic conversion as an *actual* case of productive transubstantiation.

The Natural Concomitance Problem. Aquinas repeatedly insists that transubstantiation is whole-being substance conversion in which whole substance is converted into whole substance, matter into matter, form into form. Yet, Aquinas just as often declares that Christ's intellectual soul is present, not by the power of the sacrament, but by natural concomitance. Perhaps already in his *Sentence* commentary, but at least by the time he wrote the *Summa Theologica*, Aquinas argued that the unity of a composite substance required that there be only one actuality constituent per substance and hence that prime matter be pure potentiality and that each substance have one and only one substantial form. How then could Christ's Body be the term-to-which of Thomistic productive transubstantiation? How could Thomistic transubstantiation be a conversion in which matter is converted to matter *and* form is converted into form?

The Intellect's Consideration. Aquinas's own reply is that, even if there is no really distinct substantial form of corporeity in Christ's Body, the intellectual soul virtually contains it, in the sense that it has the power (*virtus*) to produce all of the organizing effects in the matter that the form of corporeity would produce, and more besides. Moreover, we can consider priorities and posteriorities among such effects. Relevant here, we can conceive of the intellectual soul not insofar as it is intellectual, but insofar as it is a giver of corporeal being to the matter. The term of the conversion is the matter

[10] Scotus, *Op. Ox.* IV, d. 11, q. 2, n. 8; Wadding VIII. 599.

[11] Scotus, *Op. Ox.* IV, d. 11, q. 2, n. 8; Wadding VIII. 599; see d. 11, q. 3, n. 16; Wadding VIII. 619.

[12] Scotus, *Op. Ox.* IV, d. 11, q. 2, nn. 6–7; Wadding VIII. 598.

[13] Scotus, *Op. Ox.* IV, d. 11, q. 2, n. 9; Wadding VIII. 599.

insofar as it receives corporeal being from the soul and not insofar as it receives intellectual being from it.[14]

Scotus rejects Aquinas's account. First of all, Aquinas's unitarian account allows the matter to have corporeal being only so long as the intellectual soul inheres in the matter—which it does not in the Triduum between Christ's death and resurrection. If mass were said during that period, what could the term-to-which of productive transubstantiation then be?

More fundamentally, Scotus charges, the term-to-which of eucharistic conversion must be something real insofar as it is real. But the intellectual soul as giving and matter as receiving corporeal without intellectual being are abstractions and so not real.[15]

Modes and Things. Giles tried to grapple with this problem by appealing to his distinction between things (*res*) and modes, together with his contention that a thing belonging to one category can nevertheless be caused to have the mode of another. Thus, Giles proposes, the term-to-which of productive transubstantiation is matter in its quantitative mode. The actuality of matter is caused by the inherence of the substantial form in matter. The quantitative mode of the matter is caused by the inherence of quantity in the matter. But neither the substantial nor the quantitative form is part of the term of productive transubstantiation, but only matter in its quantitative mode. Giles insists that this is enough to call it "body."

Scotus retorts that it is not enough to qualify as a *human* body, which is a mixed body with flesh and bones; nor would it be enough to call it *blood*, the term of the second consecration of the wine. Not only extension but different qualities are required if Christ's Body and Blood are to be the terms.[16]

More fundamentally, Scotus is suspicious of Giles's unAristotelian distinction between modes and things. Modes are not nothing, and they are not reified—not substantial or accidental forms. So Giles must be thinking that modes are really identical with the thing whose modes they are. Scotus counters that nothing caused by the naturally posterior can be really the same as the naturally prior. By definition, the naturally posterior really depends on the naturally prior, and *not* the other way around. What is really the same as the naturally prior does not depend on the naturally posterior

[14] Scotus, *Op. Ox.* IV, d. 11, q. 3, n. 27; Wadding VIII. 630.
[15] Scotus, *Op. Ox.* IV, d. 11, q. 3, nn. 27–8; Wadding VIII. 630–1.
[16] Scotus, *Op. Ox.* IV, d. 11, q. 3, nn. 30–1; Wadding VIII. 632.

either. But quantity is an accident and so naturally posterior to its substance subject, and—Giles says—the quantitative mode is caused by the quantity. Hence, it cannot be really the same as the matter after all.[17]

A Plurality of Substantial Forms. Scotus is in a position to sidestep the Natural Concomitance Problem, because he believes that all living corporeal things are metaphysically of matter and two substantial forms—a form of corporeity or mixed body, and a soul form. Each of these is a thing really distinct from the others: matter has an intrinsic aptitude to unite with the form of corporeity to constitute a plant or animal body, and the plant or animal body has an instrinsic aptitude to unite with the soul form to constitute a plant or animal substance that is one *per se*, a complete being made up of many partial beings.[18] When the plant or animal dies, the body that is one part (composed of prime matter and the form of corporeity) remains but does not have its soul form. Because only complete beings are in the genus substance, properly speaking, the plant or animal body *sans* soul is (as an incomplete being) in the genus of substance only by reduction.[19] Thus, whether Christ is dead or alive, the Body of Christ is prime matter plus the form of corporeity, and it would be available to be the term-to-which of a productive transubstantiation during the Triduum as well as now or during Christ's pre-crucifixion earthly career.[20]

The New-Existence Problem. Scotus's defense of [T22] focuses exclusively on cases where the term-to-which is newly extant. Even if God could have produced the Body of Christ by productive transubstantiation of eucharistic bread, that is not the way God did it. Rather, the Spirit formed the Body of Christ from materials in Mary's womb.[21] Giles bases his ingenious solution to the New-Existence Problem on three assumptions: that matter as quiddity (what we might call common matter, parallel to Scotus's common nature) is found in every hylomorphic composite; that God can act directly on matter as quiddity (common matter) prior to its individuation; and matter is individuated by the inherence of (individuated?) forms. In productive transubstantiation, the bread as a hylomorphic composite includes matter as quiddity, on which God acts directly to infuse the form of Christ's Body,

[17] Scotus, *Op. Ox*. IV, d. 11, q. 3, n. 28; Wadding VIII. 630.
[18] Scotus, *Op. Ox*. IV, d. 11, q. 3, n. 46; Wadding VIII. 649.
[19] Scotus, *Op. Ox*. III, d. 11, q. 3, n. 54; Wadding VIII. 655.
[20] Scotus, *Op. Ox*. III, d. 11, q. 3, n. 28; Wadding VIII. 630.
[21] Scotus, *Op. Ox*. IV, d. 11, q. 3, nn. 16–17; Wadding VIII. 619.

thereby converting it into numerically the same matter that Christ's Body has in heaven, and converting the whole into the Body of Christ.

Scotus rejects the basic premisses of Giles's solution. First, Scotus contends, matter as subject is naturally prior to the forms that inhere in it. But nothing is individuated—made to be the very individual thing that it is—by what is naturally posterior to it. Therefore, matter cannot be individuated by inherent forms. Neither can the naturally prior receive all of its actuality from the naturally posterior. Giles's explanation of how God can get the same matter and the same composite as existed before (for example, numerically the same air as was earlier corrupted into fire) fails.

Second, however you conceive of the subject—as common matter, as numerically the same matter, as matter of the same kind—Giles's explanation of how you get the same thing as *exists already* (how you get Christ's Body that exists in heaven to exist on the altar as well) will not work. For no subject can be caused to receive a form that it already has while it has it. If F_1 has already *come to* inhere in S_1, while F_1 continues to inhere in S_1, F_1 cannot come to inhere in S_1 again. Moreover, if F_1 inheres in S_1, F_1 cannot simultaneously come to inhere in another subject S_2. Numerically the same form cannot inhere in numerically distinct subjects simultaneously, because the form's need to depend on a subject is adequately met by one such subject. (As with efficient causality, so material causal overdetermination is impossible.)

Third, Giles thinks that God is unique in acting on matter as quiddity, because he imagines that God can act on matter prior to its individuation. Scotus insists, individuation does not make natures cease to be quiddities; otherwise—since only individuals are real—they would not perform their natural functions in the nature of things. The natural function of matter is to be the subject of substantial forms. Every natural agent that causes a substantial change acts on matter as quiddity.[22]

Translative Transubstantiation. Scotus feels the force of the New-Existence Problem, because he does not see how anything could be the term-to-which of an action in the category of action (as opposed to functional operations such as understanding and willing) without acquiring some new being thereby. Christ's Body does not acquire *esse simpliciter* as a result of any eucharistic conversion; it acquired *esse simpliciter* in Mary's womb and

[22] Scotus, *Op. Ox.* IV, d. 11, q. 3, nn. 19–20; Wadding VIII. 620–1.

keeps it ever after. If the term-to-which of productive transubstantiation must be newly extant, it is too late for Christ's Body to be its term. Scotus's happy conclusion is that eucharistic conversion is a case, not of productive but of translative transubstantiation, which involves a pair of changes:

[D7] there is a translative transubstantiation from one whole substance S_1 to another whole substance S_2, when the whole substance S_1 is first here (at *P*) and then not here (not at *P*), and the whole substance S_2 is first not here (not at *P*) and then here (at *P*).

In the eucharist, the bread undergoes a loss-change (it ceases to be on the altar) without a gain-change (it does not go elsewhere), and the Body of Christ undergoes a gain-change (it comes to be on the altar) without a loss-change (it does not cease to be in heaven). Translative transubstantiation does not require that the substance mentioned in the term-to-which be newly extant, but only that it not be already here (at *P*, the place it newly acquires).[23]

Scotus draws a further important conclusion: the claim that the bread substance is translatively transubstantiated into the Body of Christ is logically independent of whether or not the bread continues to exist when it ceases to exist on the altar and the Body of Christ comes to exist there. The loss-of-place change involved in translative transubstantiation is essentially distinct from the change involved in the bread's ceasing to exist. The terms of the former are the bread's being here and the bread's not being here; the terms of the latter are the bread's existing *simpliciter* and the bread's not existing *simpliciter*. Thus, translative transubstantiation does not bring it about that the bread ceases to exist *simpliciter*. If the bread ceases to exist concomitantly, that will have to be by a distinct change![24]

II. What Happens to the Bread?

Scotus emphasizes that the most important datum to be preserved by eucharistic theorizing is that the Body of Christ is really present where eucharistic bread is consecrated. For Scotus, this is a truth of faith that must not be compromised, and he is satisfied that his own theory of translative

[23] Scotus, *Op. Ox.* IV, d. 11, q. 4, nn. 15–16; Wadding VIII. 666–7.
[24] Scotus, *Op. Ox.* IV, d. 11, q. 4, nn. 15–16; Wadding VIII. 666–7.

transubstantiation explains how this can be so. What happens to the bread is a further question, to which—Innocent III already noted—three different answers had been given: the bread remains there together with the really present Body of Christ (the "coexistence" theory, later sometimes called "consubstantiation" because the one substance remains there *together with* the other substance); the bread does not remain and is not converted but ceases to exist, whether by annihilation or by being resolved into its matter and/or corrupted into something else; the bread is transubstantiated into the Body of Christ.[25]

The Case for Coexistence. Advocates of the coexistence theory begin with a methodological premiss. Like all philosophical and theological theories, theological formulations should aim at intelligibility. Other things being equal, when there is a theoretical choice, one should take the option that involves the fewest difficulties, that does not require positing primitives, making *ad hoc* exceptions, or undertaking radical conceptual overhauls. In theology as in physics, plurality should not be posited without necessity: no more miracles than absolutely necessary! Not only does violating this rule make for non-optimal theories. It is bad apologetics, because it makes Christian faith unattractive to those who govern their beliefs by natural reason.[26]

The philosophical advantage of coexistence over transubstantiation is that it does not have to posit accidents existing without a subject. If the bread substance is there before and after consecration, the bread accidents can continue to exist in it.[27] Multiple Location and Size problems are no greater if the bread remains, because they arise, not from the presence or absence of bread substance, but from the continuing presence of the bread quantity. Nor is the absence of bread substance salient in any of the solutions canvassed so far.

Other things might not be equal. Two further factors could make it necessary to take the bread off the altar. One would be if its presence interfered with the sacramental function, whereby the eucharist signifies the really present Body of Christ. Adherents of coexistence insist, on the contrary, that the bread substance with its accidents makes an even better

[25] Scotus, *Op. Ox.* IV, d. 11, q. 3, n. 3; Wadding VIII. 605.
[26] Scotus, *Op. Ox.* IV, d. 11, q. 3, nn. 3–4; Wadding VIII. 605–6.
[27] Scotus, *Op. Ox.* IV, d. 11, q. 3, n. 3; Wadding VIII. 605.

sign than the accidents alone of the spiritual nourishment furnished by the really present Body of Christ (see Chapter 11 below).[28]

The other factor is ecclesial authority: the explicit pronouncements of the Scriptures or the Church and/or evident inferences from them furnish further data that the theologian's formulation must hold fixed. Here again, adherents claim that coexistence enjoys a positive advantage, because it seems to be required by evident inference from explicit statements in John 6: 51 ("I am the living bread that came down from heaven. Whoever eats this bread . . . ") and 1 Corinthians 10: 16 ("the bread which we break, is it not a sharing of the Body of Christ?"). Fraction and reception occur after the consecration; for bread to be broken and eaten after the words of institution, it must still be there![29]

Aquinas's Attack on the First Two Theories. Up through Albert the Great, coexistence was treated as a tolerable and tolerated if also dwindling minority report.[30] Aquinas contends, on the contrary, that coexistence is problematic, impossible, and heretical. *Sacramental Function.* Contrary to what adherents say, the continued presence of the bread would compromise sacramental function. First, still-present bread would turn eucharistic veneration into the idolatry of bread worship. Second, the sacrament of the altar should have the really present Body of Christ as its first significatum. But accidents naturally signify their substance. If the bread substance remained, it would be the first significatum instead. Third, still-present bread would turn the sacrament into bodily and not spiritual food.[31] One practical result would be that a priest could not celebrate two masses the same day without violating the fasting regulations (see Chapter 11 below).

Heresy. Worse still, Aquinas maintains, coexistence is heretical because it contradicts explicit words of Scripture. In Matthew 26: 26, Jesus institutes the sacrament with the words "this is My Body!" ("hoc est corpus meum"), But this would be grammatically incorrect if the bread were still present. Jesus would have instead said, "Here is My Body!" ("hic est corpus meum").[32]

[28] Scotus, *Op. Ox.* IV, d. 11, q. 3, n. 3; Wadding VIII. 605.
[29] Scotus, *Op. Ox* IV, d. 11, q. 3, n. 5; Wadding VIII. 606.
[30] See Burr, *Eucharistic Presence and Conversion*, I. 2, and Macy, *Treasures from the Storeroom*, ch. 5, p. 83.
[31] Scotus, *Op. Ox.* IV, d. 11, q. 3, n. 7; Wadding VIII. 607.
[32] Scotus, *Op. Ox.* IV, d. 11, q.3, n. 8; Wadding VIII. 607.

Philosophical Failure. Moreover, coexistence is theoretically inadequate, because—Aquinas argues—it cannot account for how the Body of Christ comes to be really present on the altars where mass is said. Aquinas has contended that Thomistic transubstantiation is the only way for the Body of Christ to acquire these additional locations, and what is converted does not remain.

Alternative Bread Removals. Aquinas also rejects the second option cited by Innocent III: that the bread is annihilated or resolved into its matter or corrupted into the elements. Bread is not annihilated because nothing (*purum nihil*) is the term of annihilation, while the term of Thomistic transubstantiation is something positive—namely, the Body of Christ. Bread is not resolved into bare matter, because bare matter is pure potentiality and cannot actually exist without forms. Bread is not corrupted into some new body, because either that body would exist together with the species and the Body of Christ or it would be observed to move elsewhere—both of which Aquinas rejects.[33]

Scotus's Dismissal of Aquinas's Arguments. In Scotus's judgment, none of these arguments constitutes an effective attack on the coexistence theory. *Sacramental Function*. So far as sacramental function goes, Scotus declares, the presence of the bread would do no more to make eucharistic veneration idolatrous than the undisputed presence of the accidents does. Either way, one is bowing down in a direction where mere creatures are located. Either way, one is not venerating the mere creatures but the really present Body of Christ signified by them.[34]

As for sacramental signification, Scotus makes two points. First, accidents do *naturally* signify their substances, willy nilly, but what they naturally signify is not the actual existence of such substances but their own natural aptitude to depend on them (see Chapter 9 below). Second, Scotus observes, what is at stake in the sacraments is not *natural* signification but the Divinely instituted *conventional* signification by which a sensible sign signifies the really present Body of Christ (see Chapter 1 above). The Body of Christ is the first *conventional* significatum of the bread accidents, and would be so whether or not the bread remains; just as the bread substance is their first *natural* significatum, whether or not the bread substance remains and whether or not the Body of Christ comes to be really present.

[33] Scotus, *Op. Ox.* IV, d. 11, q. 3, n. 8; Wadding VIII. 607–8.
[34] Scotus, *Op. Ox.* IV, d. 11, q. 3, n. 9; Wadding VIII. 608.

As for fasting, the continued presence of the bread substance would not give rise to a new difficulty, because experience shows that the host nourishes (see Chapter 11 below). In any event, it is not impossible for bodily food and spiritual food to be received together.[35]

Contradiction of Scripture? Likewise, Scotus finds Aquinas's grammatical argument unconvincing: Christ might have used *hoc* rather than *hic* even if the bread were still present to indicate that He was not referring to the bread substance but to what was contained under the bread.[36]

Whose Philosophical Inadequacy? So far as getting the Body of Christ on the altar is concerned, Scotus has argued, it is neither Thomistic nor productive transubstantiation but rather translative transubstantiation that is required (see Chapter 5 above). Turning to the second theory mentioned by Innocent III, Scotus denies any insuperable philosophical problems in the bread's being reduced to matter or being corrupted into something else that exists with the Body of Christ under the species or moves elsewhere. For Scotus, matter has to have an actuality of its own, naturally prior to receiving substantial forms, and so—by Divine power—could exist naked. Multiple location problems are no worse because equally solvable if other bodies besides the Body of Christ are also present, whether naturally or sacramentally.[37]

Discontinued Bread. For his own part, Scotus concedes the methodological principles sponsored by adherents of the coexistence theory. Scotus also agrees that coexistence is philosophically coherent, indeed less philosophically problematic than denying the continued existence of the bread. Scotus acknowledges that it was possible for God to institute the sacrament so that the Body of Christ came to be really present while the substance of the bread remained.[38] Scotus finds nothing to the contrary explicit in Scripture nor the evident inferences from it. Nevertheless, Scotus concludes that this is not what God in fact instituted, but rather that the Body of Christ is present under the accidents alone. The reason it is necessary to hold that the bread ceases to exist is that this is evident in the declarations of the Fourth Lateran Council. And the only reason that the Church would teach a philosophically more problematic theory is that it is true![39]

[35] Scotus, *Op. Ox.* IV, d. 11, q. 3, nn. 9–10; Wadding VIII. 608.
[36] Scotus, *Op. Ox.* IV, d. 11, q. 3, nn. 9–10; Wadding VIII. 609.
[37] Scotus, *Op. Ox.* IV, d. 11, q. 3, n. 12; Wadding VIII. 609.
[38] Scotus, *Op. Ox.* IV, d. 11, q. 3, n. 14; Wadding VIII. 618.
[39] Scotus, *Op. Ox.* IV, d. 11, q. 3, n. 15; Wadding VIII. 619.

Why not Annihilation? Scotus thinks the Holy Roman Church's decision in favor of transubstantiation (the third theoretical option on Innocent III's list) also explains majority-report insistence that, while the bread does not remain (contrary to the first, coexistence option), it is neither annihilated nor resolved into naked matter of the elements (contrary to the second options). Aquinas deals with annihilation the short way, by noting that productive transubstantiation has a positive term. But, by design, the terms of both Thomistic and productive transubstantiation are "disparate" in the sense of having no metaphysical constituent in common. How does the positive entity of the Body of Christ keep the bread from having been annihilated when—at the end of either Thomistic or productive transubstantiation—there is nothing left of the bread at all?

Henry of Ghent charged that the only way to justify denying that eucharistic bread is annihilated would be to say that something of it survived in the term-to-which transubstantiation is made. This makes no sense to Scotus, because nothing of the bread existed in the Body of Christ before transubstantiation, and the only changes in the Body of Christ due to transubstantiation are changes in external relations to place.[40]

Giles of Rome has tried to make Thomistic transubstantiation more intelligible by making it more like generation and corruption: namely, by insisting that matter as quiddity (common matter) is found in both terms. Thus, the bread is not annihilated because it continues to exist in the potency of the matter. God could convert the Body of Christ back into the bread![41] Scotus recalls how—on Giles's theory—any material thing includes the common core that makes it convertible into any other material thing by Divine power. If this sort of existence in the potency of matter is enough to avoid annihilation, God will not be able to annihilate one material thing without annihilating the whole material universe at the same time.[42]

For Scotus, the real lesson to be learned from the claim that the terms of transubstantiation do not include the non-existence of the bread is that (as above) two essentially distinct but concomitant changes are involved. Scotus thinks authority does require that the bread ceases to exist and so does demand a rejection of the coexistence theory. Scotus is willing to call

[40] Scotus, *Op. Ox.* IV, d. 11, q. 4, n. 3; Wadding VIII. 658.
[41] Scotus, *Op. Ox.* IV, d. 11, q. 4, n. 5; Wadding VIII. 659.
[42] Scotus, *Op. Ox.* IV, d. 11, q. 4, n. 5; Wadding VIII. 659.

that change annihilation, because its term-from-which is the bread existing *simpliciter* and its term-to-which is the bread not existing *simpliciter.* By free and contingent Divine volition, this change is concomitant with translative transubstantiation, in which the Body of Christ acquires presence on the altar and the bread loses presence on the altar. Thus, the eucharistic bread is annihilated, but it is not annihilated by the eucharistic conversion of translative transubstantiation.[43]

A Terminological Note. Thomistic transubstantiation is not to be identiified with either Scotistic productive transubstantiaion or Scotistic translative transubstantiation. Scotistic productive transubstantiation involves the existence of one substance followed by its annihilation and the concomitant creation of another. Scotistic translative transubstantiation involves the concomitant presence-then-absence of one substance and absence-then-presence of another. Thomistic transubstantiation purports to be a single change of a special kind, not resolvable into two changes such as the annihilation of one substance and the creation of another. Rather Aquinas holds that turning one whole into another whole is the only way to effect a place-gain for the Body of Christ, which remains in heaven. Scotus holds that the change in external relations involved in his translative transubstantiation is sufficient for that. Scotistic productive transubstantiation is not involved in the sacrament of the altar because (what he is willing to call) the annihilation of the bread is not accompanied by the creation of the Body of Christ. Commentators sometimes mark this difference between Aquinas and Scotus by saying that, while Aquinas believes in a real change of one substance into another, Scotus embraces a "substitution" theory (the Body of Christ is substituted for the bread). What they find historically noteworthy is that Fourth Lateran's language was taken by thirteenth-century authors to rule out the coexistence theory while remaining elastic enough to cover Thomistic transubstantiation and substitution theories alike.[44]

[43] Scotus, *Op. Ox.* IV, d. 11, q. 4, nn. 14–15; Wadding VIII. 666–7.

[44] See Macy, *Treasures from the Storeroom*, ch.5, pp. 81–104, esp. 89–90, 104–5. See also Burr, *Eucharistic Presence and Conversion*, who finds in Scotus's predecessors many thinkers—Richard Middleton (VI. 61, 64), William de la Mare (V. 36), Matthew of Aquasparta (V. 38–9), Peter Olivi (V. 47), William Peter de Falgar (V. 59), and William of Ware (VI. 71)—who reject Thomas's verdict, reasoning that whatever Divine omnipotence does with the aid of creatures, Divine omnipotence could do all by itself. It does not need Thomistic transubstantiation—whole-being conversion—that converts one created substance into another; Divine power can act alone to cause a place-gain for the Body of Christ.

7

Remodelling With Ockham

I. Deconstructing Aquinas's Picture

Ockham declares that, when it comes to accounting for the real presence of Christ's Body in the eucharist, everything depends on quantity![1] Certainly, Aquinas identified quantity as the heart of the multiple location problems and their solution. Aquinas's own view of material substances and their quantities is distinctive. Substance of itself is neither divided nor divisible; rather substance nature exists in the individual substance, whole in the whole and whole in each part. By contrast, quantity of itself is divisible and divided. Moreover, quantity is immediately present to and commensurate with the surrounding place, whole to whole and part to part. Substance has no immediate relation to place, but exists in place properly speaking through its own inherent dimensive quantity.[2] Dimensive quantity is also the immediate subject of the bodily qualities, which are also related to place through the quantity in which they inhere. Ockham agrees that, in the natural order of things, material substances are hylomorphic composites that are located in place. Otherwise he rejects virtually every aspect of Aquinas's picture, not least the notion that quantity is "a skin" between material substance and its qualities,[3] and reconceives their metaphysical structure from the ground up.

Ockham begins with matter. Aquinas insists that matter of itself is pure potentiality with no actuality of its own, and that matter receives actuality and its individuation from form. Ockham follows Scotus in denying both claims. The functional role of matter is to be the subject of forms, and to be

[1] Ockham, *Quaest. in IV Sent.*, q. 6; OTh VII. 72–3.
[2] Ockham, *Quaest. in IV Sent.*, q. 6; OTh VII. 81–2.
[3] Ockham, *Quodlibeta* IV, q. 31; OTh IX. 454–5.

the persistent subject that is transformed in substantial change. Both Scotus and Ockham insist that subjects are naturally prior to the forms that they receive and hence must be actual and individual prior to receiving them. What is true of the whole matter of a thing is likewise true of its parts. Moreover, Scotus and Ockham agree,

[P18] distinction and otherness are predicated of something only with respect to what primarily pertains to it.[4]

If X is the same as Y or distinct from Z, X is so through itself and not through anything really distinct from X. Aquinas and Giles are wrong to think that matter gets its individuation from really distinct inherent forms. Ockham contends that they are also wrong to think the parts of matter get their identity as parts (as this part distinct from that) from really distinct inherent quantity. Rather

[T26] material substance and its essential parts prime matter and substantial form are *divided into integral parts of themselves.*

For Ockham, this is a fundamental difference between material substances and incorporeal substances (such as an angel or the intellectual soul).

Ockham's next step is to argue that in the normal and natural case

[T27] the integral parts of material substance and its essential parts prime matter and substantial form are *at a distance from one another in place.*

The idea that material substance and its essential parts exist whole in the whole and whole in the parts of substance individuals may have appeal so long as one thinks that substance remains indivisible and undivided in substance individuals. Once it is conceded [T26] that material substance, its matter and its form, essentially have integral parts, it becomes implausible to say that these are not normally and naturally distributed in place. Ockham charges that this would undermine the contrast between material and incorporeal substances. If material substance and its essential parts were whole in the whole and whole in the parts of the individual substance, material substance and its essential parts would themselves be no more extended than the intellectual soul. On Aquinas's view, neither is extended of itself, and each has a real union to something else that is extended of itself

[4] See my *William Ockham* (Notre Dame: University of Notre Dame Press, 1987), ch. 2, pp. 13–69.

(material substance to its inherent quantity, and the intellectual soul to the body and indirectly to the quantity of the body whose substantial form it is).[5]

To help further dislodge Thomistic intuitions, Ockham forwards some cases. *Case 1.* Take a log A and divide it into two halves B and C. Place the now divided B and C a foot apart. After the division the substance of B is at a distance from the substance of C. Yet, Ockham observes, nothing new was generated in the division of A into B and C; no more wood is there after than before the division. Surely, the integral parts of A had different locations from one another before the division as well. *Case 2.* The whiteness that exists in the wood is extended. But—Ockham insists—if the subject and the inherent form each has parts, inherence requires a proper proportion between them. Therefore, the subject in which the whiteness exists must be extended. Trying to hold substance unextended by making quantity the proximate subject of the whiteness will not work, because it will be necessary to identify a subject for the quantity. Either there will be an infinite process in subjects, or the substance subject will itself turn out to be extended, whole in the whole place and parts in the parts.[6]

Aquinas held that the relation of material substance to place had to be mediated, in the normal and natural case, by its own dimensive quantity. Ockham counters,

[T28] the integral parts of material substance and its essential parts prime matter and substantial form are *related to place immediately*.

First, presence is naturally prior to inherence. Aquinas has to admit this because he says that in the eucharist the substance of the Body of Christ is related by presence without inherence to the quantity of the bread. Inherence-as-in-a-proximate-subject is not a transitive relation. For Aquinas, qualities inhere in quantity as in a proximate subject, and quantity in substance. What follows is that qualities inhere in substance, not as a proximate, but as a remote subject. By contrast, Ockham contends, immediate presence is a transitive relation.

[P19] When two are present and not spatially at a distance, whatever is immediately present to one of them is immediately present to the other.

[5] Ockham, *Quodlibeta* IV, q. 19; OTh IX. 397.
[6] Ockham, *Quodlibeta* IV, q. 19; OTh IX. 396–7.

Aquinas holds that the quantity and place are immediately present to and not at a distance from one another, whole to whole and part to part. But by [T27], if quantity is "a skin" between substance and qualities, substance and quantity will also be immediately present to one another, whole to whole and part to part. By [P19], it follows [T28] that substance will be immediately present to place through its own intrinsic parts.[7]

Holding that quantity is a thing (*res*) really distinct from substance and quality, Aquinas exploits the consequence that quantity and substance will be really distinct foundations of distinct presence relations. Thus, he says that in the eucharist the substance but not the quantity of Christ's Body is immediately present to the quantity of the bread, and that the quantity of the bread is immediately present to place when the substance of the bread and the substance of Christ's Body are not. Ockham reasons, even in the normal and natural case, substance and quantity will be really distinct foundations for presence relations. Since substance is naturally prior to quantity, the presence relation of substance to place should be naturally prior to and hence unmediated by the presence relation of quantity to place as well.[8]

Again, Aquinas admits that the substance of Christ's Body is immediately present to an alien quantity (the quantity of the bread) that does not inform it. Ockham agrees that it should be no more incompatible with matter to coexist immediately with an external quantity than with any putative "skin" quantity that informs it. But—by [T26] and [T27]—if there is a really distinct "skin" quantity, material substance, its matter and form, will have to be present to it whole to whole and part to part. Since substance is naturally prior to accident, Divine power will be able to destroy the "skin" quantity while preserving the substance immediately present to the external quantity—in which case substance would be extended in place immediately, whole in the whole and part in each part, without any mediation by quantity.[9]

Again, everyone agrees that an incorporeal substance (for example, an angel) can be present, whole in the whole and whole in each part of a divisible place. Moreover, consensus has it that an angel's presence to place does not require the mediation of any inherent absolute accident to serve as

[7] Ockham, *Quodlibeta* IV, q. 20; OTh IX. 399–400.
[8] Ockham, *Quaest. in IV Sent.*, q. 6; OTh VII.76. See *Quodlibeta* IV, q.23; OTh IX. 411–12.
[9] Ockham, *Quaest. in IV Sent.*, q. 6; OTh VII. 77.

the foundation of the presence relations. Why, then, should material substance, it prime matter and substantial form, require inherent quantity to serve as the foundation of their presence relations to place, given that—by [T26] and [T27]—inherent quantity is not needed to divide them or extend them? Here we are at the heart of Ockham's critique. If not-[T26] material substance and its essential parts had no integral parts (as Aquinas implies), then any whole-to-whole, part-to-part presence to place would have to be mediated by real union with something (pre-eminently quantity) that has parts susceptible of such commensuration. But, even if quantity is the formal cause of material substance and its essential parts having a quantitative mode (as Giles says), the parts of matter will be really distinct from the parts of quantity (as Giles also emphasizes) and hence really distinct foundations for presence relations. No further mediation by quantity would be needed to relate the parts of matter to the parts of place.[10]

Quantity's putative role in mediating the relation of material substance to place is reflected in Aquinas's definitions of *circumscriptive versus definitive placement*: a body is circumscriptively in a place when its figure is circumscribed by the figure of the place, while something to be definitively in a place is for it to be in the place and for the place to be somehow commensurate with its quantity (in the case of material things) or power (in the case of incorporeal things). Likewise, Giles defines them in terms of the commensuration of the body's quantity with the quantity of the place, so that a body is definitively in place when its quantity is commensurate with the quantity of that place alone, and it is circumscriptively in place when the commensuration is whole to whole, part to part. Ockham's nominal definitions echo Scotus's.

[D8] For something to be in place circumscriptively is for it to be whole in the whole place and part in part of the place.

[D9] For something to be in place definitively is for the whole to be in the whole place and whole in each part of place.

Absent from [D8] and [D9] are any explicit mentions of quantity. Indeed, Ockham's paradigms of definitive location are quantity-free incorporeal substances: angels are definitively in place and the intellectual soul is definitively in the body it perfects. Whether definitive or circumscriptive, such relations between a substance and a place are immediate, not brokered by

[10] Ockham, *Quaest. in IV Sent.*, q. 6; OTh VII. 76–7.

inherent accidents. Any really distinct accidents will be the foundations of their own relations to place. Likewise significant is the fact that [D9] drops out any implication that what is definitively in a place is confined to that place and hence does not exist in many places at once.[11]

Putting his own version of the circumscriptive/definitive distinction together with theses [T26]–[T28], Ockham represents his conclusion:

[T29] material substance, extended through its own intrinsic parts, is immediately in place circumscriptively and not definitively.[12]

On Ockham's definitions, Aquinas has in effect held that that material substance is itself definitively in place, while quantity is by nature circumscriptively in place. Ockham has contended that, if there were such a really distinct "skin" quantity, it would make no explanatory contribution to material substance's being circumscriptively in place. The presence of material substance and its integral parts to place will be numerically distinct from and logically independent of their presence to any putative "skin" quantity and its parts.

Against the protest—if material substance were stripped of all of its absolute accidents, it would be definitively in place like an angel—Ockham mounts a clever proof that

[C1] anything divided into intrinsic parts that exists in place definitively also exists in place circumscriptively.

Suppose that some material thing A has intrinsic parts B, C, and D; that some place P is divided into parts P1, P2, and P3; and that A exists in P definitively. It follows by [D9] that B, C, and D all exist in P1; that B, C, and D all exist in P2; and that B, C, and D all exist in P3. From the latter it follows that B exists in P1 and C exists in P2 and D exists in P3 and hence that A exists in P whole in the whole and part in each part—which by [D8] is what it means to say that A exists in place circumscriptively![13] This argument brings out a further feature of Ockham's nominal definitions in [D8] and [D9]: the only difference between definitive and circumscriptive placement is that the latter involves fewer parts in each part of place than the former.

11 Ockham, *Quodlibeta* IV, q. 21; OTh IX. 400–1.
12 Ockham, *Quodlibeta* IV, q. 21; OTh IX. 401.
13 Ockham, *Quodlibeta* IV, q. 23; OTh IX. 409.

Ockham's remodel of material substance is not quite complete, however. To prepare his next step, Ockham proposes another nominal definition:

[D10] For something to be quantified is for it to have part outside part and part situationally distant from part,

and then infers three conclusions:

[C2] whatever is *per se* one thing and is truly extended is truly and really quantified;
[C3] whatever is in place circumscriptively is quantified, because every such is whole in the whole and part in the part;
[C4] whatever is quantified is in place circumscriptively, if a place surrounds it.

Drawing these together, Ockham makes a further consequence explicit:

[T30] material substance, its essential parts matter and form, can be *quantified through their own intrinsic parts.*[14]

Really distinct "skin" quantity does not explain material substance's division into parts (by [T26]), nor their extension (by [T27]), nor their presence to place (by [T28]), and hence not their quantification (by [T29] and [T30]). Quantity as a thing really distinct from substance and quality is at best an explanatory fifth wheel.

Elsewhere and repeatedly, Ockham mounts a whole arsenal of arguments to show that the hypothesis of quantity as a really distinct thing from substance and quality is physically problematic and metaphysically incoherent.[15] Key among his contentions is that the required commensurations between a really distinct quantity accident and its material subject will—given [T26]–[T28]—be impossible to secure. Ockham concludes that 'quantity' is itself a connotative term that signifies substance and quality directly and connotes parts at a distance from one another among which there can be locomotion (distinct in place and situation).[16] It follows that

[T31] any material thing that exists circumscriptively in place is a quantity.

When Socrates sits, his substance, his prime matter and his substantial forms of corporeity and sensory soul, his sensible qualities and organic dispositions

[14] Ockham, *Quodlibeta* IV, q. 23; OTh IX. 407.
[15] Ockham excuses himself from rehearsing them yet again in *Quodlibeta* IV, q. 34; OTh IX. 466.
[16] Ockham, *Quodlibeta* VII, q. 19; OTh IX, 780–2. See *Quaest. in IV Sent.*, q. 6; OTh VII. 84.

are each and all quantities. To the objection that then—in the normal and natural course of things—many quantities would exist in the same place simultaneously, Ockham replies that cases such as sedentery Socrates pose no difficulty, because his prime matter and substantial forms are really united in his substance, which is one *per se*, while his qualities make a *per accidens* unity with him.[17]

II. Further Placement Corollaries

Ockham's remodel of material substance sidelines contrasts between *per se* and *per accidens* location in favor of a focus on circumscriptive location (whose paradigms are normally and naturally material substances and their corporeal qualities) and definitive location (whose paradigms are angels and the intellectual soul). In Ockham's hands, these definitions and cases combine with other givens from authority, to yield further startling conclusions.

The first appeals to medieval readings of Gospel stories of the virgin birth (in which baby Jesus passes through Mary's membranes without breaking them), of Christ's post-resurrection passage through closed doors and of His ascension through unriven heavens. Theological consensus concluded that

[not-T5] many whole bodies can exist circumscriptively in the same place at the same time.

Christ's body, Mary's membrane, the locked doors, and the celestial spheres were all extended bodies, existing in place whole in the whole and part in the part. Thus, we have it from a primary authority that

[T5] two bodies cannot be extended in the same place at once,

admits of exceptions.[18]

Moreover, Ockham declares, "the truth of philosophy and theology" should lead us to the converse conclusion:

[not-T6] the same whole body can exist in many places at once,

[17] Ockham, *Quaest. in IV Sent.*, q. 6; OTh VII. 87.
[18] Ockham, *Quodlibeta* IV, q. 31; OTh IX. 453.

contrary to

[T6] a single body cannot be extended in, or move toward, two distinct places at once.

Ockham argues from analogy. Suppose that A is an incorporeal substance; that P is a place divided into parts P1, P2, P3; and that A exists in P definitively. By [D9] it follows that one and the same indivisible substance A exists whole in P1, whole in P2, and whole in P3—and so exists whole in distinct places simultaneously. Why should the fact that corporeal substances have intrinsic parts be an obstacle to a single body's existing in many places at once?[19]

Next, Ockham refocuses from whole bodies onto parts and defends

[Cor 3] material substance, its essential parts and corporeal qualities, can exist in place definitively.

Evidently assuming that it ought to be harder for an indivisible substance to be whole in distinct places than for a divisible one, Ockham reasons from analogy: why—if an intrinsically indivisible substance can exist whole in many places—could not an intrinsically divisible and divided substance exist whole in the whole and whole in each part?[20] Again, beginning more evidently with [Cor 3], Ockham reasons that, if many distinct whole bodies can exist in the same place at once, why could not many parts of the same body exist in the same place at once—which is all that definitive location requires?[21] Happily, we do not even need to appeal to authority, because condensation gives us a case from nature in which multiple parts of the same body—parts that used to coexist with different parts of place—come to exist at the same place. If multiple parts can naturally exist in the same place simultaneously, why would it not be metaphysically possible—and achievable by Divine power—for all of a body's parts to do so?[22]

In the face of [Cor 3], Ockham happily bites some bullets. Material substance, its essential parts, matter and form, existing definitively in place would still be divided into parts. By [T26], they are so intrinsically. But—except insofar as definitive placement implies circumscriptive placement, as above—they would not be extended (in the sense of having only one, or in

[19] Ockham, *Quaest. in IV Sent.*, q. 6; OTh VII. 79; *Quodlibeta* IV, q. 31; OTh IX. 453.
[20] Ockham, *Quodlibeta* IV, q. 31; OTh IX. 451.
[21] Ockham, *Quaest. in IV Sent.*, q. 6; OTh IX. 79–81; *Quodlibeta* IV, q. 31; OTh IX. 453.
[22] Ockham, *Quaest. in IV Sent.*, q. 6; OTh IX. 79; *Quodlibeta* IV, q. 31; OTh IX. 452.

the case of condensation a few parts per place and not all of their parts in all of the parts of place) or figured or have categorial position (sitting, standing etc.).[23] Moreover,

[Cor 4] although it is essential to material substance, to matter, substantial form, and corporeal qualities to be divided into intrinsic parts, it is not essential to them that their parts be distinct in place and situation.[24]

In the normal and natural case they do. But because [Cor 3] their definitive placement by Divine power is metaphysically possible, they do not have to. Ockham goes so far as to declare that it is metaphysically possible for any creatable thing to exist in place definitively. If quantities were things (*res*) really distinct from substance and quality, they could—by Divine power—exist definitively in place, too. Really distinct quantities could not even explain their own quantification![25]

Ockham's [D9] combines with his Aristotelian belief in material continuity to yield the conclusion that

[Cor 5] anything that exists definitively in place, exists definitively in many places.

for, if A exists definitively in place P, which has parts P1, P2, and P3, then each of P1, P2, and P3 is divisible into parts, so that what exists whole in them also exists whole in their parts and so definitively in at least three places. Ockham's feistiness shows itself again when he infers that

[Cor 6] multiple circumscriptive locations of corporeal things should be easier to produce than multiple definitive locations, because circumscriptive location involves fewer parts in each place than definitive location does.[26]

[Cor 5] and [Cor 6] imply that

[Cor 7] it is metaphysically possible for a material substance, its essential parts, and qualities to exist circumscriptively in one or more places and definitively in one or more places at one and the same time,

which is an important consequence of eucharistic theology.

Ockham's remodel of material substance and its placement also excludes the use Giles and Scotus make of the distinction between quantitative and

[23] Ockham, *Quaest. in IV Sent.*, q. 6; OTh VII. 89.
[24] Ockham, *Quaest. in IV Sent.*, q. 6; OTh VII. 81, 87, 97–8.
[25] Ockham, *Quaest. in IV Sent.*, q. 6; OTh VII. 107–8.
[26] Ockham, *Quaest. in IV Sent.*, q. 6; OTh VII. 97–8.

categorial position. According to them, a body has quantitative position when it is quantified and its parts are ordered to one another and to the whole. Ockham reasons that the only sort of order this could be would be one in which different parts are different distances from one another (the head further from the ankle than from the neck, and so on) with different shapes and sizes from one another. Ockham agrees that it is metaphysically possible for a body with quantitative position to exist without any relation to place, because Divine power could create a body with quantitative position outside the universe and so without any surrounding place to be related to. But Giles and Scotus move from the case where the body has no relation to place because there is no place to be related to, to a case where the body as a whole is related to place but the parts of the body are allegedly not related to place. Ockham protests that this is just as contradictory as two whites existing without being similar. If the whole body is extended, with parts at different distances from one another by virtue of its quantitative position, and the whole body is present to the whole place, the parts cannot help being present to the parts of place—with the result that the body has categorial position, too.[27]

III. Christ in the Sacrament of the Altar

It follows from Ockham's analysis of material things and their placement that it is metaphysically possible for the Body of Christ at one and the same time to exist circumscriptively in heaven and definitively or circumscriptively on multiple altars where mass is said. Divine power could bring this about whether or not anything else were on the altar, whether or not anything else on the altar were simultaneously converted or ceased to exist, and whether or not anything else on the altar—substance or accident—simultaneously existed in the same place. Confronting Aquinas's worry that

> [P2] there is no passage from contradictory to contradictory—a proposition cannot be first true (false) and then its contradictory opposite be true (false)—without any change,

[27] Ockham, *Quaest. in IV Sent.*, q. 6; OTh VII. 67–8, 70; *Quodlibeta* IV, q. 18; OTh IX. 389–93.

and objectors who think [P2] requires that some thing or things (*res*) come into being or cease to exist *simpliciter* (whether naturally by generation and corruption, or supranaturally by creation, annihilation, or Thomistic whole-being conversion), Ockham replies that there are other kinds of change: namely, the actual or potential passage of time and locomotion. Sometimes there is a passage from contradictory to contradictory because of the actual passage of time (as when a law declares old forms of paper money valid through a certain date and not afterwards). For Aristotle, time is the number of motion (the number of rotations of the sun around the earth that something is simultaneous with) and so does not actually exist without the uniform motion of the heavens. But 'God creates X' is true only at the very beginning of X's existence, after which 'God created X' and 'God conserves X' are true instead. Ockham declares, if God created an angel in a world without uniformly moving bodies, 'God creates the angel' would be first true and then false because of the potential passage of time. More important for eucharistic theology, 'X is proximate to Y' can be first true and then false merely because X or Y changes place. If material substance, its essential parts matter and substantial form, are first extended and then not extended by Divine power, this happens through locomotion.[28] Likewise, when Christ's Body first is not and then is really present on the altar by Divine power, it is broad-sense locomotion (a gain-change of place) that is involved. This is a real and immediate change in Christ's Body.[29]

Divine power can and does act to place Christ's Body on the altar (to whatever extent and in whatever sense creatures function as instrumental or *sine quibus non* causes; see Chapter 3 above). In Ockham's judgment, many theological proposals about the circumstances in which God does this are metaphysically possible. Because multiple location is no problem, God could preserve the bread substance, while making Christ's Body coexist with it (sometimes called "consubstantiation").[30] So far as natural reason can prove, God could make the Body of Christ assume the bread the way the Divine Word assumes the human nature. "Impanation" is metaphysically possible by Divine power (see Chapter 11).[31] Nor would it be impossible for God to make the Body of Christ exist under the host and at the same

[28] Ockham, *Quaest. in IV Sent.*, q. 6; OTh VII. 81, 86–7.
[29] Ockham, *Quaest. in IV Sent.*, q. 8; OTh VII. 145–6; *Quodlibeta* VI, q. 3; OTh IX. 593–4.
[30] Ockham, *Quaest. in IV Sent.*, q. 8; OTh VII. 137–9.
[31] Ockham, *Quaest. in IV Sent.*, q. 8; OTh VII. 138.

time make the bread substance suddenly exist elsewhere, while preserving the bread accidents in their original position. Because prime matter has an actuality of its own, it would be possible for God instead to destroy the substantial form of bread while preserving its matter, or to reduce the bread to the elements while preserving them in the same or in a different place. Alternatively, God could reduce the bread substance to nothing.[32]

Ockham agrees with Scotus that the coexistence theory is philosophically the least problematic, especially because it avoids the difficulties involved in positing accidents without a subject (see Chapter 9 below). Aquinas to the contrary notwithstanding, neither reason, the Bible, nor the determinations of the saints force an endorsement of transubstantiation. It must be upheld only because Innocent III's council and other decretals pronounce in favor of it.[33] Miracles should not be multiplied without necessity. But sometimes in the soteriological realm, it pleases God to violate Ockham's Razor![34] The nominal definition Ockham offers in his *Sentence* commentary merely conjoins the items theological consensus had settled upon.

[D11] transubstantiation is the succession of substance to substance (of S_2 to S_1) where S_1 ceases to exist in itself and S_2 comes to exist under S_1's accidents.

Ockham declares that transubstantiation is metaphysically possible because each of its components is metaphysically possible (and evidently they are possible together): Divine power can destroy a substance S_1 in itself, Divine power can conserve the accidents without the substance, and Divine power can cause another substance S_2 to exist in the same place as S_1's accidents without S_1's accidents' informing S_2.[35]

Note: Ockham' nominal definition puts together what Scotus's [D6] and [D7] split apart: S_1's ceasing to exist and the concomitant presence-then-absence of S_1 and absence-then-presence of S_2 under S_1's accidents. But Ockham's is only a nominal definition. He is not disagreeing with Scotus about the physics or metaphysics involved. Ockhamist transubstantiation also resolves into a plurality of distinct changes.

[32] Ockham, *Quaest. in IV Sent.*, q. 8; OTh VII. 138.

[33] Ockham, *Quaest. in IV Sent.*, q. 8; OTh VII. 138–40; *Quodlibeta* IV, q. 29; OTh IX. 446–7; *Tractatus de Corpore Christi*, c. 6; OTh X. 99–101. For a survey of philosophical appeals to the relevant decretals, see Gary Macy, *Treasures from the Storeroom: Medieval Religion and the Eucharist* (Collegeville, MN: Liturgical Press, 1999), ch. 5, pp. 81–120.

[34] Ockham, *Quaest. in I Sent.*, d. 14, q. 2; OTh III. 430; *Quodlibeta* IV, q. 29; OTh IX. 449.

[35] Ockham, *Quaest. in IV Sent.*, q. 8; OTh VII. 136–7.

True to his own sense that multiple location is no problem, Ockham frames [D11] in such a way as not to specify whether circumscriptive or definitive presence is involved. If the eucharistic bread were of equal size, or Christ's Body were sufficiently condensed by Divine power, God would have no trouble placing Christ's Body on the altar circumscriptively.[36] Ockham joins theological consensus in affirming that in fact Christ's Body is on the altar definitively. Having rejected Giles's and Scotus's explanations of how Christ's Body can remain organic on the altar, Ockham explains that Christ's Body has no figure or quantity there. Nevertheless, the distinction among organic parts will not be lost, because they will retain their material dispositions and aptitudes for different functions (for example, stomach parts will still be disposed to the work of digestion, lung parts to the work of respiration, and so on).[37]

Once transubstantiation is treated as a conjunction of actions, a string of events, rather than a type of change with its own integrity (as Aquinas thought), the question about the formal term-to-which of transubstantiation is no longer apt. In his *Sentence* commentary, Ockham takes the occasion to comment on his predecessors' distinction between what is on the altar by the power of the conversion (what they identify as the formal term) and what is there by natural concomitance (what they call the *per accidens* term of the conversion). Ockham contends that this distinction is misapplied when its framers use it to conclude that the Body of Christ is the formal term of transubstantiation while the soul of Christ is present only by natural concomitance. Rather, given [D11], it is clear that there will be a distinct transubstantiation for each thing (*res*) that comes to be located on the altar. Transubstantiation to Christ's Body would have occurred without transubstantiation to Christ's soul had mass been said during the Triduum (when Christ was dead). Ockham thinks that both before and after the Triduum both occur together in the sacrament of the altar.[38] The distinction would be well used to contrast what the converting cause primarily intends to make present and what it *per accidens* intends to make present, because it cannot or chooses not to make the one present without the other.[39] Theological consensus has it that God primarily aims at the presence

[36] Ockham, *Quaest. in IV Sent.*, q. 8; OTh VII. 147–8.
[37] Ockham, *Quodlibeta* IV, q. 31; OTh IX. 453; *Tract. de Corpore Christi*, c. 7; OTh X. 104–5.
[38] Ockham, *Quaest. in IV Sent.*, q. 8; OTh VII. 141.
[39] Ockham, *Quaest. in IV Sent.*, q. 8; OTh VII. 142–3.

of Christ's Body, but—on Ockham's analysis—chooses not to make Christ's Body present without His soul, so long as He is humanly alive.

In *Quodlibeta* IV, q. 29, Ockham drops mention of natural concomitance and makes the intentions of the converting cause central. Strict-sense conversion puts on the altar what would begin to be under the species by Divine power at the utterance of the sacramental words by a priest with the relevant intentions, even if it were not really united to other things. Broad-sense conversion brings along what is really united to what strict-sense conversion puts there. Thus, strict-sense conversion locates the Body of Christ on the altar; broad-sense conversion locates His soul and accidents.[40]

Ockham thinks—by [D11]—when the bread substance is transubstantiated into Christ's Body, the bread substance altogether ceases to exist. Convinced that transubstantiation is a distinct kind of change with two positive terms, Aquinas and Giles deny that the bread substance is thereby annihilated. Ockham distinguishes two senses of 'annihilation': if 'annihilation' simply means 'being reduced to nothing', then the bread is annihilated because nothing of it remains. If 'annihilation' means 'being reduced to nothing and not converted', then bread is not annihilated. But this is merely a verbal point for Ockham, because transubstantion is just an aggregate of changes. For that reason, Ockham does not show the same interest as Scotus in what can be transubstantiated into what. Yes, on Ockham's [D11], there can be transubstantiation of body into soul. No, on Ockham's [D11], there cannot be transubstantiation into an accident, although one could frame a parallel definition of transaccidentation.[41]

IV. Causal Exposure

Governing Causal Principles. Ecclesial authority insists: Christ's Body is really present on altars where and when priests consecrate eucharistic bread. All of our authors explain: its presence there is not normal and natural; Christ's Body is present on the altar in an unusual way. On the one hand, their contention is supposed to account for our experience: if Christ's Body were present naturally and normally, surely we would see it there. On the other hand, Aquinas and Giles thought it would help with Multiple Location and

40 Ockham, *Quodlibeta* IV, q. 29; OTh IX. 448; *Tract. de Corpore Christi*, c. 5; OTh X. 97–9.

41 Ockham, *Quaest. in IV Sent.*, q. 8; OTh VII. 149–51.

Size Problems: if [T5] two bodies cannot be in the same place at once or [T6] one body in many places at once in the normal and natural manner, if [T7] an extended body cannot squeeze into a place far too small, perhaps Christ's Body could be in one place (heaven) normally and naturally and on many altars under eucharistic species in some other special way.

All of our authors agree that Christ's Body is on the altar, under the species, in such a way as not to be extended. Aquinas, Giles, and Scotus think that this obviously restricts the range of its causal interaction. Ockham recatalogs the cases of interest, distinguishing between those whose actions/passions proceed from corporeal as opposed to spiritual causal principles, and between those whose terms are some absolute form inhering in the patient as opposed to some gain or loss of relations to place.[42] Where the causal principle is corporeal and the term is an absolute form, Aquinas insists that corporeal action requires contact, which is the limit of two quantities, while Christ's Body has no order to place by means of its own dimensive quantity and so is not there in such a way as to touch or be touched by anything else. Scotus claims that what shelters Christ's Body from causal exposure is its lack of quantitative mode. Where the term of change is a relation to place, Aquinas reasons that, because Christ's Body is not located in place properly speaking but only *per accidens*, it moves when the host moves only *per accidens*. Scotus declares that, because the whole of Christ's Body is present to the whole place, but not parts to the parts, God acts alone to make the Body of Christ to be where the host is when it moves.[43] Where the causal principle is spiritual, Aquinas still insists that the presence of Christ's Body on the altar cannot be known naturally but only by faith, while Scotus allows that Christ can use His spiritual powers on the altar, because their exercise does not require the agent to exist in a quantitative mode.[44]

Ockham's analysis significantly widens the causal exposure occasioned by eucharistic presence. His rationale not only rejects much of what his predecessors assume about the metaphysics of bodily location, but also forwards fresh interpretations of Aristotelian causal principles. Ockham follows Scotus in denying the famous premiss from Aquinas's First Way:

[P20] everything in motion is moved by another.

[42] Ockham, *Quaest. in IV Sent.*, q. 7; OTh VII. 110.
[43] Ockham, *Quaest. in IV Sent.*, q. 7; OTh VII. 111–12.
[44] Ockham, *Quaest. in IV Sent.*, q. 7; OTh VII. 111–13.

Self-motion is possible, not only among intelligent agents who exercise free will, but natural agents such as water, which—when heated and left to stand—acts on itself to cool itself down. Nor does Aristotelian physics dictate (as Aquinas claims) that

[P21] contact (the touching of quantities) is necessary for corporeal action.

True, many invoked Aristotle's putative commitment to "no action at a distance" to explain why he thought seeing the white wall 10 feet away would require the wall to produce sensible species in the medium in intentional being that could be propagated through the air to the animal's eye. But Ockham's own reflections on projectile motion and magnetic attraction lead him to the contrary conclusion that action at a distance *is* possible.[45]

Ockham identifies the foundation of Scotus's position with the assumption that

[P22] causal exposure requires the relevant active and passive corporeal powers to be in place circumscriptively, both quantified and extended.

Yet, Scotus himself recognizes that substances are naturally prior to any modes of being accidental to them. He should have seen that the same goes for qualities. After all, Scotus himself cites Avicenna's claim that heat could act even if it were separated from any subject (and so from its quantitative mode in a subject). But, if active and passive causal principles are naturally prior to their quantitative mode, it takes further argument to show why lack extension in the agent or patient would obstruct causal interaction (for example, for the seeing and being seen of color).[46]

Moreover, when Scotus comes to assess the active and passive causal capacities of the Body of Christ as sacramentally present on the altar, he fails to ask whether creatures could be partial even if they could not be total causes of various changes. Divine concurrence is an efficient cause of every effect. Even where effects are not normal or natural but miraculous, active and passive created causal powers could be part of the explanatory picture.[47]

[45] See my *William Ockham*, ch. 19, 827–52.
[46] Ockham, *Quaest. in IV Sent.*, q. 7; OTh VII. 113–15; *Quodlibeta* IV, q. 13; OTh IX. 362.
[47] Ockham, *Quaest. in IV Sent.*, q. 7; OTh VII. 116–17.

Ockham's own estimates of causal exposure are grounded on a different causal axiom from Aristotelian physics:

[P23] when a sufficient agent is proximate and the patient is disposed, the action follows.

Strictly speaking, Ockham's statement of the principle is incomplete. For Aristotelian sublunary causal powers are obstructible. Aristotelian agents and patients "do their thing" always or for the most part. To make this explicit (as Ockham sometimes does), [P23] should be replaced as

[P23′] when a sufficient agent is proximate and the patient is disposed, and there is no obstacle, the action follows.

Ockham declares that no exceptions to [P23′] should be countenanced unless reason, authority, or experience requires it.[48] Where authority is silent or underdetermines the issues, reason and experience will have to decide. So far as the causal exposure occasioned by eucharistic real presence is concerned, Ockham's central question is whether definitive as opposed to circumscriptive placement constitutes a genuine obstacle to causal interaction. Working his way through his catalog of types of cases, Ockham's non-standard answer is, "in most cases, no!"

Corporeal Causal Principles/Absolute Forms as Effects. Natural reason, Ockham thinks, cannot prove that definitive rather than circumscriptive location obstructs the exercise of a thing's active and passive corporeal causal capacities.[49] On the contrary, the opposite might seem more reasonable. In Aristotelian physics, proximity and presence are salient. But definitive placement makes more parts of the agent/patient to be present in more places than circumscriptive placement does.

Focusing on the case of action, Ockham forwards the claim that

[P24] an active principle is no less able to act when it is present to a patient by its whole self than when one part is present to one part and another part to another.

Everybody has to agree that definitive placement does not in general pose an obstacle to an agent's acting on a body, because all concede (following Augustine) that the intellectual soul acts on its body to produce sickness and

[48] Ockham, *Quaest. in IV Sent.*, q. 7; OTh VII. 119–20. *Quodlibeta* IV, q. 13; OTh IX. 362.
[49] Ockham, *Quaest. in IV Sent.*, q. 7; OTh VII. 118; *Quodlibeta* IV, q. 13; OTh IX. 360.

health and in many other ways, even though the intellectual soul is whole in the whole body and whole in each part. Ockham bolsters the intuitive appeal of [P18] for corporeal agents by means of a thought experiment. Suppose the whiteness of a wall existed in the wall the way the intellectual soul exists in its body: whole in the whole and whole in the parts. Why would the presence of more rather than fewer parts of whiteness in each part of the wall render it less able to act on the medium to propagate sensible species into the eye?[50] Ockham might have added an analogy with more and less intense degrees of whiteness. More intense degrees involve more parts of whiteness in each part of the surface, but that does not keep them from causing sensible species and being seen just as much as the less intense degrees (see Chapter 9 below).

Perhaps because popular piety reported what it longed for—a *sensory* vision of the Body of Christ really present in the eucharist—philosophical discussions of this causal category (corporeal causal principles, absolute form as effect) focus on whether the sacramentally present Christ can see or be seen with the bodily eye. Applying [P24] to the Body of Christ definitively on the altar, Ockham reasons that the accidents of the Body of Christ are corporeal agents sufficiently present to human visual powers around the altar. By [P23′], vision ought to follow, so that the humans see the Body of Christ there.[51]

Ockham appeals to another Aristotelian causal principle:

[P25] If a natural active cause is related to different sufficiently close and equally disposed patients, if it can act on one, it can act on the other,

to reinforce his case with an *ad hominem* thrust against Scotus. Scotus admits—and Ockham agrees—that the Body of Christ definitively in place on the altar can cause an intuitive cognition of itself in an angel. Why should the circumscriptive placement of the patient (the human sensory power) be an obstacle to the Body of Christ's causing a corporeal vision of itself in human beings as well? Nor can Scotus consistently claim that

[P26] the placement modes of agent and patient have to be alike.

[50] Ockham, *Quaest. in IV Sent.*, q. 7; OTh VII. 118; *Quodlibeta* IV, q. 13; OTh IX. 360–1.
[51] Ockham, *Quodlibeta* IV, q. 13; OTh IX. 361.

For he admits with everyone else that the intellectual soul acts on the extended body in which it exists definitively, and he holds that extended corporeal things can cause intellectual intuitive cognitions in the unextended human soul.[52]

Unfortunately, even medieval theories made vision a particularly problematic case. If the Body of Christ is definitively in place, the different colors of its different parts will be superimposed on one another. The presence of one will obstruct the visibility of the other, just as would happen were they circumscriptively in place. Likewise, if there are many parts of the same kind present in the same place, we will not be able visually to discriminate them from one another and so to recognize that many are there. Again, vision requires seer and seen to be at a distance from one another. How then could Christ see Himself in the eucharist with His own bodily eye?[53] What these add up to is a list of ways definitive as opposed to circumscriptive placement would obstruct the process of seeing and being seen.

Ockham responds with a diagnosis, distinctions, and concessions. The diagnosis is that bodily vision requires not only location but situation in its objects. For example, the textbook on perspective lays it down that the visible object forms the base of the triangle whose apex is in the eye.[54] This is not true of other sense perceptibles such as heat, which need only be located to be sensed by nearby animals. The objector's difficulties can at least be quarantined.[55] Returning to the case of bodily vision, Ockham asserts that there is a distinction between what we can see and what we can perceptually discriminate. Humans in the vicinity of the altar in principle could see distinct parts with the bodily eye but not be able to tell them apart.[56] Second, Ockham admits problems about how well all the colors could be seen, but denies that they could not be seen at all.[57] Third, as to Christ's visual sense perception of Himself, Ockham draws on his clever conclusion that whatever exists in a place definitively thereby exists in that place circumscriptively. If the Body of Christ is definitively present to place

[52] Ockham, *Quodlibeta* IV, q. 13; OTh IX. 362–3.

[53] Ockham, *Quaest. in IV Sent.*, q. 7; OTh VII. 133–4; *Quodlibeta* IV, q. 13; OTh IX. 364.

[54] For a thorough discussion of optical theories in Ockham's day, see Katherine Tachau, *Vision and Certitude in the Age of Ockham: Optics, Epistemology, and the Foundations of Semantics 1250–1345*, in the series (Studien und Texte zur Geistesgeschichte des Mittelalters; Leiden, New York, Copenhagen, and Cologne: Brill, 1988).

[55] Ockham, *Quaest. in IV Sent.*, q. 7; OTh VII. 133–4; *Quodlibeta* IV, q. 13; OTh IX. 365.

[56] Ockham, *Quaest. in IV Sent.*, q. 7; OTh VII. 134; *Quodlibeta* IV, q. 13; OTh IX. 365.

[57] Ockham, *Quaest. in IV Sent.*, q. 7; OTh VII. 133–4; *Quodlibeta* IV, q. 13; OTh IX. 365.

P, which is divided into parts P1, P2, and P3, then the Body of Christ at P1 is at a distance from the Body of Christ at P3. Thus, it would be physically and metaphysically possible for the definitively present Christ to see Himself there![58]

Ockham is eager to drive home the general theoretical point about Aristotelian causes: that definitive versus circumscriptive placement in and of itself makes no difference to corporeal interactions whose term is an absolute form. He thereby hopes to make good on his claim that natural reason in the form of Aristotelian theoretical physics has nothing to say against this.

Where theory assessment is concerned, however, Ockham recognizes a third court of appeal: experience. Experience shows that situation matters for vision. And experience shows that in fact the Body of Christ in the eucharist is not naturally seen by humans with the bodily eye. Good theories should save the phenomena. If definitive versus circumscriptive placement really made no difference, our experience should be different.

In fact, Ockham and his predecessor opponents handle the testimony of experience in different ways. For them, what we see (the bread accidents) and fail to see (the Body of Christ) impugns the claim of real presence. They respond with theories that allow Christ's Body to be really present but naturally imperceptible. Ockham's remodel of the metaphysical structure of bodies and their placement and his understanding of Aristotelian physics lead him to deny that any sort of real presence would render a body naturally imperceptible. To save the phenomena, Ockham posits a supernatural obstruction in the natural process. God is an immediate partial cause of every effect. We do not perceive Christ's really present Body because God miraculously withdraws Divine cooperation with the created corporeal principles in causing sensory intuitive cognitions of it.[59]

Seeing the Body of Christ with the Mind's Eye. Scotus had already admitted that definitive placement is no metaphysical obstacle to a body's acting on an incorporeal substance—on intellectual souls and angels—to produce an intellectual cognition of itself. Scotus speculates that the *ante-mortem* attachment of human souls to corruptible bodies may be the obstacle that prevents us from actually seeing Christ's Body in the eucharist with the mind's eye. Ockham agrees with Scotus: the quantitative mode in the object is irrelevant for its being understood. For Ockham, [P23′] bears down with

[58] Ockham, *Quaest. in IV Sent.*, q. 7; OTh VII. 135; *Quodlibeta* IV, q. 13; OTh IX. 365–6.
[59] Ockham, *Quaest. in IV Sent.*, q. 7; OTh VII. 363; *Quodlibeta* IV, q. 13; OTh IX. 363.

presumptive force. In principle, Christ on the altar can naturally and intuitively understand everything else as if He were there quantitatively. In principle, Christ can also be understood or intuitively seen, not only by angels or separate souls, but also by *ante-mortem* human beings; not only with the intellect, but also with the bodily eye, unless there is some other obstacle (for example, the withdrawl of Divine cooperation). Of course, we do not know what Christ actually understands, but it would be remarkable if Christ existing in the host did not know where He was![60]

Change of Place. All of our authors treat as given the real presence of Christ's Body on altars where mass is said. Since Christ remains literally located in heaven after the ascension and before the judgment, this implies that Christ's Body must become newly present somehow. Medieval philosophical theologians took it as their assignment to explain how that happens and what that means. Aquinas argues that the only way for God to get Christ's Body on the altar while leaving it in heaven is to convert something already (normally and naturally) on the altar into it. But the result will be only that Christ's Body is newly present to the species and hence present to place *per accidens*. Christ's Body neither loses nor gains a place in transubstantiation, and so—insofar as it is on the altar—is not susceptible of *per se* locomotion there.

Ockham rejects Aquinas's analysis as wrong on most counts: God does not have to convert anything on the altar to make Christ's Body really present; God does not have to preserve the species to mediate the presence of Christ's Body to place; the Body of Christ and its integral parts are immediately and *per se* present to place and hence mobile *per se* as well.[61] Following Scotus, Ockham recognizes that strict-sense motion involves both the loss of one place and the gain of another, while for broad-sense motion either loss or gain will suffice. Broad-sense motion is required to get the Body of Christ on the altar: the Body of Christ undergoes a gain-change to become definitively located in a place where it was not before.[62] But what kind of motion is the definitively present Body of Christ capable of after it gets there? For Ockham as for Scotus, an answer requires some more distinctions.

[60] Ockham, *Quaest. in IV Sent.*, q. 7; OTh VII. 124–5; *Quodlibeta* IV, q. 13; OTh IX. 362–3. See *Quodlibeta* IV, q. 7; OTh IX. 135.

[61] Ockham, *Quodlibeta* IV, q. 13; OTh IX. 367.

[62] Ockham, *Quodlibeta* VI, q. 3; OTh IX. 594–5.

For Ockham, the distinction between organic and non-organic gets drawn twice over. First, between *powers*: an organic power is one that uses a bodily organ in its action (for example, the five senses), whereas a non-organic power is one that does not need a corporeal organ for its action (for example, the intellect and will). Ockham explains that, because Scotus thinks there is only one soul form in human beings, he asserts that the intellectual soul has both organic and non-organic powers. By contrast, because Ockham holds that human intellectual and sensory souls are really distinct substantial forms, he assigns non-organic power to the intellectual soul and organic power to the sensory soul.[63]

Second, between *types of motion*: to move something organically is to move first one part and then by means of its motion to move another, and so on; to move something non-organically is to move the whole and its parts all at once. Ockham explains that the intellectual soul moves its own body organically, when it first moves the heart and then by reason of the hearts motion moves another part, and by means of that a third, and so on. He explicitly notes that organic motion requires the moved object to exist in place circumscriptively, so that its parts are at a distance from one another. Ockham's example of non-organic motion is an angel moving the body it assumes. Evidently, he thinks that, because the angel exists definitively in that body, not as a perfecting form but only as a mover, it can move the body only all at once.[64] But normally and naturally, the intellectual soul as a form perfecting its body has non-organic power (exercised by understanding and willing) to move it only organically (first one part and then by means of its motion to move another, and so on).[65]

The intellectual soul of Christ in heaven (where Christ's Body exists circumscriptively) has the same kind of motive power as any other intellectual soul with respect to its own body: non-organic power to move its body organically.[66] The soul of Christ under the host has non-organic power to move its Body under the host only non-organically (all of its parts at once). The soul of Christ under the host does not have power to move Christ's Body under the host organically, because Christ's Body is not extended there. But the soul of Christ under the host does have non-organic power to

[63] Ockham, *Quaest. in IV Sent.*, q. 7; OTh VII. 121; *Quodlibeta* IV, q. 14; OTh IX. 368–9.
[64] Ockham, *Quaest. in IV Sent.*, q. 7; OTh VII. 122; *Quodlibeta* IV, q. 15; OTh IX. 371–2.
[65] Ockham, *Quodlibeta* IV, q. 15; OTh IX. 372–3.
[66] Ockham, *Quaest. in IV Sent.*, q. 7; OTh VII. 123; *Quodlibeta* IV, q. 15; OTh IX. 372–3.

will that its Body be moved non-organically (all the parts at once) when the host moves, and—*pace* Scotus—this willing can be a partial cause, concurring with the Divine will, of such motion.[67] If, however, the soul of Christ ceased to will to move when the host moved, Divine power would act alone to make it move that way. The soul's ability to will this or not has nothing to do with whether the Body of Christ is in place definitively or circumscriptively, however.[68]

Retaming Multiple Location. Scotus worried that multiple location might widen causal exposure too much, in ways that would subject the same thing to contrary properties simultaneously. Nutshelled, his main solution was that, wherever and in however many places a thing exists, it has all of its properties that are naturally prior to its location in place. Thus, Scotus infers, a thing has the same absolute properties wherever it is located, while its relative properties may vary from place to place. So far as absolute properties are concerned, the resultant of some causes acting to heat the water in London and others acting to cool the same water in Rome, is the same as if all causes were acting on the water in London. Scotus also distinguishes the absolute properties a thing has primarily as here from those it has by natural concomitance on the basis of whether or not the cause of the substance's having that property is here rather than some other place where it also exists.

Surprisingly, Ockham gives this topic shorter shrift. He does insist with Scotus that places (and relations to different places) are not themselves contraries. Nor does the idea that locomotion itself requires a kind of contrariety prove that they are. True, one could hardly speak of change if the term-from-which and the term-to-which did not differ. But there are two ways to explain how locomotion meets this requirement without supposing that places (and relations to different places) are contraries themselves. Sometimes Ockham follows Scotus in breaking changes down into their components whose terms are contradictory opposites: X's strict-sense motion from P1 to P2 analyses into a loss-change (whose term-from-which is *being at P1* and whose term-to-which is *not being at P1*) and a gain-change (whose term-from-which is *not being at P2* and whose term-to-which is *being at P2*); X's broad-sense motion from P1 to P2 involves the gain-change without the loss-change. Alternatively, Ockham explains that what locomotion—like

[67] Ockham, *Quaest. in IV Sent.*, q. 7; OTh VII. 123; *Quodlibeta* IV, q. 15; OTh IX. 373.

[68] Ockham, *Quaest. in IV Sent.*, q. 7; OTh VII. 124; *Quodlibeta* IV, q. 15; OTh IX. 373–5.

the intensification and reduction of forms—requires is distance (the non-identity of terms), not contrariety.[69]

When Ockham turns to consider the causal exposure cases, he does not give Scotus's proposals a detailed review. Instead, he declares that Scotus is right about what in fact obtains—*de facto*, if a body exists in two places circumscriptively or definitively, every absolute thing that pertains to the integrity it has in one place, it also has in the other place[70]—and hurries on to another proposal that interests him more. On Ockham's analysis, a material substance—such as Socrates or the Body of Christ—is constituted by really distinct things (prime matter, substantial form(s), and absolute accidental forms) metaphysically glued together by different kinds of real union. Ockham has already insisted that each really distinct thing is the foundation of its own relations, not least of its relation to place. If so, there is no metaphysical impossibility in a substance being located somewhere one way (circumscriptively or definitively) and its accidents not being located there or being located there the other way (definitively instead of circumscriptively, or vice versa).[71] In an effort to solidify our intuitions, Ockham offers an analogy: Christ's human nature is really distinct from but really united to the Divine Word, in a manner analogous to the real union between substantial form and prime matter or that between absolute accidents and substance. Yet, Christ's human nature is not everywhere just because it is assumed by the omnipresent Divine Word.[72] So also, Ockham reasons, the accidents of Christ's Body could be located where Christ's Body exists circumscriptively (in heaven) but not where Christ's Body exists sacramentally; and the accidents of Christ's Body could be located in one place where it exists circumscriptively and not another (say in the place where the accident is caused and not elsewhere). In the first case, if whiteness inheres in Christ's Body, 'Christ's Body is white *simpliciter*' and 'Christ's Body is white in heaven' will be true, while 'Christ's Body is not white here (on the altar)' is also true. But this gives rise to no contradiction, because 'Christ's Body is not white here' does not entail 'Christ's Body is not white *simpliciter*'. Drawing the inference would commit the fallacy of *secundum quid et simpliciter*.[73]

69 Ockham, *Quaest. in IV Sent.*, q. 6; OTh VII. 102–3.
70 Ockham, *Quaest. in IV Sent.*, q. 7; OTh VII. 130.
71 Ockham, *Quaest. in IV Sent.*, q. 6; OTh VII. 99–101; q. 7; OTh VII. 130–3.
72 Ockham, *Quaest. in IV Sent.*, q. 6; OTh VII. 99–100.
73 Ockham, *Quest. in IV Sent.*, q. 6; OTh VII. 101; q. 7; OTh VII. 130–3.

Independent Accidents?

8

Accidents Without Substance: Aquinas and Giles of Rome

I. Can God Make Any Accidents without a Subject?

On Aquinas's theory, the Body of Christ is placed on the altar by transubstantiation, a whole-being conversion, with the result that at the end of the consecration the substance of the bread is not there. Sense experience testifies that the accidents of the bread are still there. Divine power must somehow enable both to be so simultaneously. The most straightforward way would be for God to conserve the accidents in existence without their substance. Yet, Aquinas maintains, only the metaphysically possible is doable. And Aquinas recognizes four principal arguments to the effect that accidents cannot exist without their subject even by Divine power.

The first three are metaphysical. *The "Definition Problem."* It is contradictory to separate the definition from what it defines. But it belongs to the definition of a substance to exist *per se*, and it belongs to the definition of an accident to inhere in a substance.[1] *The* "Esse *Problem."* It is metaphysically impossible for a thing to exist without its act of existing (*esse*). But the act of existing (*esse*) of an accident is its inherence in a subject (*inesse*).[2] *The "Individuation Problem."* Just as form is individuated by its matter, so is an accident by its subject. The accidents on the altar are individuated; otherwise they would not be sense perceptible. Therefore, they must still have a subject.[3] Derivative from these is a fourth, semantic objection, the *"Natural*

[1] Aquinas, *Sent.* IV, d. 12, q. 1, a. 1, qc. 1 [15587–15588]; *Summa Theologica* III, q. 77, a. 1, arg. 2.

[2] Aquinas, *Sent.* IV, d. 12, q. 1, a. 1, qc. 1 [15586].

[3] Aquinas, *Sent.* IV, d. 12, q. 1, a. 1, qc. 3 [15598]; *Summa Theologica* I, q. 77, a. 1, arg. 3.

Signification Problem." The eucharist is a sacrament of truth. But accidents naturally signify that their subjects exist under them. They would signify a falsehood if the bread substance were no longer there.[4]

Aquinas moves to dissolve all four difficulties. He charges that the Definition Problem and the *Esse* Problem are products of metaphysical confusion. True, Aristotle famously declares that being is divided into being in the mind and being outside the mind, and being outside the mind is divided into the ten categories, of which the first is substance and the remaining nine are accidents. But Aquinas denies that this makes being a genus, with substance and accident its proximate species. One fundamental reason is that genus and differentiae are both positive principles that must be taken from something outside the genus (otherwise the differentiae would not be *distinct* principles). Being cannot be a genus because no positive principle can fail to participate in being. Through itself (*per se*) cannot be a differentia either, because it is a pure negation (the negation of dependence on another). Two further consequences follow from the fact that being is not a genus. First, the ten categories are themselves the highest genera. As such, they are genera that are not species and so are not constituted by genus and differentia. Since proper Aristotelian definitions are in terms of genus and differentiae, the highest genera are not definable properly speaking. Second, because being is not a genus, the quiddities that fall under the ten categories do not include any act of existence (*esse*) in their intelligible content.[5]

What does naturally belong to substance and accident respectively is that substance ought (*debere*) by nature to exist *per se*, while accidents ought (*debere*) by nature to exist in (*inesse*) a substance.[6] *Per se* and inherence are modes of being that are naturally appropriate to substance and accident respectively, and are normally conferred upon them by their proximate causes. But what is naturally appropriate can be miraculously taken from a thing by Divine power (as when God miraculously obstructs the fire in Nebuchadnezzar's furnace from even singeing the three young men thrown into it).[7]

[4] Aquinas, *Sent.* IV, d. 12, q. 1, a. 1, qc. 2 [15592]; *Summa Theologica* III, q. 77, a. 1, arg. 1.

[5] Aquinas, *Summa Contra Gentiles* I, ch. 25, arg. 4; *De Potentia* q. 7, a. 3; cf. John Wippel, *The Metaphysical Thought of Thomas Aquinas: From Finite Being to Uncreated Being* (Washington: Catholic University of America Press, 2000), pt. two, ch. 7, sect. 3, pp. 228–37.

[6] Aquinas, *Sent.* IV, d. 12, q. 1, a. 1, qc. 1 [15606]; IV, d. 12, q. 1, a. 1, qc. 3 [15617]; *Summa Theologica* III, q. 77, a. 1 ad 2um &ad 4um.

[7] Aquinas, *Sent.* IV, d. 12, q. 1, a. 1, qc. 1 ad 2um [15606–15607].

In his *Sentence* commentary and elsewhere, Aquinas expands upon the causal chains normally involved in the production and conservation of accidents. God stands as first cause of all creatures. So far as proximate causes are concerned, some accidents are produced by the principles that constitute the substance itself. Thus, accidents proper to substance (for example, dimensive quantity for bodies or the soul's powers for animals) are "naturally consequent upon," "emanate," or "flow from" the genus and differentiae of the substance nature. Other accidents (for example, being male or female) are naturally consequent upon or concomitant with the individuating principles of the substance. Still others (separable accidents) are caused by external agents: some that are contrary to the principles of the substance (for example, heat caused by fire in naturally cold water) and others that perfect it (for example, light in the air, theological virtues in the soul). Normally and naturally, Aquinas thinks that the substance subject is a conserving cause of all of its accidents, whether they are internally or externally produced. Thus, inherence (*inesse*) is the mode of existence that pertains to an accident in relation to its proximate productive and conserving efficient cause—that is, they produce and conserve the accident inhering in its subject. But, when the substance subject is taken away, its order to the first cause remains, and that order is, not to exist in (*inesse*) the first cause as in a subject (as its material cause), but to be from the first cause (*ab alio esse*) as from an efficient cause.[8]

So far as the Individuation Problem is concerned, Aquinas explains in his *Sentence* commentary that to be an individual is [a] actually to exist, whether *per se* or in another, [b] to be divided from others that do or can exist in the same species, and [c] to be undivided from itself. In corporeal things, the first principle of individuation is matter in which corporeal forms acquire [a] actual *esse*. But matter of itself is indivisible. The secondary principle of individuation is quantitative dimension, which is *per se* [b–c] divided into numerically distinct but specifically the same parts. The inherence of quantitative dimension in matter divides matter into parts that may be inhered in by different substantial forms. Thus, the inherence of quantitative dimension in matter is naturally prior to the inherence of other accidents, which are founded on substance by means of quantity and are individuated thereby. Normally and naturally, quantitative dimensions are not said to be individuated *per se*, because—although quantitative parts are [b] divided

[8] Aquinas, *Sent.* IV, d. 12, q. 1, a. 1, qc. 1 [15605].

from others of the same species and [c] undivided from themselves *per se*—[not-a] they have their actual existence only through inhering in matter. But in the sacrament, Divine power makes the quantitative dimensions actually to exist *per se*, so that they are individuated *per se*, and the other accidents are individuated through them as before.[9] In the *Summa Theologica*, Aquinas simply says that accidents acquire their individuated being in a subject (*inesse*) and that they are conserved in that same individuated act of existence by Divine power.[10]

Having dealt with the metaphysical difficulties, Aquinas finds the semantic Natural Signification Problem easy to dispatch. The senses veridically perceive the accidents. But it belongs to the intellect, not the senses, to judge the presence or absence of substance. Because faith informs the intellect not to rely on natural signification in this case, no deception is involved.[11]

II. Accidents without Substance: What Sort of Active and Passive Causal Powers?

Experience shows that what is left on the altar remains causally interactive in just the same ways as bread and wine are. These are phenomena that a good Aristotelian would want to save. But Aquinas's understanding of Aristotelian agency makes this difficult, thrice over. First, Aquinas contends that, strictly speaking, it is only the whole substance—not its matter, not its forms—that is said to act. Strictly speaking, it is Ferdinand the bull who acts by reason of his form, which is the principle of action. The bread accidents are all forms. Even if Divine power preserves them in existence, how can they be causally engaged even as principles of action when their substance agent is gone? Call this the *No Substance Agent Problem*.

Second, Aquinas envisions a hierarchy or essential order of causal principles within the individual substance itself. But, normally and naturally, the substantial form is not the immediate but a remote principle of action. The substantial form activates the substance by means of active and passive qualities that function as its instruments. How often does Aquinas tell us: take away the

[9] Aquinas, *Sent.* IV, d. 12, q. 1, a. 1, qc. 3 [15612, 15615]. See *Summa Theologica* III, q. 77, a. 2 c.
[10] Aquinas, *Summa Theologica* III, q. 77, a. 1 ad 3um.
[11] Aquinas, *Sent.* IV, d. 12, q. 1, a. 1, qc. 2 [15610]; *Summa Theologica* III, q. 77, a. 1 ad 1um.

first cause, take away the secondary causes? When the substantial form of bread is gone, how can the qualities of the bread do any activating on their own? Call this the *No Substantial Form Problem.*

Finally, there is the *No Prime Matter Problem.* Aristotelian changes require a subject, a material cause that persists through the change and is first a constituent of the term-from- which and then a constituent of the term-to-which. But consecrated bread species undergo putrefaction into worms and combustion into ashes; consecrated wine species sour into vinegar and are diluted into water. If the prime matter of the bread and wine are gone, where does prime matter for worms and ashes, for vinegar and water, come from when these new substances appear?

Aquinas burrows down beneath the theoretical surface to bring up his answers. As for the *No Substance Agent Problem*, his fundamental principle about agency is not that, strictly speaking, only substances act, but rather that only what exists *per se* acts. In the sacrament, quantity exists *per se* and so can count as an agent. Just as Ferdinand the bull acts by reason of his form, so quantity acts only by means of qualities that are *per se* principles of action. Since quality still exists in the quantity as its proximate subject, it retains the same mode of existence as it had when the bread existed. Aquinas concludes that quality also retains the same functional role in acting.[12]

For an answer to the *No Substantial Form Problem*, Aquinas recalls his own analysis of instrumental causality (see Chapter 3 above). Aquinas thinks that instrumental power is something that inheres in the instrument. Just as Divine power preserves the accidents numerically and specifically the same when the substance is removed, so also Divine power preserves the same instrumental powers in the qualities. Since the instrumental power is ordered to the effect of the principal agent, qualities can remain proximate causal principles not only of accidental but also of substantial changes.[13]

Aquinas works out his answer to the *No Prime Matter Problem* within the framework of theological majority report, which understood it to be Divine policy to preserve the Body and Blood of Christ really present and the quantity *per se* extant so long as the species continue to be of a sort suitable to bread (wine). The Body and Blood of Christ do not depart at any and every change. Thus, the *per se* extant quantity can play the role of material cause

[12] Aquinas, *Sent.* IV, d. 12, q. 1, a. 2, qc. 1 c [15651].

[13] Aquinas, *Sent.* IV, d. 12, q. 1, a. 2, qc. 2 c [15655]; IV, d. 12, q. 1, a. 2, qc. 2 ad 1um &ad 2um [15656 &15657]; cf. *Summa Theologica* III, q. 77, a. 3. args. 2–3 &ad 2um &ad 3um.

persisting through qualitative changes. Just as qualities existing in *per se* extant quantity can act on other things in the same ways they did before, so they can be acted upon by other things in the same way as they were before. But, when the qualities change to become unsuitable for bread (wine), or when the quantity is divided into parts too small to be bread (wine), then the Body and Blood of Christ cease to be there, and the resultant quantity does not continue to exist *per se*.[14]

Facing the *No Prime Matter Problem*, Pope Innocent III had forwarded a suggestion that everyone had to mention: namely, that, when the qualitative change in the host goes so far, the substance of the bread returns, so that the worms or ashes can be generated from it. Aquinas rejects this explanation as unscientific, because it founders on timing problems. *When* would the substance of the bread return? Not while the accidents remain bread suitable, because the Body of Christ is there then and bread substance does not exist together with it. Not when the accidents become unsuitable for bread, because bread substance would not naturally remain under such conditions; worms or ashes would be there then. From Aquinas's point of view, Innocent III's proposal is also theologically unacceptable: if whole-being conversion gets the Body of Christ on the altar by converting the substance of the bread into it, the only way to get the bread back would be to convert the Body of Christ into it![15]

In the *Summa Theologica*, Aquinas simply insists that the species can do whatever they could do existing in the substance of bread and wine. Therefore, they can be converted into whatever their previously existing substances can be converted into.[16] In his *Sentence* commentary, however, he draws on Averroes' distinction between indeterminate and determinate quantity to fill out his picture of how it might happen. Averroes understands indeterminate dimensions to inhere in matter (which is indivisible in itself) and to render matter divisible with part at a distance from part. Determinate dimensions (determinate size and shape, extension with determinate boundaries) are naturally consequent upon the naturally posterior inherence of substantial form. In this passage, Aquinas appears to adopt Averroes' picture according to which indeterminate dimensions are the proximate

[14] Aquinas, *Sent.* IV, d. 12, q. 2, a. 3 c [15658]; IV, d. 12, q. 1, a. 2, qc. 3 ad 2um [15660]; see *Summa Theologica* III, q. 77, a. 4 c.

[15] Aquinas, *Sent.* IV, d. 12, q. 1, a. 2, qc. 4 c [15662]; see *Summa Theologica* III, q. 77, a. 5 c.

[16] Aquinas, *Summa Theologica* III, q. 77, a. 5 c; III, q. 77, a. 6 ad 3um.

subject of substantial forms. Normally and naturally, what persists through substantial change is not prime matter alone but prime matter informed by indeterminate dimensions. In the case of putrefying or burning bread accidents in the sacrament, the indeterminate dimensions that were originally in the bread would become the indeterminate dimensions of worms or ashes. Aquinas envisions two possibilities. Either prime matter would come back because prime matter is naturally concomitant with the substantial form of worms or ashes (the way the soul of Christ is present by natural concomitance in the sacrament). Or Divine power supplies the prime matter, not because it is required for the actual existence of the new substantial form (of worms or ashes), but because of the functional affinity of indeterminate dimensions with prime matter. Either way, matter would be newly created, but this would not swell the sum total of matter in the universe, because only as much would return as was lost when the bread was converted into the Body of Christ.[17]

With this explanation of how new substances can be generated from sacramental species, Aquinas applies his general conclusion to three special, eucharist-related cases. To the question whether sacramental species can nourish those who consume them, Aquinas answers "yes," because it is as easy for them to be converted into new parts of a human body as into worms or ashes![18]

A second puzzle involved diluting the contents of a consecrated chalice. Normally and naturally, adding a different kind of liquid of greater or equal volume to a volume of wine, thereby bringing every part of the wine into contact with part(s) of the added liquid so that they were thoroughly mixed, would change the wine into liquid of another species. If the added liquid were of lesser volume so that not all parts of wine were touched by parts of the added liquid, then only the touched parts would change. If the added liquid were of the same kind, the result would be a numerically distinct volume of wine. Since the wine species causally interact in all the same ways the wine would, adding non-wine liquid to a consecrated chalice will result in the same pattern of changes to new substance parts. Where only some of the parts in the consecrated chalice change, there will be a mixture of sacramental species (under which the Blood of Christ is present after the

[17] Aquinas, *Sent.* IV, d. 12, q. 1, a. 2, qc. 4 c [15662–15663]; IV, d. 12, q. 1, a. 2, qc. 4 ad 4um [15666].

[18] Aquinas, *Sent.* IV, d. 12, q. 1, a. 2, qc. 5 [15667]; *Summa Theologica* III, q. 77, a. 6 c.

manner of substance) with parts of the new type of liquid. Aquinas says that the parts will share one common dimension of quantity (for example, the same surface), but the quantity will not have one common mode of being, because some of its parts will exist without a subject and others of its parts will exist in a subject. Where additions would not make for a numerically distinct liquid, then the sacramental species and the Blood of Christ would remain. But, where they are sufficient to make a numerically distinct liquid, then the Blood of Christ would not remain.[19]

The third puzzle probes the effects of the fraction, which occurs after the consecration in the eucharistic rite. In the eleventh-century eucharistic controversy, Berengar of Tours had been made to swear that in the eucharist the real Body of Christ, the one that Mary bore and that was crucified under Pontius Pilate, is broken by the hands of priests and torn by the teeth of the faithful. Aquinas denies that this formula is to be taken literally. Because the Body of Christ is not really present on the altar by its own dimensions, it is not there in such a way that it can be touched or broken. Nor can it be literally torn, chewed, or eaten. What is literally touched and broken and eaten are the sacramental species. The Body of Christ remains present to the species after the manner of substance as long as the species remain the kind of accidents suitable to bread, and hence the Body of Christ may accompany them all the way down the digestive track into the stomach. But it is the sacramental species that are literally digested and provide bodily nourishment, while the really present Body of Christ furnishes spiritual nourishment (see Chapter 11 below).[20]

III. Complicating the Picture

Varieties of Accidents. For Giles of Rome as for Aquinas, whole-being conversion gets the Body of Christ onto the altar, while leaving the bread accidents without their substance. Giles acknowledges that this seems philosophically problematic insofar as accidents normally and naturally exist in (*inesse*) substance. Indeed, it is essential to all types of accidents to have *a*

[19] Aquinas, *Sent.* IV, d. 12, q. 1, a. 2, qc. 6 [15671]; *Summa Theologica* III, q. 77, a. 8 c &ad 1um, 2um, 3um, 4um.

[20] Aquinas, *Sent.* IV, d. 12, q. 1, a. 3, qc. 1 c &ad 1um [15695–15696]; *Summa Theologica* III, q. 77, a. 7 ad 3um.

natural aptitude to exist in a subject, so that what it is to be an accident is humanly inconceivable without reference to a subject.[21] Nevertheless, Giles insists, where *actual* existence in a subject is concerned, not all accidents are on a par. This is because, where accidents are concerned, there are several different theoretical roles that a subject may play. Put the other way around, there are three different ways an accident may depend upon a subject: formally for its essential unity; material causally for its individuation; and efficient causally for its production and/or conservation in existence. Normally and naturally, all accidents depend on subjects for their efficient causal preservation in existence. Giles distinguishes among accidents that are permanent things whose parts can all exist simultaneously (for example, quantity and quality) and successives (for example, motion and time) whose parts cannot all exist simultaneously.

[1] Giles maintains that the unity of a successive depends on two factors: the order of their parts to one another, and their subject.[22] Suppose there are two simultaneous motions, one whose parts are A, B, C, and the other whose parts are M, N, O, where A is simultaneous with M, B with N, and C with O. What makes A, B, and C (M, N, and O) to be parts of one motion, while M, B, and O are not, is that A, B, and C (M, N, and O) successively inhere in numerically the same subject X (Y), whereas M and O both inhere in Y and B inheres in X. Giles says that, although the subject does not, properly speaking, pertain to the definition (*ratio formalis*) of the accident, the subject is nevertheless the formal ground of its unity and so does somehow pertain to its quiddity.[23] Consequently, it is not possible—whether naturally or miraculously—for successives to exist without a subject (for example, for motion to exist without a mobile subject).

[2] Among permanent accidents, some (namely, qualities) depend material causally on their subjects for individuation. They do not have individual existence and hence do not have actual existence except insofar as they exist in a subject. They are numerically multiplied insofar as they exist in different subjects. Therefore, it is not possible—whether naturally or miraculously—for such subject-individuated accidents to exist *per se* without existing in a

[21] Giles of Rome, *Theoremata*, Propositio XL, fo. 28vaD–vbA.

[22] Giles of Rome, *Theoremata*, Propositio XXXV, fo.23vaABC; Propositio XXXVI, fo. 24raB; Propositio XXXVIII, fo. 25vbAB; Propositio XXXIX, fo. 26rbD.

[23] Giles of Rome, *Theoremata*, Propositio XXXVIII, fo. 25vbAB, fo. 26raCD.

subject either.[24] Giles notes the question whether God could not individuate these accidents that are naturally individuated by their subjects in another way. Giles registers his own scepticism but refuses to pursue the issue because he will argue that the individuation of qualities in the sacramental species can be accounted for in something close to the normal way (namely, by their inherence in quantity).[25]

[3] Other permanent accidents (namely, dimensive quantity) are self-individuating and so depend on their subjects only efficient causally for their production and/or conservation.[26] Whether or not these could exist without a subject thus depends on whether something else could take the place of the subject's efficient causal power.

Solo Divine Action. Accordingly, Giles next turns his attention to the causal roles that God is thought to play. Philosophically uncontroversial in the late thirteenth century was the thesis that God is the first efficient, first final, and exemplar formal cause of everything else. Likewise generally agreed were models of explanation that required the first efficient cause to be metaphysically simple and so rendered it impossible for the first efficient cause to inhere or to be inhered in by anything else. The evident inference was that God could not be either a material or an inherent formal cause of anything else. Thus far, Christians were on common ground with their Muslim and Jewish philosophical sources.

Moreover, Christian Aristotelians insisted on secondary causality: that things other than God are subjects of active and passive causal powers and that these powers come into play so that creatures regularly act together with God in the natural course of the world. God, the first cause, acts together with the revolving sun, a secondary universal cause, and with the generative powers of Ferdinand the bull and Beulah the cow to engender Elsie the cow. But Christian thinkers took a step away from Avicenna and Averroes when they contended that, while God normally acts together with created causes, God could act alone to bring about any and all such collaborative products. Giles formulates the Solo Divine Action principle more precisely:

[24] Giles of Rome, *Theoremata*, Propositio XXXVIII, fo. 24raC &fo. 25vaAB; Propositio XXXIX, fo. 264rbD–vaA.

[25] Giles of Rome, *Theoremata*, Propositio XXXVIII, fo. 25vaBC.

[26] Giles of Rome, *Theoremata*, Propositio XXXVIII, fo. 25rbBCD.

[T32] For every genus of cause with respect to which God is a cause of a creature, whatever God can do by means of creatures, God can do without them.[27]

It follows from [T32] that whereas God usually acts together with the substance subjects of accidents to produce andòor conserve them in existence, God could act alone—without substance subjects—as an efficient cause to produce and/or conserve those accidents unless there were some other obstacle. In the case of successives, there is another obstacle to the accidents existing without their substance subjects—namely, that the subjects formally ground the unity of those accidents. And God cannot substitute as the mobile subject that unifies a motion. Likewise, in the case of subject-individuated permanent accidents, there is another obstacle—namely, that the accidents actually exist only as individuated and they are individuated by the subjects in which they inhere. And it is metaphysically impossible for God to substitute as their subject of inherence. But, in the case of self-individuating permanent accidents, there is no further obstacle. Divine power could act to make dimensive quantity exist *per se*, independently of any substance subject of inherence.[28] Giles reinforces his conclusion by reminding us of his earlier point: that no metaphysical impossibility is involved in a thing (*res*) that belongs to one category existing in a mode that belongs to another category (for example, with matter or substance existing in a quantitative mode).[29]

Quantity Akin to Matter. Dimensive quantity is metaphysically eligible for *per se* existence because it is self-individuated and so depends on its subject for production/conservation only. Having made that point, Giles expands on the suitability of dimensive quantity to be the subject of the other accidents in the eucharist. Of the nine categories of accident, quantity and quality are internal; others are relatives that are consequent on quantity or quality (for example, place, time, situation) and/or externals (for example, action and passion in relation to an agent). Giles says that the internal, non-relative accidents are more real (have more *ex parte rei*) than those that pertain to their subject in relation to externals, and that all of the other accidents are founded on quantity and quality.[30] Of the latter two, Giles

[27] Giles of Rome, *Theoremata*, Propositio XXXVII, fos. 24vbABCD–25raAB.

[28] Giles of Rome, *Theoremata*, Propositio XXXVII, fo. 25raCD; Propositio XXXVIII, fo. 25raD–rbACD, 25vbD.

[29] Giles of Rome, *Theoremata*, Propositio XL, fo. 27vaD–vbA.

[30] Giles of Rome, *Theoremata*, Propositio XXXIX, f. 26vaD–vbD.

contends, quantity is closer to matter twice over. First, matter cannot actually exist without quantity, although—Giles thinks—it can exist without other accidents.[31] Giles infers that quantity must therefore exist in matter *prior* to other accidents.[32] Second, quantity is more like matter insofar as quantity is never an immediate principle of action and never changes except insofar as it is informed by qualities. Thus, Giles thinks quantity is more apt to play the role of matter (as ultimate subject of inherence) while quality is more suited to play the role of substantial form (as the active causal principle).[33]

Drawing these reflections together, Giles concludes that, whereas substance persists through accidental change and prime matter through substantial change, what persists through transubstantiation is the bread accidents. By Divine power, quantity is conserved in being so that it exists *per se* apart from any subject, and so does not exist in the mode of accident but in the mode of substance. By contrast, the other permanent non-relative and relative accidents do continue to exist in the mode of accidents, because qualities exist in quantity as in a subject, and relatives are founded on qualities and quantity as before.[34]

IV. Elaborating on the Causal Consequences

Earlier Giles considered what sorts of causal interaction the Body of Christ was able to engage in by virtue of being located on the altar in a non-standard way. According to Giles, changes in the Body of Christ, like the real presence of the Body of Christ under the species, are neither empirically observed nor observable. So any conclusions drawn were a product of theoretical speculation. By contrast, the eucharistic species remain literally located on the altar. Like Aquinas, Giles knows that many changes are empirically observable and observed: the host moves off the altar into the mouths of communicants; the host changes temperature, the wine species undergo condensation and rarefaction; at times the bread species are putrefied into worms or reduced to ashes, the wine species are soured into

[31] Giles of Rome, *Theoremata*, Propositio XXXIX, fos. 26vbD–27raABCD.
[32] Giles of Rome, *Theoremata*, Propositio XXXIX, fo. 27rbAB.
[33] Giles of Rome, *Theoremata*, Propositio XXXIX, fo. 26rbBCD.
[34] Giles of Rome, *Theoremata*, Propositio XL, fo. 27vbBC.

vinegar.[35] Like Aquinas, Giles recognizes two problems that arise from Aristotelian physics about how these phenomena can be saved if the substance subject is not there.

Like Aquinas, Giles is sensitive to the *No Prime Matter Problem*: in Aristotelian physics, there must be a persistent subject to function as the material cause of the change. Substance is the mobile that moves, that changes quantity and quality. Prime matter persists through substantial change and is informed by first one substantial form and then another. But, if the substance, the prime matter, and the substantial form of the bread are not there, what can the material cause of such changes be?

Like Aquinas, Giles recognizes and wrestles with the *No Substantial Form Problem*. Like Aquinas, Giles identifies a hierarchy of causes within the Aristotelian substance itself, so that the substantial form is the principal active cause and the accidents are secondary or instrumental causes in relation to it. Giles explains that one might think that accidents act in virtue of substantial form, because of the principal that

[T33] action (*agere*) pertains to a thing the way existence (*esse*) pertains to it.

Normally and naturally, accidents inhere in the composite substance as in a subject and so depend on the substance subject for their existence. Therefore, by [T33], accidents that could not exist without substantial form could not act without substantial form either.[36]

Alteration. So far as qualitative changes are concerned, Giles responds that in the sacrament quantity plays the role of matter and quality the role of form. Quantity can play the role of matter, because—by Divine power—it exists *per se* independently of any subject. Where quality is concerned, Giles applies [T33] to draw the opposite conclusion: since quality actually exists without substantial form, it can—by [T33]—act without substantial form to produce qualitative change. For, in acting to produce qualitative change, quality does not over-reach its species.[37]

Condensation and Rarefaction. If dimensive quantity is the subject that persists through qualitative change and as such is subject first to one qualitative form and then to another, what is the subject that persists through changes in dimensive quantity, when the sacramental species are rarefied or condensed? Like Aquinas, Giles picks up on Averroes'

[35] Giles of Rome, *Theoremata*, Proposition XLII, fo. 29vaAB–vbD.
[36] Giles of Rome, *Theoremata*, Propositio XLIII, fo. 30vbB.
[37] Giles of Rome, *Theoremata*, Propositio XLIII, fo. 30vaB–vbB.

distinction between two kinds of dimensive quantity: indeterminate dimensions through which matter is so much; and determinate dimensions through which a body occupies so much place. Indeterminate dimensions are prior to determinate dimensions, and the latter are founded on the former. In the order of explanation, matter is first of a given quantity (so much); then it exists in larger or smaller determinate volumes and accordingly is rarer or denser. Giles concludes that indeterminate dimensions are what persist through the change of determinate dimensions in condensation and rarefaction of the eucharistic species.[38]

Giles pauses to consider the objection that matter is necessary even for accidental changes because there is a third theoretical role for it to play: whether the change is substantial or accidental, forms are *educed from the potency of the matter.* Giles's reply is significant: he reduces a form's eduction from the potency of the matter to the fact that the form does not exist *per se* but depends on the efficient causality of matter for its production/conservation. In this sense, forms could be educed from anything else that could be their subject of inherence *and* play that efficient causal role. If indeterminate dimensions could exist *per se*, accidental forms could be founded on and educed from them. Giles concludes that this is what happens in the sacrament of the altar.[39] Already Aquinas has maintained that the role of the substance subject as material cause is to exercise efficient causality in the production and conservation of the accidents that inhere in it as in a subject. In this passage, Giles breaks the substance subject down into components and applies the same reasoning to the matter and to the indeterminate dimensions. This is surprising, because matter is otherwise associated with potentiality and with not active but passive efficient causal power. Likewise, quality is usually contrasted with quantity on the ground that quality is but quantity is not a principle of action. To Giles, both conclusions seem to be logical consequences of Aquinas's move to analyze the theoretical role subject-of-inherence in terms of exercised efficient causal power in the production and/or conservation of what inheres.

Generation and Corruption. Giles notes two problems that arise regarding the species' role in generation and corruption: one from the side of matter, and the other from the side of substantial form. First, the *No Prime Matter Problem*: normally and naturally, when X is corrupted into Y (fire into air;

[38] Giles of Rome, *Theoremata*, Propositio XLIV, fo. 31rbD–vaAB.
[39] Giles of Rome, *Theoremata*, Propositio XLIV, fo. 32raCD.

Beulah the cow into a corpse), the prime matter of X persists through the change, loses one substantial form and acquires another. How can eucharistic species be putrefied into worms or reduced to ashes, when the bread matter is gone? Second, the *No Substantial Form Problem*: even if (as Giles claims) qualities that exist independently of substantial forms could act independently of substantial forms to produce other qualities, such independent qualities surely could not over-reach their species and act alone to produce a different substantial form in anything else. By the *Causal Nobility Principle*, equivocal causes must be nobler than their effects, and substantial form is nobler than accidents. The qualities of X must act in the power of the substantial form of X, if they are to produce a new substantial form in Y. How could the eucharistic species act to produce new substantial forms in other things when the substantial form of bread is gone?

Turning into Worms and Ashes. So far as the *No Prime Matter Problem* is concerned, Giles follows the lines laid down by Aquinas. Giles agrees that the generated worms and ashes are hylomorphic composites that have a material component, but rejects a long list of previous proposals as to where the matter comes from. Not the normal and natural way from bread substance, because the bread is no longer there, having been transubstantiated into the Body of Christ.[40] Like Aquinas, Giles rejects various proposals to supply the matter by having the bread or the prime matter of the bread return because—given eucharistic constraints—there is no way to return them in time. For Giles joins Aquinas in denying that anything else is present under the species while the Body of Christ is there. And the Body of Christ remains under the species so long as accidents naturally compatible with bread substance are there. Thus, the bread or prime matter of the bread do not return so long as accidents naturally suitable to bread are there. But it would be incongruous for bread substance to return at a time when accidents that cannot belong to bread substance are there. Indeed, the first instant of such qualities is the instant at which the new substance (matter–form composite) appears. Normally and naturally, when worms or ashes are produced from putrefying or burning bread, the instant at which worms or ashes appear is the first instant at which the bread substance is no more.[41]

Timing problems also beleaguer Abelard's suggestion that worms and ashes are generated from the surrounding air. For the generated substance

[40] Giles of Rome, *Theoremata*, Propositio XLV, fo. 32vaCD.
[41] Giles of Rome, *Theoremata*, fo. 32vbC.

comes to be where the corrupted substance was. If worms and ashes come to be where the bread species were, the surrounding air will have to move into that place from the surround. Since—Giles maintains—two quantities could not be in the same place at once, the air could not move there so long as species suitable to bread lasted. But the worms or ashes are generated instantaneously in the first instant at which the bread-suitable species no longer exist. And the air could only then begin to move to the relevant place. Because locomotion takes time, the air could not get there in time to do any good! Giles adds that, even if it could, air is an element and it is physically impossible for mixed bodies (such as worms) to be generated from a single element![42]

Giles has tried to explain how God could convert any hylomorphic composite X into another hylomorphic composite Y by miraculously reaching beneath the individuation of the matter in X and informing matter as quiddity with the substantial form of Y. But this analysis could not be adapted to show how indeterminate dimensions could be converted into matter.[43]

Embracing the common methodological principle that miracles should be kept to a minimum in accounting for natural phenomena, Giles forwards an alternative account that he hopes will put the mind to rest. Up until the instant at which the worms are generated, no matter is there but only the eucharistic species. At the temporal instant of worm generation, five things happen simultaneously: many bread-suitable accidents are corrupted; new accidents are introduced; the Body of Christ ceases to be there; matter begins to be there; and the substantial form of worms is educed from the potency of the matter. Among the temporally simultaneous, there are natural priorities and posteriorities: the introduction of accidents unsuitable to bread substance is naturally prior to and disposes the matter for receiving the substantial form of worms.[44]

Despite the fact that the matter (in the amount the bread would have had) has to be newly created by God, Giles cleverly contends that the generation of the worms is no more miraculous than the ensouling of a human fetus is. Giles maintains that it is not supernatural for one human being to beget another. Yet, natural processes do not educe the intellectual soul from the

[42] Giles of Rome, *Theoremata*, Propositio XLV, fo. 32vbAB.
[43] Giles of Rome, *Theoremata*, Propositio XLV, fo. 33raC.
[44] Giles of Rome, *Theoremata*, Propositio XLV, fo. 34rbA.

potency of the matter, because no combination of internal or external created efficient causes suffice to produce the intellectual soul in matter. Rather intellectual souls require to be created by God. The process remains natural, because, when the fetus is sufficiently developed, the matter is naturally disposed for the introduction of the intellectual soul. Giles insists that, so far from being miraculous when God introduces the intellectual soul by creation, it would be a miracle if the intellectual soul were not introduced into such naturally disposed matter.[45]

Generalizing, Giles maintains that

> [T34] when something X, according to its nature and existence, has an order to another Y, it is not miraculous for X to be conjoined to Y, even if X's conjunction with Y involves something's being newly created by God. On the contrary, it would be a miracle for X not to be conjoined to Y in such circumstances.

Returning to the sacrament of the altar, it is a miracle when God confers *per se* existence on the bread accidents. But no new miracle is involved when these permanent accidents continue to exist without any matter to inhere in. Giles compares this to a blind man: it is a miracle when he receives his sight, but no new miracle is involved in his continuing to see afterwards. Moreover, no new miracle is involved when external causes act to change the accidents to the point that they are no longer compatible with bread substance. But the new accidents of themselves have a natural aptitude to inhere in matter, and the first miracle did not confer *per se* existence on them. Rather it conferred *per se* existence on the indeterminate dimensions of the bread for only so long as they remain subject to qualities suitable to bread substance. Since the new accidents have a natural order to matter, by [T34], no new miracle is involved in matter's coming to be there when they do.[46] It is a matter of Divine concurrence.

Producing New Substantial Forms in Something Else. Giles is firmly committed to the *Causal Nobility Principle*: what is lower on the scale of being has less causal power and so cannot act alone and unassisted to produce anything higher. Ontological eminence and quantity of causal power are positively correlated and directly proportional. *The No Substance Agent Problem* raises its head. Eucharistic species, including the active qualities, are all accidents.

[45] Giles of Rome, *Theoremata*, Propositio XLV, fo. 33rbD–vaB.

[46] Giles of Rome, *Theoremata*, Propositio XLV, fos. 33vaC–34raA.

However they may be able to act alone to produce qualities, they cannot act alone and unassisted to produce substantial forms in other things. Rather, qualities cannot change matter to generate a substance unless they act in the power of their own substantial form.[47]

Giles turns to the case where a drop of water is added to a consecrated chalice. Naturally and normally, according to medieval applications of Aristotelian science, when a drop of water is added to a chalice of wine, the wine accidents will act in the power of their substantial form to change the drop of water into wine. But in the consecrated chalice, the wine—prime matter and substantial form—is no longer there, because it has been converted into the Blood of Christ. The indicated conclusion seems to be that the wine accidents will be able to change the accidents of the water drop but will be unable to corrupt its substantial form. Giles hesitates, however, since the senses testify that the added water drop becomes indistinguishable. Even if it does not belong to the senses to make judgments about substance, Giles thinks the phenomena would be better saved by admitting that the water has been turned into wine. Giles reaches for an example from biology to illustrate how accidents might act in the power of their substantial form even though they are no longer joined with it. Lion semen cannot dispose matter to receive a lion soul without acting in virtue of the substantial form of lion. Yet, the power in the semen has to do this when it is no longer conjoined to the lion soul of the father. Giles is imagining that somehow substance-generating power has been conferred on the lion semen through its previous connection. Likewise, for wine accidents![48]

[47] Giles of Rome, *Theoremata*, Propositio XLVIII, fo. 36vbCD.
[48] Giles of Rome, *Theoremata*, Propositio XLVIII, fo. 37raB–rbA.

9

Independent Accidents: Scotus and Ockham

I. 'Accident' as a Denominative Term

Categories theory divides the highest genera into substance and accidents. The doctrine of the Incarnation makes us wonder, does it follow from what it is to be a substance that any and every individual substance exists *per se*? Likewise, eucharistic doctrine drives us to ask, does it follow from what it is to be an accident that any and every accident exists in a subject? This way of putting the question makes it sound as if 'substance' and 'accident' are both natural-kind terms that receive real definitions.

Scotus emphasizes, 'substance' is an absolute term that names the first and chief category. But 'accident' is a denominative term like 'white', so that it is necessary to distinguish what it signifies *per se* from what is denominated by it. 'White' *per se* signifies whiteness, but 'white' denominates a wide variety of things that are modified by whiteness—a wide variety of whiteness-haver's such as Nordic humans, stones, walls, and paper. Likewise, 'accident' *per se* signifies a relation to a foundation or a subject of inherence, but 'accident' denominates things of many different genera (of the remaining nine categories) to which such a relation might pertain. When the question is asked, whether any accident might exist independently of inhering in a subject, the issue is whether any of the things denominated by the term 'accident' might actually exist without having the relation that the term 'accident' *per se* signifies.[1]

[1] Scotus, *Op. Ox.* IV, d. 12, q. 1, nn. 5–6; Wadding VIII. 711.

General Arguments that Accidents Essentially Depend on a Subject. Like Aquinas and Giles, Scotus rehearses general arguments from *Categories* theory that appear to support the negative conclusion that it is not metaphysically possible for any accident to exist without a subject. But Scotus's objectors frame the difficulties in a somewhat different way. [1] *The Division of Being* argument declares that being is fundamentally divided into being *per se* and being in another. Since the former pertains to substance and the latter to accidents, it is impossible for substance not to exist *per se* and impossible for substance to exist in another. Likewise, it is impossible for an accident to exist *per se* and impossible for an accident to exist without existing in another. [2] *The Natural Priority* argument begins with the self-evident proposition that what is essentially naturally posterior cannot exist without what is essentially naturally prior to it. 'X is naturally posterior to Y' means that X depends for X's existence on Y and Y does not depend for Y's existence on X. If it is essential to X to be naturally posterior to Y, then it is impossible for X to exist without depending on Y and hence impossible for X to exist without Y. But *Categories* theory makes accident naturally posterior to substance, while substance is the principle of all beings. Therefore, it is impossible for an accident to exist without a substance whose accident it is. [3] Another *Definitional Connection* argument notes that there are many kinds of definitional connections: sometimes X is included in the definition of Y because X is the genus or differentia of Y and so one of Y's essential constituents. Other times, X is included in the definition of Y *as something added*, say because X is a necessary cause of Y. This argument contends that substance is a necessary cause of accidents, just as much as God is of creatures, and so occurs in the definition of accidents as something added. It concludes that a substance subject is something that no accident can exist without. [4] Finally, Scotus cites a semantic argument, different from the Natural Signification argument considered by Aquinas. *The Same Significatum* argument maintains that 'whiteness' and 'white' have the same significatum—namely, whiteness. Likewise, for other corresponding absolute and denominative terms—for example, 'quantity' and 'quantum.' But there is no quantum without a subject. Therefore there is no quantity without a subject either.[2]

Scotus counters these arguments and their conclusion by first distinguishing *aptitudinal versus actual* (in)dependence. The natural aptitude to exist one

[2] Scotus, *Op. Ox.* IV, d. 12, q. 1, n. 2; Wadding VIII.702.

way as opposed to another does pertain to a thing essentially. Thus, it is essential to substance to be naturally apt to exist *per se*, and essential to any and every accident to be naturally apt to exist in another. Consequently, re [1] the Division of Being argument, *aptitudinal per se* existence and *aptitudinal* existence in another do divide being. But many Aristotelian natural aptitudes are naturally obstructible (for example, the natural aptitude of earthen objects to seek the center is obstructed by the floor of the house or the baseball bat propelling the ball high over the stadium). Even more natural aptitudes are obstructible by Divine power (for example, fire's power to destroy the three young men in Nebuchadnezzar's fiery furnace). Scotus holds that Divine power can likewise obstruct the natural aptitude of substance to exist *per se* (as happens with the human nature of Christ in the Incarnation) and—in some cases—the natural aptitude of accidents to exist in another. Consequently, *actual* being *per se* does not pertain to substance essentially, and *actual* being in another does not pertain to every kind of accident essentially. Scotus concludes that *actual* being *per se* versus *actual* being *per accidens* is not a fundamental division of being.[3]

Likewise, re [2] the Natural Priority argument, *aptitudinal* natural posteriority and *aptitudinal* natural priority are essential, but *actual* natural posteriority and *actual* natural priority are not.[4] Divinely obstructible aptitudinal natural posteriority does not make a thing as dependent on its subject as any and every creature is on God. For not only is any and every creature *apt* to depend on God; it is metaphysically impossible for a creature to exist without so depending. Consequently, [3] the Definitional Connection argument fails to show that substance is included in the definition of any and every accident thing as something added. Finally, so far as [4] the Same Significatum argument is concerned, it confuses the two types of signification that belong to denominative terms. The *per se* signification of 'quantity' and 'quantum' is the same. But 'quantum' also *denominates* the subject of the quantity (the quantity-haver). 'Quantity' does not share this denominative signification.[5] Thus, none of these arguments shows that inherence in a subject is essential to whatever 'accident' denominates.

Redividing Being: Absolute versus Relative. Seizing the initiative, Scotus reminds us that being can be divided many ways, not only into aptitudinally

[3] Scotus, *Op. Ox.* IV, d. 12, q. 1, n. 23; Wadding VIII. 724.
[4] Scotus, *Op. Ox.* IV, d. 12, q. 1, n. 26; Wadding VIII. 725.
[5] Scotus, *Op. Ox.* IV, d. 12, q. 1, n. 27; Wadding VIII. 726.

independent versus aptitudinally dependent, but also into absolute versus relative. [1] *Absolutes* include the Divine essence, substance, quantity, and quality. It is a fundamental contradiction to suppose that any absolute being essentially includes a relation.[6] It follows that absolute accidents do not essentially depend on their subjects, and that actual inherence does not pertain to absolute accidents *per se* the first way (as genus or differentia) or *per se* the second way (as proper *passio).* At most, Scotus reasons, the subject pertains to an absolute accident only as an external cause. For the power of the created external cause (for example, the subject) can always be supplied by Divine power.[7]

[2] By contrast, it follows from what it is to be *a relation or a relative* that no relation or relative can exist without a foundation-in/on-which and a term-to-which. The similarities of two whites to one another require to be founded on their whitenesses as proximate subjects of inherence. When fire causes heat in the log, the relation of causation requires to be founded on fire's calefactive power (= its heat). Even relations in the Godhead (Paternity, Filiation, and Spiration) require a foundation (namely, the Divine intellect or Divine will power) and/or a supposit (which—together with the Divine essence—they constitute). Thus, Scotus insists, it follows from what it is to be *a relation, not* from what it is to be *an accident*, that it is metaphysically impossible for an accidental relation or relative to exist without a proximate subject of inherence.[8] It follows further that some accidents (namely, relations or relatives) can exist in others (for example, qualities) as in their proximate subjects of inherence. Without such inherence, no created absolute substance or accident would be related to anything else.[9]

Objections and Replies. Scotus's response to the by now predictable protest—that the subject is the material cause of an accident, and as material cause is not an external but an internal cause—returns to *Categories* theory. If in general subjects were essential to accidents, then the union of subject and accident would always be essential or *per se.* For adding to something what pertains to its essence does not yield a being *per accidens* but a being *per se.* But white Socrates constitutes a *per accidens* union. Therefore, the dependence of

[6] Scotus, *Op. Ox.* IV, d. 12, q. 1, n.10; Wadding VIII. 717.

[7] Scotus, *Op. Ox.* IV, d. 12, q.1, n.10; Wadding VIII. 717; IV, d. 12, q.1, n. 21; Wadding VIII. 723.

[8] Scotus, *Op. Ox.* IV, d. 12, q. 2, nn. 9, 14, 18–19; Wadding VIII. 731, 733–5.

[9] Scotus, *Op. Ox.* IV, d. 12, q. 2, nn. 2, 16; Wadding VIII. 733–4.

absolute accidents on their subjects is not absolutely necessary—it is not contradictory that an absolute accident exist independently of its subject.

Scotus holds, and he interprets the philosophers as holding, that normally and naturally subjects are efficient partial causes of the accidents that inhere in them. When the philosophers claim that accidents cannot exist without their subjects, this is not because they believe that it belongs to the essence of accidents actually to inhere in a material cause. Rather it is because the philosophers reject the Solo Divine Action principle and maintain that the essential order of efficient causes is absolutely necessary. The philosophers deny that the first cause can cause the caused without the secondary cause. Thus, Scotus explains, the philosophers do not think it is possible for anything else to supply the subject's efficient causality with respect to its accident. That is why they deny that accidents can exist without subjects.[10]

Scotus acknowledges that if inherence is not essential to absolute accidents, then it is an external relation, which pertains to them contingently through the action of an external cause.[11] Opponents try to turn this consequence into a refutation of Scotus's position. Take white Socrates. If inherence is an external relation (one that foundation and term could each and both exist without), then the inherence of whiteness in Socrates will be a relative accident really distinct from and inhering in the whiteness. But then the inherence of whiteness in Socrates will inhere in the whiteness by a further relation of inherence that is really distinct from and inhering in it, and so on ad infinitum. If inherence is not essential to absolute accidents, there will be an infinite progression of really distinct inherence relations. But a simultaneously existing actual infinity is impossible. Opponents conclude that inherence must be really the same as and essential to whiteness.[12]

Scotus's own theory of relations averts these conclusions. Where real relations are concerned, Scotus reasons that, if the foundation could exist without a relation, the relation is really distinct from the foundation; but if the foundation could not exist without the relation, the relation is really the same as but distinct formally from the foundation. Thus, if two white things could not exist without being similar, still each of the two could exist without the other and so without its relation of similarity to the other.

[10] Scotus, *Op. Ox.* IV, d. 12, q.1, n. 10; Wadding VIII. 717. See also *Op.Ox.* IV, d. 12, q. 3, n. 33; Wadding VIII. 754.

[11] Scotus, *Op. Ox.* IV, d. 12, q. 1, n. 21; Wadding VIII. 723.

[12] Scotus, *Op. Ox.* IV, d. 12, q. 1, nn. 11–12; Wadding VIII. 718.

Likewise, if this fire causes heat in that log, the fire could nevertheless exist without being the cause of heat in that log (say, if the log never existed or were always placed too far away). The similarity relation and causal relation are really distinct from the white and from the fire respectively. By contrast, neither a white thing nor fire could exist without essentially efficient causal dependence on God. Therefore, Scotus concludes that a creature's efficient causal dependence on God is really the same as the creature. But that does not mean that God or dependence on God pertains to the quiddity of any and every creature. If it did, then all creatures would be relatives; among creatures there would be no absolutes to be found. Rather, the creature and its dependence, while really the same, remain distinct formally.

Returning to the case of white Socrates, the inherence of whiteness in Socrates (call it I_1) is really distinct from the whiteness, because Socrates and the whiteness could both exist without the whiteness inhering in Socrates. But, because relations by their very nature cannot exist without a foundation and a term, I_1 could not exist without inhering in the whiteness (call that inherence relation I_2). Since I_1 could not exist without I_2, I_1 is really the same as I_2, and there is no infinite progression of really distinct relative things. But I_1 remains formally distinct from I_2, because the foundations and terms of the two relations are distinct: the foundation of I_1 is the whiteness and the term of I_1 is Socrates, but the foundation of I_2 is I_1, and the term of I_2 is the whiteness.

Thus, on Scotus's theory of relations, absolute accidents may be contingently related to their subjects by really distinct external relations without running any risk of an infinite series of really distinct things. And, even where the foundation is really the same as its real relation of dependence, the foundation and the relation remain formally distinct.[13]

Despite all of this, Scotus does make a concession to those who want to insist on a *conceptual* connection between any and all accidents and subjects of inherence. He distinguishes between a definition that analyzes the whole quiddity of a thing into genus and differentia that pertain to the definiendum *per se* the first way, from a perfect concept of the definiendum that "puts the mind to rest." Scotus has admitted that aptitudinal dependence is

[13] Scotus, *Op. Ox.* IV, d. 12, q.1, nn. 17–18; Wadding VIII. 720–1. For a fuller discussion of Scotus's theory of relations and Ockham's critique of it, see my *William Ockham* (Notre Dame, IN: University of Notre Dame Press, 1987), ch.7, pp. 217–50. See also Mark G. Henninger, SJ, *Relations: Medieval Theories 1250–1325* (Oxford: Clarendon Press, 1989), ch. 5, pp. 68–97.

essential to any and all accidents. They differ in this from substance that is aptitudinally independent. Even when thinking of aptitudinal as opposed to actual dependence, Scotus reasons, the mind will not rest without thinking of the term of dependence. So, in that sense, the subject of inherence is included in the perfect concept of any accident.[14]

Quantity versus Quality. Scotus has argued from what it is to be *absolute* that an absolute being cannot essentially include any relations. But, for Aquinas and Giles, the Individuation Argument was decisive in proving the metaphysical impossibility of sensible qualities existing without a subject. All agree: only individuals really exist. But sensible qualities are individuated by inhering in dimensive quantity. Further, experience shows that the bread qualities are sense perceptible and divisible. But it is metaphysically impossible for qualities to be sense perceptible and divisible without being extended.[15]

For his part, Scotus rejects the theory of individuation through quantitative dimensions, different versions of which were sponsored by Aquinas, Giles of Rome, and Godfrey of Fontaines. Scotus takes it to be metaphysically fundamental that

[P27] no being is singular formally through something of another genus.

Quantity and quality are distinct categories. Aquinas, Giles, and Godfrey all take it that indeterminate and/or determinate quantities are things really distinct from sensible qualities. Therefore, quantities cannot be the formal reason that makes the sensible qualities the very individuals they are.[16]

Another argument against the metaphysical possibility of sensible qualities existing independently of quantity begins with the plausible premiss that what distinguishes sensible from spiritual qualities is that the former are by nature sense perceptible while the latter are by nature not sense perceptible. It continues with the thesis that only what is quantified is sense perceptible, and concludes that sensible qualities are essentially quantified in the sense that it is metaphysically impossible for them to exist without inhering in quantity as in a subject.

[14] Scotus, *Op. Ox.* IV, d. 12, q. 1, nn. 19–20; Wadding VIII. 721–2; IV, d. 12, q. 2, a. 1; Wadding VIII. 734.

[15] Scotus, *Op. Ox.* IV, d. 12, q. 2,a. 5; Wadding VIII. 729–30.

[16] Scotus, *Op. Ox.* IV, d. 12, q. 2, n. 6; Wadding VII. 730.

Scotus's response is that 'sense perceptible' is ambiguous between a proximate and a remote potency for being sensed. A thing is in remote potency for being sensed if it has a sufficient form but does not exist under the mode suitable for being sensed (that is, under the quantitative mode); in proximate potency, when it is also quantified. It is essential to sensible qualities generally (for example, to whiteness) to be in proximate-or-remote potency for being sensed, and it is essential to spiritual qualities generally (for example, to wisdom) not to be in either proximate or remote potency with respect to being sensed. Likewise, it is essential to whiteness to be naturally apt to perfect a body, but it does not actually do so except when it exists in the quantitative mode. The fundamental reason why whiteness cannot perfect an angel is that there is an immediate repugnance between the two forms. Scotus counts the fact that an angel cannot be the subject of quantity as only a secondary reason.[17]

Theological consensus—that the bread accidents exist on the altar without substance—drove the common conclusion that some bread accident must exist there and so be metaphysically capable of existing there without a subject. But—having rejected his predecessors' "individuation" arguments that quantity and only quantity would be metaphysically capable of *per se* existence—Scotus finds it necessary to reconsider whether the independent existence of sensible qualities is metaphysically possible. Scotus first considers the question within the framework of the common opinion that quantities are things really distinct from substance and qualities. He draws his arguments from the essential orders of dependence and of eminence, in turn.

[1] In an essential order of dependence, relatives depend on the posterior and proximate more than on the prior and remote, because it follows from what it is to be relative that the relative exists in a foundation, but nothing further follows about whether that foundation constitutes or exists in an individual substance. With absolutes, however, it is the other way around: an absolute thing essentially depends more on the prior and remote than on the posterior and proximate. The common opinion holds that sensible qualities inhere immediately in dimensive quantity, which is their proximate subject, and indirectly in substance, which is their remote subject. Scotus infers that sensible qualities depend more on substance than they do on dimensive quantity. But theological consensus has it that—after

[17] Scotus, *Op. Ox.* IV, d.12, q. 2, nn. 7–8; Wadding VIII. 730.

consecration—the bread qualities exist on the altar without the bread substance. Therefore, it is metaphysically possible for sensible qualities to exist without inhering in quantity, their proximate and posterior subject.[18]

[2] So far as the essential order of eminence is concerned, Scotus reckons that a being's place in the hierarchy is a function of its intensive actuality. Scotus advances several more and less persuasive arguments that qualities are just as noble as or nobler than dimensive quantity. [a] Substance has more intensive actuality than either quantity or quality. Like Aquinas and Giles, Scotus suggests that quantity is more substance-like in its capacity to stand under and serve as the subject of other forms, while qualities are more substance-like in being principles of action. His conclusion—that quantity is more like prime matter, while qualities are more like substantial form—puts quality at least even and maybe ahead of quantity in the eminence rankings. Unfortunately, this piece of reasoning makes the problematic assumption that qualities are active principles, but quantities are not. But Scotus himself joins the consensus that the subject of inherence exercises efficient causality with respect to producing and/or conserving what inheres. Scotus also sometimes claims that—normally and naturally—quantitative dimensions exercise efficient causal power to make their body fill the place it occupies and to exclude other bodies from being there at the same time.[19]

[b] A second argument from eminence contends that there is a closer correspondence between substance and quality than between substance and quantity, because the nobler substance has nobler qualities, but the nobler substance does not necessarily have greater quantity. The reason is that greater size seems to be inversely correlated with permanence (for example, larger bodies are more generable and corruptible than the elements).[20] [c] Again, qualities are part of what constitutes a thing's reaching its end (for example, the qualities that constitute beatific vision and enjoyment), but quantity is not.[21] [d] Again, some qualities—for example, wisdom, justice—are absolute perfections (that is, good-making features that do not imply any bad-making features) and share a formal principle (*ratio*) with Divine wisdom and Divine justice. But no quantities are absolute perfections.[22]

[18] Scotus, *Op. Ox.* IV, d. 12, q. 2, n. 9; Wadding VIII. 731.
[19] Scotus, *Op. Ox.* IV, d.49, q.16, nn.5–6; Wadding X. 612–13.
[20] Scotus, *Op. Ox.* IV, d. 12, q. 2, a. 9; Wadding VIII. 731.
[21] Scotus, *Op. Ox.* IV, d.12, q. 2, n. 9; Wadding VIII. 731.
[22] Scotus, *Op. Ox.* IV, d. 12, q. 2, n. 10; Wadding VIII. 731.

Overall, even if the common opinion—that quantities are things (*res*) really distinct from substance and qualities—were accepted, Scotus would see no reason to regard qualities as ontologically inferior to quantities where intensive actuality is concerned. If quantity is metaphysically capable of existing without a subject, quality should be, too. On the other hand, Scotus mentions but does not develop another opinion: that quantity is not really distinct from substance and quality. Scotus remarks that its adherents have to hold that the bread qualities exist in the eucharist without inhering in any really distinct quantity, and hence that qualities are metaphysically capable of independent existence.[23]

II. What Effects Can Eucharistic Species Cause?

Here it is possible to distinguish two questions. First, how are the causal capacities of eucharistic accidents affected by their separation from any substance subject? Second, are the causal capacities of the eucharistic accidents sufficient to explain the range of observed phenomena? Scotus dwells on both at length.

Instrumental Causality? Aquinas defends his bold answer to both questions at once—that separating eucharistic accidents from their substance subject has no impact on their causal capacities and that eucharistic accidents are sufficient to explain the range of observed phenomena—by appeal to his doctrine of instrumental causality. When the bread accidents inhered in the bread substance, the bread accidents were instruments of the bread substance and as such participated in the principal agent's causal power. According to Aquinas, this instrumental causal power is something that inheres in the instrument and thus—he imagines—is something that Divine power can preserve in the accidents after the substance is no more. Hence, Aquinas declares, the separate accidents can continue to act in the power of the substance.

Scotus dismisses Aquinas's account of instrumental causality as patent nonsense. The notion that instrumental causal power is anything in the

[23] Scotus, *Op. Ox.* IV, d. 12, q. 2, n.15; Wadding VIII. 734. Scotus may be referring to the opinion of Peter John Olivi, but condemnations of his theological works meant that masters could not mention him by name in their public disputations or written work. See David Burr, *Eucharistic Presence and Conversion in Late Thirteenth-Century Franciscan Thought* (Philadelphia: American Philosophical Society, 1984), p. 86.

instrument while the principal agent is acting is already riddled with difficulties (see Chapter 3 above). So also, and all the more so, any idea that instrumental causal power is something that can outlast the existence and action of the principal agent. Scotus mocks Aquinas's suggestion that the separate accidents continue to act in the power of substance, with the retort that nothing acts in the power of anything that does not exist![24]

Do Supposits Have a Monopoly on Agency? Some formulations of the No Substance Agent Problem appeal to philosophical authorities in support of the thesis that only supposits (that is, only individual substances such as Socrates or this fire) act. Even if Divine power makes eucharistic accidents to exist independently, they are not supposits because they are not substances. After the consecration, the bread substance will be gone, and there will be no relevant supposit there. Hence, all causal interaction should cease—which is contrary to experience.

Scotus's response is to deny that 'action pertains only to a supposit' is a correct construal of Aristotle's claim in *Metaphysics* I. Rather Aristotle is insisting that only *singulars* (as opposed to universals) act. But substance supposits are not the only singulars: the Divine essence, human souls, substantial and accidental forms, and chunks of prime matter are singular as well. Again, Boethius says that what is (*quod est*) and that by which it is (*quo est*) are distinct. Certainly, in many cases the substance supposit (for example, this fire) is the ultimate subject to be denominated from the action (for example, heating), while the form (for example, the substantial form of fire and its proper accident heat) is the formal principle by which the action occurs. But—Scotus contends—it is not generally true of creatures that what acts and the formal principle by which it acts are distinct. Assuming—as Scotus elsewhere argues against Aquinas—that the human soul is a simple essence and really identical with its powers, what acts (that is, the soul) and that by which it acts (that is, intellect and will) are not different. Thus counter-exampled, the quote from Boethius should not be allowed to settle the question whether the separate accidents (all of which are forms) can be subjects of action. Normally and naturally, both the supposit (for example, this fire) and the formal principle by which it heats (for example, the substantial form of fire and/or its proper accident heat) can be denominated from the action (for example, heating)—the form(s) proximately and the supposit remotely. Normally and naturally, there is a substance supposit;

[24] Scotus, *Op. Ox.* IV, d. 12, q. 3, nn. 6–8; Wadding VIII. 741–2.

and, where there is, we usually prefer to speak of the substance supposit as acting. But where there is no substance supposit, where (as happens in the eucharist) the accidents exist in the mode of a supposit, why should there be any problem about denominating them from the action in question?[25]

Abstract Accidents? Some argue that separating eucharistic accidents from their substance subject would rob them of all agency, because separate quantity would be mathematical (because it would not inhere in any material substance). In contemporary philosophical parlance, separating quantity from its substance subject would turn it into an abstract object, and abstract objects are causally inert. Scotus replies that mathematical quantities abstract not only from matter but from natural qualities that are formal principles of causal interactions. But, on the common opinion, the dimensive quantity of the bread continues to be the proximate subject of natural qualities. Mere abstraction from a material subject is not enough to keep eucharistic quantity from being denominated as an agent![26]

The logic of Scotus's position takes him further. Substantial and qualitative forms of the third species (= sensible qualities) are the formal principles by which an agent acts. In themselves, these forms *are* certain causal powers. What a thing is *per se* remains unaffected by its external relations. But Scotus has argued that inherence is an external relation where absolute accidents are concerned. Therefore, the identity of these causal powers is unaffected by whether or not the forms in question in fact inhere in anything (in the case of accidental forms) or combine with matter to make something one *per se* (in the case of substantial forms). Provided sensible qualities exist in a mode suitable for action (namely, quantified), it makes no difference whether or not they inhere in a substance subject; they will produce the action for which they are a total active principle. On the common opinion, sensible qualities are quantified (and so exist in a mode suitable for action) only if they inhere in dimensive quantity. On the minority report, quantity is not anything really distinct from substance and quality. Qualities are quantified if they have one part at a distance from another, even if they do not inhere in anything at all.[27]

[25] Scotus, *Op. Ox.* IV, d. 12, q. 3, nn. 34–6; Wadding VIII. 755. For further discussion of Scotus and Ockham on supposits, see my "What's Metaphysically Special about Supposits?" *Proceedings of the Aristotelian Society*, supplementary volume 79 (2005), pp. 15–52.

[26] Scotus, *Op. Ox.* IV, d. 12, q. 3, n. 36; Wadding VIII. 756.

[27] Scotus, *Op. Ox.* IV, d. 12, q. 3, n.17; Wadding VIII. 745.

Eminence Issues. Scotus's answer to the first question is that separation from their substance subject has no impact on the causal capacities of eucharistic accidents. For Scotus, the real difficulties that separate accidents pose for saving the phenomena have to do with the second question and arise because of the Causal Nobility Principle. What a form's causal power is a function of is its intensive actuality, its degree of ontological eminence. Like Giles, Scotus is wedded to the thesis that

[P28] the total active cause must have as much intensive actuality as or more intensive actuality than the effect,

and advances it as one "as well known as any in philosophy." [P28] implies that the total active cause must be at least as perfect as or more perfect than the effect. Negatively, if X is more imperfect than Y, then X cannot be the total active principle with respect to the production of Y. Denying [P28] would make it impossible to establish an order of eminence among beings, or to prove that the first efficient cause is also the most eminent being, or to disprove that the whole universe was produced by a fly![28] Scotus holds that where a univocal and an equivocal cause concur for the same effect (for example, Ferdinand the bull and Beulah the cow concur with the sun in producing Elsie the cow), the equivocal cause is more perfect and explains the continuation of generative and corruptive activities by the univocal causes here below (for example, the rotations of the heavenly bodies explain the continuing succession of bovine generations). Where the equivocal cause (for example, the sun) could not produce the effect (for example, a perfect animal such as Elsie the cow) without the univocal cause (for example, the bovine parents Ferdinand and Beulah), that equivocal cause (for example, the sun) is less perfect than an equivocal cause (for example, God, the first efficient cause) that could produce the effect without the univocal cause (by the Solo Divine Action principle). Solo action requires more intensive actuality in an equivocal cause than merely collaborative action does, because in collaborative action some of the intensive actuality and hence causal power is supplied by the univocal agent.[29]

Returning to questions about the causal interactions of eucharistic species, Scotus calculates from [P28] that the sensible qualities there cannot be *total* active causes of effects more perfect than they are. Since substances are more

[28] Scotus, *Op. Ox.* IV, d. 12, a. 3, n. 13; Wadding VIII. 744.
[29] Scotus, *Op. Ox.* IV, d. 12, q. 3, nn. 14–16; Wadding VIII. 744–5.

perfect than qualities, sensible qualities cannot be the *total* active causes of generating or destroying substances. By contrast it seems *prima facie* as if the intensive actuality of sensible qualities would empower them to reduce or corrupt contrary qualities of equal or lesser degrees.

Scotus, however, goes beyond Giles of Rome to notice a problem about saying that sensible qualities in the eucharist are or have causal power to corrupt nearby contrary qualities of equal or lesser degree. For substances determine themselves to a certain degree of their proper accidents, so that, when the proper accidents fall below the requisite degree, the substance is corrupted. Moreover,

[P29] normally and naturally, the corruption of one substance involves the generation of another.

If, no matter how high its degree, a sensible quality cannot be the *total* active principle in the generation of substance, then—by [P29]—not in the corruption of substance; and if not in the corruption of substance, then how could it be the *total* active principle in the corruption of the limit degree of the proper accident either? Scotus goes so far as to concede, if the whole substance of the sphere of fire were corrupted and its heat accidents conserved, those accidents would not, by themselves, constitute enough causal power to corrupt a single drop of water![30]

Scotus tries on two responses to this question. (1) His first suggestion is that the sensible quality can corrupt all the degrees of its contrary up to the limit degree, but only the cause that corrupts the one substance and generates another can corrupt the limit degree. (2) Alternatively, Scotus distinguishes the contrary quality considered in itself from the contrary quality considered in relation to its substance. If the contrary quality is considered in itself, a eucharistic quality of overall greater degree has as much power to corrupt one degree of the contrary quality as another. But, if the contrary quality is considered in relation to its substance, then the eucharistic quality may lack power to corrupt the limit degree. For the substance subject that determines itself to the limit degree exercises efficient causal power to preserve the limit degree and to prevent its proper quality from falling below the limit. The eucharistic quality does not have sufficient intensive actuality to overcome the combined resistance of the contrary quality and its

[30] Scotus, *Op. Ox.* IV, d. 12, q. 3, n. 22; Wadding VIII. 748.

substance subject.[31] Thus, if heat and cold existed in quantities without a substance subject, the more intense degree of heat could corrupt any degree of the cold and a more intense degree of cold could corrupt any degree of the heat. The reason is that quantity does not determine itself to any degree of a quality. But, if heat existed in fire and cold in water, then the substance subjects would resist the corruption of the limit degree of their proper quality. In that case the limit degree would not be corrupted unless there were some other cause there to corrupt the substance itself.[32]

(3) Scotus suggests a third answer in the course of explaining the fact that eucharistic species do causally interact in ways that at least occasion the corruption and generation of substances. Since eucharistic qualities cannot be the *total* active principle of such generation and corruption, Scotus speculates that perhaps the universal cause—the rotating heavens—can introduce a substantial form such as fire or worms, when a particular cause disposes the matter. If the new substantial form were of too perfect a sort for the heavens to cause, one would have to appeal to the absolutely first cause to introduce the substantial form to which the natural agent disposes. Either way, one could say that the eucharistic qualities are able to corrupt whatever degree of the contrary quality, even the limit degree, because the universal cause and/or the absolutely first cause are/is always there to corrupt the one substance and produce the new substance when the materials are disposed, just as God regularly infuses the intellectual soul when the organic body is disposed.[33] The hypothesis would be that supplying the substantial forms when the matter is disposed would be part of Divine policy for this present state (see Chapter 2 above).

III. What Changes Can Other Causes Produce in Eucharistic Species?

Salient Distinctions. Turning from what effects eucharistic species can cause to what other causes can produce by acting on the eucharistic species, Scotus distinguishes [D1] the questions what changes in the eucharistic species are *metaphysically possible* from what changes are *producible by created*

[31] Scotus, *Op. Ox.* IV, d. 12, q. 3, n. 24; Wadding VIII. 751.

[32] Scotus, *Op. Ox.* IV, d. 12, q. 3, n. 31; Wadding VIII. 753.

[33] Scotus, *Op. Ox.* IV, d. 12, q. 3, nn. 22, 24; Wadding VIII. 748–9, 751.

causes acting on the eucharistic species. Scotus maintains that metaphysically possible changes include those whose term-to-which includes substance, those whose term-to-which is nothing, those whose term-to-which is a different quantity or quality, and those whose term-to-which is place. Giles of Rome argues that it is metaphysically impossible for successives to exist without a substance subject, because existence in the same substance subject is what makes the successive parts to be part of one and the same successive (for example, parts of numerically the same motion). Scotus joins Godfrey of Fontaines in begging to differ. If it is metaphysically possible for an accident to exist at rest (*in esse quieto*) without a subject, it is metaphysically possible for that accident to flow (for example, for the form of whiteness to undergo a continuous process of intensification from a lesser degree to a greater degree of intensity) without existing in a substance subject (for example, without Socrates or any other whiteness-haver). The flux of the form (*fluxus formae*) or the form in process (*in fieri*) does not require a substance subject any more than the form's existing at rest (*in esse quieto*) does,[34] although presumably there could not be sheer flux that takes away not only the subject but also the form that flows (for example, intensification not only without the whiteness-haver but without the whiteness). Nevertheless, not everything metaphysically possible is producible by created causes. The reason is what we may call the "Presupposed Subject Principle" that

[P17] created active causal powers are powers to transform a subject and thus require as a co-cause the passive power of the subject to be acted upon.[35]

[D2] Scotus distinguishes those changes that can be caused in the eucharistic species and the eucharist remain (that is, the Body and Blood of Christ remain really present where the species are) from those whose occurrence marks an end to real presence. Scotus merely joins the theological majority report when he advances the criterion that

[P30] the real presence lasts as long and only so long as the accidents on the altar remain bread (wine) suitable.[36]

[34] Scotus, *Op. Ox.* IV, d. 12, q. 4, n. 3; Wadding VIII. 760; IV, d. 12, q. 4, n.18; Wadding VIII. 765–6; IV, d. 12, q. 4, n. 27; Wadding VIII. 770.

[35] Scotus, *Op. Ox.* IV, d. 12, q. 4, n. 18; Wadding VIII. 765; IV, d. 12, q. 4, nn. 23–4; Wadding VIII. 768; IV, d. 12, q. 5, n. 4; Wadding VIII. 773–4.

[36] Scotus, *Op. Ox.* IV, d. 12, q. 5, n. 4; Wadding VIII. 774; IV, d. 12, q. 6, nn. 3–4; Wadding VIII. 776; IV, d. 12, q. 6, nn. 11–12; Wadding VIII. 782.

Finally, [D3] Scotus distinguishes four kinds of change: change as to where something is (locomotion); qualitative change that involves no concomitant quantitative change; qualitative change that does involve concomitant quantitative change; and changes that are primarily changes in quantity.[37]

With these distinctions in hand, Scotus returns to the eucharist to sort the types of changes: which could be produced only by Divine power, and which can be produced by created causes and how?

Qualitative Changes without Concomitant Quantitative Changes. Those who think that quantity is a really distinct thing from substance and quality—to use Ockham's mocking language, normally and naturally a kind of "skin" between substance and qualities—would seem to have an easy time explaining how created causes can produce qualitative changes that do not involve any accompanying change in quantity, because they can identify the quantity as the persistent subject on which created causes can act to produce different qualitative forms from before. Minority reporters who deny that quantity is really distinct from substance and quality would seemingly have to deny—by [P17]—that created causes can produce qualitative changes in the eucharist, because they do not recognize any persistent subject there.

As before, the issue is not quite so straightforward, because substance kinds determine themselves to certain degrees of their proper qualities, so that normally and naturally the corruption of the substance is concomitant with the corruption of the limit degree of the proper quality. But [P29], normally and naturally, the corruption of one substance involves the generation of another. It seems to follow that, normally and naturally, the causal package involved in corrupting the limit degree of the quality must be sufficient to generate the new substance as well. Earlier, in considering what effects the eucharistic accidents can produce, it was the Causal Nobility Principle that raised the problem: accidents do not by themselves have enough intensive actuality to generate substance.

Here an inverse problem—about whether and how created causes can corrupt the eucharistic accidents—is raised by [P17] the Presupposed Subject Principle and Divine policies for this present state (see Chapter 1 above). By [P30], real presence lasts only so long as bread-suitable accidents last. Likewise, the companion Divine policy is that

[37] Scotus, *Op. Ox.* IV, d. 12, q. 4, n. 19; Wadding VIII. 766.

[P31] the accidents on the altar exist *per se*, independently of substance, only so long as the real presence lasts.

So, corrupting the limit degree of bread-suitable qualities will mean the generation of a new substance (worms or fire) to be the subject of the bread-unsuitable accidents. But created causes cannot by themselves generate a new substance from the eucharistic accidents—not because of the Causal Nobility Principle, since the substance fire and its proper accident heat may have the same intensive actuality as the effect; and not because there is no passive subject present, since—on the common opinion—the quantity is there. Rather, it is because there is no *appropriate* subject present. Scotus contends—against Aquinas and Giles of Rome—that no quantity, whether indeterminate or determinate, can be the proximate subject of a substantial form; only prime matter is (see the very next section below). And, so long as real presence lasts, there is no prime matter under the accidents on the altar. Scotus concludes that since [P30] and [P31] are not naturally necessary but consequences of free and contingent Divine policy, created causes can act to corrupt the limit degree of bread-suitable qualities, because of God's corollary policy to generate a relevant substance subject for the bread-unsuitable accidents and to do so at the instant at which the bread-suitable accidents are corrupted.[38]

Condensation and Rarefaction. Some qualitative changes carry concomitant quantitative changes: notably, condensation and rarefaction, where heating and cooling bring on expansion and contraction of the volume occupied. Scotus reviews several theories and finds condensation and rarefaction a difficult case. *The Indeterminate Quantity Theory*. Giles of Rome (and sometimes Aquinas) try to save the phenomena of created causes producing condensation and rarefaction by appealing to Averroes' distinction between indeterminate quantity that inheres immediately in prime matter and renders it divisible into parts from determinate quantity that is consequent upon the substantial form and confers determinate size, shape, and density on the substance subject. On this picture, Aquinas and Giles reason, even if the substance is gone, indeterminate quantity is there to persist through changes in determinate quantity.

Scotus rejects this idea as unAristotelian. Form essentially determines itself to a subject that can receive it, just as subjects essentially determine

[38] Scotus, *Op. Ox.* I, d. 12, q. 5, n. 4; Wadding VIII. 774; IV, d. 12, q. 6, nn.11–13; Wadding VIII. 781–2.

themselves to a range of forms that they can receive. Matter is the proximate subject of substantial form, not of quantity, indeterminate or otherwise. Substantial form is essentially determined to substantial matter as its proximate subject. It is by nature incapable of perfecting anything in the genus of quantity. The reason is that substance is naturally prior to quantity and does not perfect quantity but rather (in the case of corporeal substances) the other way around. Again, substantial form is naturally apt to combine with what it perfects to make something one *per se*, but obviously substantial form cannot combine with anything in the category of quantity to make something one *per se*! Again, that on which accidents have a natural aptitude to depend cannot itself actually depend on them![39] From the point of view of *Categories* metaphysics, the Indeterminate Quantity Theory is ridiculous!

Intensification and Reduction Analogies. Another approach to understanding what happens in condensation and rarefaction is to see them as analogous to the intensification and reduction of qualities. Some qualities (such as heat and cold and colors) seem to come in degrees and can change from one to another. Three main theories were current in Scotus's time. The Succession or Generation and Corruption Theory saw each degree of a quality as a numerically distinct form in its own right, and treated the intensification and reduction of qualities as the continuous generation and corruption of successive froms from the initial degree (the term-from-which) up to and including the final degree (the term-to-which). Addition and Subtraction Theories saw higher degrees of qualities as made up of parts, and treated the intensification and reduction of qualities as the addition or subtraction of quality parts. Finally, the Mixture Theory understood lower degrees of qualities to involve a mixture with their contraries (for example, of heat with cold, of black with white), while higher degrees involved the presence in the subject of less of the contrary.

(1) *Godfrey of Fontaines's Flux of Quantitative Forms.* Scotus interpreted Godfrey of Fontaines to extend a Succession Theory of intensification and reduction of qualities to the quantative changes involved in condensation and rarefaction.[40] Godfrey reasons that the forms must be numerically distinct, because

[39] Scotus, *Op. Ox.* IV, d. 12, q. 6, n. 8; Wadding VIII. 779.

[40] Scotus's attribution of the Succession Theory to Godfrey was the subject of twentieth-century scholarly puzzlement that failed to locate texts in which Godfrey clearly sponsored that position. See Anneliese Maier, *Zwei Grundprobleme der scholastischen Naturphilosophie*, 'Das Problem der intensiven Grösse' (Rome: Edizioni di Storia e Letteratura, 1968), pp. 3–109; John F. Wippel,

[P32] the terms of motion must be incompossible.

Otherwise there would be no genuine change. Where condensation and rarefaction are concerned, Godfrey seems to maintain that [A] these involve a continuous flow of numerically distinct *quantitative* forms between the term-from-which to the term-to-which, a flux of the form (*fluxus formae*) that—*pace* Giles of Rome—requires no subject in which the successive forms inhere. Scotus agrees with Godfrey against Giles that this is metaphysically possible: it does not pertain to the essence of motion to have a substance subject. But Godfrey wants to agree with Giles that [B] the condensation and rarefaction of eucharistic species can be produced by created causes. Accordingly, Godfrey goes on to contend that this flow of quantitative forms can be produced by created causes, despite the fact that there is no persistent subject of inherence. Godfrey agrees that the passage from nothing (*nihil, non esse*) to being (*esse*) is out of reach for created causes. But he insists that, because of the continuous flux, new degrees of form do not follow from nothing (*nihil, non esse*). Rather, continuity means that each degree follows and is followed by another degree until the term-to-which is reached. Just as a substance subject has a potency for a different degree, so the earlier form has a potency to be succeeded by a later form, and the later form has a certain disposition (*habitudo*) to the previous form. If it did not, if the succession were discontinuous, it would be right to say that the later form came to be from nothing and therefore that it has to be created. But, in the continuous flux of quantitative forms involved in condensation and rarefaction, this is not the case.[41]

Godfrey tries to keep the condensation and rarefaction of eucharistic species within the range of created causes another way, by contending that the essential or *per se* change involved in condensation and rarefaction is the qualitative change, while the concomitant quantitative change is *per accidens*. On the common opinion that quantity is the proximate subject of the

"Godfrey of Fontaines on Intension and Remission of Accidental Forms," *Franciscan Studies* (1979), pp. 316–55; Edith Dudley Sylla, "Godfrey of Fontaines on Motion with Respect to Quantity of the Eucharist," in A. Maieru and A. Paravicini Bagliani (eds.), *Studi sul XIV Secolo in Memoria di Anneliese Maier* (Rome: Edizioni di Storia et Letteratura, 1981), pp. 105–41. Happily, this issue has been sorted out and Scotus's attribution verified by reference to fourteenth-century sources and to Godfrey himself in Stephen D. Dumont's "Godfrey of Fontaines and the Succession Theory of Forms at Paris in the Early Fourteenth Century," in S. Brown, T. Kobusch, and T. Dewender (eds.), *Philosophical Debates at Paris in the Early Fourteenth Century* (Leiden: Brill, 2009), pp. 39–125.

[41] Scotus, *Op. Ox.* IV, d. 12, q. 4, nn. 5–7; Wadding VIII. 761–2.

qualities (which Godfrey accepts), the *per se* change involved in condensation and rarefaction will have a subject.[42]

Contra [*B*]. Scotus attacks both of Godfrey's attempts to assign the condensation and rarefaction of eucharistic species to created causes. First, Scotus contends, the fact that an individual form is part of a continuous flow of temporally successive forms has no impact whatsoever on how much causal power it takes to produce it. The latter is a function of its intensive actuality, which will be the same whether or not it succeeds or is succeeded by anything else. It is not essential to a quantity or quality of a given degree that it be preceded or succeeded by quantities or qualities of other degrees. If a quality succeeded its contrary opposite, one would agree that it came into being from nothing. So also with subject-free degrees of quantity in the case at hand. Morever, genuine causes are simultaneous with their effects. Neither the earlier form nor its natural aptitude to be succeeded exists at the time the successor form requires to be produced. Again, there would be no temptation to posit any disposition (*habitudo*) of a form to its predecessor if the forms existed in a subject. But—Scotus insists—nothing positive exists in the separated forms that would not exist in them if they existed in a subject. Talk of a disposition (*habitudo*) reduces to the fact of succession, and mere succession does not keep the production of the subject-less forms from counting as creation.[43]

To Godfrey's second argument—that there is no problem with creatures causing condensation and rarefaction in the eucharistic species, because the *per se* change there is qualitative, and the qualitative change (that is, the heating and cooling) does have a subject—Scotus counters that the problem remains, because the quantity is the subject of the qualities, and subjects are naturally prior to that of which they are subjects. Therefore, the new quantity cannot be acquired only *per accidens* when the new quality is acquired. The new quantity is *presupposed* as already acquired when the new quality is acquired.[44]

Contra [*A*]. Scotus finds Godfrey's Succession Theory *philosophically* problematic even as an account of what goes on normally and naturally in rarefaction. For in nature accidents "cannot migrate from substance to substance": for example, this individual whiteness cannot first belong to

[42] Scotus, *Op. Ox.* IV, d. 12, q. 4, n. 3; Wadding VIII. 760.

[43] Scotus, *Op. Ox.* IV, d. 12, q. 4, nn. 14–16; Wadding VIII. 764–5.

[44] Scotus, *Op. Ox.* IV, d. 12, q. 4, n. 18; Wadding VIII. 766.

Socrates and then belong to Plato. But Godfrey holds the common opinion that quantity is the proximate subject of the qualities. If there is a continuous succession of numerically distinct quantitative forms in condensation and rarefaction, it follows that the sensible qualities that inhere in them will be likewise continuously generated and corrupted. And there will be no explanation of why—as experience shows—the qualities that inhere in degree-*n* quantity are of the same species as those that inhered in degree-*m* quantity. For example, within limits, sweet white wine in London remains sweet and white as it rarefies, while red bitter wine in Rome remains red and bitter while it rarefies. Fire does have power to heat and thereby expand the volume wine occupies. But it does not also have power to cause whiteness and sweetness in London and redness and bitterness in Rome. Call this the "Same Quality" Problem.[45]

Moreover, Godfrey's Succession Theory of quantitative change combines with his conviction that quantity individuates material substances to jeopardize another *theological* desideratum: that moderate condensation and rarefaction of the eucharistic species does not bring the real presence of Christ's Body and Blood to an end. The theological majority report has it [P30] that real presence lasts only so long as the species remain bread suitable. Scotus adds a further precision [P30′]: it lasts only so long as the accidents remain accidents that could pertain to *the very individual* bread over which the prayer of consecration has been said. Numerically distinct quantitative forms result in accidents that are not suitable to the bread that was prayed over, but to a numerically distinct bread. Hence, on Godfrey's theory of individuation, any condensation or rarefaction would bring real presence to an end.[46]

Addition and Subtraction Theories. Godfrey's principal philosophical argument for his Succession Theory begins with [P32] Aristotle's claim that the terms of motion must be incompatible and concludes that the term-from-which and the term-to-which must be numerically distinct qualitative (quantitative) forms. Scotus agrees with [P32] but rejects the inference. Strictly speaking, the terms of motion are privation (not-F) and form (F), not two incompatible forms (F and G).[47] In other contexts, Scotus himself

[45] Scotus, *Op. Ox.* IV, d. 12, q. 4, nn. 8–10; Wadding VIII. 762–3.

[46] Scotus, *Op. Ox.* IV, d. 12, q. 4, n. 10; Wadding VIII. 762–3; IV, d. 12, q. 4, n. 17; Wadding VIII. 765.

[47] Scotus, *Op. Ox.* IV, d. 12, q. 4, n. 11; Wadding VIII. 763.

favors an Addition and Subtraction Theory of intensification and reduction that sees intensifiable and reducible qualitative forms as made up of more or fewer parts. In the intensification of F-ness, a qualitative form with m F-parts has added to it $n-m$ F-parts. F_m, the qualitative form with only m F-parts, is not F_n. F_n is not wholly distinct from F_m, however, because F_m is contained in F_n as a part of it. *Mutatis mutandis* for reduction that involves the subtraction of parts. This model applied to quantities would treat quantities as made up of forms and larger quantities as having more parts than smaller quantities, where larger quantities might be obtained by addition and smaller quantities by subtraction of parts.[48]

Godfrey charges that the Addition and Subtraction Theory as applied to quantity is incoherent. Suppose air has a volume Q_m with m-quantitative parts and that the air is rarefied to a volume Q_n. If the old quantity Q_m remains, it would have to have the same subject as before, because in nature accidents do not migrate from substance to substance. But what would be the subject of the new $n-m$ quantity parts? They cannot share a subject with the old quantity, because the same part cannot be quantified by two quantities simultaneously. Nor could they find a subject in some newly produced air, because then the old air would not occupy any larger volume than it did before and so would not be rarefied after all. Being continuous with more air parts does not make the original air parts any rarer.[49]

However that may be, Scotus acknowledges that the Addition Theory of rarefaction cannot save the desideratum that eucharistic species are rarefied by created causes. For—on the Addition Theory—rarefaction involves the addition of new parts of quantity existing without a subject, and—according to Aristotelian physics—[P17] created causes cannot produce accidents without a subject on which to act.[50] Although Scotus does not say so, it would also seem to suffer from the Same Quality Problem: could fire or the sun explain why—when sweet white wine is rarefied—the new quantity parts are subject to whiteness and sweetness instead of redness and bitterness?

The Mixture Theory. Of the models of quantitative change based on analogies with the intensification and reduction of qualities, only the

48 Scotus, *Op. Ox.* IV, d. 12, q. 4, n. 11; Wadding VIII. 763.
49 Scotus, *Op. Ox.* IV, d. 12, q. 4, n. 4; Wadding VIII. 761.
50 Scotus, *Op. Ox.* IV, d. 12, q. 4, n. 22; Wadding VIII. 767–8.

Mixture Theory avoids positing the creation of new subject-less accident parts. Why not suppose that rarefaction involves putting subtler bodies in between, so that the parts of the original body are at a greater distance from one another than before? Scotus sees the appeal of this solution, but still finds it doubly problematic. First, could the created causes—for example, the fire or the sun—thought to be salient in rarefaction really bring it about that such subtle bodies move in between the rarefied species? Second, if the rarefaction of the wine species in the eucharist involved mixing it up with other subtler substances, then the resultant mixture would be one under some of whose parts the Blood of Christ would be really present and under others of whose parts it was not. Overall, Scotus is not attracted to the Mixture Theory, because he finds it counter-intuitive to say that a substance could not itself be rarefied without mixing in anything else.[51]

Scotus thus seems to bite the bullet and concede that the condensation and rarefaction of eucharistic species have to be produced by God.

Merely Quantitative Change. Far easier, Scotus thinks, are merely quantitative changes. The eucharistic species cannot literally be subject to growth and diminishment, because—in Aristotelian biophysics—these pertain only to living things. What *is* possible is the addition or subtraction of parts. The eucharistic rite brings two cases prominently to mind. The first is the fraction, when the priest breaks the consecrated host into pieces. On Scotus's analysis, this involves the actual division of parts of a continuum. The positive entity of the parts remains the same. Before the fraction, they are divisible but not actually divided; they are united into a continuous whole. At the fraction, there is a "quasi-corruption without generation" in that their continuity ceases to be, but no new positive entity is produced.[52] The second case is the addition of the contents of one consecrated chalice to the contents of another consecrated chalice. When two things that were separate are made to be continuous, the positive identity of the parts remains the same. In this case, Scotus thinks that something is acquired: namely, a disposition (*habitudo*) to being united or continuous with the positive entity of the other part.[53]

[51] Scotus, *Op. Ox.* IV, d. 12, q. 4, n. 20; Wadding VIII. 766.
[52] Scotus, *Op. Ox.* IV, d. 12, q. 4, n. 25; Wadding VIII. 769.
[53] Scotus, *Op. Ox.* IV, d. 12, q. 4, n. 26; Wadding VIII. 770.

IV. Ockham's Reassessment

Separate Accidents? In assessing the metaphysical possibility of separate accidents, Ockham follows lines laid down by Scotus. He observes the distinction between absolutes versus relatives: created relations necessarily signify an order to their subject, but accident terms in general do not.[54] Where absolutes are concerned, individual substances have their prime matter and substantial forms as *internal* causes. But all absolute accidents are related to their absolute subjects as *external* causes, and God can suspend and replace the causality of external causes. Therefore, God can make one absolute accident exist without its subject as much as any other—not only sensible qualities, but also acts of intellect and will.[55]

Ockham recognizes that some substances determine themselves to certain accidents (for example, material substances to quantity; animate substances to soul powers), while some accidents determine themselves to certain substances (for example, color to corporeal substance). A substance cannot be the subject of just any accident, and an accident cannot inhere in just any substance. But—*pace* Henry of Ghent—that fact does not prove that the substance could not exist stripped of any and all accidents or that the accident could not exist separate from any and all substance subjects.[56]

Eminence and Action. Turning to the active causal powers of separate accidents, Ockham targets Scotus's reliance in his calculations on Causal Nobility principles:

[P28] the total active cause must have as much intensive actuality as or more intensive actuality than the effect,

and

[Cor 8] the total active cause must be at least as perfect as or more perfect than the effect.

Ockham does not deny [P28] and [Cor 8]. He agrees that they underlie the only way we have of proving that God is a supremely perfect being: for any thing (*res*) X, if X is producible, God is or can be the *total* efficient cause of X's existence; and Divine omnipotence is power enough to be the *total*

[54] Ockham, *Quaest. in IV Sent.*, q. 9; OTh VII. 155–6.
[55] Ockham, *Quaest. in IV Sent.*, q. 9; OTh VII. 155–6, 159–60.
[56] Ockham, *Quaest. in IV Sent.*, q. 9; OTh VII. 156–8.

efficient cause of any combination of compossible producibles together. Thus, by [Cor 8], an omnipotent God will have to be at least as perfect as any combination of compossible producibles. If one adds Scotus's further principle that

[P33] an equivocal cause capable of solo action without the collaboration of univocal causes is more perfect than the effect,

one can draw the further conclusion that an omnipotent God is more perfect than any combination of compossible producibles.[57]

What Ockham wants to emphasize is that these eminence principles are of no use in calculating whether or not a given *created* thing could be *a* causal principle in the production of some effect. The reason is that no creature is the *total* cause of any effect, because God concurs with every created action. Wherever created efficient causes act as partial causes, Divine power also acts as a partial cause. Because Divine power is by itself more perfect than any created effect, Divine power already ensures that the *total* package of efficient causes will be more perfect than the created effects, no matter what the collaborating created efficient causes are. [P28], [Cor 8], and [P33] cannot be used to disqualify creatures as *partial* efficient causes, because partial causes need not be equally perfect as or more perfect than their effects. Cognitive psychology furnishes many illustrations: a rock is an efficient partial cause of sensory and intellectual intuitive cognitions of itself, but the rock as non-living is less perfect than those cognitive acts.

Thus, eminence principles entitle Scotus to infer that no mere accidents, separate or inherent, are *total* causal principles in the corruption of substances, but this does not prevent the accidents' being *partial* causes. Ockham reasons that experience suggests that they are: for there are some accidents at whose presence the corruption follows and absent whose presence the corruption does not follow. But experience cannot *demonstrate* that accidents make a causal contribution. If we had experience of substances existing without accidents (for example, fire without heat), we could test whether or not substances were sufficient by themselves, quite apart from any action by their accidents, to corrupt other substances. As things are, we have no experience of substances existing without accidents, and so

[57] This is a slightly cleaned-up version of the argument toward which Ockham gestures in *Quaest. in IV Sent.*, q. 9; OTh VII. 171–2.

are unable to run the experiment to discover for certain what they can do acting alone.[58]

Corrupting the Species and Generating Substances therefrom. To the question whether created causes can corrupt eucharistic accidents or generate substances from them (for example, worms or ashes from consecrated hosts), Ockham responds with his own fresh estimates.

Beginning with the old, Ockham reminds that, strictly speaking, no production of worms or ashes from eucharistic species could count as Aristotelian generation, because of the No Prime Matter problem. Generation is a change in which the efficient causal agent transforms matter, but in the eucharist the bread matter is no longer present (indeed, no longer extant) and the bread accidents include no matter to transform. Rather, the production of worms and ashes requires creation, and Ockham forwards his own distinctive argument for why creatures cannot create. Barring obstructions, created *natural* agents act to the limit of their powers to produce effects within their causal range. Of itself, created causal power to generate *F*'s is unlimited: is as much power to generate this *F* as that *F* and so on for infinitely many particular *F*'s. But Ferdinand the bull is not "equally related" to all of the reproducibles that his bovine reproductive power is power to produce, because his actual exercise of bovine reproductive power is restricted by whether and what hunks of matter are available to be transformed. Because Beulah is the only cow nearby, and because her menstrual matter is properly disposed only sometimes, Ferdinand does not produce infinitely many, but begets only Elsie and Bruno and not Sally and Sam. Power to *create* cows likewise ranges over infinitely many particulars, but its exercise does not presuppose nearby matter. This means that the creative agent is equally related to any and all of the particulars its creative power ranges over. Thus, if Ferdinand had natural active power to create cows, he would act to the limit of his powers and impossibly overpopulate the world with a simultaneous actual infinity of bovines. Even created *voluntary* powers of bovine creation would be metaphysically dangerous, because intellectual creatures are not infallible and can efficaciously will what is in fact metaphysically impossible: for example, to create all of the cows they had power to create. When consecrated hosts putrefy or burn, the worms and ashes are God's doing, products of solo Divine action![59]

[58] Ockham, *Quaest. in IV Sent.*, q. 9; OTh VII. 169–70; see *Quaest in II Sent.*, qq. 3–4; OTh V. 62, 314.

[59] Ockham, *Quaest. in IV Sent.*, q. 9; OTh VII. 178–80. For a longer discussion of Ockham and his predecessors on this topic, see my "Can Creatures Create?" *Philosophia*, 34 (2006), 101–28; DOI 10.1007/s11406-006-9020-1.

Nevertheless, Ockham takes issue with the consensus that the No Prime Matter Problem keeps created agents from being able to *corrupt* separate accidents. Ockham contends that there is a difference between destruction and production. His argument that creatures cannot be creators does not show that creatures cannot annihilate. Suppose Leo the lion had power not only to eat but to annihilate cows. Of itself, this power would range over infinitely many bovines and would be power to annihilate any one as much as any other. Nevertheless, Leo would not be equally related to any and all of infinitely many, because only the finitely many bovines that actually exist would be available to be destroyed and only some of these would be relevantly proximate to Leo! Coming closer to the eucharistic case, suppose a quality—low-intensity coldness—exists separately from any subject of inherence. *Pace* Scotus, it would be remarkable if a great fire with high-intensity heat could not corrupt that coldness. So also in the eucharist, external created causes can corrupt separate accidents, because, in destroying, created causes do not require matter to transform![60]

Condensation and Rarefaction. It is a fact of experience that eucharistic species are condensed and rarefied. But for those who held separate quantity to be the subject of eucharistic qualities, this change was among the most difficult to explain. Condensation and rarefaction seem to involve quantitative changes. Since creatures cannot create and there is no matter to transform, Divine creative power would have to be invoked to produce the new qualities or parts of quantity; likewise to explain why qualities of the same species survive in successive new-quantity subjects. Godfrey of Fontaines tries to avoid saying that new quantities or quantity parts are *created* by supposing that the new quantity has a disposition (*habitudo*) towards the previous one. Like Scotus, Ockham rejects this as silly: the coming into existence of X from nothing at all (*purum nihil*) counts as creation, no matter what external relations (for example, of temporal succession) X bears to other creatures (for example, to the previous quantity).[61]

Calculating first what would have to be said according to the common opinion—that quantity is a thing really distinct from substance and quality—Ockham argues that condensation and rarefaction cannot be accounted for by the addition or subtraction of parts of quantity, but only by the corruption of the whole previous quantity and the production of a whole new one. He

[60] Ockham, *Quaest. in IV Sent.*, q. 9; OTh VII. 178–9.
[61] Ockham, *Quaest. in IV Sent.*, q. 9; OTh VII. 175.

reasons that the quantitative changes in the condensation and rarefaction of eucharistic species will be the same as those that would occur if the bread/wine substance were there. Suppose that at T1 the substance S is divided into four parts—S1, S2, S3, and S4—which are inhered in by four commensurate parts of quantity—Q1, Q2, Q3, and Q4. Suppose S is rarefied, and suppose that this involved the addition of a new quantity Q5. What would the immediate subject of Q5 be? Not any of S1, S2, S3, or S4, because they already have quantities—Q1, Q2, Q3, and Q4, respectively—and

[P34] it is naturally impossible that two quantities primarily inform the same subject simultaneously.

Nor can the prior quantities scoot over and crowd together to make room for the new quantity part, because

[P5] it is naturally impossible for accidents to migrate from subject to subject.

[P5] would also explain why condensation cannot involve the loss of Q4 and the rearrangement of Q1, Q2, and Q3. Ockham infers—and he takes this to be Scotus's final position—that, in condensation and rarefaction, the whole of the preceding quantity is corrupted and a whole new one produced. The same type of change would be involved in the eucharist; only the substance subject is subtracted. But, given the absence of matter to be acted upon, the new quantity would have to be Divinely produced.[62]

Ockham's considered opinion is that quantity is not a thing really distinct from substance and quality (see Chapter 7 above). If so, condensation and rarefaction are easily accounted for by the locomotion of substance and/or quality parts to occupy ("coexist with") a lesser or a larger place than before.[63] Nevertheless, dense and rare are not a simple function of volume occupied, so that any two corporeal items of equal volume would be equally dense or rare. Rather, Ockham clarifies, material things are divided into parts in and of themselves, and different substantial forms subsume more or fewer parts of matter. The substantial form in a cubic liter of earth is divided into the same number of parts as the substantial form in a cubic liter of fire. But the cubic liter of earth is denser than the cubic liter of fire, because there is enough matter under the substantial form of earth to be converted into

[62] Ockham, *Quaest. in IV Sent.*, q. 9; OTh VII. 175–7.
[63] Ockham, *Quaest in IV Sent.*, q. 9; OTh VII. 175.

one hundred cubic liters of fire.[64] A volume of earth might itself become denser or rarefied as its parts are moved to occupy lesser or greater place.

Ockham identifies substantial form and proper qualities as efficient causes in condensation and rarefaction. He offers two hypotheses as to how this happens. According to the first, the qualities of earth are wholly corrupted while the substantial form of earth remains; then the qualities of fire are introduced while the substantial form of earth remains, and the qualities of fire rarefy the earth; then the substantial form of fire is introduced; finally, the introduced substantial form of fire causes the ultimate degree of rareness. According to his second and slightly preferred proposal, the qualities of earth are expelled; then the qualities of fire are introduced, while the matter remains as dense as before; then the substantial form of fire acts together with the qualities of fire to cause rareness suitable to fire. This last step would involve locomotion and so would take a little time, but—Ockham speculates—it would happen very quickly.[65]

[64] Ockham, *Quaest. in IV Sent.*, q. 9; OTh VII. 183–5.
[65] Ockham, *Quaest. in IV Sent.*, q. 9; OTh VII. 187.

Morals of the Story

10

Theology Provoking Philosophy

I. Theoretical Remodelling

Transplanting the Canon. In the marketplace of ideas, competing theories are assessed for consistency and coherence, explanatory power and fruitfulness. Both in late antiquity and in the thirteenth-century Latin West, Aristotle's corpus appeared to be a system of thought that possessed these features in high degree. Because of the scope and analytical rigor of his achievement, Aristotle's works bid fair not only to take their place in, but to dominate, the canon of philosophy. Professional competence in philosophy required thorough familiarity with them. Tackling philosophical problems meant serious engagement with ideas and approaches found in them. To achieve credibility, disagreements and departures had to be explained and defended. Aristotle's philosophy had the *gravitas* to set the agenda for philosophy, to define a research program: first to interpret the texts, then to reconcile the *prima facie* inconsistencies, then to work out the details and develop his theories in new directions by applying them to new problems. For thirteenth- and fourteenth-century school theologians and students of the liberal arts, Aristotle's authority in his field was so evident that he could be nicknamed "the Philosopher"!

Even highly articulate theories confront data that they have not been designed to incorporate, data that are not readily subsumed under their general principles or analyzed by the conceptual machinery already in place. When this happens, adherents may try to explain away or at least marginalize the recalcitrant phenomena. Alternatively, they may discover that the theory—whether as was or as modified, whether altered ad hoc or systematically—has the resources to manage the findings after all. Most radically, insistent but misfitting data may topple the old theory and provoke a conceptual revolution.[1]

Where Aristotle's philosophy was concerned, the Neoplatonists of late antiquity had a competing Platonic philosophical system to set up against it, one not so rich in analytical detail but nevertheless compelling in its overall cosmic picture. Jewish and Christian philosophical theologians brought with them the claims of biblical religion. These thinkers all worked to integrate their various commitments into new theories that also displayed the marks of consistency and coherence, explanatory power and fruitfulness. Nor was harmonizing Plato with Aristotle or either with biblical religion a simple matter of adjusting minor details. No! It involved taking sides on fundamentals. What they sought to do was to transplant chunks of Aristotle's analysis into metaphysical frameworks significantly different from his own, in such a way that—despite these differences—Aristotle's account could be taken as a reliable guide to understanding what normally happens here below. Once again, the twentieth-century parallel is with Einstein's theory of relativity and Newtonian mechanics. Einstein's theory contradicted Newton's premiss of absolute space–time, but did so in such a way as to leave Newton's laws as workable approximations in the region for which they were originally developed.

First Efficient Causality. Neoplatonic philosophers and patristic theologians agreed: Aristotle's understanding of the unmoved mover's relation to the rest of the world was ripe for revision. Aristotle thought that it was not the *existence* of the world that required explanation: the heavens, prime matter, the sublunary species of things, were eternal and necessary, incapable of coming into being or passing away. What needed accounting for was motion or change. Efficient causes act to cause locomotion or to effect the transformation of some matter. Cosmological arguments rise from particular movers here below to universal causes such as the heavenly bodies to the unmoved mover that functions, not as an efficient but as a first final cause, as an object of desire.

Neoplatonists insisted, on the contrary, that being does need to be explained, and that the top of the metaphysical hierarchy is the source of the being of everything else that necessarily emanates from it in a hierarchy of descending perfection. Under the influence of such Neoplatonic notions, Avicenna (980–1037 CE) and Averroes (1126–98 CE) insisted [1] that

[1] See Thomas Kuhn, *The Structure of Scientific Revolution* (Chicago: Phoenix Books, 1962).

the first being is the *efficient* as well as the final cause of everything else. Moreover, they maintained that the first effect of the first efficient cause is another spiritual being. Taken together, these claims forced [2] a second fundamental modification: namely, in Aristotle's notion of efficient causality. Efficient causal power could not be merely the power to transform matter. Spiritual beings do not produce other spiritual beings by transforming matter, because spiritual beings are not hylomorphic composites. Spiritual beings produce other spiritual beings out of nothing (*ex nihilo*). Accordingly, Avicenna and Averroes reconceived efficient causal power as power to produce something in existence. Material agents here below produce other material things in existence by transforming matter. Aristotle's Presupposed Subject Principle applies to them. But the Presupposed Subject principle is not generally true, because it does not apply to the production of spirits. The Arab commentators envisioned a "great chain" of naturally necessary emanation of spiritual beings, one from another, and of material things from various spiritual beings. They drew the conclusion [3] that not only the first cause but also other spiritual beings have power to produce out of nothing (*ex nihilo*).[2] Our authors all had access to these ideas insofar as Avicenna and Averroes (nicknamed "the Commentator") joined Aristotle as part of their philosophical canon.

Divine Omnipotence. Aquinas, Giles of Rome, Scotus, and Ockham all seek to make Aristotelian ideas at home in a metaphysical theory that features Divine omnipotence. Roughly speaking, Divine power is power to bring about anything the bringing-about of which does not involve a contradiction.[3] It includes power to do whatever is possible absolutely, but it does not—according to them—include power to do anything that is metaphysically impossible (for example, make contrary qualities to inhere in the same proximate subject at the same time). Nevertheless, theological consensus imposes further commitments regarding what does and does not involve a contradiction. (1) First, where Avicenna and Averroes assume that the first cause acts by natural necessity to produce its proximate effect,

[2] See Herbert A. Davidson, *Proofs for Eternity: Creation and the Existence of God in Medieval Islamic and Jewish Philosophy* (New York and Oxford: Oxford University Press, 1987). See also *John Duns Scotus: A Treatise on God as First Principle*, trans. and ed. with commentary by Allan B. Wolter, OFM (Chicago: Franciscan Herald Press, 1966), chs. 2–3, pp. 187, 247–8.

[3] Omnipotence puzzles are notorious. For a discussion of how thirteenth- and fourteenth-century philosophical theologians refined their analyses to meet them, see my *William Ockham* (Notre Dame: University of Notre Dame Press, 1987), ch. 28, pp. 1151–1229.

Christians insisted that Divine power is voluntary, exercised freely and contingently in the production of everything else. Not only do created things not exist by the necessity of their own natures; God does not create them by natural necessity either. Their existence is contingent upon Divine free choice. It is metaphysically possible for God not to create at all and for God to have created other individuals, maybe even—if there are creatable natures not represented in this world—things of other kinds.

(2) Second, where Avicenna and Averroes think that the first cause is power to produce one and only one proximate effect, so that the first cause does not and could not act alone to produce further effects, but acts only mediately, by means of creatures, to produce them, Christians maintain that God acts immediately in the production of every creature, and endorse the Solo Divine Action principle—that whatever God can efficient causally produce by acting together with created causes, God can produce acting all by Godself.

(3) Third, where Avicenna and Averroes allowed some creatures power to create out of nothing (*ex nihilo*), medieval Christians hold that God alone has that power. Aristotle's Presupposed Subject Principle applies to all created agents. Moreover, Divine omnipotence includes power not only to create *ex nihilo*; Divine omnipotence is power to annihilate, to reduce any created being to nothing without remainder.

(4) Fourth, not only does the exercise of any created causal power essentially depend on Divine concurrence; omnipotence also includes the power to obstruct any created natural active or passive power. Aristotle himself taught that natural powers are obstructible: fire cannot burn damp paper or piles of leaves that are too far away; a rock is naturally apt to seek the center of the universe, but its fall is stopped by the roof of the house. All creatures come with built-in natural active and passive powers, aptitudes and tendencies. But our authors all say that every creature is in *obediential potency* to Divine power, which can obstruct their natural doings and undergoings (for example, God keeps the fire from even scorching the three young men in the fiery furnace).

(5) Fifth, theological consensus adds that for each state (era of salvation history; see Chapter 2 above) God establishes distinctive policies regarding Divine concurrence and Divine obstruction. For this present state, God always-or-for-the-most-part concurs with natural causes. Miracles are rare. God could do things that God does not do, such as make other worlds or

always obstruct natural activity. Likewise, God can do things that God mostly does not do—violate Archimedes' principle to make iron axeheads float and humans walk on water, multiply loaves and fishes, interfere with the weather either to blow up or suddenly to calm a storm. Moreover, God can do things that God will do only later—burn up the whole sublunary world, make the heavens to cease their motion, make human bodies impassible, resurrect the elect into beatific vision and enjoyment (see Chapter 12 below).

Over all, this understanding of Divine omnipotence means both that Aristotelian natural regularities do not have the last word on what is metaphysically possible (what is contrary to natural aptitudes might nevertheless be metaphysically possible and producible by Divine power), and that what actually happens is always-or-for-the-most-part what Aristotelian physics or metaphysics would lead us to expect. The former opens theoretical room to maneuver, while the latter guarantees that Aristotle's analyses do not lose their usefulness.

Real Presence. Eucharistic theology barges in and sits down at a table already set by Divine omnipotence. Sacramental causality insists that spiritual benefits and/or real presence bear a non-accidental connection to the performance of and participation in new-law sacramental rites. The doctrine of eucharistic real presence stipulates that, after eucharistic consecration, the Body (Blood) of Christ is present on the altar where the eucharistic species still are; that the substance of the bread (wine) is no longer there; and that the Body (Blood) of Christ still exists in heaven. Sacramental causality and real presence provoked our authors to give Aristotelian philosophy further development and revision. It is time to overview the moves that they made.

II. Bodies Extended in their Places

Quantity as Divider and Locator. Philosophically speaking, Aquinas and Giles of Rome think that matter is what makes corporeal substance fundamentally different from spiritual substance. Considered in themselves, both spiritual substance and matter are undivided and indivisible. One fundamental difference is that matter can be the subject of quantity, while spiritual substance cannot. For Aquinas and Giles of Rome, it is quantity that is *of itself* divisible and divided into parts. Both the subject of quantity (matter, corporeal substance) and what inheres in quantity as in a subject (for example, the sensible qualities) are rendered divisible and actually divided by virtue of quantity's inhering in and being subject to them. Matter, corporeal substance, and sensible qualities cannot actually exist without being subject to or inhering in quantity, and so cannot actually exist without being divisible and divided into parts. But their divisibility and division are derivative from their quantity.

Aquinas also holds that it is quantity that is *of itself* present to place immediately. Normally and naturally, the presence to place of matter, corporeal substance, and sensible qualities is mediated by their own determinate quantity. Thus, the natural impossibility of [T5] two bodies being extended in the same place at once, and of [T6] one body's being extended in two places at once, is rooted in the alleged impossibility of two quantities being commensurate (whole with the whole and parts with the parts) with the same place at once and of one quantity's being commensurate with two places at once. The impossibility of the multiple location of bodies is also derivative from their quantities.

When he turns to eucharistic theology, Aquinas sticks to his philosophical view that bodily placement is mediated by quantity and to his endorsement of [T5] and [T6]. For him, the metaphysical impossibility of multiple extended location remains philosophically entrenched. His conclusion is that the Body (Blood) of Christ cannot be on the altar *per se*, through its own determinate quantity, but only *per accidens*.

In the Supplement to *Summa Theologica* III, q. 83, the author (probably one of Aquinas's students) explicitly connects [T5] and [T6] to the role of quantity in individuation. Aquinas maintains that, when quantity divides matter into integral parts, these parts can serve as numerically distinct subjects for substantial forms. When the form of bovinity exists in this hunk (matter "signed" by quantity Q1), the result is Beulah the cow; when the form of bovinity exists in that hunk of matter (matter "signed" by quantity Q2), the result is Elsie, a numerically distinct cow from Beulah. Since it is naturally impossible for two quantities Q1 and Q2 to be commensurate with the same place at the same time, if Beulah and Elsie did exist in the same place at the same time, they would have to have the same quantity and so would not be numerically distinct after all. Hence, [T5]. Likewise, if Beulah could be extended in both P1 and P2 at one and the same time, that would either require Beulah to have two quantities—which is impossible, because two quantities would make two numerically distinct cows—or necessitate Beulah's single quantity Q1 being commensurate with both P1 and P2 at once—which Aquinas also finds naturally impossible. So far, for Aquinas and the author of the Supplementary questions, their philosophical analysis is driving their conclusions.

Other theological counter-examples to [T5] (for example, when Christ was born of a Virgin, walked through closed doors, and ascended through the unriven heavens) provoke the author of the Supplementary questions to find a difference between [T5] and [T6], however. He claims that [T5] is true only about what is the case *normally and naturally*, but can be contravened by Divine power, while it is contradictory to suppose that there could be an exception to [T6]. The author appeals to Aquinas's own theologically prompted distinction between what it takes to originate the being (*esse*) of a thing and what it takes to conserve it. From a philosophical point of view, it might seem straightforward to assume that

[P35] if something X depends on a material subject to acquire individual existence (*esse*), it would depend on a material subject to retain it.

Human intellectual souls are individuated by virtue of a relation to matter (S1 is apt to exist in M "signed by" Q1, while S2 is apt to exist in M "signed by" Q2) and take their individuated act of existence (*esse*) on the occasion of their original union with matter. Yet Christian theology insists in the face of Arab philosophical commentators that individual souls survive death, which brings separation from their material subject. Aquinas's solution is to override the prima facie plausibility of [P35] by insisting that, however much something may acquire its individuated act of existence (*esse*) on the occasion of its coming to exist in a material substance, God can preserve that act of existence (*esse*) numerically distinct from others, even when the soul no longer exists in matter as in a subject. Analogously, the author of the Supplementary questions suggests, if B1 originates in P1, and B2 originates in P2, God can conserve B1's act of existence (*esse*) numerically distinct from B2's while moving B1 to exist with B2 at P2. What is unclear is why the author of the Supplementary questions does not think an analogous solution would work for B1's existing at both P1 and P2 at one and the same time. Why could not God originate B1 at P1 and preserve that act of existence (*esse*) at P2 as well?

Bodily Division, Revised. For Aquinas and the author of the Supplementary questions, a body's quantity is the means of its being in place, and the natural impossibility of two quantities commensurate with the same place or one quantity commensurate with two places at once is what naturally rules out multiple location. Scotus and Ockham find these philosophical explanations to be flawed philosophically, because they rest on mistaken pictures of the relation of matter and corporeal substance to quantity and a false understanding of the metaphysics of bodily individuation. Scotus and Ockham insist that a subject is naturally prior to what inheres in it. As naturally prior, the subject is what it is and is the very individual it is, and its parts are the very individuals they are, prior in the order of explanation to the inherence of any and every form. It follows that the individuation of a subject and its parts cannot be accounted for by any inherent forms.

Reflection on the eucharist provokes Scotus to ask whether there is any sound philosophical case to be made for the metaphysical impossibility of multiple location. He contends that—so far as [T5] is concerned—the putative impossibility of multiple bodies or body parts in the same place at once is not to be explained in terms of the *formal* incompatibility of their quantities. Suppose B1 is quantified by Q1 and B2 by Q2, and that B1 is related to P2 by the location relation (the *ubeitas* or "whereness") U1 and that B2 is related to P2 by U2. There would be a formal incompatibility in two quantities existing in the *same* body at once (for example, both Q1 and Q2 in B1, or both Q1 and Q2 in B2) just as—on Aristotelian metaphysics—there would be a formal incompatibility in blackness and whiteness existing in the same parts of the same body at once. But in this case, the different quantities are in numerically distinct subjects. There is no formal incompatibility in B1's having Q1 when B2 has Q2 than there is in B1's being white and B2's being black at one and the same time. Nor would any formal incompatibility between Q1 and Q2 arise, just because their numerically distinct subjects B1 and B2 were in the same place P2.

Moreover, Scotus continues, no formal incompatibility would arise because of their wherenesses. U1 and U2 are not formally incompatible *of themselves*, because they are of the same species: they are individual instances of the relation "located in P2." Nor in this case does any formal incompatibility between U1 and U2 arise *in relation to their subjects*. Even if there were a formal incompatibility involved in U1 and U2 both existing in B1 or both existing in B2, no formal incompatibility is generated by U1 existing in B1 and U2 in B2. If there were any formal incompatibility between U1 and U2, it would have to be because *of the term of these relations*. But there is not in general any problem with two external relations having the same term. This happens with internal relations. If Socrates is white and two walls are newly painted white, each wall will be similar to white Socrates and there will be two similarity relations to the same term. If two volumes of air are newly condensed to fit into 3 square foot containers, they will be equal in volume to the air that was condensed into 3 square feet yesterday. A fortiori there is no general principle against two *external* relations to the same term at once![4]

Why Solo Location, Normally and Naturally? If high-level metaphysical principles do not generate any reasons [T5] against multiple bodies or body parts in the same place at once, how can we explain what experience seems to show: that one body in a place excludes others being in that place at the same time, that one body entering a place has to evict the body that was already there? Scotus replies that there are two ways for X and Y to be incompatible: formally and virtually. X and Y are *formally* incompatible if X and Y are incompatible of themselves—if the what-it-is-to-be X is incompatible with the what-it-is-to-be Y (as is the case, for example, with contrary qualities such as whiteness and blackness). X and Y are *virtually* incompatible if X is a sufficient natural cause of E1 and Y is incompatible with E1. Natural causes always act to the limit of their power (*virtus*) unless obstructed. The opposite of the natural cause's effect is virtually incompatible with the natural cause, because it is incompatible with that natural cause's exercising its causal power (*virtus*) to produce its effect. Where bodies and their placement are concerned, the quantity Q2 of body B2 naturally acts to make body B2 fill the place P2 where it is located to the degree that P2 is naturally apt to be filled. This effect of Q2 is incompatible with B1's existing at P2 at the same time. Thus, the quantity of one is virtually incompatible with the location of another body in the same place. Normally and naturally, Q1 and Q2 cannot both exist in P2, because Q1 would naturally act to make B1 fill up P1 to its limit and Q2 would naturally act to make B2 fill up P2 to its limit, but P2 cannot be filled to its limit by B1 and filled to its limit by B2 both at once![5]

Theology provokes the philosophical reasoning that brings Scotus to these startling conclusions. His philosophical analysis proves theologically fortuitous, however, because, while Divine omnipotence does not extend to what is formally incompatible, it does range over what is virtually incompatible. The reason is that all created causal powers stand in obediential potency to, in the sense of being obstructible by, Divine power. God can produce natural causes without their natural effects (for example, the

[4] Scotus, *Op. Ox.* IV, d. 49, q. 16, n. 18; Wadding X. 621.

[5] Scotus, *Op. Ox.* IV, d. 49, q. 16, nn. 5–6; Wadding X. 612–13.

three boys unsinged in the fiery furnace). If God wants multiple bodies or body parts in the same place at once, all God has to do is to obstruct the natural causal powers (*virtus*) of their quantities so that their quantities do not cause them each to fill up place to its limit![6]

Ockham refuses to reify quantities—that is, to treat them as things really distinct from substances and qualities—for *philosophical* reasons. Accordingly, he does not join Scotus in explaining the phenomenon of one body's excluding another from the same place in terms of any natural causal powers (*virtus*) that quantity things are supposed to have. Nevertheless, Ockham himself agrees with Scotus's conclusion—that there is no formal incompatibility in multiple bodies or body parts being in the same place at once—and even insists that condensation furnishes a natural example in which this happens![7]

As for [T6], Scotus and Ockham agree: Aristotle is right that no created cause can make a body or body part to be in two places at once. Nevertheless, the natural priority of bodies and body parts to their location is enough to remove metaphysical objections to its possibility, which—for Scotus and Ockham—arise not from problems about making a quantity thing commensurate with two places, but from causal exposure (see Chapters 5 and 7 above).

III. Varieties of Location

What our authors have to say about eucharistic real presence is both philosophically and theologically odd. Where eucharistic theology is concerned, our authors count real presence as a *desideratum* of prime importance. But our authors all deny that Christ's Body and Blood are on the altar in the normal and natural way. Where Aristotelian natural philosophy is concerned, [T5] and [T6] are taken for granted. Our authors all agree with Aristotle that (with the possible exception of condensation) multiple location of extended bodies cannot be produced by natural causes. But they explain real presence by appeal to an idea that is equally unAristotelian: namely, that bodies can be present to a place without being extended in it.

[6] Scotus, *Op. Ox.* IV, d. 49, q. 16, n. 6; Wadding X. 613.
[7] Ockham, *Quaest. in IV Sent.*, q. 6; OTh VII. 79–80.

For Aquinas, it is his *philosophical* analysis of "normal and natural" bodily placement that forces him to posit some other sort of presence. But what sort? Aquinas's distinctions among circumscriptive, definitive, and repletive ways of being in place are of no use, because—on Aquinas's definitions—each and all of them entail that a body placed that way is related to the place through its own determinate quantity and so extended there (see Chapter 4 above). Aquinas does recognize that God and the angels may be said to be located in places without being extended in them. But Aquinas explains that spiritual beings and bodies are said to be in place equivocally, because spiritual beings are not in place through any contact of their dimensive quantities (because they have none) but rather through contact of their power. Thus, a spiritual being S is said to be in a place P if and only if S exercises its efficient causal power to produce an effect in place P. God exercises Divine power everywhere anything exists;[8] angels as finite can exercise power in only one place at a time.[9] But it would be counterproductive for Aquinas to liken the real presence of Christ's Body and Blood on the altar to that of God's or an angel's, because Aquinas insists that Christ's Body and Blood are on the altar in such a way as not to be causally interactive there.

Aquinas's account of how Christ's Body and Blood are there *per accidens* depends on his assumption that immediate presence is not a transitive relation: that is, that 'X is immediately present to Y and Y is immediately present to Z' does not entail 'X is immediately present to Z' (where X = the substance of Christ's Body, Y = the bread quantity, and Z = the place). An "alien" quantity (i.e., the bread quantity) is located in the place P *per se*, and—by being present to that alien quantity—the Body of Christ is located in P through another, *per aliud* or *per accidens*. Giles of Rome takes basically the same approach, explaining that the Body of Christ is neither definitively nor circumscriptively in place on altars where mass is said, but it is determined to place there, not through its own, but through an alien quantity (that is, the bread quantity) (see Chapter 4 above).

Aquinas and Giles, of course, recognize that such *per accidens* placement through alien quantities is as unAristotelian as multiple location through a body's own determinate quantity would be. What they wish to urge is that the former but not the latter is possible absolutely and so within reach of

[8] Aquinas, *Summa Theologica* I, q. 8, a. 1 c & ad 3um; a. 2 c; a. 3 c.
[9] Aquinas, *Summa Theologica* I, q. 52, a. 2 c; q. 53, a. 1 c.

Divine power. What wrecks this strategy, according to Ockham, is the fact that immediate presence *is* a transitive relation. If immediate presence is transitive, the quantity of Christ's Body is just as immediately present to the bread quantity as its substance is; and both the quantity and the substance of Christ's Body are as immediately present to place as the bread quantity is. Aquinas's and Giles's maneuver does not avoid Christ's Body being present on altars by its own determinate quantity and so—by their lights—extended in the place.

Giles of Rome introduces his distinction between quantitative placement (the order of the parts of a body to one another within the whole) and categorial placement (and the order of the body to place) to explain how a body can avoid losing its structure in places where it is only *per accidens* located. Scotus seizes on the distinction as a way to explain how a body can be somewhere without being extended there. For Scotus, placement relations are external relations, and external relations are reified. He reasons that Divine power could make a body with quantitative but no categorial position simply by making an organic body without any other body surrounding it (and so without any place to which it could be related). If so, why could not God make an organic body (a body with quantitative position) and relate it whole to the whole of a place without relating its parts to the parts of the place (and so make it to be in place as a whole without being extended in place)? Would not that merely mean God's making fewer rather than more placement relations? Ockham thinks there is a reason why Scotus's proposal is a non-starter: it would be contradictory for a body with quantitative position to be related whole to the whole place, without its parts being related parts to the parts of place; just as it would be impossible even for God to make two white things without their being similar. This is a fact to which the reification of accidents makes no difference.

Aquinas, Giles of Rome, and Scotus all hope to locate bodies in places where they are not extended without turning them into structureless heaps there. Ockham finds the appeal both to *per accidens* location and to the distinction between quantitative and categorial position to be philosophically inadequate. So how can Christ's Body be really present on altars without being extended? Aquinas and Giles of Rome build 'commensuration through its own determinate quantity' into the definitions of circumscriptive and definitive location. Ockham simplifies the contrast: X is circumscriptively in P if and only if the whole of X is in the whole of P and the parts of X are in the parts of P, while X is definitively in P if and only if X is whole in the whole of P and whole in the parts of P. Normally and naturally, bodies are in place circumscriptively. The Body of Christ exists circumscriptively in its heavenly place and definitively on altars where mass is said. Where bodies are concerned, definitive placement involves multiple location: many body parts in the same place at once. For Ockham, the conclusion is evident: *eucharistic real presence cannot be accounted for without giving up [T5] and [T6]! The multiple location of bodies and body parts must be metaphysically possible for Divine power.*

Ockham bites another bullet: definitive placement in P takes away from the body insofar as it is in P any structural features that depend on actual extension. When all of Christ's body parts are in P, it is not the case that the neck parts in P are closer to the head parts in P than they are to the foot parts in P. Insofar as all of the parts are in P and in all of the parts of P, none is in a place from which another is missing. That does not turn the Body of Christ into an undifferentiated heap, Ockham claims, because the parts continue to differ in their natural propensities (stomach parts for digestion, lung parts for absorbing oxygen, and so on). Feisty as he is, Ockham also points out that any body that exists definitively in place also exists circumscriptively in place. Suppose that P is divided into four parts, P1, P2, P3, and P4. All of Christ's Body parts exists in each place, so that the head at P1 would be at a distance from the foot at P4 and closer to the neck at P2 than to the ankle at P3! Thus, *even Ockham's analysis does not give us an account that puts Christ's Body on the altar, altogether unextended.* All the same, these ideas would have left Aristotle very surprised!

IV. How Does It Get There?

Real presence as our authors understood it required one substance to succeed another on the altar, while leaving Christ's Body and Blood in heaven and the eucharistic species on the altar, where they were before. Our authors deployed two different strategies to explain this: Aquinas formulates "Thomistic transubstantiation," relative to Aristotle's taxonomy a new kind of change to which Giles of Rome tried to give further conceptual development, while Scotus and Ockham resolve transubstantiation into component changes of types Christian Aristotelians had recognized before.

None of the changes featured in Aristotle's physics and metaphysics can sufficiently account for real presence. Locomotion requires a body to leave one place while gaining another in continuous succession between the term-from-which and the term-to-which. Likewise, Aristotle teaches that a body cannot proceed via locomotion to two destinations (distinct terms-to-which) at once. But mass can be said in London and Rome simultaneously. Nor does the Body of Christ get there by quantitative or qualitative change: not its own, and not—experience shows—in the bread. Not by generation and corruption, because the term-to-which of generation is newly extant, while the Body of Christ has existed for centuries, since the Holy Spirit formed it in Mary's womb. Christian understandings of creation already went beyond Aristotle to assign Omnipotence power over the whole being of things: power to create *ex nihilo* and power to reduce to nothing (see Section I above). But it is too late for Christ's Body to be created, and annihilation would get the bread off the altar without doing anything to get Christ's Body onto the altar. Aquinas's solution is that Divine power is capable of whole-being conversion. In Thomistic transubstantiation, God converts the whole being of the bread into the whole being of the Body of Christ: the bread matter into the matter of Christ's Body and the bread form into the form of Christ's Body. Thus, Aquinas finds, Aristotle was right about the scope of created powers and correctly catalogued the kinds of changes of which they are capable. But real presence requires whole-being conversion that falls within the scope of Divine power alone.

Giles of Rome subjects Thomistic transubstantiation to *philosophical* scrutiny. Even if such changes are "theological" in that doctrinal data motivate us to posit them and Divine power alone can effect them, the idea of God's doing so has to make philosophical sense. Giles reasons that we can be the more confident that it does so, the more closely transubstantiation is modelled on Aristotelian change. Giles zeroes in on the fact that the generation of S2 by the corruption of S1 puts S2 in roughly the place where S1 used to be, only because matter persists through the change—the matter of S1 comes to be the matter of S2—and remains in roughly the place where it was before. Giles concludes that Thomistic transubstantiation can get the Body of Christ onto the altar only if God effects it by doing something to the matter: not individuated matter signed by quantity, but matter as quiddity, prior to any and every individuation. Giles also confronts the philosophical consequences of Aquinas's doctrine of the unity of substantial forms, to conclude that the term-to-which of transubstantiation is not a matter–form composite but only the matter of Christ's Body, matter in a quantitative mode. Scotus meets Giles philosopher-to-philosopher and dismisses Giles's analysis of whole-being conversion as nonsense on philosophical grounds.

Scotus and Ockham opt for transubstantiation over coexistence or consubstantiation, even though they find the latter less problematic, because they believe that Innocent III at the Fourth Lateran Council declared it to be the correct explanation of real presence. Their strategy is to save this theological datum by analyzing locomotion and transubstantiation into complexes of changes. Normally and naturally, locomotion involves loss-changes (body B1 ceases to be at P1) and gain-changes (body B1 comes to exist at P2), indeed a continuum of these between the term-to-which and the term-from-which. But *once multiple location is recognized as metaphysically possible, it is possible to see gain-changes as logically independent of loss-changes, and vice versa.* In particular, it is metaphysically possible for the Body of Christ to gain a place (on an altar) without losing any place (in heaven). Aristotle was right about changes of place producible by created causes, but Divine power can produce gain-change without loss-change where place is concerned. Aristotelian locomotion is locomotion, properly speaking, but gain-change without loss-change and loss-change without gain-change can be counted locomotion broadly speaking, insofar as they do involve a change of place.

Likewise, Scotus and Ockham analyze transubstantiation into a complex of changes. For Scotus, productive transubstantiation involves S1 first existing (before T) and then ceasing to exist at T (a loss-change) and S2 first not existing (before T) and then coming to exist at T (a gain-change). Translative transubstantiation involves S1's first existing at P and then not existing at P (a loss-change) and S2's first not existing at P and then existing at P (a gain-change). Ockham also reduces transubstantiation into the succession of substance to substance: first S1 exists under S1's accidents and then (at T) S1 ceases to exist under S1's accidents; first S2 does not exist under S1's accidents and then (at T) S2 comes to exist under S1's accidents. Both Scotus and Ockham recognize a change of substances and their placement, but no whole-being conversion of one thing into another is involved! Therefore, Scotus is eager to emphasize, translative transubstantiation is logically independent of the ceasing to be of the bread substance.

V. Independent Accidents?

Categories theory can be read to imply that primary substances are ontologically basic and accidents are "adverbial"—that is, how something else is. If adverbial, accidents would be ontologically parasitic on the existence of other things (on this reading of the *Categories*, on primary substances) that are that way. *How* something is cannot exist without *something* that is that way, any more than the Cheshire cat's smile can exist without the cat! All of our authors reject the notion that all Aristotelian accidents are adverbial. They all "reify" at least some Aristotelian accidents: that is, they count them as things (*res*) really distinct from substance and the essential parts of substance (that is, prime matter and substantial forms). Aquinas, Giles of Rome, and Scotus all reify the absolute accidents, quantity and quality. Ockham contends that quantity is nothing (no *res*) really distinct from substance and quality but how some substance and quality are. Nevertheless, Ockham reifies some qualities. If our authors all distinguish real relations from relations of reason, Scotus is the only one to reify some categorial relations, in the sense of counting them things (*res*) really distinct from substance and absolute accidents. In all cases, our authors' motivation for reifying such accidents is first and foremost *philosophical*, a metaphysical consequence of the principle

[P2] there is no passage from contradictory to contradictory—a proposition cannot be first true (false) and then its contradictory opposite true (false)—without any change.

This means that the reified accidents are things (*res*) with some sort of essence of their own, a what-it-is-to-be that pertains to them in and of themselves (*de se*). By virtue of what they are in themselves, they also characterize any proximate and remote subjects to which they are united. Normally and naturally, any really extant accidents would exist in a primary substance as in a subject. For Aquinas, such accidents exist in (*inesse*) or inhere by participating in the *esse* of their substance subject. For Scotus, the relation between reified accidents and their substance subject resolves into two: essential non-efficient causal dependence and potency actualization. The principal relation between an accident and the subject in which it exists is not captured by efficient causality, because the accident does not exist in all of its efficient causes (for example, this fire and its heat are efficient causes of heat in that water). Rather, there is another type of relation of essential dependence of which the substance subject is the term. Second, the accident actualizes a potentiality of its substance subject. The natural kind of the substance subject determines a range of types of accident for which it will be in potency. Bodies are in potency to colors, but angels are not; angels are in potency to intellectual thoughts, but rocks and trees are not. Where inherent reified accidents are concerned, the substance subject is denominated from what the accident is of itself (for example, when whiteness inheres in Socrates, Socrates is white).

Normally and naturally, accidents always exist in a subject. Scotus explains that the philosophers think that the way things normally and naturally are is the way they necessarily are. This is because the philosophers do not recognize any cause in the universe that could make them to be any other way. Theological consensus that the bread substance does not survive transubstantiation drove our authors all to the conclusion that it must not be metaphysically necessary for really extant accidents to exist in a subject, and that independent accidents must be possible by Divine power. Thus provoked by theology, Aquinas and Scotus both discover philosophical arguments why actual inherence (*inesse*) does not pertain to the real definition of accidents (and so is not predicated of them *per se* the first way) or belong to them as a proper *passio* (and so is not predicated of them *per se* the second way). Aquinas explains that to treat inherence (*inesse*) as included in the real definition of accidents is to suppose that being is a genus while inherence and *per se* are differentiae. But being cannot be a genus, because differentiae have to be taken from outside the genus, and nothing is outside being. Likewise, differentiae are positive, but *per se* is merely a negation of dependence. Scotus notes that 'accident' is not a natural kind term with a real definition, but a denominative term. If existing in a subject were essential to the things that are accidents, then the union of the accident with its subject (for example, whiteness with Socrates) would—like the union of substantial form with prime matter—constitute a *per se* unity, whereas it constitutes a *per accidens* unity. Likewise, if inherence pertained to the things that are accidents essentially, then all accidents would be relatives and none would be absolute.

All of our authors so embrace *Categories* metaphysics that they very much want to preserve the contrast between substance and accident. If actual inherence does not pertain to any and all accidents necessarily (because eucharistic species do not actually inhere), and actual independence does not pertain to any and all individual substance natures necessarily (because

Christology stipulates that the human nature of Christ is not actually independent), then actual independence versus actual inherence cannot mark the contrast. Instead, Aquinas and Scotus conclude, substance differs essentially from the things that are accidents in that substance is—in the language of Scotus—aptitudinally independent, or—as Aquinas puts it—*ought* to be independent, while accidents are aptitudinally dependent or *ought* to be inherent.

Aristotelian natural aptitudes are obstructible, some by created agents, while others are in obediential potency to God alone. Divine power can make an individual substance nature depend on an "alien" supposit (the way God makes an individual human nature depend on the Divine Word), and Divine power can preserve some accidents in existence while obstructing their natural tendency to inhere (quantities, for Aquinas and Giles of Rome; quantities and possibly qualities, for Scotus; and qualities, for Ockham). To explain how Divine obstruction of an accident's aptitudinal dependency works, Aquinas, Giles of Rome, and Scotus bring out of the closet another startling idea: that normally and naturally, the substance subject of an accident plays two roles. On the one hand, it functions as the material cause of the *per accidens* unity. Socrates is the *material* cause of white Socrates insofar as whiteness actualizes a potency in Socrates, and Socrates is the term of the whiteness's relation of essential non-efficient-causal dependence. In addition, the substance subject is a proximate and partial *efficient* cause of the production and conservation of the accident. Normally and naturally, Socrates is an efficient partial cause of the production and conservation of his whiteness. As Giles of Rome explains, it is metaphysically impossible for a simple God to take over the role of material cause from substance. But Divine power can fill in for any created efficient cause. This is what happens when God conserves the eucharistic species on the altar when their substance is gone.

VI. Non-Standard Agents and Patients

For Aristotle, bodily agents come in complete hylomorphic packages—prime matter and substantial forms, an array of accidents—and all (with the possible exception of the outermost sphere of the heavens that has no containing body) exist in place circumscriptively, extended whole in the whole place and part in the parts. Eucharistic real presence forces our authors to widen the domain of corporeal agents and patients to include bodies that are somehow in place but not extended in it (the way the Body of Christ exists under the bread accidents) and accidents that do not exist in any substance. Experience showed a range of causal interactions around consecrated host and chalice, but gave no information about what the really present Body and Blood of Christ might be doing or suffering on the altar. Theological consensus stipulated that [T4] the risen and ascended Body of Christ is glorified and hence impassible. To carry out their analysis, our authors had to extrapolate answers from general causal principles that they had already taken on board.

Further Causal Assumptions. We have already noted (in Section I above) their understanding of Divine omnipotence and its efficient causal implications: that God is the first efficient cause, that God acts freely and contingently in relation to others, that God is able to create and annihilate, to concur and to obstruct, to act alone to produce whatever God in fact produces in cooperation with creatures (the Solo Divine Action Principle). Moreover, our authors endorse Aristotle's Presupposed Subject Principle

[P17] created active causal powers are powers to transform a subject and thus require as a co-cause the passive power of a subject to be acted upon,

for created causes generally, and Aristotle's Proximate Presence Principle

[P23] when a sufficient agent is proximate and the patient is disposed, the action follows,

where created natural (as opposed to voluntary) agents are concerned.

Other causal ideas were commended by Arab and Jewish commentators, whose Neoplatonic sources featured a metaphysical vision of the "Great Chain of Being" and Goodness. Our authors also recognize an excellence hierarchy with Godhead at the top and creatable natures ranked according to their degree of Godlikeness. Natural goodness is—in Scotus's language—a function of intensive actuality, and different natures confer different amounts of it: intelligent natures more than non-rational animal natures, animal natures more than plant natures, living more than non-living. Likewise, our authors agree that substance has more intensive actuality than accidents, and debate whether quantity has more than corporeal qualities (Aquinas and Giles may think so, while Scotus doubts it and Ockham does not believe in really distinct quantity things at all). Scotus reifies most categorial relations but counts them "little things," because they are incapable of existing apart from their foundations. Giles of Rome might say the same about successives, which—he believes—derive their unity and identity from their subject. If what efficient causes do is confer being on their effects, and if—as is intuitively plausible—nothing can give more than it has got, such excellence hierarchies seem to underwrite "Causal Nobility" Principles:

[P28] the total active cause must have as much intensive actuality as or more intensive actuality than the effect,

so that

[Cor 8] the total active cause must be at least as perfect as or more perfect than the effect,

which figure prominently in the reasoning of Aquinas, Giles of Rome, and Scotus. Without such principles, Scotus contends, cosmological arguments would not allow us to conclude that the first cause is more perfect than its effects! Ockham credits these principles, but finds them less useful in calculating what can be produced through any package of created causes, because the created causal package is always at most a partial cause of any effect. God is the other partial cause, thus guaranteeing that the excellence of the total causal package swamps the excellence of any merely created effect.

Avicenna and Averroes envisioned a "great chain" of naturally necessary emanation of the less excellent from the more excellent. Aquinas and Scotus forward cosmological arguments that rely on essentially ordered causal chains in which—as Scotus makes explicit—the prior cause is of a more excellent kind and the posterior depends on the prior in causing their common effect (see Chapter 3 above). If it takes a descending hierarchy of causal contributors on the outside to produce an individual substance (for example, Beulah the cow) here below, Aquinas reasons by analogy to find a hierarchy of causal involvement within the individual substance itself: substantial principles emanate necessary accidents and potencies for others. Moreover, if substances act or suffer through their accidents, still the substance itself and/or its essential components (prime matter and substantial form) play (what Aquinas and Scotus would recognize as prior) causal roles.

Ockham critiques Scotus's notion of hierarchical essentially ordered causal chains, because he thinks no workable account has been given of what it means to say that one cause is prior to the other, or of what it is for the posterior cause to depend essentially on the prior cause *in causing*. For Ockham, the dependence of one cause on another in causing reduces to their being immediate partial causes of the same effect. Ockham argues—*pace* Aquinas and Scotus—that natural reason cannot prove what faith must nevertheless assert: that God is an immediate partial cause of every effect. Which creatures are efficient partial causes of other creatures is something to be discovered empirically through observed correlations.

Independent Accidents. Ockham observes that the fact that—normally and naturally—creatures come in complete substance-accident packages prevents us from doing any systematic "separation" experiments to determine on empirical grounds what substance could cause without accidents and how accidents would interact all by themselves. But ecclesial consensus against the coexistence theory (or consubstantiation) enables faith to recognize the interactions of consecrated host and chalice as sites where independent accidents act and are acted upon. Our authors both use and extend their philosophical causal principles to sort out what the accidents contribute and what has to be supplied by God.

For Aquinas, the causal interactions of consecrated host and chalice can be explained if we suppose that God does four extra things. Before the consecration, bread accidents participated in the bread's own act of existence (*esse*). As a substance subject, the bread had that act of existence (*esse*) *per se*, while the accidents had it through another (that is, the substance). After the consecration, [1] God conserves all of the eucharistic species in the same *esse* they had before, and—since the bread is no more, having been converted—[2] God makes the quantity to be no longer dependent but to have that act of existence (*esse*) *per se*. Aquinas then precisions the allegedly Aristotelian principle that only primary *substances* act: philosophically, what is true is that only what exists *per se* acts. Before the consecration, the bread acted by reason of its substantial form, and the bread accidents were instrumental causes acting in the power of the substance. After consecration, causal interactions can go on much as before, because [3] God conserves in the accidents, not only the act of existence (*esse*) they had before, but the instrumental powers they had before, powers whose terms-to-which are the ends at which the substance agent aims. By these two maneuvers, Aquinas hopes to skirt the apparent consequences of the Causal Nobility Principles. The bread accidents—although mere accidents—can act on other things to produce any effects that the complete hylomorphic package—bread substance together with its accidents—could produce before, including the corruption and generation of other substances. Giles of Rome picks up on this idea when he suggests that something (lion semen) might act in the power of another (the lion or the substantial form of lion) even when separated from it (when the semen is in the womb of the lioness) to produce the effect of the principal agent (a lion soul)! So far as the action of other causes on the eucharistic species is concerned, Aquinas thinks that [4] God creates the matter of the new substance when the eucharistic species are corrupted beyond bread (wine) suitability.

Scotus and Ockham do not believe, and do not think Aristotle believed that properly speaking only primary substances act. Rather, Aristotle meant to emphasize (against Plato) that only *individual* things act. Scotus reasons that, since the intensive actuality of an accident will not vary because of its external relations, inherence makes no difference to how much causal power an accident has in itself. Nevertheless, excellence hierarchies and Causal Nobility Principles loom large in Scotus's metaphysics. Accidents have less intensive actuality than substantial forms or substance composites. Because accidents are less perfect, they cannot—by [P28] and [Cor 8]—be the total effective principles in producing them. Althugh accidents in themselves should be perfect enough to corrupt contrary accidents of the same or lesser intensity, Scotus brings up the difficulty that corruption of the substance is naturally consequent upon the corruption of the limit degree of qualities pertaining to that substance kind, and corruption of one substance is naturally followed by the generation of another. There is not enough to accidents either to destroy one substantial form or to produce another! Scotus equivocates as to whether eucharistic accidents can corrupt even the limit degrees of contrary qualities, but is clear that the new substantial form will have to be introduced by some universal cause, whether the sun or God.

For Scotus, the Presupposed Subject Principle means that created causes need something to act upon, but he denies that it has to be a substance subject. On the common theory that quantity is something really distinct from substance and quality, the bread qualities still exist in a subject and can be corrupted at least up to the limit of bread suitability. Scotus wrestles with the problem of condensation and rarefaction, but is clear that, if new quantities or quantity parts are involved, Divine power will have to produce them, just as Divine power will have to produce the prime matter and substantial forms when the eucharistic species are corrupted into vinegar, worms, or ashes. The separation and uniting of eucharistic continua pose no Causal Nobility or Presupposed Subject problems, because no new intensive actualities are involved.

In assessing what separate accidents can cause, Ockham emphasizes that Causal Nobility Principles rule them out as *total* but not as *partial* causes of substances. As for what external causes can do to eucharistic species,

Ockham defends the Presupposed Subject Principle for creatures, from the Aristotelian principle that natural causes act to the limit of their powers, and concludes that creatures cannot *create* vinegar, worms, or ashes out of eucharistic species. But Ockham denies that analogous arguments prove that creatures are unable to *destroy* eucharistic species. Creatures might be able to destroy even if Divine power would be required to maintain the sequence in which the destruction of bread (wine) accidents is followed by the production of vinegar, worms, or ashes.

Extension in Place and Causal Exposure. In Aristotle's physics, material agents and patients must both be extended in place and proximate to one another, if they are to interact causally. Aristotle thought it metaphysically impossible that a body be located in a place without being extended in it, and so did not consider that proximity and extension might break apart. The theological doctrine—[T4] that Christ's resurrection body is impassible—gave our authors incentive to find a way for Christ's Body to be located on the altar (and thus proximate to many created causes in the environment) without being causally exposed. To secure this conclusion, Aquinas, Giles of Rome, and Scotus think it will be enough to deny that Christ's Body is extended in place on the altar. Rejecting their analyses of real presence (see Section III above), Ockham's own conviction—that Christ's Body is definitively in place on the altar—provokes him to challenge the philosophical consensus that ordinary extension (whole in the whole and only parts in the parts) is required of material agents and patients. If causal power is a function of intensive actuality, and definitive placement puts more intensive actuality (because more parts of the body) in each part of place than circumscriptive placement does, why should definitive placement be a metaphysical obstacle to causal efficacy? Ockham concludes that proximity is sufficient for causal exposure: material objects that are unextended but present will interact the same way as they would if they were extended unless—as in the eucharist—this is obstructed by Divine power.

VII. Sacramental Causality and Essential Connections

Aquinas interpreted the traditional tag—that new-law sacraments effect what they figure—as the demand to identify a non-accidental explanatory connection between new-law rites and/or participation in them, on the one hand, and spiritual benefits and/or real presence, on the other. No link as loose as that between the white and the sculpture in Aristotle's example will do. Our authors all agreed that neither the material stuffs, nor the outward and inward acts involved in the rites, were the right kinds of things to possess grace- or real-presence-producing powers naturally, through their own forms. All agreed that that the non-accidental explanatory connection had to be established by an alien causal power. They divided over how this happens, in particular over whether the alien power does or does not have somehow to exist in the sacramental cause.

Alien Forms and Powers. Aquinas, Henry of Ghent, Bassolis, and Mayronis all maintain that real efficient causes must have in themselves, and exercise, efficient causal power to produce the effect. They infer that sacraments can effect what they figure only if grace- and/or real-presence-producing causal power exists in them. Bassolis and Mayronis are content to draw the further conclusion that sacraments are not real causes of grace and real presence, where 'cause' is understood the way it is in natural philosophy. Henry of Ghent says that real efficient causal power is in the sacrament, because God is the subject of such power and God is present in them to produce that effect. Aquinas's approach is much more imaginative, insofar as it draws on an analogy with cognitive psychology to explain how alien forms and powers can exist in something as in a subject.

So far as Great Chain and Causal Nobility Principles are concerned, Aristotelian cognitive psychology seemed already to blur the divide between material and spiritual. For Aristotle, cognition is quite literally "information": the receiving of the form of the thing known without its matter. Aquinas can say that "knowers differ from non-knowers in this: that knowers can receive the forms of others."[10] Non-knowers such as rocks and grass have their own substantial and accidental forms and are characterized by them: rocks are hard and heavy, grass is green and chewable. Knowers (such as cows, humans, and angels) also have their own substantial and accidental forms and are characterized by them. In addition, knowers can receive alien forms, the forms of other things (for example, of colors, flavors, odors, textures, temperatures; of different substantial kinds). These alien forms do not exist in the knowers in such a way as to characterize them (if they did, those forms would not be merely *alien*), but in such a way that the receiver cognizes them. Thus, Aquinas contrasts the natural

[10] Aquinas, *Summa Theologica* I, q. 14, a. 1 c.

existence of a form in a subject (natural *inesse*) with the intentional existence of a form in a subject (intentional *inesse*). The natural existence of Fness in X makes X to be F, while—where X is a knower—the intentional existence of Fness in X enables X to cognize Fness. Since—for Aquinas—the proper subject of sensation is the living sense organ, this theory already posits that *animate material* things can be the subjects of forms in intentional being.

Because the proximity requirements of Aristotelian physics were also thought to rule out action at a distance (or at least action beyond a determinate distance), Averroes concluded and Aquinas agreed that colored objects did not act on the eye directly, but by propagating the sensible species (the sensible form without the matter) through the medium. The redness that has natural existence in the wall was said to cause redness to have intentional existence in the proximate air, and that redness having existence in the air next to the wall caused redness to have intentional existence in the air just ahead of it, and so on up to the eye. The philosophical doctrine of the propagation of species through the medium posited that *inanimate* material could be the subject of forms in intentional being. Not only knowers, but certain non-knowers, were said to be able to receive alien forms.

Not only was Aristotelian cognitive psychology read as allowing material things to be *subjects* of forms that do not characterize them. Aristotle's doctrine that human knowing begins with sensation seemed to give material things some sort of *causal* role in human intellectualizing as well. Aristotle teaches that the agent intellect abstracts the intelligible species of material quiddities from sorted sense images, which are themselves modifications of material things. Later interpreters disagreed (Aquinas himself seems to forward different suggestions in different passages) as to whether the sorted sense images serve as a material or an instrumental or an efficient partial cause of the intelligible species.

For Aquinas, this philosophical analysis of cognition furnished the model for his handling of sacramental causality. Just as the agent intellect is the principal cause of intelligible species and sorted phantasms are the material or instrumental cause, so God is the principal cause of grace and real presence, and sacraments are the instrumental cause. Material things involved in sacramental rites have their own forms and are thereby furnished with active and passive causal powers, including powers to produce effects of which they are principal causes. But instrumental causes differ from causes that have not been taken up as instruments in this: that instrumental causes have not only their own powers through their own forms; while they are being used, they participate in alien powers, the powers of their principal agent, powers that have temporary and transient intentional existence in them as in a subject.

These theories of cognitive psychology and instrumental causality were *philosophically* controversial in themselves. But Aquinas's contemporaries found his attempts to analyze sacramental causality as instrumental causality as multiply muddled for philosophical reasons (see Chapter 3 above).

Essential Dependence through the Power of Another. What makes Aquinas so eager to locate efficient causal powers in the sacraments themselves is his conviction that otherwise the sacraments will be causes of grace and real presence at most *per accidens*, the way the white is a *per accidens* cause of the sculpture. The principal cause acting through its own form is the *per se* cause of the effect. The instrumental cause does not have such power through its own form. But—during the causal transaction—the instrumental cause participates in the power of the principal agent so that the principal agent's power has intentional existence in the instrumental cause. For Aquinas, it is this power that the instrumental cause has existing in it through another (that is, through the principal agent) that keeps it from being a merely *per accidens* cause of the principal agent's intended effect.

Scotus's alternative strategy is to integrate the conclusion of the Assistance Theory—that there is neither grace- nor real-presence-producing power in the sacraments—into his own metaphysical picture of the cosmos as unified and structured by the essential orders of eminence and dependence. The order of eminence is comprehensive: for every pair of natures Nm and Nn, either Nm is more excellent than Nn or vice versa. But it is not obviously the case that every pair of natures or extant things is ordered by essential dependence: that one has power to be the *per se* cause of another, or that one essentially depends on the other in causing a third. Thus, Scotus's philosophical project motivates him to discover "non-obvious" categories of essential dependence. Suppose X's are correlated with Y's. When all is said and done, what makes the difference for Scotus between essential dependence and merely *per accidens* causal connection is whether or not the correlation is underwritten by the structured intentionality of some causal power or powers. The result is that Y may essentially depend on X, even if X neither has nor exercises any efficient causal power to produce Y, provided that there is something else Z the intentionality of whose causal power is so structured as to produce Y only when X is present.

For Scotus, it is systematic metaphysical preoccupations that lead him to focus on putative cases of "non-obvious" essential dependence in nature. He then extends his insight to sacramental causality, where it is the structured intentionality of God's will that underwrites the connection. For Ockham, positing non-obvious essential dependence in nature would lead to scepticism in natural science: what evidence would enable us to tell which were the cases of non-obvious and which others of obvious essential dependence? Ockham returns to the political analogies forwarded by the Assistance Theory and highlighted by Mayronis: the connection between sacraments and grace on the soul and/or real presence on the altar is established, not by any power in the sacraments, but by the will of another. Overall, then, our authors respond to the philosophical challenges of eucharistic real presence with significant conceptual remodels wrought by massive efforts of integration.

PART THREE

What Sort of Union

11

Eucharistic Eating and Drinking

I. "Take! Eat! This is My Body!"

For the authors we have been considering, sacraments are sensible *signs* of the sanctification of human beings. Their *use* results in a spiritual change in suitable receivers. For Christian sacraments other than the eucharist, the sacrament *is* its use. Baptism *is* someone's being baptized; confirmation, someone's being confirmed; extreme unction, someone's being anointed and strengthened. In the eucharist, the use is in the eating and drinking of Christ's Body and Blood in obedience to Christ's command, a consumption that has spiritual consequences for suitable receivers.

Nevertheless, Aquinas and Scotus emphasize, the eucharist is different from other sacraments. It is perfected not in its use, but in the real presence of the Body and Blood of Christ under forms of bread and wine. Every eucharistic consecration puts Christ's Body and Blood on the altar where the forms of bread and wine seem to be, whether or not anyone eats or drinks. This is the way Christ keeps His promise to be with us always—not only spiritually, but present in body, to the close of the age (cf. Matt. 28: 20). For our authors, to be in the presence of Christ's Body and Blood is itself a great honor, just as many subjects would consider it a privilege to join crowds along the parade route of earthly monarchs, even if their interaction did not go beyond that. Eucharistic reception is supposed to be a further step that takes the worthy worshipper into even more intimate communion. Eating and drinking are the way we take Christ in. Eating is consummated when the eater and what is eaten become one.[1]

[1] *Aquinas, Summa Theologica* III, q. 65, a. 3 c & ad 3um; III, q. 73, a. 1 c & ad 1um & 3um; III, q. 73, aa. 1–2 c; III, q. 73, a. 3 c & ad 2um; III, q. 73, a. 5 c; *Sent.* IV, d. 8, q. 1, a. 3, qc.3.c [14821]; Scotus, *Op. Ox.* IV, d. 8, q. 1, n. 5; Wadding VIII. 408–9.

The question is, how to put eucharistic perfection and eucharistic use—real presence and eucharistic eating and drinking—together? Back in 1059, Cardinal Humbert of Silva Candida ("right hand man" to Pope Nicholas II) thought he knew. Suspecting Berengar of Tours of a merely "symbolist" view of the eucharist—that the sacrament is merely a sign of Christ's passion, and that sacramental eating and drinking are merely a sign of some spiritual transformation in soul—Cardinal Humbert forced Berengar to swear that

> the bread and wine which are placed on the altar are after consecration not only a Sacrament but also the real body and blood of our Lord Jesus Christ, and that with the senses [*sensualiter*], not only by way of Sacrament but in reality, these are held and broken by the hands of priests and are crushed by the teeth of the faithful.

Although the species of bread and wine remain, so that the faithful "may not shrink through perceiving what is raw and bloody,"[2] it is the same body that Mary bore and that was crucified, that is bitten into, torn, and chewed.[3] Taken at face value, *Ego Berengarius* (as this formula came to be known) seems to imply that the priests literally break Christ's Body the way they might break a stick, and that the faithful literally eat the flesh of Christ the way they might consume a piece of chicken or lamb!

Cardinal Humbert's ecclesiastical position made it awkward for theologians to dismiss his formula directly. All the same, the most intellectually sophisticated thinkers—including both Berengar and his vigorous opponent Lanfranc—were revolted by it. They maneuvered to evade its starkest consequences and/or to explain them away.

[2] Bonaventure cites this rationale for veiling the really present Body of Christ with the sacramental species in *Sent.* IV, d. 10, p. 1, a.u, q. 1, arg. 4; Quaracchi IV. 217.

[3] Gregorius VII 1073–85, Proceedings of his Sixth Council at Rome in 1079, "De ss. Eucharistia: Ius iurandum a Berengario praestitum," in *Enchiridion Symbolorum: Definitionum et Declarationum de Rebus Fidei et Morum*, ed. Heinrich Denzinger (Freiburg in Breisgau: B. Herder, 1911). Berengar's position was condemned repeatedly: by Leo IX at Rome in 1050, Victor II at the synod of Florence in 1055, by Nicholas II at Rome in 1059, and by Gregory VII at Rome in 1078 and again in 1079. For useful historical discussions of Berengar's controversial career, see Henry Chadwick, "Ego Berengarius," *Journal of Theological Studies*, NS 40/2 (Oct. 1989), pp. 414–45, and "Symbol and Reality: Berengar and the Appeal to the Fathers," in Peter Ganz, R. B. C. Huygens, and Friedrich Niewöhner (eds.), *Auctoritas und Ratio: Studien zu Berengar von Tours* (Wiesbaden: Otto Harrassowitz, 1990), pp. 25–45. See also in the latter volume H. E. J. Cowdrey, "The Papacy and the Berengarian Controversy," pp. 111–38, and Gary Macy, "Berengar's Legacy as Heresiarch," pp. 47–67.

II. Manifold Improprieties

Ego Berengarius made explicit the picture that lay behind even earlier worries that it would be unfitting for God to expose Christ's Body and Blood to eucharistic eating and drinking.[4] *Biological Processing?* (1) If Christ's Body is literally torn by the teeth in eucharistic eating, will it not also descend to the stomach for digestion with the usable parts being turned into the eater's body while the rest passes out through the intestines like other bodily waste? Fasting regulations required the faithful to receive on an empty stomach, so that at least Christ's Body would not be mixed in the stomach with ordinary food. (2) If the healthy digest Christ's Body, what about those sick with indigestion, who swallow the host only to vomit it up or excrete it whole? Penitential practices counted this a serious offense and instructed confessors to impose heavy penances on those who received the host but failed to keep it down. *Inappropriate Subjects.* Again, if the eucharist makes Christ's Body to be really present for literal eating, will it not be taken in by any animal that puts the hosts in its mouth, regardless of the eater's inner states? (3) What about *unwitting* receivers—mice nibbling the reserved sacrament or unbelievers who think they are ingesting ordinary bread or wine? Some argued that eucharist-fed mice should be caught and burned, along with consecrated hosts on the verge of molding. (4) What about *unworthy* receivers—the unbaptized or believers who have committed but not yet been absolved from mortal sin? Uncleanness is "caught" by contact. Would not putting the host into a mortal sinner's mouth contaminate the Body of Christ?[5] Disciplines of rigorous self-examination and confession hedged against that prospect.

If Cardinal Humbert's formula revolts in the detail, it also appears to contradict the dogma that Christ's resurrection body is glorified and impassible. During His earthly career, Christ's human body was—like other

[4] Gary Macy, in *The Theologies of the Eucharist in the Early Scholastic Period: A Study of the Salvific Function of the Sacrament according to the Theologians c.1080–c.1220* (Oxford: Clarendon Press, 1984), notes how critics of Paschasius' view—that there is salvific nature-to-nature contact between the Body of Christ and the body of the recipient—attempted to discredit it by pointing out that an over-literal understanding of the presence of the Body of Christ might expose it to digestion (I. 27–34).

[5] Cited by Bonaventure as an erroneous opinion in *Sent.* IV, d. 9, a. 2, q. 1.c; Quaracchi IV. 207–8. See also Lombard, *Sent.* IV, d. 9, cc. 2–3; Grottaferrata II. 288–90.

animal bodies—as vulnerable to being torn by teeth as by whips, as subject to literal cannibalism, digestion, and excretion as to crucifixion and rotting in the grave. But Christ is raised incorruptible. To make sense of eucharistic eating, some other understanding is needed that allows the faithful to receive Christ's Body and Blood without doing His human flesh any harm!

III. Impanation, or Christ's Body Breaded!

Berengar of Tours was adamant that the Body of Christ that Mary bore and that died on a cross remains impassible in heaven, no matter where or how many masses are said. Moreover, he maintains against Lanfranc that the substance of bread and wine remains, because accidents without substance are impossible in Aristotelian metaphysics. Sacraments are signs. In the eucharist, the bread and the wine are the signs of Christ's Body and Blood. Take away the signs and you take away the sacrament! Sometimes Berengar suggests that the sacrament is not merely a sign, because at the consecration the bread and wine undergo a change: there comes to be a union between the sign and the thing signified analogous to that between human and Divine in the Incarnation. The Body of Christ becomes bread (impanation) the way the Divine Word becomes flesh (Incarnation).[6]

The texts left to us contain no detailed analysis of exactly what Berengar or some of his followers understood by this, and in any event rigorous accounts of the metaphysics of the Incarnation were the work of the thirteenth- and fourteenth-century Aristotelians (Aquinas, Scotus, and Ockham notable among them). Relative to these later developed discussions, it is easy to see why the parallel leapt to mind. For underlying such theories of Incarnation is the assumption that

[T35] one and the same individual X can have two natures N_1 and N_2: one nature N_1 that belongs to X essentially, the nature that makes X the very thing X is and without which X could not exist; another N_2 that X assumes contingently.

Aristotelian natures are constituted by or give rise to characteristic sets of active and/or passive powers. The individual does through each nature

[6] Henry Chadwick, "Ego Berengarius," pp. 424–5; "Symbol and Reality," pp. 32–5, 37. Macy notes how Guitmund of Aversa listed impanationists as one of four kinds of Berengarians (in "Berengar's Legacy as Heresiarch," p. 50).

what the powers of that nature enable it to do and suffers through each nature what the powers of that nature enable it to suffer. Thus, Godhead is only active power and is immutable and impassible. God the Son is essentially Divine but contingently assumes human nature and makes it His own. God the Son acts through both of His natures, doing Divine things (for example, creating and sustaining the world) through His Divine active power and human things (for example, eating bread and taking a walk) through His human active power. But He suffers and dies only through His human passive power. The suffering and death through the human nature leave the Divine nature intact.

Likewise, the Body of Christ is essentially human; it could not exist and be the very body that it is without being human. Through its human active powers the Body of Christ does characteristically human things such as taking a walk, making mud pies with saliva, using a rope whip to knock animal cages and money off tables. Through its passive power, the Body of Christ suffers hunger and thirst, pain and death. In the eucharist, the Body of Christ contingently assumes the bread nature on the altar and through its bread nature acts to produce sense perceptions in nearby animals and suffers the fate of any bread that is eaten: it is broken, torn, and chewed; it descends through the gastrointestinal track to be digested and/or excreted. Thus, Christ's Body is broken by the hands of priests and torn by the teeth of the faithful only through the passive powers of its bread nature. Its being eaten and destroyed through its bread nature leave its human nature intact.

God the Son cannot lay down His Divine nature: it belongs to Him essentially; He could not exist without it. God the Son could lay down His human nature, because it belongs to Him contingently: He could and did exist without it, and could cease to assume it at any time. Nevertheless, according to medieval theological consensus, God the Son in fact assumes His human nature "once and for all"; He takes it up at conception and will never lay it down. Likewise, the Body of Christ is essentially human and so could not lay aside its human nature without ceasing to exist. But the Body of Christ assumes not only one but as many particular bread natures as there are altars on which mass is said, and so would assume many bread natures at once. Moreover, the Body of Christ assumes them only to lay them down as soon as they are somehow destroyed, whether by the digestive process, by putrefaction, or by fire.

The doctrine of *communicatio idiomatum* states that

[T36] when an individual X has two natures N_1 and N_2, propositions that describe X in terms of N_1 in the subject and in terms of N_2 in the predicate can come out true.

Thus, it is true that God the Son suffers and dies, because the individual that suffers and dies in His human nature is God the Son essentially. Likewise, it is true to say that the faithful receive and eat the Body of Christ, because the individual body that enters the mouth and suffers the fate of ordinary food through its bread nature is—through its human nature—the very body that Mary bore, that died on a cross, and is now impassible in heaven.

Impanation seems to enjoy a theoretical economy over transubstantiation. It does not have to modify Aristotle's *Categories* metaphysics to allow for actually independent accidents. Instead, it borrows from Christology another modification of Aristotle's *Categories* metaphysics that allows individual substance natures actually to depend on something else as on a subject. Christology requires only that *Divine* persons can assume extra natures that are not essential to them. Impanation posits that this is possible for individual creatures. Christology does not have to go beyond the claim that God the Son assumed a single created nature. Impanation has to assign the Body of Christ the metaphysical capacity to assume many extra natures at once.

Commenting on this, Ockham says that natural reason could not show it to be metaphysically impossible for individual creatures to assume extra natures.[7] Scotus sees no metaphysical impossibility in a Divine person's assuming many extra natures at once.[8] Since "alien assumption"—whether by a Divine person or a creature—is achieved by an exercise of Divine power, these philosophers would see no convincing argument against the possibility of Christ's Body assuming many individual bread natures at once.[9] Nevertheless, already in the eleventh and twelfth centuries, metaphysically inchoate forms of impanation were being crowded out as theologically dubious[10] by

[7] Ockham, *Quaest in Sent.* IV. q. 8; OTh VIII. 138. Scotus's long discussion of the issue (in *Op. Ox.* III, d. 1, q. 4, nn. 2–3; Wadding VII. 1.47–50) proves inconclusive.

[8] Scotus, *Op. Ox.* III, d. 1, q. 3, n. 2; Wadding VII. 1. 44.

[9] For a more detailed discussion of these issues, see my *Christ and Horrors: The Coherence of Christology* (Cambridge: Cambridge University Press, 2006), ch. 5, pp. 108–43, and ch. 9, pp. 296–307. See also Richard Cross, *The Metaphysics of Christology: Thomas Aquinas to Duns Scotus* (Oxford: Oxford University Press, 2002).

[10] Rupert of Deutz got into difficulties, among other things, for holding a version of impanation. See John H. Van Engen, *Rupert of Deutz* (Berkeley, Los Angeles, and London: University of California Press, 1983), ch. IV, pp. 140–1. See also Henry Chadwick, "Ego Berengarius," pp. 437–9;

philosophically underdeveloped versions of transubstantiation. Pope Innocent III's generic sponsorship of transubstantiation at the Fourth Lateran Council in 1215 contributed significant momentum. Franciscus Mayronis, an "independent-minded Scotist" and slightly older contemporary of Ockham, could almost mock impanation for having the vices of its virtues: it would mean that Christ's Body was still corruptible after the resurrection (that is, through its bread nature), and it would confront believers with a really present but "breaded Christ"![11]

IV. Transubstantiation, Another *Via Media*?

Developed in terms of the later metaphysics of hypostatic union, impanation opens a *via media*. On the one hand, impanation concedes what Cardinal Humbert required—that eucharistic fraction and reception involves the literal breaking and tearing of Christ's Body. Likewise, impanation accommodates the further implications of *Ego Berengarius*—that eucharistic eating leads to the digestion or vomiting or defecation of Christ's Body. On the other hand, impanation's two-nature theory removes the scandal by quarantining such effects to the bread nature of Christ's Body. Transubstantiation charted a different *via media*. As Henry Chadwick argues, in the midst of the eleventh-century controversies, it appealed because of its ability to explain how Christ's Body is really present on the altar and really enters suitable receivers, without running the risk of any harm or corrupting changes at all.[12] The cost of this benefit is that transubstantiation has to explain away Cardinal Humbert's evident insistence that Christ's Body is literally broken, torn, and chewed.[13]

likewise, Darwell Stone, MA, *A History of the Doctrine of the Holy Eucharist* (2 vols.; London, New York, Bombay, and Calcutta: Longmans, Green, & Co, 1909), who traces views of eucharistic presence from the New Testament to the early twentieth century. The theory only sometimes *called* impanation—with its putative parallel between the Incarnation and eucharistic presence—is strongly suggested by Theodoret (Stone I. 3. i. 99–102); Gelasius (I. 3. i. 101–2); Leontius of Byzantium (I. 4. i. 135); Ephraim of Antioch (I. 4. i. 135–6); John of Paris (*c.*1300) (I. 8. i. 361–2); and the Anglican divine Lancelot Andrews (1555–1626) (II. xiii. ii. 258, 265). It was attributed to Luther by the 1552 session of the Council of Trent (Stone II. 9. x. 88) and the 1672 Council of Jerusalem/Bethlehem (II. 4. vi. 181–2).

11 Franciscus Mayronis, *Sent.* IV, d. 8, q. 7, a. 19; 1520, fo. 186va L.

12 Henry Chadwick, "Ego Berengarius," p. 418; "Symbol and Reality," p. 27.

13 Henry Chadwick, "Ego Berengarius," pp. 440–2, 445; "Symbol and Reality," p. 29.

Salient Distinctions. From Lombard onwards, philosophical sponsors of transubstantiation meet the problem of eucharistic eating by drawing some crisp distinctions. *Sign versus Thing Signified.* For every sacrament, it is necessary to distinguish between the sacrament (that is, the sign itself) and "the thing of the sacrament" (that is, the thing signified). Where the eucharist is concerned, however, there are three levels. The eucharistic species are sacrament only insofar as they signify the true Body and Blood of Christ. The true Body and Blood of Christ are the things signified by the eucharistic species, but they are also sacraments insofar as they signify the mystical body of Christ. That mystical body politic is only a "thing of the sacrament," because—in the eucharist at least—it is not a sign of anything else. With these distinctions in hand, adherents of transubstantiation explain that it is the eucharistic species (the signs) that are literally eaten and swallowed, digested, vomited, or excreted. Neither of the things signified—not the true Body and Blood of Christ and not the mystical body of Christ—is literally broken by the hands of the priest or torn by the teeth of the faithful![14]

Varieties of Eating. Likewise they distinguish three kinds of eating. [1] Eaters eat the eucharistic species *carnally* when they eat taking them to be ordinary bread and wine. Mice and humans eat carnally when they do not recognize what is on the altar or in the tabernacle as consecrated. [2] Eaters eat the eucharistic species *sacramentally* when they eat believing them to be, or even believing only that others believe them to be, veils of the true Body of Christ. The unbaptized and unrepentant mortal sinners might eat sacramentally, just as much as the faithful who are well prepared. [3] Eaters eat *spiritually* when they not only have faith in Christ's saving work but also are stirred (Bonaventure says "inflamed") with a love of Christ that unites them and more deeply engrafts them into the mystical body of Christ. This knowledge and love of Christ are their spiritual eating, and their union in the mystical body of Christ is their spiritual nourishment. Thus, as Augustine declared, where carnal eating turns what is eaten into the body of the eater, spiritual eating turns the eater into what is eaten, insofar as it unites the eater to Christ and incorporates the eater into the mystical body of Christ, which is the Church.[15]

[14] Aquinas, *Summa Theologica* III, q. 73, a. 6 c; Bonaventure, *Op. Ox.* IV, d. 8, p. 2, a. 2, q. 1.c; Quaracchi IV. 196; IV, d. 11, q. 2, a. 1, q. 1.c; Quaracchi IV. 254–5.

[15] Hugh of St Victor, *De sacramentis* bk. II, pt. 8, c. 5, p. 307; bk. II, pt. 8, cc. 7–8, 309–11; Bonaventure, *Sent.* IV, d. 8, p. 2, a. 2, q. 1 c & d. 8, p. 2, a. 2, q. 2 c; Quaracchi IV. 196–8; IV, d. 9, a. 1, qq. 2–3; Quaracchi IV. 203–5; *Breviloquium* pt. VI, c. 9; Quaracchi V. 273–5; Aquinas, *Summa Theologica* III, q. 73, a. 3 c & ad 2um; *Sent.* IV, d. 8, q. 1, a. 3, qc.1 c & ad 3um [14813; 14816]; Scotus, *Op. Ox.* IV, d. 8, q. 3, n. 2; Wadding VIII. 445.

Thus, the Body of Christ is really present under the eucharistic species *ex opere operato*, independently of whether or not it is received. But the type of eucharistic eating possible for an eater depends on the eater's inner (cognitive and affective) states. Mice and ignorant humans eat carnally, but not spiritually or sacramentally. Any who recognize the eucharistic species as a sign of Christ's true Body may eat sacramentally, but only baptized persons who are free from mortal sin win any spiritual benefit from sacramental eating. And only baptized persons who are free from mortal sin and are stirred with a love for Christ eat spiritually and enjoy union with the mystical body of Christ.

Philosophical Underpinnings. This solution, forwarded by Lombard and Bonaventure, rests on two key assumptions:

[T37] the eucharistic species can be broken, eaten, and converted into the eater;

and

[T38] the Body of Christ is really present in such a way as not to be vulnerable to breaking or to corruption by the eating and the digestion process,

both of which turned out to be non-trivial when the doctrine of transubstantiation is probed in philosophical detail.

[T37] is prima facie problematic, because—according to the theory of transubstantiation—the eucharistic species are bread accidents and wine accidents existing without a subject. According to Aquinas, Giles of Rome, and Duns Scotus, the bread and wine qualities have the bread and wine quantities for their proximate subjects. Aquinas and Giles of Rome even hold that the qualities are individuated by the quantity in which they inhere. Eucharistic fraction involves a quantitative change, which—for them—raises the question of whether the same qualities remain, or whether fraction would not simply destroy the eucharistic species, so that they would not be there to be eaten! Again, even if the eucharistic species were to survive the fraction, there is the problem that digestion involves substantial changes. But the No Substance Subject, No Substantial Form, and No Persistent Prime Matter problems seem to pose obstacles to regarding separate accidents as the *terminus a quo* of substantial change. [T38] is also prima facie problematic, because explanations are owed of how the Body of Christ can be really present without being causally exposed. While conceding both [T37] and [T38], Aquinas, Giles of Rome, Scotus, and Ockham resolve the difficulties in different ways.

Digestible Accidents? Aquinas admits that the bread accidents do nourish and so must be digested by the eater. Like the reduction of hosts to ashes or worms, this is one more case of the bread accidents being the *terminus a quo* of a change whose *terminus ad quem* is a substance or substance part. Aquinas explains that *terminus a quo* will be *per se* extant because the bread quantity exists *per se* in the sacrament, and the bread qualities are its *per se* principles of action. The missing substantial form is no problem, because Divine power conserves in the bread accidents whatever instrumental power they would have had if the bread were there. Sometimes Aquinas deals with the No Persistent Prime Matter problem by adopting Averroes' view that indeterminate quantity is the proximate subject of the substantial form. Normally and naturally, it is not prime matter alone but prime matter informed by indeterminate dimensions that persists through substantial change. Where changes in the eucharistic species are concerned, the indeterminate dimensions that formerly belonged to the bread persist through the change, and the prime matter returns either as a natural concomitant or miraculously by Divine power (see Chapter 8 above).

On Giles of Rome's analysis, the following five things happen at one and the same time but are ordered as to natural priority and posteriority: many bread-suitable accidents are corrupted; new accidents are introduced; the Body of Christ ceases to be there; matter begins to be there; the new substantial form is educed from the potency of the matter. Giles picks up on Aquinas's first suggestion to maintain that the return of the matter in the generation of substances from eucharistic accidents (in the case of eucharistic eating, the conversion of bread accidents into the eater's flesh) is no more miraculous than the infusion of the intellectual soul into the suitably formed fetus (see Chapter 8 above).

Focusing on cases of hosts being reduced to ashes or worms, Scotus leads with the Causal Nobility Principle:

[P28] the total active cause must have as much intensive actuality as or more intensive actuality than the effect,

and its corollary:

[Cor 8] the total active cause must be at least as perfect as or more perfect than the effect.

Since accidents have less intensive actuality than substantial form and substance, eucharistic accidents cannot be the *total* active cause in the production of a new substance. Presumably, because created efficient causes presuppose a subject on which to act, any substantial and qualitative forms in the digestive juices could not be the *total* active cause of the conversion of bread accidents into the eater's flesh either. Accordingly, Scotus concedes that such changes require the additional activity of some universal cause, whether God or the heavens to produce the substantial form, and presumably God to restore the prime matter that underlies it.

When it comes to eucharistic eating, Ockham's approach finds no metaphysical problem with digestive juices corrupting the eucharistic accidents, indeed with reducing them to nothing. Because creatures cannot create, however, the production of new flesh in the eater will have to be solo Divine action!

Causal Inaccessibility. Aquinas, Giles of Rome, and Scotus deal with the difficulties around [T38] by contending that, in Aristotelian physics, a body is causally exposed only if it and/or its accidents are *extended* in the place. But the Body of Christ is not present that way in the place where the bread accidents are. According to Aquinas and Giles of Rome, a body is extended in a place only if it is present to that place through its own determinate quantity, which is present whole to the whole of the place and part to the part of the place. The Body of Christ is not present to the place by means of its own determinate quantity, but rather is present to the eucharistic species in the mode of substance (whole to the whole and whole to each part). Scotus draws on Giles of Rome's distinction between quantitative placement (the order of the parts of a body to one another) and categorial placement (the order of the body to place). For Scotus, a body is extended in a place if and only if the whole body has an external placement relation to the whole of the place and each part of the body has an external placement relation to a part of the place—that is, only if the body's parts enjoy categorial as well as quantitative placement. Scotus contends that the whole Body of Christ bears an external relation to the whole place where the bread accidents are, but the parts of the Body of Christ do not bear external relations to the parts of the place. Therefore, the Body of Christ is not extended under the bread accidents. Either theory makes it metaphysically possible for the Body of Christ to be present to the bread accidents wherever they go, so long as they exist, and to be there without causal exposure to qualitative or substantial change. Aquinas and Giles would contend that the Body of Christ is not broken when the host is broken, because the Body of Christ is not present to that place by its own determinate quantity. What is revolting about

Humbert's formula is its suggestion that eucharistic eating might change the relation of the parts of Christ's Body to one another (that is, their quantitative position). Scotus's thought would be that the quantitative position of body parts is vulnerable only in places relative to which those body parts have categorial position. On Scotus's theory, that is precisely what Christ's Body parts do not have!

Ockham understands Aristotelian physics a different way, as prioritizing proximity and presence:

[P23′] when a sufficient agent is proximate and the patient is disposed, and there is no obstacle, the action follows.

Normally and naturally, bodies are also extended in the places where they are located. But Ockham understands the Body of Christ to be in the place where the bread accidents are definitively—that is, whole in the whole place and whole in each part of the place. Given Ockham's argument that whatever is in a place is immediately present to the place, each part of the definitively placed body will be immediately present to the place so that in no case is the presence of one part to the place mediated by the presence of another part to the place. (We are not to imagine a queue of body parts in the place!) He reasons, therefore, that such supranatural definitive placement should be no barrier to causal exposure:

[P24] an active principle is no less able to act when it is present to a patient by its whole self than when one part is present to one part and another part to another.

If anything, it is more present, in the sense that more of its parts are present at each place! Although Ockham does not explicitly draw this conclusion, his arguments would rationalize the corresponding principle for passive power:

[P36] a passive principle is no less liable to be acted upon when it is present to an active principle by its whole self than when one part is present to one part and another to another.

Thus, for Ockham, the manner of placement of Christ's Body under the bread accidents cannot be what shields it from qualitative or substantial change. If Christ's Body is not digested when it descends down the receiver's gullet, that will be for the same reason that we have no intellectual intuitive cognition of it present on the altar: namely, Divine power fails to concur with the interaction!

For Ockham, definitive placement *does* explain why Christ's Body is not broken when the species are broken, however. Suppose a consecrated host has four parts—P1, P2, P3, and P4. Definitive placement means all of Christ's Body parts are under P1, all under P2, all under P3, and all under P4. Ockham himself draws the conclusion that the parts at P1 will be at a distance from the parts at P4. This means Christ's head at P1 will be at a distance from Christ's foot at P4. But it also means that Christ's head at P1 will be at a distance from Christ's head at P4. Multiple location puts bodies at a distance from themselves! If the consecrated host is broken so that P1 and P2 are now no longer continuous with P3 and P4, but P1 and P2 are a foot away from P3 and P4, then each of Christ's Body parts will be newly distant from itself and from all of the other parts. But that will not keep each and all of Christ's Body parts from being under each and all of P1, P2, P3, and P4, wherever they may be. Eucharistic fraction will not separate muscle from bone so that the muscle is in a place where the bones are not and the bones in a place where the muscle is not, such as happens when a leg of lamb is carved![16]

V. Insult in Place of Injury?

Human beings were created for worship, which gives honor to God. For the typical wayfarer—notwithstanding a few saints (for example, St. Paul) who are taken further—holy eucharist is the ultimate in worship in this world between birth and the grave. Even if the various theories of transubstantiation shield Christ's Body from causal exposure in eucharistic eating, a rite that insulted would be as counter-productive as one that did concrete harm. The literal breaking and tearing of Christ's Body suggested by Cardinal Humbert's formula conjured the prospect of Christians doing Christ violence in eucharistic eating. But, even if teeth and digestive processes cannot literally destroy Christ's Body, are there not depths to which it would be unfitting for Majesty to descend and places where it would be indecent for Majesty to go?

Worries about honor pressed the question, if consecration puts the Body of Christ in the same place as the bread accidents, how long and under what conditions does it remain and continue to go where the accidents go? *Only*

[16] Hugh of St Victor, *De sacramentis* bk. II, pt. 8, c. 11, p. 312.

So Far Down? Hugh of St Victor thinks that Christ is with us "corporeally" when we eat and taste the species, and remains so long and only so long as the senses are corporeally affected by them. The mouth is fit to receive a lover, but the gastrointestinal track is not![17] *Non-Human Receivers?* Bonaventure draws back from the idea that the Body of Christ might remain really present to the eucharistic species, when they are nibbled, chewed, and swallowed by mice. Bonaventure declares that the real presence of the Body of Christ under the species is for the sake of human eating. Even though consecration makes the Body of Christ to be really present whether or not anyone receives it, it will remain only if the eater is human.[18] Aquinas disagrees, insisting that the Body of Christ remains under the eucharistic species so long as they remain bread suitable—and that whether or not they are eaten and no matter who or what consumes them.[19]

Sinful Receivers? Some held that the true Body of Christ no more remains under the species when received by unshriven mortal sinners than it does when the species are eaten by mice.[20] Bonaventure notes that this position was condemned: eucharistic real presence is supposed to be a continuation of the Incarnation. Christ came to the righteous and to sinners during His earthly career when He died on a cross. Likewise, the true Body of Christ remains as really present to the eucharistic species when received by the wicked as when received by the faithful who have prepared.[21] But this very fact of sustained real presence makes unworthy reception dangerous. For unworthy reception gives offence (it is irreverent and shows contempt), because it receives the worthiest of guests into a filthy hostel to share space with His enemies. The person who has sinned mortally and does not bother to prepare, sins mortally in receiving.[22] Contrary to ancient etiquette that warns commoners not to look emperor or monarch in the face, Bonaventure thinks that the person does not give

[17] Hugh of St Victor, *De sacramentis* bk. II, pt. 8, c. 13, p. 314.

[18] Bonaventure, *Sent.* IV, d. 13, a. 2, q. 1, c; Quaracchi IV. 308.

[19] Aquinas, *Summa Theologica* III, q. 80, a. 3 ad 3um. See Gary Macy, in *Treasures from the Storeroom: Medieval Religion and the Eucharist* (Collegeville, MN: Liturgical Press, 1999), ch. 3, who sees a sharp divide between those who—like Alexander of Hales and Bonaventure—tie continued real presence to the subjective states and capacities of receivers and those who—like Aquinas—let the metaphysical change stand until another metaphysical change occurs, regardless of the receiver's subjective states or capacities (III. 36–51).

[20] Bonaventure, *Sent.* IV, d. 9, a. 2, q. 1; Quaracchi IV. 207.

[21] Bonaventure, *Sent.* IV, d. 9, a. 2, q. 1; Quaracchi IV. 207–8.

[22] Bonaventure, *Sent.* IV, d. 9, a. 2, q. 2 c & ad 4um & ad 8um; Quaracchi IV. 209–10.

offense merely by looking—that is, by witnessing the elevation of the host. Touching comes in between. It is a sin for the spiritually unclean to touch the consecrated host, but not as great a sin as taking it in and swallowing it down.

Worthy reception requires sweeping of the soul's house by self-examination and confession. Sufficient preparation involves accurately confessing all of the sins (especially all of the serious sins) one has committed. Those who prepare "according to truth" win the spiritual benefits that the sacrament affords. Those who prepare with probability and insufficiently do not sin, but do not win a spiritual benefit either.[23]

With the stakes so high, Bonaventure's thoughts naturally turn to the priest's responsibility as shepherd of his flock who is charged with their spiritual well-being. As confessors and/or as leaders otherwise in the know, priests may recognize that someone is an unshriven mortal sinner, when the wider community does not. But Church law requires a priest to give communion to any baptized persons who present themselves. Bonaventure recognizes a distinction between what a person has a right to in truth and absolutely, and what he or she has a right to under canon law. If the secretly unrepentant mortal sinner presents him or herself, the priest must give communion in order not to scandalize the community. But if an open sinner presents him or herself, the priest should withhold the sacrament.[24]

Scotus also examines the perils of sacramental eating when the eater is in a state of mortal sin. He distinguishes a range of cases. First there is the distinction between those who are presently committing mortal sin (whether by an internal or external act), and those who have committed mortal sins in the past. Anyone who receives while committing mortal sin thereby commits another mortal sin. Where past mortal sins are concerned, one may not have tended to them—through repentance, doing penance, confession and absolution by the Church—because of crass negligence, in which case ignorance is no excuse. Alternatively, one may have forgotten having committed them, despite sufficient self-examination, contrition, and confession of remembered sins. In this case, one does not sin in receiving, even though one has failed to remember. Scotus declares that, where self-examination is concerned, there is no certainty for pilgrims (*viatores*). If there has been diligent examination, confession, and contrition, not only does one

[23] Bonaventure, *Sent.* IV, d. 9, q. 2, q. 3 c & ad 2um & ad 3um; Quaracchi IV. 210–11.
[24] Bonaventure, *Sent.* IV, d. 9,a. 2, q. 4; Quaracchi IV. 212.

avoid sin in receiving, but the forgotten sin is remitted by the sacrament. Where there is opportunity, the faithful should always go to confession before sacramental eating. Scotus explains that this is because the goal of sacramental eating is spiritual eating, which is union with the mystical Body of Christ. Therefore, if possible, one should prepare by being reconciled with the Church and not only with God. Where no worthy confessor is available, it is best not to receive until one has confessed, if scandal can be avoided. Sometimes, however, clergy on duty cannot delay receiving without scandal, in which case it is permissible for him to receive, so long as he is contrite and has the intention of confessing when he gets the chance. Likewise for non-celebrants, where not following local customs about reception would raise scandal. Contrition and the intention of confessing give him "the affect of actual confession" as he fulfils his obligation not to scandalize his neighbor. Scotus adds that even venial sins give offense to God, so that it is appropriate to receive only if one approaches without the will of sinning venially and has made satisfaction for venial sins with prayers and tears.[25]

Fasting with Respect. Scotus declares that, even though the Body of Christ risks no causal exposure as it slides down the eater's digestive track, the Church has instituted fasting rules on Christ's authority, because it would be irreverent to mix the sacrament with ordinary food. A non-faster may receive carnally or sacramentally, but—except in special circumstances—he or she will not receive spiritually if he or she has not kept the fast. Where fasting is concerned, however, Scotus distinguishes the fast of nature, which ensures that there is nothing in or on the way to the stomach by consuming nothing from the beginning of the day, and the fast of the Church, which allows for the fast of nature to be compromised by certain sorts of eating. Normally, the fast of nature is required. But when someone is ill, he or she may receive without offense even though he or she has taken medicine, and those who are gravely ill may receive even if they have eaten, lest they die without their *viaticum*. Priests also may receive, even though they have broken the fast of nature. For example, if the priest consumes left-over consecrated hosts, eating the first one means that he does not receive the second one fasting. Again, if a liturgical mistake were made and the priest thought he was saying the prayer of consecration over a cup of white wine,

[25] Scotus, *Op. Ox.* IV, d. 9, q. u, n. 4; Wadding VIII. 476.

but when he received he found it to be water, he would be required to reconsecrate and receive the wine species after having already taken a drink. In this case, Scotus believes, the rules that the priest must consecrate in both kinds, and that the consecrating priest must receive, take precedence over the norm of observing the fast of nature.[26]

[26] Scotus, *Op. Ox.* IV, d. 8, q. 3, nn. 4–7; Wadding VIII. 460–1.

12

Sacraments, Why Ceasing?

I. "The End of the World as We Know It!"

Medieval Christian consensus held that human history is divided into states, which differ as to Divinely instituted framework policies. This present state will come to an end, not only for human beings as individuals, but for the whole cosmos once the perfect number of the elect has been reached. There will be an end of the world as we know it. The world as it will be will be very different. In the world as it will be, sacraments will cease.

"Separate" Souls. Where human individuals are concerned, death is the end of the world as we know it. Death involves the separation of the soul from the body. By contrast with cow souls, the human soul is immortal and—by Divine decree—enters immediately into its destiny. The elect who die pure in heart (if there are any besides the soul of Christ) enter immediately into beatific vision and enjoyment.[1] The elect who require further purification from venial sins (doubtless the majority) are plunged into purgatorial punishments, which are temporary and aimed at producing the deiformity needed for union with God. For the souls of the damned, the torment begins: they are located in the fire (whole in the whole fire and whole in the parts of the fire) and bound to it so that they cannot move; their thoughts are controlled so that fire is what they principally think about and they cannot shift their attention; likewise, their wills are controlled so that they hate where they are and hate the direction of their thoughts and hate the fact that they can change neither of them. Already, as soon as their souls are separated from their bodies, the pure in heart are rewarded; the

[1] Bonaventure, *Sent.* IV, d. 48, p. 1, a.u, q. 3; Quaracchi IV. 1005; IV, d. 49, p. 1, a.u, q. 5; Quaracchi IV. 1009.

damned are punished; and the incompletely sanctified dive into their final bath.[2]

Cosmic Last Things. When enough elect human beings to fill heaven have been produced and have completed their earthly careers, when purgatorial rehabilitation is complete, Christ will return to judge the world. His appearance will be fierce and terrifying and seen alike by the elect and the damned. "Fire will go forth from His face" to kindle the great conflagration in which all of the material stuff of the world will be reduced to the elements.[3] Even school theologians steeped in Aristotle will depict this as "a cosmic cleansing ritual" that burns away the taint that "rubbed off" on the material world through human sin. From the "purified" elements, a stripped-down cosmos will be re-created. Human bodies will be reassembled, so that each and every human soul will be permanently reunited with numerically the same body that it animated before.[4] All human bodies will be raised metaphysically complete, with all of their essential parts, in the natural condition that corresponds to youthful vigor. The heavenly bodies will be brighter than before, but will cease to move.[5] There will be a concomitant end to generation and corruption. The elements will remain, but will no longer interact to be converted into one another or to corrupt non-homogeneous human bodies. Plants and non-human animals will not be re-created. The supposed reason is that non-human material creatures do not exist to praise God on their own.[6] Rather, the material universe was "made for humankind." In this present state, plant and non-human animals are useful for food and for cosmic ornamentation. But in the final state of things human bodies will be raised impassible and incorruptible, so that there will be no need of bodily food. Simplicity will replace variety as the aesthetic excellence in the material world to come.[7] Judgment will "separate the sheep from the goats" (Matt. 25: 31–46). Elect souls will continue in

[2] Bonaventure, *Sent.* IV, d. 43, a. 1, q. 3; Quaracchi IV. 887; Aquinas, *Sent.* IV, d. 45, q.u, a. 1; Parma XXII. 423; *Summa Contra Gentiles* IV, c. 91.

[3] Bonaventure, *Sent.* IV, d. 48, a. 2, q. 3; Quaracchi IV. 993; Aquinas, *Sent.* IV, d. 47, q.u, a. 4; Parma XXII. 428; Scotus, *Op. Ox.* IV, d. 4 7, q. 2, nn. 1–4; Wadding X. 300–1.

[4] Bonaventure, *Sent.* IV, d. 43, a. 1, q. 4; Quaracchi IV. 888–9; d. 43, a. 1, q. 5; Quaracchi IV. 893; Aquinas, *Sent.* IV, d. 43, q.u, a. 2; Parma XXII. 417.

[5] Scotus, *Op. Ox.* IV, d. 48, q. 2, n. 2; Wadding X. 312; IV, d. 48, q. 2, n. 9; Wadding X. 315–16; IV, d. 48, q. 2, nn. 16–17; Wadding X. 320.

[6] Bonaventure, *Sent.* IV, d. 48, q. 2, n. 4; Quaracchi IV.994; Aquinas, *Summa Theologica* III, q. 60, a. 4 ad 2um.

[7] Bonaventure, *Sent.* IV, d. 48, q. 2, a. 1; Quaracchi IV. 990; IV, d. 48, q. 2, n. 4; Quaracchi IV. 994.

their state of beatific vision and enjoyment, while their re-created and reunited bodies will participate in the rewards of union with God through "a dowery" of excellences: impassibility to ward off corruption, brightness to enhance beauty, subtlety and impassibility to perfect their mobility at the soul's command.[8] The torments of the damned will be increased: not only their souls but their bodies will be permanently and involuntarily located in the fire,[9] where God will concur with the fire to produce sensory suffering without destroying their bodies.[10]

Ceasing Sacraments. Given this picture of the world as it will be, our authors find it logical that sacraments will cease. Their reasoning is straightforward. Sacraments properly speaking are *efficacious signs.* God institutes sacraments insofar as it is fitting for God and useful for us. Sacraments generally are useful for us insofar as participation in them admits us to the company of worshippers, repairs psycho-spiritual damage done by the fall, and advances us toward the deiformity required for union with God. Among new-law sacraments, the eucharist is an anticipation of heaven twice over: eucharistic consecration keeps Christ's promise to be with the disciples always, to the end of the age, by making Christ's Body to be really present under forms of bread and wine; eucharistic eating that is not only carnal but sacramental, not only sacramental but spiritual, unites the faithful to the mystical body of Christ.

Yet, "types and shadows have their ending." Just as inchoate signs are replaced by more explicit ones (old-law sacraments by new-law rites), so signs generally "stand in" for the thing signified. *Signs are useful when the thing signified is absent or hidden. When the thing signified is obviously present, there is no need for a sign.* In the world as it will be, every eye will have an unmediated vision of Christ's Body when He comes to judge the world. His real presence will be unveiled, obvious, and unmistakeable (Rev. 1: 7). Likewise, the elect will have an intuitive cognition of the Divine essence. The elect

[8] Bonaventure, *Sent.* IV, d. 49, p. 2, a. 1, q. 2; Quaracchi IV. 1014, 1016; Aquinas, *Sent.* IV, d. 44, q. 1, a. 3; Parma XXII. 420; *Summa Contra Gentiles* I, c. 86; Scotus, *Op. Ox.* IV, d. 49, q. 13, nn. 9–11; Wadding X. 587–8; IV, d. 49, q. 14, nn. 2–9; Wadding X. 593–6; IV, d. 49, q. 15, nn. 2–5; Wadding X. 606, 608–9; IV, d. 49, q. 16, n. 17; Wadding X. 620–2.

[9] Scotus, *Op. Ox.* IV, d. 44, q. 2, nn. 9, 12–13; Wadding X. 452–3; IV, d. 46, q. 4, nn. 4–6; Wadding X. 270–2, 274.

[10] Bonaventure, *Sent.* IV, d. 44, p. 2, a. 2, qq. 1–2; Quaracchi IV. 926–8; IV, d. 44, p. 2, a. 3, q. 1; Quaracchi IV. 929; IV, d. 44, p. 2, a. 3, q. 2; Quaracchi IV. 933–4; Aquinas, *Sent.* IV, d. 44, q. 1, a. 4; Parma XXII. 420; IV, d. 44, q. 2, a. 4; Parma XXII. 422; *Summa Contra Gentiles* IV, c.89.

body-politic will be separated out and gathered in the heavenly city. In the world as it will be, material signage for really present Godhead and for the mystical body will be obsolete!

Nor will sacraments be any longer useful for their *efficacy*. For, according to the history of the human race as our authors understand it, this present state and our passage through it is the time of testing, the time frame designated by Divine dispensation for members of Adam's fallen race to respond or not to the offer of salvation through Christ. Time runs out on God's new-law provision of restorative and deiforming grace, for individuals at death and for the world at the judgment. The elect will already have received sacramental benefits, and—after death—God will immediately and non-sacramentally cause and preserve what else they need for beatific vision and enjoyment. For the damned, it will be too late to receive sanctifying grace, although God will continue to show mercy by making them suffer less than they deserve.

II. End-Time Incongruities

Our authors readily concur in concluding that sacraments will cease, because—as skillful means—they will have "had their day"! Nevertheless, the end-time picture that motivates their argument startles with its failure to fit with other important theoretical commitments that our authors make.

Bodies: Still Useful or Merely Ornamental? First and foremost, this picture and the accompanying reasoning underwrite the more radical conclusion that in the future state—as our authors envision it—material stuff generally will become dysfunctional: not only the *material* signs that sacraments are, but the human body and the material cosmos itself! Reconsider their contentions. Not only is the material cosmos stripped down to include only the heavens, the elements, and human bodies. These remaining material items are prevented from engaging in most of their natural functions. The heavenly bodies cease to move. The elements cease to interact to produce "chemical" changes.[11] Impassibility makes the human body more durable, but robs it of all vegetative functions—digestion, respiration, excretion, reproduction—as well as some sensory functions—vision and touch will

[11] Bonaventure, *Sent.* IV, d. 48, p. 2, q. 4; Quaracchi IV. 991–4; Aquinas, *Sent.* IV, d. 48, q. 2, a. 2 ad 2um; Parma XXII. 430–1; *Summa Contra Gentiles* IV, c. 97.

remain, but taste and smell involve generation and corruption in the sense organs and hearing may involve such in the air or other media. And, in the world as it will be, all generation and corruption will come to an end.[12] Moreover, the future state is to be the scene of reward and punishment. But all agree that elect souls can be supranaturally happy and damned souls thoroughly miserable while still separate from their bodies. If the material world was made for the sake of human beings, what use will either the material cosmos or human bodies be then? Sun and moon, stars and planets, human bodies—will they not all be relics of a bygone age, vestigial but made more ornamental by the gift of supranatural brightness?[13]

Yet, belief in bodily resurrection is central to Christian theology. St Paul declares that faith is vain without it (1 Cor. 15: 14), and both Jesus's and the general resurrection are explicitly affirmed in the Nicene and Apostles' creeds. Moreover, all of our authors are of the philosophical opinion that human beings are essentially soul–body composites. Dualists (such as Bernard of Clairvaux, Hugh of St Victor, and Bonaventure) think that soul and body are distinct substances united in one person. Aristotelians regard humans as hylomorphic composites (like other animals), with the intellectual soul as the form of the body and apt to unite with it to make an individual substance that is one *per se*. How then can they endorse an understanding of the end-time that gives material stuff so little point?

Two strategies for handling this worry can be found in their works. (1) The first accepts that it is less for utility than for honor that bodies are included in the future state. However subsistent, separate souls are essentially human fragments. Metaphysical completeness confers ontological dignity in that the composite whole is a better being than any part taken by itself. Likewise, it is a mark of Divine prowess as re-creator that God is able, not only to conserve human souls after death, but to restore the whole composite by resurrection. Thus, God raises each and every member of Adam's race into metaphysical completeness, both the elect and the damned.[14]

[12] Bonaventure, *Sent.* IV, d. 49, p. 2, sec. 1, a. 3, q. 1; Quaracchi IV. 1019; Aquinas, *Sent.* IV, d. 48, q. 2, a. 2; Parma XXII. 431; *Summa Contra Gentiles* IV, cc. 83, 85–6.

[13] Aquinas, *Summa Contra Gentiles* IV, c. 86.

[14] Bonaventure, *Sent.* IV, d. 43, a. 1, q. 1; Quaracchi IV. 883; d. 43, a. 1, q. 4; Quaracchi IV. 889; d. 44, p. 1, a. 1, q. 2; Quaracchi IV. 909–10; IV, d. 44, p. 1, a. 3, qq. 1–2; Quaracchi IV. 915–16; Aquinas, *Sent.* IV, d. 44, q. 1, a. 1; Parma XXII. 418; IV, d. 44, q. 1, a. 2; Parma XXII. 419; IV, d. 44, q. 1, a. 4; Parma XXII. 420; Scotus, *Op. Ox.* IV, d. 11, q. 3, nn. 46, 54; Wadding VIII. 649, 653; IV, d. 45, q. 2, n. 14; Wadding X. 182.

Where the elect are concerned, re-embodiment restores another dimension of god-likening dignity: namely, dominion. The human body gives the soul something to govern. Subtlety and agility in the resurrected body put the elect soul in a better position to command its movements.[15] By contrast, damned souls are degraded by being denied such dominion and by being forcibly confined to the fire instead. Here the principal reward lies in the power of governance rather than any benefit obtained by it; our authors' end-time picture gives the elect no reason to want to move around! Likewise, the chief punishment is being deprived of autonomy, although the damned do have reasons of advantage for wanting to get out of the fire!

(2) The second strategy tries to show that soul–body reunion does—contrary to appearances—enhance *post-mortem* functioning. Bernard of Clairvaux and Bonaventure insist that soul–body reunion is necessary for maximal happiness. They reason that the soul develops such a strong affection for the body it animates, the very body that is its birth-to-death partner in doing and suffering, that the soul will pine after it, so much so that sorrow over separation could keep the soul from enjoying the beatific vision as much as it otherwise could. Perhaps they mean it metaphorically, but Bernard and Bonaventure speak as if the soul's desire for its body were a conscious deliberative appetite.[16] Aquinas and Scotus draw back from any such notion; the soul's inclination for its body is just that of any substantial form for the constituents with which it is naturally apt to unite to make something one *per se*, and as such it is unconscious. Where beatific vision and enjoyment are concerned, neither Aquinas nor Scotus thinks that soul–body reunion removes conscious distractions or makes the *acts* of intellect and will involved more perfect. Soul–body reunion serves only to make the *subject* of such acts more perfect because metaphysically complete.[17] As for the reprobate in hell, all agree that soul–body reunion adds the further dimension of sensory suffering. Bonaventure declares that the elements are all weapons in the hand of the Creator for the torment of the damned![18]

[15] For the idea that humans were to imitate Divine providence by exercising providence over their material bodies and the material world generally, see Hugh of St Victor, *De sacramentis*, bk. I, pt. 1, c. 19, p. 23; bk. I, pt. 1, c.25, p, 25; bk. I, pt. 2, c. 1, 28–9; bk. I, pt. 6, c. 1, p. 94.

[16] Bonaventure, *Sent.* IV, d. 43, a. 1, q. 1; Quaracchi IV. 883–4; IV, d. 43, a. 1, q. 5; Quaracchi IV. 894; IV, d. 44, p. 1, a. 2, q. 1; Quaracchi IV. 910; IV, d. 49, p. 2, a. 1, q. 1; Quaracchi IV. 1012.

[17] Aquinas, *Sent.* IV, d. 49, q. u, aa. 2, 4; Parma XXII. 432–4; *Summa Contra Gentiles* IV, c. 79; Scotus, *Op. Ox.* IV, d. 45, q. 2, n. 14; Wadding X. 182; IV, d. 49, q. 2, nn. 15, 18; Wadding X. 339; IV, d. 49, q. 8, n. 7; Wadding X. 503.

[18] Bonaventure, *Sent.* IV, d. 44, p. 2, a. 2, q. 2; Quaracchi IV. 938.

The Superfluity of Signs? Sacraments properly speaking are liturgical rites that function as efficacious signs. For our authors, Christian sacraments function to carve out a company from Adam's fallen race and unite them in the mystical body of Christ. It seems reasonable to conclude that such rites—baptism, confirmation, ordination, penance, eucharist, unction, and marriage—will be outmoded in the world that will be. But any and all kinds of creatures are sacraments in the broad sense, because any and all are natural signs of the Divine essence. Given our authors' understandings of human cognitive psychology, it is far from clear that an intuitive cognition of the Divine essence would eliminate any and all need or use for such natural signs.

Both Neoplatonists and Aristotelians emphasize how human differs from angelic cognition in being essentially *discursive*. For Aquinas, separate intelligences or angels intuitively see and thereby understand whatever they understand. By contrast, humans may acquire a simple cognition of material quiddities by abstraction from sense images. But human beings do not understand what it is to be a cow until they can spell out what they see by defining it in terms of genus and differentia. Even then, their knowledge of what it is to be a cow remains underdeveloped, until they combine premisses into arguments and reason to conclusions. *Given human cognitive psychology, simple vision does not take away the need but rather gives rise to a demand for articulation.* Why then suppose that this would not be the case with the elects' intuitive cognition of the Divine essence?

Bonaventure, in his *The Mind's Journey into God*,[19] maps out the contemplative's ascent into ecstatic contemplation of the sort experienced by St Francis and others of the early friars. The human mind begins by turning outward to the material world to contemplate God at first through and then in material things. The next step requires the mind to turn inward to contemplate God through and then in its own activities of thinking and willing. The further step turns the soul upward to contemplate Divine Being and Divine Goodness in turn, then to let the mind boggle over the coincidence of opposites in God Incarnate, and finally to "pass over" into ecstacy through meditation on the crucified God![20]

[19] Bonaventure, *Itinerarium Mentis in Deum*; Quaracchi V. 293–313.

[20] See also Aquinas, *Summa Theologica* II. 2, q. 180, a. 4 ad 3um, who offers a different list of six steps by which we ascend to contemplation of God: perception of sensibles; perception of intelligibles; judgment of sensibles according to intelligibles; absolute consideration of intelligibles which are arrived at through sensibles; contemplation of intelligibles that cannot be arrived at through sensibles but can be grasped by reason; consideration of intelligibles that reason can neither discover nor grasp, which pertains to the sublime contemplation of Divine truth.

What is important for present purposes is that—according to Bonaventure—in this present state, ecstatic contemplatives always "fall back": after a period of being "dead to the world," they "come to." When they do, Bonaventure imagines, they are better able "so to pass through things temporal that they lose not things eternal," because their ecstatic union with God sharpens their vision to see God through and in created things. Cast into a general principle, the claim would be that *acquaintance with the thing signified (significatum) enables the knower to recognize natural signs of the thing signified as natural signs.*

Putting Bonaventure's observations about the mind's ascent together with a roughly Aristotelian account of the discursive character of human knowledge (*scientia*), could commend a further conclusion: that recognizing and appreciating how creatable kinds are natural signs of the Divine essence (say, through extensive comparison and contrast) is a human way of "digesting" what beatific vision sees. It is a human way of turning that cognition into knowledge. Moreover, such comparisons and contrasts would be the stuff of syllogistic reasoning toward further conclusions. This point was not entirely lost on late-thirteenth and early fourteenth-century authors. Scotus and Ockham responded to the question of whether theology is a science by contrasting the theological systems possible for wayfarers (*viatores*) with those that could be developed by the blessed who see God face to face!

Thus, the very cognitive psychologies forwarded by our authors commend the picture of heaven as a classroom, a scene of eternal learning in which the blessed are always growing in the knowledge and love of God. Gregory of Nyssa (whom they probably never read) suggests that the blessed will forever remain in the tension between joy in what they see and insatiable desire, which sets them striving to know more. A stripped-down universe, bereft of plants and non-human animals, would not serve, because variety in creatures would continue to be useful to us. In the heavenly classroom, humans would have an eternal (or at least long-standing) need for such broad-sense sacraments or natural signs. Perhaps Aquinas recognizes this when he suggests that the glorified bodies remaining will be more Godlike than they were before.[21]

Neglecting Christ? Likewise puzzling is how our authors can subscribe to an end-time narrative that gives Christ such short shrift. Not only do they

[21] Aquinas, *Sent.* IV, d. 48, q. 2, a.2; Parma XXII. 430.

affirm Christ's bodily resurrection. They also hold to His perpetual assumption of His human nature: that is, there was a particular moment in history at which God the Son assumed a particular human nature as His own, but once He had assumed it He would—as a matter of Divine policy—never lay it down. The risen Christ, God the Son, will remain embodied for eternity. Yet, given our authors' projection of the world as it will be, we may ask, whatever for? Only in debates about the judgment do they spend time on the fact that Adam's descendants will all see Christ's Body with bodily eyes. They do so then only to dwell on the terror that it will inspire and to make an invidious comparison: the damned will see only Christ's humanity but the elect will see His Godhead as well![22]

Doubtless our authors follow tradition in appreciating that Godhead is infinite being while Christ's human nature is "almost nothing" in comparison. But, even if Christ's sudden return to judge the earth will scare us out of our wits to begin with, it seems incongruous for them not to mention the joy the elect would find in seeing Christ's human face, once they had recovered from the shock. After all, they have identified the eucharist as the climax of worship for the typical wayfarer, among other things, because the eucharist involves being and seeing *where* the Body of Christ is really present. Moreover, they have exercised considerable philosophical imagination to make out just how such real presence is metaphysically possible (see Chapters 4–9 above). If real presence under forms of bread and wine is so wonderful, how much more would unveiled real presence be a joy to behold? Again, if Bonaventure's birth-to-grave spiritual exercises boggle the mind by inviting us to contemplate the infinite being and boundless goodness of Godhead joined to human nature in unity of person, would not the elect be eternally fascinated by the unmediated view of each and both in juxtaposition? If a "burning love of the crucified" is presupposed for the mind's ascent, if what triggers the "passover" into ecstacy for humans in this present state is the thought of God crucified, so also and all the more so for those who eternally gaze on His glorious scars!

Heaven as A-Social? The Bible's God has social purposes. Just as God orders chaos to create a cosmos (Gen. 1), so God forms a nation by the giving of the law. Prophets recall Israel to life together under Divine governance. In the Gospels, Jesus proclaims that the Kingdom of God is

[22] Bonaventure, *Sent.* IV, d. 48, q. 1, aa. 2–3; Quaracchi IV. 985–8; Aquinas, *Summa Contra Gentiles* IV, c. 97.

at hand. From Lombard forward, our authors themselves say that eucharistic spiritual eating incorporates eaters into the mystical body of Christ, evidently into Christ's body-politic. Yet, their end-time scenario seems almost a-social. People are not ushered into heaven or herded into hell on the basis of race or national origin. Adults qualify or not as individuals, *de facto* on the basis of sacramental participation and moral performance, on the basis of their record of meritorious or demeritorious acts. Although Aquinas and Scotus[23] mention in passing that God aims at community, the focus of their discussions can easily leave the impression that the blessed will be absorbed in God and the damned preoccupied with their own misery, that togetherness for the blessed will not go beyond that among art-museum visitors staring at the same painting or that of a theater audience enjoying the same show.

III. The Contemplative Ideal

Many "misfitting" features of our authors' end-time scenario find their explanation in the tradition that distinguishes the active from the contemplative life and treats the latter as far superior to the former. This distinction was pressed into service as a rationale for Christian monasticism, but in fact found its philosophical expression much earlier in Aristotle's *Nicomachean Ethics*, book X, chapters 7–8.

Two Kinds of Happiness. Aristotle famously defines happiness as activity of the soul in accordance with virtue. He infers that the highest happiness will be activity in accordance with the highest virtue, which will pertain to what is best in us. Reason is what is best in us, and reason taking thought over things noble and divine (that is, contemplation) is the highest activity.[24] Other marks of its superiority are that it is the easiest to sustain (insofar as it requires minimal physical effort) and is the most self-sufficient (insofar as the sage can do it all by him or herself).[25] Aristotle explicitly says that the contemplative life is too high for us, that living that way does not pertain to us insofar as we are human beings, but insofar as there is something divine present in us.[26] Nevertheless,

[23] Scotus, *Op. Ox.* IV, d. 46, q.1, n. 11; Wadding X. 253; IV, d. 46, q. 4, n. 9; Wadding X. 274; IV, d. 47, q. 1, n. 5; Wadding X. 294.

[24] Aristotle, *Nicomachean Ethics* 7 1177^{a}12–18.

[25] Aristotle, *Nicomachean Ethics* 7 1177^{a}19–1177^{b}25.

[26] Aristotle, *Nicomachean Ethics* 7 1177^{b}26–30.

he thinks we ought to do our best to rise above our nature and to strive to live such a contemplative life[27] the way the gods do.[28]

Besides this Godlike happiness, there is a second-class happiness that befits the human condition: activity of the soul in accordance with the cardinal virtues, prudence, temperance, courage, and justice. As Aristotle sees it, these moral virtues have to do with our composite nature, insofar as they tame the passions to make them subordinate to reason as it deliberates concerning external actions that relate one human being to another. The exercise of moral virtues depends on circumstances beyond one's control (for example, one cannot act with liberality if one lacks resources to distribute or courageously if no real or apparent danger is at hand). Thus, the active life in society with others is less independent.[29] Since the needs of our animal nature will have to be met willy nilly, Aristotle identifies moderation as the key to approximating self-sufficiency as much as we can.[30]

Higher and Lower Life Styles. In *Summa Theologica* II-2, qq. 179–82, Aquinas reshapes this distinction for a Christian context. Aristotle sees full-time contemplation as a super-human ideal toward which the fortunate in life may be able to approximate. For Aquinas, contemplation of Divine truth is the supranatural end of all human beings, which the elect will reach after death in a face-to-face vision of God.[31] In this present state, not everyone can be a full-time contemplative, because some people have to organize society and see to it that the necessities of life are provided.[32] Those who embrace the active life will be perfected through the moral virtues that essentially pertain to it, ordering as they do the passions to reason[33] and humans to one another in society.[34] "Activists" will become expert in their fields of endeavor, and their judgment about what is to be done in external affairs may well be better than that of some contemplatives would be. By the same token, "movers and shakers" are too busy to pay much attention to intellectual issues that do not bear on their spheres of action, so that their judgment will be less reliable about them.[35]

[27] Aristotle, *Nicomachean Ethics* 7 1177^{b}30–1178^{a}1.
[28] Aristotle, *Nicomachean Ethics* 8 1178^{b}9–23.
[29] Aristotle, *Nicomachean Ethics* 8 1178^{a}8–1178^{b}8.
[30] Aristotle, *Nicomachean Ethics* 8 1178^{b}33–1179^{a}33.
[31] Aquinas, *Summa Theologica* II. 2, q. 180, a. 4 c; II. 2, q. 181, a. 1 c.
[32] Aquinas, *Summa Theologica* II. 2, q. 179, a. 2 c&ad 3um; II. 2, q. 181, a. 1 c.
[33] Aquinas, *Summa Theologica* II.2, q. 182, a.3 c&ad 3um.
[34] Aquinas, *Summa Theologica* II. 2, q. 181, a.1 ad 1um.
[35] Aquinas, *Summa Theologica* II. 2, q. 181,a. 2 ad 2um.

Nevertheless, Aquinas emphasizes, the end is *supra*natural. Contemplation by an act of simple intuition is an activity naturally more suited—as Aristotle says—to the gods, or—as Aquinas thinks—to the Trinity and to the angels.[36] Aquinas concludes that those who devote themselves to contemplation of the truth already in this present state embark on a lifelong ascetical discipline aimed at "alienating" themselves from bodily sensation (and thereby becoming more like God and the angels). Even if the moral virtues do not pertain to the contemplative life essentially, they are a help, insofar as they subordinate sensory passions to reason's rule. Because—Aquinas believes—human cognitive powers are naturally built to abstract intelligible contents from sense images, *ante-mortem* contemplation will never entirely break free of its dependence on the senses.[37] Only in the future state will contemplation be completely independent of the body. In heaven, contemplation will reach perfection in a supranatural vision of God unmediated by natural cognitive processes or mental representations of any kind.[38]

In the world as it will be, all of the elect will be full-time contemplatives. Eating, drinking, and death being things of the past, any need for distracting outward action will come to an end. Aquinas quotes Augustine as allowing that there might be some external action pointed toward the end of contemplation, which is vision, love, and praise.[39] But elsewhere Aquinas himself opines that heavenly worship will be entirely internal. There will be no further need for external rites!

In *Proslogion* 25 and *Epistolae* No. 112, Anselm does try—in ways that our later authors would probably approve—to find some social dimension to heaven. If the heavenly city is a community of contemplatives, Anselm likens it to an ideal monastic community, which he understands to be an ideal society of friends. Anselm declares that mutual friendship-love will be the tie that binds God and the citizens of heaven together. Humans and angels will love God more than themselves and others as themselves. God will love each and all more than they love themselves, because God is the Love through which lovers love their beloved(s)—One over Many![40] Loving God above all and for God's own sake, each rational creature will

[36] Aquinas, *Summa Theologica* II. 2, q. 180, a. 3 c&ad 1um; II. 2, q. 180, a. 6 ad 2um.
[37] Aquinas, *Summa Theologica* II. 2, q. 180, a. 5 c&ad 2um.
[38] Aquinas, *Summa Theologica* II. 2, q. 182, a. 2 ad 2um.
[39] Aquinas, *Summa Theologica* II. 2, q. 181, a. 4 ad 2um.
[40] Anselm, *Proslogion*, c. xxv; S 1.119, 4–7.

will only what God wills (or what God wills them to will), with the result that everyone in the whole society wills the same thing. Anselm speaks of the elect being "welded in love" into unity with God and all of the holy angels and humans—willing the same, nilling the same (*idem velle, idem nolle*). Because God gets what God wants, each and all will be like perfect kings in getting whatever they want, too.[41] Moreover, if each will have joy in its own well-being, friendship that loves the other as self is a joy-multiplier, because each will rejoice in the happiness of the others as much as in his or her own. Friendship love for God more than self puts each in a position to enjoy God's own happiness immeasurably more than his or her own and that of the whole company of holy humans and angels combined.[42] Nevertheless, taking satisfaction in the contemplative enjoyments of others is minimally social, however refined the sentiment may be.

Supranatural End. What lies behind the end-time picture inherited but embraced by our authors is a vivid appreciation of the metaphysical size gap between God and creatures: Godhead is boundless Goodness; any and all creatures are "almost nothings." "Forget natural human flourishing! How could that begin to compare with union with God?" If the end is supranatural, how unsurprising if human nature will have to be "bent out of shape" to reach it. Beatific vision and enjoyment of Godhead are *spiritual* activities. Already in this present state, full-time contemplatives take on the assignment of stretching beyond natural human capacities to become as much like the angels and God as they can. Christian ascetics did not look forward with Socrates to *metaphysical* amputation in the form of permanent soul–body separation. Rather the goal for humans was to achieve deiformity by perfecting two subordination relations: independence and dominion. Independence would make the soul's cognitive and affective functions independent of the senses (a fortiori of any reliance on material signs), and so effect a kind of *psycho-spiritual* amputation. Dominion would put the body completely under the soul's voluntary control and so "out of the way," incapable of distracting the soul from contemplative enjoyment of the one thing needful.

Resolving Plots. Also distinctive is how this end-time scenario is governed by the narrative structure of journey/destination, of labor/rest, of process/perfection. In this present state, Adam's race are wayfarers (*viatores*) on a

[41] Anselm, *Proslogion*, c. xxv; S 1. 120, 9–11; *Epistolae* No. 112; S III.244–6, 21–72.
[42] Anselm, *Proslogion*, c. xxv; S I. 120, 14–17.

difficult and dangerous journey; but at death the elect will arrive home (*in patria*). In this present state, Adam's race works hard to survive and to cooperate with God to revive God's image; but in the future state the elect will rest from their labors. In this present state, the faithful strive to grow in the knowledge and love of God; but heaven will greet them with contemplative perfection. It makes no difference that *natural* human cognitive functions are discursive, because contemplative perfection is *supra*natural. For Aquinas, beatific vision will be a simple intuitive apprehension that supranatural light will make clear to us, so that we see in something of the way angels do, without any discursive reasoning. Bonaventure would add that our supranatural end is not understanding, but contemplative ecstacy: our goal is not to grasp Godhead, but to be grasped by what is infinitely more than we could ask or imagine. Bonaventure himself appropriates the philosophical narrative of a cosmic *exitus-redditus*: all things go out from God in creation, and all things are led back to God to rest in their origin. On any and all of these storylines, the end-time means an end to narrative tension and plot complication. The end-time is when the plot resolves!

IV. Coherent Alternatives

Taking Stock. When I set out to write this book, I guessed that—according to my medieval authors—sacraments were made to match human nature: material signs efficaciously mediating spiritual benefits fit the essential soul–body composition of human beings. Their view that humankind has a history as well as a nature forced me to revise that estimate. Sacraments suit human beings not simply because of their nature but because of their state. They are useful for us, not in Eden or in the future state, but in this present state in which we find ourselves, fallen in a fallen world, journeying between the womb and the grave.

By now, it has emerged that their motive for writing human history as they did arises from the contemplative ideal, from the conviction that human beings—while remaining soul–body composites—were made to become as much like the angels as we can. Elect humans and angels are alike destined sooner or later to enter into a permanent state of clear, simple intuitive cognition and enjoyment of the Divine essence. This sort of contemplative union is what our authors take to be ideal life together with God.

Given this present state in which we find ourselves, in which the human condition generally and Divine–human relations in particular are non-optimal, our authors envision a sequel in which contemplative union is permanently perfected. Because they do not want to say that God created us and the world in our present condition, they also posit a prequel. Because they are attracted to a plot with narrative development, they imagine that God's "Plan A" was for us to begin with soul–body dominion and a supranatural degree of contemplative enjoyment and to progress to perfect contemplative enjoyment after passing through a trial that offers us the opportunity to be somehow self-determined—to choose that condition for ourselves (see Chapter 2 above).

This spin on human history gives humankind a supranatural beginning and a supranatural ending. Only in this present state are humans left to being human. Sacraments are of no use to souls that are supranaturally elevated to a condition of cognitive and affective independence of the senses and dominion over their bodies. What material rites are suited for is human nature left to itself. The sacraments were made to match human nature after all!

Letting the contemplative ideal dictate the prequel and the sequel has the effect of *spiritualizing* God's interest in creation. Hugh of St Victor and Scotus are explicit. God's primary purpose is that there should be a company of created intellects who could join the Trinity in contemplative enjoyment of the Divine essence. God does not value *composite* human nature for itself. God values human *souls*, and creates the material world for the sake of humans. God has no interest in the material world except insofar as it is involved in preparing human souls for or holding human souls back from contemplation. It is created to provide a positive occasion for humans to grow in deiformity, but the downside of this upside is that it can also become a stumbling block that leads to sin and the frustration of the contemplative ideal. Hence, this present state between Adam's fall and the Judgment! The sacraments were made for humankind. But human beings were created to become—while remaining soul–body composites—as angelic as possible. According to the contemplative ideal, the elect are destined to outgrow, not only any need for sacraments, but any intrinsic interest in external activities in which their bodies would be involved.

Refocusing the Picture. Usually, complexes of philosophical and theological commitments can be focused in many ways. In fact, our authors let the normative priority of the contemplative life control their picture of human destiny, of the place of human bodies, the use of sacraments, and the point of the material cosmos itself. I want to close by sketching an alternative focus, already hinted at in Section II above, that would give greater dominance to their own sometimes positive estimate of the worth of material things.

(1) The first step toward a more "material" picture would reassert the thesis—so often celebrated by Bonaventure and Aquinas—that God loves variety. Because God is infinite and creatable natures are finite, a variety of natural signs is required to declare what God is. Every nature reflects Godhead from a distinctive angle—angels from one, human composites from another—and thereby valuable because of the very what-it-is-to-be of that kind. The next step would recall something that Bonaventure and Aquinas make so much of: that the very composite nature of humankind is of special interest. Because human nature includes both soul and body, it stands at the metaphysical borderline in creation. Precisely because human being is not pure spirit and not merely material either, human being microcosms the macrocosm. God can unite with the whole creation by taking an individual human nature for His own.

(2) The second step is to reconsider the idea that near cosmic stasis is the goal. One trouble with the variety of kinds is that they "run interference" with each other: one corrupts the other in order to sustain and reproduce itself. Plants use up soil minerals; animals devour plants and other animals; all material life dies. The final solution posited by the traditional end-time picture is drastic. It brings all generation and corruption to an end, and with it most material natural functions. It even strips plants and non-human animals out of the universe, because they would no longer be needed for food. Lurking in the background is the old fallacious argument that any change would be a change for the worse, once perfection has been reached. What if some perfections themselves involve process?

Prima facie, it would seem possible to make the cosmos more hospitable to living creatures without bringing most changes to an end. Our authors themselves suggest that death was prevented in Eden by the provision of better food. Flesh bits get used up in bodily functions and require to be replaced. Food in this fallen world converts into flesh that is inferior to what was there in the first place, and thereby contributes to the general run-down toward death. Allegedly, the food in Paradise would have sustained life indefinitely by replacing used flesh with bits of equal vigor. Biblical end-time prophecies speak of orchards fed by crystal-pure water, with trees to provide fruit for every month. True, natural eating is a hostile act, insofar as the eater destroys what he or she eats. But, where non-personal material life is concerned, individual death need not be tragic. Divine goodness to plants and non-human animals might be secured by re-creating them in an environment where each specimen has a chance to flourish as a thing of the kind that it is, before it dies. Aristotle reckoned that the repeated cycle of birth, growth, and death in an unending series of generations was the way material life imitates immortality, just as the perpetual rotation of the heavens was a moving likeness of eternity.

(3) A third and related step is to revisit the idea that the cosmic plot must resolve in such a way as to eliminate all tension. Is not the idea that stories ought to have a beginning, middle, and end a psychological projection of the shape of our animal lives that begin in birth, middle in growth, which reverses into decline, and ends in death? "World without end" explodes this narrative structure. Why scramble to reclaim it by robbing the future state of all drama? Why suppose that eternal joy requires peace that rests on its laurels instead of the excitement of discovery? Why not suppose that the tension of stretching for more of God, of the mind boggling over the Incarnation's bridging the size gap between humanity and Divinity, of fiery wonder over the cross of Christ, will last forever? For that matter, why not suppose that resurrected bodies embrace new challenges and adventures as well?

(4) The fourth step is to question whether perfect contemplation requires a near monopoly on human functioning. This idea gains credence from our experience in this present state, where external action and intense sensations do distract from contemplation. The explanation—modern as well as medieval—is that finite human psyches have limited energy and attention spans. Contemplative enjoyment has to compete for available resources with other cognitive activities and affections. Nevertheless, medievals all admit that pure contemplation is already supranatural. Aquinas thinks (although Scotus disagrees) that beatific vision involves a way of seeing for which we naturally lack even the passive capacity. If contemplating God is going to involve cognitive upgrades, why could they not be in the direction of intensifying the powers that we have to enable us to pay careful attention to more things at once?

In fact, our authors are already committed to the idea that this is metaphysically possible. For their own Christologies affirm both that the human soul of Christ experienced beatific enjoyment throughout His earthly career, and that the human soul of Christ exercised such cognitive and appetitive functions as are natural to human beings. Aquinas and Scotus both emphasize how the human soul of Christ had sense experience and abstracted intelligible contents on the basis of it, even though at the same time He saw God and saw all (actual) things in God. Fullness of grace and perfection in virtue meant that the human soul of Christ could not experience emotions that ran contrary to right reason. But, according to them, He did experience anger (for example, over the money changers in the Temple) and sorrow (for example, over His impending death).[43] Their point was that Christ's earthly career somehow recapitulates all of the states of human being, and so includes the innocence of Eden, the natural functioning and vulnerability of this present state, and the beatitude of the elect in heaven. They declared that Christ is simultaneously a wayfarer (*viator*) who shares our present predicament and a *comprehensor* who experiences beatific vision and enjoyment.

These claims could equally well be taken as a measure of how much human cognitive and affective capacities can be expanded. Their picture of what Christ's earthly life was like ought to serve them as a model of what is metaphysically possible for us. What is clear is that—on their account—Christ is not only *viator et comprehensor*. During His earthly career He combines the active and the contemplative life (that is, He leads what Aquinas calls a "mixed" life), full of social interactions.[44] Why not suppose that in the world to come the elect will enjoy similarly widened psychological capacities, so that contemplative enjoyment and attention to human relationships no longer compete?

(5) The fifth step would give analytical attention to the social side (to the Kingdom) of heaven, to life in the mystical body-politic of Christ. Once the horizontal dimension is taken seriously, it will not be enough to say that there will be peace in heaven because all of the elect are so absorbed in union with God that they do not think about anything or anyone else, or because they all "rubber-stamp" whatever God wills, or even because they will all rejoice in one another's contemplative enjoyments. Where action joins contemplation (the way it did during Christ's earthly career), there will have to be further explanations about how God orders humans to one

[43] For a fuller discussion of these issues in Bonaventure, Aquinas, Scotus, and Luther, see my *What Sort of Human Nature? Medieval Philosophy and the Systematics of Christology* (Milwaukee, WI: Marquette University Press, 1999).

[44] Aquinas, *Summa Theologica* II. 2, q. 179, a. 2 ad 2um.

another in a utopic community, where what is good for each does not conflict with what is best overall.

(6) Merely human friends might agree that their togetherness peaks with intense personal presence to one another. But they would not conclude that material expressions of their love—a handshake or a hug or a kiss—were pointless. Likewise, the contemplative ideal assumes that union with God is something that happens best "spirit to spirit" without any material mediation. But where God is relating to human soul–body composites, contemplative enjoyment would not have to put an end to materially mediated interactions—experiencing the majesty of God in mountain scenery or God's caress in a gentle breeze. Moreover, Scotus recognizes how, in this present state, external rites help to bind embodied persons into a common society. The Bible imagines harps and incense and a choir of thousands (Rev. 4: 1–11; 5: 6–14) with heavenly liturgies of which earthly ones are pale copies (Heb. 9–10). Overall, then, if our authors had taken post-mortem embodiment and society as seriously as they did eucharistic real presence, they might have been less confident that sacraments will cease!

List of Numbered Propositions

[P1] Substance individuals are naturally prior to accidents.

[P2] There is no passage from contradictory to contradictory—it is not the case that a proposition is first true and then its contradictory opposite is true—without any change.

[P2′] There is no passage from contradictory to contradictory without the generation or corruption of some thing.

[P3] If A is wholly and completely in B, and C is wholly and completely in D, and B and D are wholly and completely outside one another, then A is not numerically the same as C.

[P4] If X is similar to Y, there is something else Z that is the respect of their similarity.

[P5] Accidents cannot migrate from subject to subject.

[P6] Contradictories cannot be simultaneously true.

[P7] No thing (*res*) that through its nature is in a category can be in a category really different from it.

[P8] A thing in one category can have the mode of another category, because it is joined to another or related to another that pertains to that other category.

[P9] If a nature is contingently related to each form of another genus taken absolutely, then it is contingently related to the whole genus.

[P10] Wherever God can make a natural substance to exist not under its natural mode or under a mode opposite to its natural mode, God can make it to exist under its natural mode.

[P11] It is impossible for the same matter to be under two substantial forms simultaneously.

[P12] Efficient causal overdetermination is impossible.

[P13] A natural agent does not *per se* intend the corruption of the term-from-which, but only *per accidens*, because the term-from-which is incompatible with the term-to-which.

[P14] Natural power is less over more than over fewer, and over many than over one.

[P15] Nothing X essentially depends on another Y unless either [a] Y pertains to the essence of X, or [b] Y is a cause of X.

[P16] Wherever a temporal thing can have real existence, there it can begin to be.

[P17] Created powers all presuppose a subject on which to act and so are powers only to transform a subject.

[P18] Distinction and otherness are predicated of something only with respect to what primarily pertains to it.

[P19] When two are present and not spatially at a distance, whatever is immediately present to one of them is immediately present to the other.

[P20] Everything in motion is moved by another.

[P21] Contact (the touching of quantities) is necessary for corporeal action.

[P22] Causal exposure requires the relevant active and passive corporeal powers to be in place circumscriptively, both quantified and extended.

[P23] When a sufficient agent is proximate and the patient is disposed, the action follows.

[P23′] When a sufficient agent is proximate and the patient is disposed, and there is no obstacle, the action follows.

[P24] An active principle is no less able to act when it is present to a patient by its whole self than when one part is present to one part and another part to another.

[P25] If a natural active cause is related to different sufficiently close and equally disposed patients, if it can act on one, it can act on the other.

[P26] The placement modes of agent and patient have to be alike.

[P27] No being is singular formally through something of another genus.

[P28] The total active cause must have as much intensive actuality as or more intensive actuality than the effect.

[P29] Normally and naturally, the corruption of one substance involves the generation of another.

[P30] The real presence lasts as long and only so long as the accidents on the altar remain bread (wine) suitable.

[P30′] The real presence lasts only so long as the accidents remain accidents that could pertain to *the very individual* bread over which the prayer of consecration has been said.

[P31] The accidents on the altar exist *per se*, independently of substance, only so long as the real presence lasts.

[P32] The terms of motion must be incompossible.

[P33] An equivocal cause capable of solo action without the collaboration of univocal causes is more perfect than the effect.

[P34] It is naturally impossible that two quantities primarily inform the same subject simultaneously.

[P35] If something X depends on a material subject to acquire individual existence (*esse*), it would depend on a material subject to retain it.

[P36] A passive principle is no less liable to be acted upon when it is present to an active principle by its whole self than when one part is present to one part and another to another.

⋆ ⋆ ⋆

[T1] The bread accidents or "species" are still there on the altar, where they were before the consecration.

[T2] By means of the consecration, the true Body of Christ (the very one that was born of Mary and crucified) comes to be "on the altar," "contained by the sacrament" "under the species" of bread that remain.

[T3] The Body of Christ has ascended into heaven, where it will remain until Judgment Day.

[T4] The risen and ascended Body of Christ is glorified and hence impassible.

[T5] Two bodies cannot be extended in the same place at once.

[T6] A single body cannot be extended in, or move toward, two distinct places at once.

[T7] A body is located in a place, only if its dimensions are commensurate with the dimensions of the place.

[T8] Multiple things whose relations to place have the same kind of foundation (*ratio*) cannot thereby be in the same place at once.

[T9] Quantitative position is essential to *quantified* bodies.

[T10] Quantitative position is logically and metaphysically independent of categorial position.

[T11] Categorial position is *not* essential to quantified body.

[T12] Whatever are essentially prior to place relations (*ubi*) inhere in the body uniformly, even though the place relations are diverse.

[T13] Just as a patient existing in one place receives a form from two agents acting on it, so the patient existing in two places will suffer from proximate agents in both places.

[T14] Just as a body existing in one place is related as an active power to different things close to it in that place, so the same body existing in two places would be related to the same things existing in two places close enough to it.

[T15] It is *not* absolutely necessary that, if something has parts and properties under the natural mode, it has the same parts and properties under the sacramental mode.

[T16] It is *not* absolutely necessary that, if a body has parts and properties under the sacramental mode, it has the same parts and properties in natural existence.

[T17] Every action that pertains to Christ primarily as in heaven pertains to Christ as in the sacrament concomitantly.

[T18] No sensation pertains primarily to Christ as in the sacrament.

[T19] The spiritual functions of intellect and will can inhere in Christ primarily as in the sacrament.

[T20] Christ in the eucharist cannot use any active corporeal power, whether it is merely corporeal (as those conseqent on the nature of mixed bodies are) or corporeal (as those consequent on the nature of animate bodies are).

[T21] Christ in the eucharist can use any active spiritual power.

[T22] Productive transubstantiation is possible.

[T23] Productive transubstantiation is possible only for Divine power acting immediately.

[T24] Deity cannot be converted into any creature.

[T25] It is metaphysically possible for any creature to be wholly converted into any other.

[T26] Material substance and its essential parts prime matter and substantial form are *divided into integral parts of themselves.*

[T27] The integral parts of material substance and its essential parts prime matter and substantial form are *at a distance from one another in place.*

[T28] The integral parts of material substance and its essential parts prime matter and substantial form are *related to place immediately.*

[T29] Material substance, extended through its own intrinsic parts, is immediately in place circumscriptively and not definitively.

[T30] Material substance, its essential parts matter and form, can be *quantified through their own intrinsic parts.*

[T31] Any material thing that exists circumscriptively in place is a quantity.

[T32] For every genus of cause with respect to which God is a cause of a creature, whatever God can do by means of creatures, God can do without them.

[T33] Action (*agere*) pertains to a thing the way existence (*esse*) pertains to it.

[T34] When something X, according to its nature and existence, has an order to another Y, it is not miraculous for X to be conjoined to Y, even if X's conjunction with Y involves something's being newly created by God. On the contrary, it would be a miracle for X not to be conjoined to Y in such circumstances.

[T35] One and the same individual X can have two natures N_1 and N_2: one nature N_1 that belongs to X essentially, the nature that makes X the very thing X is and without which X could not exist; another N_2 that X assumes contingently.

[T36] When an individual X has two natures N_1 and N_2, propositions that describe X in terms of N_1 in the subject and in terms of N_2 in the predicate can come out true.

[T37] The eucharistic species can be broken, eaten, and converted into the eater.

[T38] The Body of Christ is really present in such a way as not to be vulnerable to breaking or to corruption by the eating and the digestion process.

* * *

[D1] A body B is *definitively* in place P, if and only if the quantity of B is commensurate with the quantity of P and the quantity of B is not commensurate with that of any place other than P.

[D2] A body B is *circumscriptively* in a place P, if and only if the quantity of B is compared with the quantity of P, whole to whole and part to part.

[D3] A body B is *determined* to a place P, if the magnitude through which it is said to be in P is finite and that magnitude is not its own substance.

[D4] The quantitative position of a body is the order of the body parts to one another and to the whole and of the whole to the parts.

[D5] Categorial position is the order of the parts of body to place.

[D6] Productive transubstantiation is the transition of a whole substance into a whole substance.

[D7] There is a translative transubstantiation from one whole substance S_1 to another whole substance S_2, when the whole substance S_1 is first here (at *P*) and then not here (not at *P*), and the whole substance S_2 is first not here (not at *P*) and then here (at *P*).

[D8] For something to be in place circumscriptively is for it to be whole in the whole place and part in part of the place.

[D9] For something to be in place definitively is for the whole to be in the whole place and whole in each part of place.

[D10] For something to be quantified is for it to have part outside part and part situationally distant from part.

[D11] Transubstantiation is the succession of substance to substance (of S_2 to S_1) where S_1 ceases to exist in itself and S_2 comes to exist under S_1's accidents.

* * *

[Cor 1] The eucharist could have been before the Incarnation just as much as now, both so far as its signification and insofar as the contained and signified thing is concerned.

[Cor 2] After the Incarnation, the Body of Christ could cease in its natural mode and yet remain truly in the eucharist, both so far as the truth of the sign and the reality of the contained thing are concerned.

[Cor 3] Material substance, its essential parts and corporeal qualities, can exist in place definitively.

[Cor 4] Although it is essential to material substance, to matter, substantial form, and corporeal qualities to be divided into intrinsic parts, it is not essential to them that their parts be distinct in place and situation.

[Cor 5] Anything that exists definitively in place, exists definitively in many places.

[Cor 6] Multiple circumscriptive locations of corporeal things should be easier to produce than multiple definitive locations, because circumscriptive location involves fewer parts in each place than definitive location does.

[Cor 7] It is metaphysically possible for a material substance, its essential parts, and qualities to exist circumscriptively in one or more places and definitively in one or more places at one and the same time.

[Cor 8] The total active cause must be at least as perfect as or more perfect than the effect.

⋆ ⋆ ⋆

[C1] Anything divided into intrinsic parts that exists in place definitively also exists in place circumscriptively.

[C2] Whatever is *per se* one thing and is truly extended is truly and really quantified.

[C3] Whatever is in place circumscriptively is quantified, because every such is whole in the whole and whole in the part.

[C4] Whatever is quantified is in place circumscriptively, if a place surrounds it.

⋆ ⋆ ⋆

[R1] Change-expressing statements that merely imply an *order* of term to term should be conceded.

[R2] Change-expressing statements that imply an *identity* of subject in the term-from-which and the term-to-which should not be granted properly speaking, but at most taken improperly and in an extended sense.

Bibliography

PRIMARY SOURCES

Abaelardus, Petrus, *Opera Theologica: Commentaria in Epostolam Pauli ad Romanos et Apologia contra Bernardum*. (Corpus Christianorum, Continuatio Mediaevalia XI; Turnholt: Brepols, 1969).

Aegidius Romanus, *Theoremata de Corpore Christi* (Rome: Antonius Bladus, 1554).

Anselm of Canterbury, *Opera Omnia*, ed. Franciscus Salesius Schmitt (Stuttgart-Bad Cannstatt: Friedrich Frommann Verlag [Günther Holzboog], 1968).

Aquinas, Thomas, *De Veritate*, in *Quaestiones Disputate ad Fidem Optimarum Editionum* (Paris: P. Lethielleux, 1882), ii. 455–iii. 602.

——*De Potentia*, in *Quaestiones Disputate ad Fidem Optimarum Editionum* (Paris: P. Lethielleux, 1882), i. 1–370.

——*Scriptum super Sententiis* IV (Parma, 1858), vols. 7 and 22. www.corpusthomisticum.org/iopera.html [referenced by online paragraph numbers as opposed to volume and pages].

——*Summa Contra Gentiles*, ed. Laureano Robles Carcedo, OP, and Adolfo Robles Sierra, OP (2 vols.; Madrid: Biblioteca de Autores Cristianos, 1967–8).

——*Summa Theologiae*, ed. Petrus Caramello (3 vols.; Turin and Rome: Marietti, 1952–6).

Aristotle, *Ethica Nicomachea*. A Revised Text with Critical Notes by I. Bywater (Oxford: Clarendon Press, 1894).

Aristotle's 'Categories' and 'De Interpretatione', trans. with notes by J. L. Ackrill (Oxford: Clarendon Press, 1963).

Aristotle's Metaphysics. A Revised Text with Introduction and Commentary by W. D. Ross (2 vols.; Oxford: Clarendon Press, 1924).

Aristotle's Physics. A Revised Text with Introduction and Commentary by W. D. Ross (Oxford: Clarendon Press, 1936).

Bassolis, John, *Opera . . . a quatuor sententiarum libros (credite) aurea* (Paris, 1516–19).

Bonaventure, *Opera Omnia*, ed. Studio et Cura PP. Collegii a S. Bonaventura (Quaracchi: Typographia Collegii S. Bonaventurae, 1883–1902).

Franciscus de Mayronis, *In quatuor libros sententiarum* (Venice: Impensa . . . Octaviani Scoti, 1520) [Unveränderter Nachdruk, Frankfurt/Main: Minerva GmbH, 1966].

Henry of Ghent, *Quodlibeta* (Paris: I. Badius Ascensius, 1518).

Hugh of St Victor, *De Sacramentis.*, trans. Roy Deferrari (Cambridge, MA: Medieval Academy of America, 1951).

Lombard, Peter, *Sententiae in IV Libris Distinctae*, ed. the fathers of the College of St Bonaventure (Grottaferrata: Editiones Collegii S. Bonaventurae, 1971, 1981).

Ockham, William, *Opera Philosophica et Theologica*, ed. G. Gál, S. Brown, G. Etzkorn, C.Grassi, F. Kelly, F. del Punta, J. Wey, and R. Wood (St Bonaventure, NY: Franciscan Institute Publications, 1969–88).

Pseudo-Dionysius, *The Complete Works*, trans. Colm Luibheid (New York: Paulist Press, 1987).

Scotus, John Duns, *Opera Omnia*, ed. L. Wadding (Lyons, 1639; repr. Hildesheim 1968–9).

——*A Treatise on God as First Principle*, trans. and ed. with commentary by Allan B. Wolter, OFM (Chicago: Franciscan Herald Press, 1966).

SECONDARY LITERATURE

Adams, Marilyn McCord, "Can Creatures Create?" *Philosophia*, 34 (2006), 101–28.

——*Christ and Horrors: The Coherence of Christology* (Cambridge: Cambridge University Press, 2006).

——*What Sort of Human Nature? Medieval Philosophy and the Systematics of Christology* (Milwaukee, WI: Marquette University Press, 1999).

——"What's Metaphysically Special about Supposits?" *Proceedings of the Aristotelian Society*, supplementary volume 79 (2005), 15–52.

——"Why Bodies as Well as Souls in the Life to Come?" forthcoming in a volume for the Wippel-fest medieval colloquium series, School of Philosophy, Catholic University of America.

——*William Ockham* (Notre Dame: University of Notre Dame Press, 1987).

Burr, David, *Eucharistic Presence and Conversion in Late Thirteenth-Century Franciscan Thought* (Philadelphia: American Philosophical Society, 1984).

Chadwick, Henry, "Ego Berengarius," *Journal of Theological Studies*, NS 40/2 (Oct. 1989), 414–45.

——"Symbol and Reality: Berengar and the Appeal to the Fathers," in Peter Ganz, R. B. C. Huygens, and Friedrich Niewöhner (eds.), *Auctoritas und Ratio: Studien zu Berengar von Tours* (Wiesbaden: Otto Harrassowitz, 1990), 25–45.

Cowdrey, H. E. J., "The Papacy and the Berengarian Controversy," in Peter Ganz, R. B. C. Huygens, and Friedrich Niewöhner (eds.), *Auctoritas und Ratio: Studien zu Berengar von Tours* (Wiesbaden: Otto Harrassowitz, 1990), 111–38.

Cross, Richard, *The Metaphysics of the Incarnation* (Oxford: Oxford University Press, 2002).

——*The Physics of Duns Scotus: The Scientific Context of a Theological Vision* (Oxford: Clarendon Press, 1998).

Davidson, Herbert A., *Proofs for Eternity: Creation and the Existence of God in Medieval Islamic and Jewish Philosophy* (New York and Oxford: Oxford University Press, 1987).

De Lubac, Henri Cardinal, *Corpus Mysticum: The Eucharist and the Church in the Middle Ages*, trans. Gemma Simmonds, CJ, with Richard Price (London: SCM Press, 2006).

Denzinger, Heinrich (ed.), *Enchiridion Symbolorum: Definitionum et Declarationum de Rebus Fidei et Morum* (Freiburg in Breisgau: B. Herder, 1911).

Dumont, Stephen D., "Did Duns Scotus Change his Mind on the Will?" in Jan A. Aertsen, Kent Emery Jr. and Andreas Speer (eds.), *Nach der Verurteilung von 1277: Philosophie und Theologie an der Universität von Paris im letzten Viertel des 13. Jahrhunderts. Studien und Texte* (Berlin and New York: Walter de Gruyter, 2001), 719–94.

——"Godfrey of Fontaines and the Succession Theory of Forms at Paris in the Early Fourteenth Century," in S. Brown, T. Kobusch, and T. Dewender (eds.), *Philosophical Debates at Paris in the Early Fourteenth Century* (Leiden: Brill, 2009), 39–125.

Furth, Montgomery, *Substance, Form, and Psyche: An Aristotelian Metaphysics* (Cambridge: Cambridge University Press, 1988).

Goering, Joseph, "The Invention of Transubstantiation," *Traditio*, 46 (1991), 147–70.

Grant, Edward, "Place and Space in Medieval Thought," in Peter K. Machamer and Robert G. Turnbull (eds.), *Motion and Time, Space and Matter* (Columbus, OH: Ohio State University Press, 1976), 137–67.

——"The Medieval Doctrine of Place: Some Fundamental Problems and Solutions," in *Studi sul XIV Secolo in Memoria di Anneliese Maier* (Rome: Edizioni di Storia e Letteratura, 1981), 57–79.

Henninger, Mark G., SJ, *Relations: Medieval Theories 1250–1325* (Oxford: Clarendon Press, 1989).

Hubert, Henri, and Mauss, Marcel, *Sacrifice: Its Nature and Function*, trans. W. D. Halls; foreword E. E. Evans-Pritchard (Chicago: Chicago University Press, 1898/1964).

Kuhn, Thomas S., *The Structure of Scientific Revolution* (Chicago: Phoenix Books, 1962).

Macy, Gary, "Berengar's Legacy as Heresiarch," in Peter Ganz, R. B. C. Huygens, and Friedrich Niewöhner (eds.), *Auctoritas und Ratio: Studien zu Berengar von Tours* (Wiesbaden: Otto Harrassowitz, 1990), 47–67.

——*The Theologies of the Eucharist in the Early Scholastic Period: A Study of the Salvivic Function of the Sacrament according to the Theologians c.1080–c.1220* (Oxford: Clarendon Press, 1984).

——*Treasures from the Storeroom: Medieval Religion and the Eucharist* (Collegeville, MN: Liturgical Press, 1999).

Maier, Anneliese, *Metaphysische Hintergründe der spätscholastischen Naturphilosophie*, 'Das Problem der Quantität' (Roma: Edizioni di Storia e Letteratura, 1955), 141–224.

——*Zwei Grundprobleme der scholastischen Naturphilosophie*, 'Das Problem der intensiven Grösse' (Rome: Edizioni di Storia e Letteratura, 1968), 3–109.

Moore, John C., *Pope Innocent III (1160/61–1216): To Root up and to Plant* (Leiden and Boston: Brill, 2003).

Pini, Giorgio, *Categories and Logic in Scotus* (Leiden, Boston, and Cologne: Brill, 2002).

Pseudo-Dionysius: The Complete Works, trans. Colm Luibheid (New York: Paulist Press, 1987); *The Celestial Hierarchy* and *The Ecclesiastical Hierarachy*.

Roland-Gosselin, M. D., OP, *Le "De Ente et Essentia" de S. Thomas D'Aquin: Texte établi d'après les manuscrits parisiens, introduction, notes, et études historiques* (Paris: Librairie Philosophique J. Vrin, 1948).

Sylla, Edith Dudley, "Autonomous and Handmaiden Science: St Thomas Aquinas and William of Ockham on the Physics of the Eucharist," in J. E. Murdoch and E. D. Sylla (eds.), *The Cultural Context of Medieval Learning* (Dordrecht-Holland: D. Reidel Publishing Company, 1975), 349–96.

——"Godfrey of Fontaines on Motion with Respect to Quantity of the Eucharist," in A. Maieru and A. Paravicini Bagliani (eds.), *Studi sul XIV Secolo in Memoria di Anneliese Maier* (Rome: Edizioni di Storia et Letteratura, 1981), 105–41.

Stone, Darwell, *A History of the Doctrine of the Holy Eucharist* (2 vols.; London, New York, Bombay, and Calcutta: Longmans, Green, & Co, 1909).

Tachau, Katherine, *Vision and Certitude in the Age of Ockham: Optics, Epistemology, and the Foundations of Semantics 1250–1345* (Studien und Texte zur Geistesgeschichte des Mittelalters; Leiden, New York, Copenhagen, and Cologne: Brill, 1988).

Trifogli, Cecilia, "La Dottrina del Luogo in Egidio Romano," *Medioevo*, 14 (1988), 235–90.

——*Oxford Physics in the Thirteenth Century (ca.1250–1270): Motion, Infinity, Place, and Time* (Leiden, Boston, and Cologne: Brill, 2000).

——"Thomas Wylton on the Immobility of Place," *Recherches de Théologie et Philosophie médiévales: Forschungen zur Theologie und Philosophie des Mittelalters*, 65/1 (1998), 1–39.

Van Engen, John H., *Rupert of Deutz* (Berkeley, Los Angeles, and London: University of California Press, 1983).

Wippel, John F., "Godfrey of Fontaines on Intension and Remission of Accidental Forms," *Franciscan Studies* (1979), 316–55.

——*The Metaphysical Thought of Thomas Aquinas: From Finite Being to Uncreated Being* (Washington: Catholic University of America Press, 2000).

Zavalloni, Roberto, *Richard de Mediavilla et la controverse sur la pluralité des formes: Textes inédits et étude critique* (Louvain: Éditions de l'Institute Supérieur de Philosophie, 1951).

Index

Made in the USA
Middletown, DE
05 May 2018